GW01255367

The History of the Jews [By H.H. Milman]

You are holding a reproduction of an original work that is in the public domain in the United States of America, and possibly other countries.You may freely copy and distribute this work as no entity (individual or corporate) has a copyright on the body of the work.This book may contain prior copyright references, and library stamps (as most of these works were scanned from library copies).These have been scanned and retained as part of the historical artifact.

This book may have occasional imperfections such as missing or blurred pages, poor pictures, errant marks, etc. that were either part of the original artifact, or were introduced by the scanning process. We believe this work is culturally important, and despite the imperfections, have elected to bring it back into print as part of our continuing commitment to the preservation of printed works worldwide. We appreciate your understanding of the imperfections in the preservation process, and hope you enjoy this valuable book.

THE

HISTORY OF THE JEWS.

———◦◦◦———

VOLUME II.

THE

HISTORY OF THE JEWS.

FROM THE EARLIEST PERIOD DOWN TO
MODERN TIMES.

By HENRY HART MILMAN, D.D.,

DEAN OF ST. PAUL'S.

IN THREE VOLUMES.—VOL. II.

FIFTH EDITION.

LONDON:
JOHN MURRAY, ALBEMARLE STREET.
1883.

LONDON:
PRINTED BY WILLIAM CLOWES AND SONS, LIMITED,
STAMFORD STREET AND CHARING CROSS.

CONTENTS OF VOL. II.

90

BOOK XIV.

PREPARATIONS FOR THE WAR.

BOOK XV.

THE WAR.

BOOK XVI.

SIEGE OF JERUSALEM.

BOOK XVII.

TERMINATION OF THE WAR.

BOOK XVIII.

BARCOCHAB.

BOOK XIX.

THE PATRIARCH OF THE WEST, AND THE PRINCE OF THE CAPTIVITY.

HISTORY OF THE JEWS.

BOOK X.

THE ASMONEANS.

Mattathias — Judas the Maccabee — Jonathan — Simon — John Hyrcanus — Aristobulus I. — Alexander Jannæus — Alexandra — Aristobulus II. — Hyrcanus II.

AT this crisis Divine Providence interposed, not as formerly, with miraculous assistance, but by the instrumentality of human virtues : the lofty patriotism, adventurous valour, daring and sagacious soldiership, generous self-devotion, and inextinguishable zeal of heroic men in the cause of their country and their God. In Modin, a town on an eminence, commanding a view of the sea, the exact site of which is unknown,* lived Mattathias, a man of the priestly line of Joarib, himself advanced in years, but with five sons in the prime of life, Johanan, Simon, Judas, Eleazar, and Jonathan. When Apelles, the officer of Antiochus, arrived at Modin to enforce the execution of the edict against the Jewish religion, he made splendid offers to Mattathias as a man of great influence, to induce him to submit to the royal will. The old man not only rejected his advances, but publicly proclaimed his resolution to live and die in the faith of his fathers ; and when an apos-

---

* It was on a height on the road from Jerusalem to Joppa, the Talmudists say not far from Lydda.

tate Jew was about to offer sacrifice to the heathen
deity, in a transport of indignant zeal, Mattathias struck
him dead upon the altar.   Mattathias then fell on the
king's commissioner, put him to death, and summoned
all the citizens who were zealous for the Law to follow
him to the mountains.[b]   Their numbers rapidly increased; but the Syrian troops having surprised 1000
in a cave, attacked them on the Sabbath day, and meeting with no resistance, slew them without mercy. From
thenceforth Mattathias and his followers determined to
break through this over-scrupulous observance of the
Sabbath, and to assert the legality of defensive warfare
on that day.[c]

The insurgents conducted their revolt with equal
enterprise and discretion. For a time they lay hid in
the mountain fastnesses : and, as opportunity occurred,
poured down upon the towns; destroyed the heathen
altars; enforced circumcision; punished all apostates
who fell into their hands; recovered many copies of the
Law, which their enemies had wantonly defaced; and
re-established the synagogues for public worship; the
Temple being defiled, and in the possession of the
enemy. Their ranks were swelled with the zealots for
the Law, who were then called the Chasidim. For, immediately after the return from Babylonia, two sects
had divided the people: the Zadikim, the righteous,
who observed the written Law of Moses; and the more
austere and abstemious Chasidim, or the holy, who added
to the Law the traditions and observances of the fathers,
and professed a holiness beyond the letter of the covenant. From the former sprang the Sadducees and
Karaites of later times; from the latter, the Pharisees.

---

[b] 1 Macc.; 2 Macc.; Joseph. Ant. xii. 6, 7.   [c] Summer, B.C. 166.

But the age of Mattathias was ill suited to this laborious and enterprising warfare: having bequeathed the command to Judas, the most valiant of his sons, he sank under the weight of years and toil. So great already was the terror of his name, that he was buried, without disturbance on the part of the enemy, in his native city of Modin.

If the youth of the new general added vigour and enterprise to the cause, it lost nothing in prudence and discretion. Judas unfolded the banner of the Maccabees, a name of which the derivation is uncertain. Some assert that it was formed from the concluding letters of a sentence in the eleventh verse of the fifteenth chapter of Exodus, " Mi Camo Ka Baalim Jehovah," signifying, *Who is like unto thee among the Gods, O Jehovah?* Some, that it was the banner of the tribe of Dan, which contained the three last letters of the three names of Abraham, Isaac, and Jacob: others that it was the personal appellation of Judas, from a word signifying a hammer, like that of Charles Martel, the hero of the Franks. Having tried his soldiers by many gallant adventures, surprising many cities, which he garrisoned and fortified, Judas determined to meet the enemy in the field. Apollonius, the governor of Samaria, first advanced against him, and was totally defeated and slain. Judas took the sword of his enemy as a trophy, and ever after used it in battle. Seron, the deputy-governor of Coelesyria, advanced to revenge the defeat of Apollonius, but encountering the enemy in the strong pass of Beth-horon, met with the same fate. The circumstances of the times favoured the noble struggle of Judas and his followers for independence. By his prodigal magnificence, both in his pleasures and in his splendid donatives and offerings, Antiochus had exhausted his finances. His eastern

B 2

provinces, Armenia and Persia, refused their tribute. He therefore was constrained to divide his forces, marching himself into the East, and leaving Lysias, with a great army, to crush the insurrection in Judæa. The rapid progress of Judas had demanded immediate resistance. Philip, the Syrian governor in Jerusalem, sent urgent solicitations for relief. The vanguard of the Syrian army, amounting to 20,000, under the command of Nicanor and Gorgias, advanced rapidly into the province: it was followed by the general in chief, Ptolemy Macron; their united forces forming an army of 40,000 foot and 7000 horse. In their train came a multitude of slave merchants; for Nicanor had suggested the policy of selling as many of the insurgents as they could take, to discharge the arrears of tribute due to the Romans.[d] Judas assembled 6000 men at Mizpeh: there they fasted and prayed; and the religious ceremony, performed in that unusual place, though of old one of the sanctuaries of God, sadly reminded them of the desolate state of the holy city, the profanation of the sanctuary, the discontinuance of the sacrifices.[e] But if sorrow subdued the tamer spirits, it infused loftier indignation and nobler self-devotion into the valiant.[f] Judas knew that his only hope, save in his God, was in the enthusiastic zeal of his followers for the law of Moses. In strict conformity to its injunctions, he issued out through his little army the appointed proclamation, that all who had married wives, built houses, or planted

---

[d] 2 Macc. viii. 10. They were to have 90 slaves for a talent: 11.

[e] 1 Macc. iii. 46 et seqq.

A characteristic circumstance is here noted, " and laid open the book of the Law, *wherein the heathen had sought to paint the likeness of their images.*" 48.

[f] " For it is better for us to die in battle, than to behold the calamities of our people and our sanctuary. Nevertheless as the will of God is in heaven, so let him do." 1 Macc. iii. 59, 60. Compare 2 Macc. c. viii.

vineyards, or were fearful, should return to their homes. His force dwindled to 3000 ill-armed men.[g] Yet with this small band Judas advanced towards Emmaus, where the enemy lay encamped. Intelligence reached him, that Gorgias had been detached with 5000 chosen foot and 1000 horse to surprise him by night. He instantly formed the daring resolution of eluding the attack by falling on the camp of the enemy. It was morning before he arrived; but, animating his men to the onset, they rushed down, all their trumpets clanging, upon the Syrians, who, after a feeble resistance, fled on all sides, unto Gazera, and unto the plains of Idumea, and Azotus, and Jamnia. Three thousand fell in battle.[h] Judas was as wary as bold; his troops were as well-disciplined as enterprising. He restrained them from the plunder of the camp till the return of Gorgias with the flower of the army, who came back weary with seeking the Jewish insurgents among the mountains, where they had hoped to surprise them. To their astonishment they beheld their own camp a blaze of fire. The contest was short but decisive: the Syrians fled without striking a blow, and in their flight suffered immense loss. The rich booty of the camp fell into the hands of the Jews, "much gold and silver, and blue silk and purple of the sea, and great riches."[i] The Jews, with just retribution, sold for slaves as many of the slave-merchants as they could find. A due share of the spoil was given to the maimed, the widows, and the orphans; the rest divided among the conquerors.[k] The next day was the Sabbath, a day indeed of rest and rejoicing. But success only excited the honourable am-

---

[g] "Who nevertheless had neither armour nor swords to their minds." 1 Macc. iv. 6.

[h] Verse 15.
[i] Verse 23.
[k] 2 Macc. viii. 28

bition of the Maccabee.   Hearing that a great force was
assembling beyond the Jordan under Timotheus and
Bacchides, he crossed the river, and gained a great victory and a considerable supply of arms.   Here two of
the chief oppressors of the Jews, Philarches and Cal-
listhenes, perished; one in battle; the other burnt to
death in a house, where he had taken refuge.   Nicanor
fled in the disguise of a slave to Antioch.   So closed the
first triumphant campaign of the Maccabees.

The next year Lysias appeared in person, at the
head of 60,000 foot and 5000 horse, at Bethsura, a
little north of Hebron[1] towards the southern frontier of
Judæa; having perhaps levied part of his men among
the Idumeans.   This tribe now inhabited a district to
the west of their ancestors, the Edomites, having been
dispossessed of their former territory by the Nabathæan
Arabs.   Judas met this formidable host with 10,000
men; gained a decisive victory, and slew 5000 of the
enemy.   Thus on all sides triumphant, Judas entered,
with his valiant confederates, the ruined and desolate
Jerusalem.[m]   They found shrubs grown to some height,
like the underwood of a forest, in the courts of the
Temple; every part of the sacred edifice had been profaned; the chambers of the priests were thrown down.
With wild lamentations and the sound of martial trumpets they mingled their prayers and praises to the God
of their fathers.   Judas took the precaution to keep a
body of armed men on the watch against the Syrian
garrison in the citadel; and then proceeded to install
the most blameless of the priests in their office, to
repair the sacred edifice, to purify every part from the
proïanation of the heathen, to construct a new altar. to

---

[1] 1 Macc. iv. 28-35.   [m] 1 Macc. iv. 36-60.

replace out of the booty all the sacred vessels, and at length to celebrate the feast of Dedication—a period of eight days—which ever after was held sacred in the Jewish calendar.[n] It was the festival of the regeneration of the people, which, but for the valour of the Maccabees, had almost lost its political existence.

The re-establishment of a powerful state in Judæa was not beheld without jealousy by the neighbouring tribes.[o] But Judas, having strongly fortified the Temple on the side of the citadel, anticipated a powerful confederacy which was forming against him, and carried his victorious arms into the territories of the Idumeans and Ammonites. Thus discomfited on every side, the Syrians and their allies began to revenge themselves on the Jews who were scattered in Galilee and the trans-Jordanic provinces. Judas revenged a cruel stratagem of the inhabitants of Joppa, who decoyed 200 Jews or families on board their ships and threw them into the sea. He made a descent and burned many houses on the harbour, and many of their ships. In Jamnia the same hostile measures were threatened. He fell on Jamnia, set the town on fire, the blaze of which was seen in Jerusalem.[p] A great force from Tyre and Ptolemais advanced into the neighbouring country. Timotheus, son of a former general of the same name, laid waste Gilead with great slaughter.[q] Judas, by the general consent of the people, divided his army into three parts. 8000 men, under his own command, crossed the Jordan into Gilead; 3000, under his brother Simon,

---

[n] Herzfeld observes that they would use no profaned fire for the lamps and lights which were henceforth to burn in the Holy Place. According to 2 Macc. x. 3 : "Striking stones, they took fire out of them."—Herzfeld, ii.

p. 271.
[o] 1 Macc. v. 1. Compare 2 Macc x. 1-8. Joseph. Ant. xii. 7. 6.
[p] 2 Macc. xii. 3. 9.
[q] 1 Macc. v. 3.

marched into Galilee; the rest, under Joseph the son of
Zacharias, and Azarias, remained to defend the liberated
provinces; but with strict injunctions to make no hostile movement. The Maccabees, as usual, were irresistible: city after city fell before Judas and Jonathan.[r]
At length, having subdued the whole country, Judas
found it prudent not to extend his kingdom to the
bounds of that of David, and with that view removed
all the Jews beyond the Jordan to the more defensible
province of Judæa. Simon was equally successful in
Galilee; he drove the enemy before him to the gates of
Ptolemais. But the commanders who were left at home,
in direct violation of orders, undertook an ill-concerted enterprise against Jamnia, a sea-port. They were opposed by
Bacchides, the most skilful of the Syrian generals, and
met with a signal defeat.[s] The defeat was before long
revenged by the indefatigable Judas, but not without
loss. When they proceeded, after observing the Sabbath
in Adullam, to bury the dead, small idols were found in
the clothes even of some of priestly race. A sin-offering
was sent to Jerusalem, not only to atone for the guilt of
these men, but for the dead, in whose resurrection the
Maccabean Jews, no doubt the Chasidim, had full faith.[t]

In the mean time the great oppressor of the Jews,
Antiochus, had died in Persia. That his end was miserable, both the Jewish and Roman historians agree. He
had been repulsed in an assault on a rich and sumptuous temple in Persia, called by the Greeks that

---

[r] "Bosora (Bosra), and Bosor, and
Alema, Casphor, Maked, and Carnaim,
all these cities are strong and great."
—v. 26.

[s] 1 Macc. v. 55-61.

[t] 2 Macc. xii. "For if he had not
hoped that they that were slain should
have risen again, it had been superfluous and vain to pray for the dead."
v. 44. This is the earliest *distinct*
assertion of the Jewish belief in the
resurrection.

of Diana; perhaps the female Mithra or the moou. Whether he had been incited by the desire of plunder, or by his bigoted animosity against foreign religions, does not appear; but at the same time he received intelligence of the disastrous state of his affairs in Palestine. Hastening homeward, he was seized with an incurable disorder, in a small town among the mountains of Paretacene. There, consumed in body by a loathsome ulcer, afflicted in mind by horrible apparitions and remorse of conscience, for his outrage on the Persian temple, says Polybius—for his horrible barbarities and sacrilege in Judæa, assert the Hebrew writers—died the most magnificent of the Syro-Macedonian monarchs.[n]

Lysias, who commanded in Syria, immediately set a son of the deceased king, Antiochus Eupator, upon the throne; Demetrius, the rightful heir, being a hostage in Rome. The first measure of Lysias was to attempt the subjugation of Judæa, where in Jerusalem itself the garrison of the unsurrendered fortress on Mount Sion joined to a strong party of

---

[n] 1 Macc. vi. 1-16; 2 Macc. ix.; Joseph. Ant. xii. 9. 1; Polybius, xxxi. 11. Josephus is indignant with Polybius for ascribing the death of Antiochus to the violation of the Temple of Diana. The comparison of the simpler pathos in the account of his death in the first book of Maccabees with the passionate and relentless exaggeration of the account in the later second book is an instructive illustration of the growth of popular traditional history. The dying speech of Antiochus in his remorse (in the Second Maccabees) is very curious, " and as touching the Jews whom he had judged not worthy so much as to be buried, but to be cast out with their children to be devoured of the fowls and wild beasts, he would make them all equals to the citizens of Athens: and the holy Temple, which before he had spoiled, he would garnish with goodly gifts, and restore all the holy vessels, with many more, and out of his own revenue defray the charges belonging to the sacrifices: yea and that also he would become a Jew himself, and go through all the world that was inhabited, and declare the power of God." The other account is strange enough, but more like the Greek, and utterly irreconcileable with the foregoing. It is simple and pathetic, and therefore seemingly truthful. 1 Macc. vi. 11, 13.

the apostate Jews anxiously awaited his approach.[x] The royal army formed the siege of Bethsura, on the Idumean frontier, not far from Hebron, which Judas had strongly fortified. Their force consisted of 80,000 or 100,000 foot, 20,000 horse, and 32 elephants. Bethsura made a valiant defence, and Judas marched from Jerusalem to its relief. The elephants seem to have excited great terror and astonishment. According to the Jewish annalist each beast was escorted by 1000 foot, splendidly armed, and 500 horse; each bore a tower containing 32 men: and to provoke them to fight, *they showed them the blood of grapes and mulberries.* The whole army, in radiant armour, spread over the mountains and valleys, so that the *mountains glistened therewith, and seemed like lamps of fire.* Yet wherever Judas fought, the Israelites were successful; and his heroic brother, Eleazar, excited the admiration of his countrymen by rushing under an elephant, which he stabbed in the belly, and was crushed to death by its fall. Still Judas found himself obliged to retreat upon Jerusalem.[y] Bethsura, pressed by famine (it was the Sabbatic year, the land lay fallow, and supplies were scarce), capitulated on honourable terms; and the royal army joined the siege of that part of the capital which was in the possession of Judas. Jerusalem resisted all their assaults; the Syrians began to suffer from want of provisions;

---

[x] The narrative of the affairs after the accession of Antiochus Eupator in 1 Macc. vi. 18-63 is perfectly clear and distinct. That in 2 Macc., from x. 10, is a mass of inextricable confusion. In that account the same Timotheus is twice defeated and killed, x. 21, 38; xii. 15, 25. The whole is a series of repetitions, some of events before the death of Antiochus, some after. Josephus mainly follows 1 Macc. He however sets the King himself at the head of the army of Lysias.

[y] According to 2 Macc. xi., Lysias was totally defeated and fled; but afterwards proposed a treaty Ch xiii. repeats this invasion.

and intelligence arrived that affairs at Antioch demanded their immediate presence.[a]   A treaty was concluded, full liberty of worship was guaranteed to the
Jews, they were to be henceforth permitted to live
according to their own laws.[a] Antiochus was admitted
into the city; but, in direct violation of the terms, he
threw down the walls and dismantled the fortifications.

Demetrius in the mean time, the lineal heir to the
throne of Antioch, had escaped from Rome. After some
struggle, he overpowered Lysias and Antiochus, put
them to death, and became undisputed master of the
kingdom.   The new king adopted a more dangerous
policy against the independence of Judæa than the invasion and vast armies of his predecessor. The looser
and less patriotic Jews ill brooked the austere government of the Chasidim, who formed the party of Judas:
many, perhaps, were weary of the constant warfare in
which their valiant champion was engaged. Menelaus,
the renegade High Priest, had accompanied the army of
Lysias, and endeavoured to form a faction in his favour;
but, on some dissatisfaction, Lysias had sent him to
Berea, where he was thrown into a tower of ashes, and
suffocated—a fit punishment, it was said, for one who had
polluted the altar fires and holy ashes of God's shrine.[b]
Onias, son of the Onias murdered by means of Menelaus,

---

[a] Philip, who had been appointed guardian of his son by Antiochus Epiphanes, had reached Antioch and seized the government.

[a] 1 Macc. vi. 58-61.

[b] 2 Macc. xiii. 3; Joseph. Ant. xii. 9-7. The tower ὄργανον εἶχε περιφερὲς πάντοθεν ἀπόκρημνον εἰς τὸν σκόδον. It must therefore have been different from that, according to Val. Maximus, built by King Ochus as a place of punishment. "Ochus . . . septum altis parietibus locum cinere complevit, suppositoque tigno promi-uente benignè cibo et potione exceptos in eo collocabat, e quo somno sopiti decidebant." These were not burned, but smothered by the vapours. Val. Max. ix. 2-6. Compare Herod. ii. 100.

the heir of the priesthood, fled to Egypt, and Alcimus, or Jacimus, was raised to the High-priesthood.[c] By reviving the title of the High Priest to the supreme authority, Demetrius hoped, if not to secure a dependent vassal in the government of Judæa, at least to sow discord among the insurgents. He sent Alcimus, supported by Bacchides. his most able general, to claim his sacerdotal dignity. The zealots for the Law could not resist the title of the High Priest.[d] Jerusalem submitted. But no sooner had Alcimus got the leaders into his power than he basely murdered sixty of them. Bacchides followed up the blow with great severities in other parts. Still, immediately that Bacchides had withdrawn his troops, Judas again took arms, and Alcimus was compelled to fly to Antioch. Demetrius despatched Nicanor, with a great army, to reinstate Alcimus. Jerusalem was still in the possession of the Syrians; and Nicanor attempted to get Judas into his power by stratagem, but the wary soldier was on his guard. A battle took place at Capharsalama.[e] Nicanor retreated, with the loss of 5000 men, to Jerusalem, where he revenged himself by the greatest barbarities: one of the elders, named Raziz, rather than fall into his hands, stabbed himself with his own sword; but the wound not proving mortal, he ran forth and destroyed himself by other means, too horrible to describe.[f] By these cruelties, and by a threat of burning the Temple and consecrating the spot to Bacchus, Nicanor endeavoured to force the people to surrender their champion. All these treacherous and cruel measures proving ineffectual, he was forced to revert to open war.

---

[c] 2 Macc. xv. 3. "Alcimus, who had been high priest, and had defiled himself wilfully in the times of their mingling with the Gentiles."

[d] 1 Macc. vii. 14.
[e] 1 Macc. vii. 31.
[f] 2 Macc. xiv. 37. 41.

A second battle took place, in which the superior forces of Nicanor were totally routed, and he himself slain.[f] His head and his right hand were cut off and hung in scorn and triumph—the head over one of the towers, the hand over one of the gates of the Temple, called afterwards the gate of Nicanor.[h] After this final victory Judas took a more decided step to secure the independence of his country; he entered into a formal treaty of alliance with Rome. The Jews had heard great things of Rome: that the Romans had subdued Gaul, were masters of the silver and gold mines of Spain; that kings from all parts of the world had trembled at their mandate; that Philip and Perseus and the great Antiochus had been defeated by, and paid tribute to this mighty people; that to their allies or vassal kings they granted empires—Lydia, Media, even India (such were the reports); yet none of them wore crown or purple, and every year they changed their Captains (their consuls). One, the mightiest, had subdued Greece.[i] The ambitious Roman senate—steadily pursuing their usual policy, of weakening all the great monarchies of the world, by all means, whether honourable or treacherous; and ever, as Justin observes, ready to grant what did not belong to them[j]—

---

[f] 1 Macc. vii. 43.

[h] 1 Macc. vii. 37; 2 Macc. xv. 32, 33. The eastern gate of the inner court of the Temple retained the name of the gate of Nicanor. "Nicanor was one of the captains of the Greeks, and every day he wagged his hand towards Judæa and Jerusalem, and said, 'Oh, when will be in my power to lay thee waste?'" But when the Asmonean family prevailed, they subdued him and slew him, and hung up his trunk and great toes upon the gates of Jeru-salem. Hence Nicanor's Day in the Jewish calendar.—From Baba Taanith, fol. xviii. 2. Lightfoot, vol. x. p. 65.

[i] 1 Macc. viii. The whole account of the prowess and victories of the Romans is very curious. See the offensive and defensive treaty.

[j] "A Demetrio cum descivissent, amicitiâ Romanorum petitâ, primo omnium ex Orientalibus libertatem receperunt, facile tunc Romanis de alieno largientibus."—Justin, Hist., xxxvi. 3.

eagerly ratified the independence of Judæa, and received under their protection these useful confederates.

Before, however, the treaty was made known, the glorious career of the Maccabee had terminated. Demetrius had sent Alcimus and Bacchides, with the whole force of his kingdom, into Palestine. Judas was abandoned by all his troops, all but 800 men, yet could not be prevailed on to retreat. Having discomfited one wing of the enemy's army, he fell nobly, as he had lived, the Martyr, as the champion of his country (B.C. 161). His body was rescued and buried in Modin. Among those lofty spirits who have asserted the liberty of their native land against wanton and cruel oppression, none have surpassed the most able of the Maccabees in accomplishing a great end with inadequate means; none ever united more generous valour with a better cause.

The faction of Alcimus now triumphed, the partisans of the Maccabees were oppressed, and the unrelenting Bacchides put to death the bravest of their adherents with the most cruel indignities. Jonathan, the brother of Judas, assembled a small force, and lay concealed in the wilderness of Tekoa, defended by the Jordan on one side, and by a morass on the other. A third of this gallant race, John, had fallen in an affray with an Arab tribe, who surprised him while escorting some of their effects to the friendly Nabathæans.[k] To revenge his death was the first object. During a splendid marriage ceremony, the Jews fell on the bride and bridegroom, and put them and all their attendants to the sword. Soon after this they repelled an attack of Bacchides with great loss, but finding their numbers unequal to the contest, they swam the Jordan and escaped. Bacchides, to secure military possession of the country, fortified and

---

[k] 1 Macc. ix. 35.

garrisoned all the strong towns. In the mean time, the unworthy High Priest, Alcimus, having begun to throw down one of the partition walls in the Temple, was seized with a mortal disorder, and died. On his death, Bacchides retired to Antioch, and Jonathan immediately broke out of his hiding-place. On the re-appearance of Bacchides at the head of a considerable army, the Maccabee again took refuge in the wilderness; where he kept up a desultory guerrilla warfare, he himself hovering about the camp of Bacchides, while his brother Simon defended the strong post of Bethhasi. At length Bacchides, wearied of this inglorious and harassing campaign, or perhaps by orders from his court which began to tremble at the danger of oppressing an ally of Rome, entered into honourable terms of peace.[1]

Some years passed away in quiet. Jonathan thus became master of Judæa; though Jerusalem, and many of the stronger towns, occupied by garrisons, either of Syrians or apostate Jews, defied his authority.

A revolution in the kingdom of Syria gave Jonathan new strength and importance. An adventurer, Alexander Balas, announcing himself as the son of Antiochus Epiphanes, laid claim to the crown of the Seleucidæ.[m] The Romans admitted his title, and Jonathan found himself courted by the two competitors for the kingdom of Antioch. It was a strange reversal in the state of a people which seemed but a few years before to have been doomed to utter extinction; their country overrun by vast irresistible armies; their city walls razed, and the city commanded by a strong garrisoned fortress; their Temple defiled and dedicated to strange gods; their few defenders, freebooters in caverns and in the clefts of their mountains. Now they are the arbiters, it might seem, of

---

1 Macc. ix. 70.   ■ 1 Macc. x.

conflicting rivals for the magnificent throne of the Seleucidæ; and all this by the valour, the military conduct, the prudence, the patriotism, the religious faith of
one family.   The offers of king Demetrius were lavish,
even to desperation; exemption from all tribute, *customs
from salt, and crown taxes, the third part of the seed,
and half of the fruit of the trees.*   Not only the city of
Jerusalem, even the commanding fortress is evacuated.
The terms include the surrender of all prisoners and all
captives who had been compelled to migrate with their
cattle: not only perfect freedom of religion, but the full
observance of all their feasts and Sabbaths; the enrol-
ment of 30,000 Jews to be paid by the king, but these
troops are to occupy under their own officers the strongholds of the land; certain districts of Samaria and the
noble seaport of Ptolemais are to be added to their territory; munificent donatives promised for the repair and
sustentation of the Temple, and the rebuilding the walls of
the city.[n]   Still, from mistrust of the promises of Demetrius, and larger advances from Alexander, or foreseeing
his prevailing power, or perhaps knowing him to have the
support of Rome, the Jews continued faithful to the alliance with Alexander; and Jonathan, conscious of his
own strength, with the common consent, tacit or avowed,
of the contending kings, assumed the pontifical robes,
and in his person commenced the reign of the Priest-
Kings of the Asmonean line.

The impostor, Alexander Balas, met with the greatest
success; defeated and slew Demetrius (B.C. 150);
mounted the throne of Syria; and received the daughter
of the king of Egypt in marriage.   All this the Jews had
foreseen.   Jonathan, who appeared at the wedding, was

---

[n] 1 Macc. x. 35.

received with the highest honours the court could
bestow. These distinctions were not thrown away on a
useless or ungrateful ally. Apollonius, the general of
young Demetrius, who laid claim to his father's crown,
was defeated by Jonathan; the victorious High Priest
stormed Joppa, took Azotus, and there destroyed the
famous temple of Dagon. The reign of Alexander Balas
was short. He was overthrown by his father-in-law,
Ptolemy, against whose life he had conspired. He fled
into Arabia; the Arab chief, Zabdiel, with whom he
had taken refuge, sent his head to the conqueror. But
Ptolemy, who had won two crowns, those of Syria
and Egypt, died, having been mortally wounded in the
decisive battle which overthrew Balas; and Demetrius, surnamed Nicator, obtained the throne of Syria.
Jonathan seized the opportunity of laying siege to the
citadel of Jerusalem. The opposite faction endeavoured
to obtain the interference of Demetrius; but Jonathan,
leaving his troops to press the siege, went in person to
the court in Antioch. He was received with great
honour, and a treaty was concluded, still more advan-
tageous to his power than that with Alexander Balas.
In return, a body guard of 3000 Jews saved Demetrius
from a dangerous conspiracy, and suppressed a turbulent
sedition in Antioch.° The conspiracy took its rise from
the claims of Antiochus, son of Alexander Balas, who was
supported by Tryphon, an officer equally crafty and ambitious. But the good understanding between Demetrius and Jonathan did not last long: and no sooner
was the support of his powerful vassal withdrawn, than
the Syrian king was constrained to fly, and yield up the

° This part of the history is very
obscure. The conspiracy was organ-
ised by Ammonius, the minister and
favourite of Alexander. It is doubtful
whether Antiochus was privy to it.—
Joseph. Ant. xiii. 4. 6.

throne to his rival, young Antiochus. Jonathan was treated with great distinction by this new sovereign, Antiochus Theos; he was confirmed in his dignity as High Priest. Simon, his brother, was appointed captain-general of all the country from the ladder of Tyre to the river of Egypt. The activity of Jonathan mainly contributed to the security of Antiochus. He gained two signal victories over the armies in the service of Demetrius,[p] strengthened many of the fortresses in Judæa : he built a wall to separate the tower or fortress which the Syrians still held on Mount Sion, to insulate it from the city; and he renewed the treaty with Rome, as also with Lacedæmon.[q] His prosperous career was suddenly cut short by treachery. Tryphon, the officer who had raised the young Antiochus to the throne, began to entertain ambitious views of supplanting his king. The great obstacles to his scheme were the power and integrity of Jonathan. With insidious offers of peace, he persuaded Jonathan to dismiss a large army which he had assembled to assist Antiochus, and allured him within the walls of Ptolemais, with a few followers, under pretence of surrendering to him the town. He then suddenly closed the gates, took Jonathan prisoner, and poured his troops over the great plain of Galilee. The Jews were struck, but not paralysed, with consternation. Another of the noble race of Mattathias remained, and Simon was immediately invested with the command.

Simon, the last of the five brethren, was not the least glorious for the vigour and wisdom of his administration.[r]

---

[p] 1 Macc. xi. 67; xii. 27.

[q] The singular connexion between Jerusalem and Lacedæmon is related with too much particularity. Yet it may perhaps be supposed to contain some truth. But I have seen no satisfactory explanation of it; and there are great difficulties in the documents as compared with the history of Sparta.

[r] It is remarkable that in the investiture of Simon with the supremacy we

The crafty Tryphon began to negotiate: he offered to yield up Jonathan at the price of 100 talents of silver and two of his children, as hostages for his peaceful conduct. The money and the hostages were sent, but the perfidious Tryphon refused to surrender Jonathan. The two armies watched each other for some time. The Syrians being prevented by a heavy fall of snow from relieving their garrison in the fortress of Jerusalem, Tryphon, having first put to death the brave Jonathan,[s] hastened into Syria, where he treated the unhappy Antiochus with the same treachery and atrocity. Simon recovered the body of his brother, which was interred at Modin in great state. A sepulchre, with seven pillars, for the father, mother, and five Maccabean brethren, was raised on an eminence; a sea-mark to all the vessels which sailed along the coast.[t]

Simon openly espoused the party of Demetrius against Tryphon, and received from that monarch a full recognition of the independence of his country. Instead, therefore, of interfering in foreign affairs, he directed his whole attention to the consolidation and internal security of the Jewish kingdom. He sent an embassage, which was honourably received at Rome. He fortified Bethsura on the Idumean frontier, and Joppa, the great port of Judæa; reduced Gazara; and at length having made himself master of the fortress in Jerusalem, not merely dismantled it, but, with incredible labour, levelled the hill on which it stood, so that it no longer commanded the hill of the Temple. Simon executed the law with

---

read these words, which show the full development of the expectation of a Messiah—a religious Messiah:—" the Jews and priests were well pleased that Simon should be their governor and High Priest for ever, until there should arise a faithful prophet."—1 Macc. xiv. 41; compare iv. 46; ix. 27.

[s] 1 Macc. xiii. 23.
[t] 1 Macc. xiii. 27.

great impartiality and vigour; repaired the Temple, restored the sacred vessels. The wasted country began, under his prudent administration, to enjoy its ancient fertility. In the picturesque language of their older poets, the historian says, *The ancient men sat all in the streets, communing together of the wealth of the land, and the young men put on glorious and warlike apparel.*[u] To secure the alliance of the Romans, the great safeguard of the new state, he sent a golden shield, weighing 1000 pounds, to Rome. The Romans, in return, sent a proclamation to many of the kings of the East, to all the cities in the empire in which the Jews were settled, announcing their recognition of Simon as the Prince of Judæa; and while on the one hand the Jews at their command were to acknowledge Simon, on the other they haughtily intimated to the kings and cities under their dominion that the Jews were under their protection and in alliance with Rome. These imperious mandates were addressed to the kings of Syria, Pergamus, and Cappadocia, even to Parthia; to Sparta, Sicyon, Delos, Gortyna in Crete, to Samos, Cos, and Rhodes, to Myndus, Halicarnassus, and Cnidus; to the cities in Lycia and Pamphylia, in Cyprus, the Island of Aradus, the Phœnician territory and Cyrene. This is a singular illustration of the widespread dispersion of the Jews even in those times, and of the all commanding policy of Rome.[x] In the mean time, Demetrius, the rightful sovereign of Syria, had been taken prisoner in an expedition against the Parthians. Antiochus Sidetes, his brother, levied an army to dispossess the usurper and murderer, Tryphon. In a short time Antiochus gained the superiority in the field,

---

[u] 1 Macc. xiv. 9.

[x] 1 Macc. xv. 22–24. The edict was issued in the name of the consul Lucius. Lucius Cæcilius Metellus, with Appius Claudius Pulcher, was consul A.U. 612, B.C. 141.

and besieged Tryphon in Dora.[y]   Simon openly espoused
his party; but Antiochus considered Simon's assistance
dearly purchased at the price of the independence of
Palestine, and above all, the possession of the important
ports of Gazara and Joppa.   Athenobius, his ambassador,
sent to demand tribute and indemnification, was struck
with astonishment at the riches and splendour of Simon's
palace;[z] and on the Jewish sovereign refusing all submission, and only offering a price for the possession of
Joppa, Antiochus sent his general, Cendebeus, to invade
the country.   Simon, now grown old, entrusted the command of his forces to his sons, Judas and John Hyrcanus.
They, having defeated Cendebeus, and taken Azotus,
returned crowned with victory.

But the Maccabean race seemed destined to perish by
violence (B.C. 134).   Ptolemy, son of Abubus, the son-
in-law of Simon, under a secret understanding with Antiochus, king of Syria, formed a conspiracy to usurp the
sovereignty of Judæa.   At a banquet in Jericho, he contrived basely to assassinate Simon and his elder son; and
at the same time endeavoured to surprise the younger,
John Hyrcanus, in Gazara.[a]   But John inherited the
vigour and ability of his family; he eluded the danger,
appeared in Jerusalem, and was unanimously proclaimed
the High Priest and ruler of the country.   His first
measure was to march against Jericho to revenge the
base murder of his father; but Ptolemy had in his power
the mother and brethren of Hyrcanus.   He shut himself
up in a fortress, and exposed his captives on the walls,
scourging them, and threatening to put them to death.
The noble-minded woman exhorted her son, notwithstand-

[y] 1 Macc. xv. 10 et seqq.
[z] 1 Macc. xv. 32.

[a] Rather Gezer, not to be confounded with Gaza.

ing her own danger, to revenge his father's murder : but Hyrcanus hesitated; the siege was protracted; and, at length, according to the improbable reason assigned by Josephus, the year being a Sabbatic year, entirely raised the siege.   Ptolemy fled to Philadelphia; of his subsequent fate we know nothing.   The rapid movements of Hyrcanus had disconcerted the confederacy between the assassin and Antiochus. Still, however, the Syrian army overran the whole country.   Hyrcanus was besieged in Jerusalem, where he was reduced to the last extremity by famine.   He had been compelled to the hard measure of expelling from the city all those, the old and young, of both sexes, who were incapable of contributing to the defence.   The besiegers refused to let them pass; many perished miserably in the ditches and on the outworks.[b] But Antiochus proved a moderate and generous enemy; on the feast of Tabernacles, he conceded a week's truce, furnished the besieged with victims for sacrifice, bulls with golden horns, and gold and silver vessels for the Temple service.   He was gratefully compared with his impious ancestor, Antiochus Epiphanes, and called Antiochus the Pious.[c]   Finally he concluded a peace, of which the terms, though hard, were better than Hyrcanus, in the low condition to which he was reduced, could fairly expect.   The country was to submit to vassalage under the kings of Syria, tribute was to be paid for Joppa and other towns held by grants from the predecessors of Antiochus, and Jerusalem was dismantled. But Hyrcanus, it is said, opened the sepulchre

---

[b] In this siege Jerusalem, for the only time it should seem, suffered for want of water.   Probably the excellent system of wells, conduits, and tanks for the supply of water in the days of Solomon, restored in later times (and which did not fail in the last fatal siege), had been neglected or wilfully destroyed.

[c] Joseph. Ant. xii[i]. 8. 2.

of king David, where he found three thousand talents of silver.

Four years after, John Hyrcanus was summoned to attend his liege lord on an expedition into Parthia, under the pretence of delivering Demetrius Nicator, brother of the king, formerly possessor of the crown, and long a captive in Parthia. Hyrcanus returned before the defeat, which lost Antiochus his throne and life. Demetrius escaped, and recovered the throne of Antioch. Hyrcanus seized the glorious opportunity of throwing off the yoke of Syria, and the Jewish kingdom reassumed its independence, which it maintained until it was compelled to acknowledge the Roman dominion —first under the Asmonean dynasty, then under the house of Herod.

The Syrian monarchy being distracted by rival competitors for the throne, the prudent and enterprising Hyrcanus lost no opportunity of extending his territory and increasing his power. He took Samega and Medaba, in the trans-Jordanic region. But his greatest triumph, that which raised him the highest in the opinion of his zealous countrymen, was the capture of Sichem, and the total destruction of the rival temple on Gerizim.[d] It was levelled to the earth; not a vestige remained. For two hundred years this hated edifice had shocked the sight of the pious pilgrim to Jerusalem. Now the Temple of Jerusalem resumed its dignity as the only sanctuary where the God of their fathers was worshipped, at least within the region of Palestine. The Samaritan temple had always seemed a usurpation upon the peculiar property of the Jewish people in the universal Deity; now they were again undisputed possessors, as of the Divine Presence, so they conceived of the Divine protection.

---

d Joseph. Ant. ix.

Yet, at a more remote distance, another temple had arisen, which excited great jealousy in the more rigid. This was in Egypt, where, in fact, another nation of Jews had gradually grown up. On the capture of Jerusalem by Nebuchadnezzar, a great number of Jews, under Gedaliah, fled to Egypt. Alexander is reported to have encouraged their settlement in his new city of Alexandria by privileges which put them on the same footing with the Macedonians. Ptolemy, founder of the Egypto-Grecian kingdom, transported from Judæa 30,000 families; some he settled in Cyrene, most in Alexandria. During the oppressions of the Syrian kings, many, envying the peaceful and prosperous state of their brethren in Egypt, abandoned Judæa, and took refuge under the protection of the Ptolemies, who, either as useful subjects, or never entirely abandoning their ambitious views on Palestine, generally endeavoured to secure the attachment of the Jews.[e] They lived under their Ethnarch, and occupied a separate portion of the vast city; not as in a Ghetto in later days in the cities of Europe, but in a quarter vying in extent, splendour, and wealth with the other quarters of prosperous Alexandria. Under the reign of Ptolemy Philometor, as has been stated, Onias, (son of that Onias who was murdered by Menelaus,) the rightful heir of the High-priesthood, fled into Egypt. He rose high in favour with the king and his queen, Cleopatra; and, being deprived of his rightful inheritance, Onias conceived the design of building a temple for the use of the Egyptian Jews. The king entered into his views,

---

Herzfeld has a full and valuable chapter on the rise and history of the Alexandrian-Jewish community.—iii. p. 486 et seqq.

On the persecutions attributed to Ptolemy Philopator and Ptolemy Physcon see below.

whether to advance his popularity with his Jewish subjects, or to preserve the wealth, which, as tribute or
offering to the Temple, flowed out of his dominions to
Jerusalem. He granted to Onias a ruined temple in
Leontopolis, in the Heliopolitan nome, and a tract of
land for the maintenance of the worship. Both temple
and domain remained unviolated till the reign of Vespasian. Onias reconciled his countrymen to this bold
innovation by a text in Isaiah (xix. 18, 19). In this
passage it is predicted that *there should be an altar to the
Lord in the midst of the land of Egypt.* According to the
interpretation of Onias, the very place was designated.
That which in our translation appears as " the city of
destruction," was interpreted, perhaps not inaccurately,
the City of the Sun (Heliopolis). Thus then the Jews
of Alexandria claimed divine authority for their temple,
and had unquestionably the legitimate High Priest as
their officiating minister. The Aramean Jews looked on
their Egyptian brethren with assumed contempt, but
inward jealousy: perhaps the distance only prevented
a feud, almost as deadly as that with the Samaritans.[f]

Alexandria being the retreat of Grecian learning, the
Jews turned their attention to literature, and even to
philosophy. But in some respects they were in an
unfortunate situation, with great temptations and great
facilities to substitute fiction for truth. They were
pressed on all sides, by Egyptians, by Greeks, and by
the Aramean Jews. The former denied their antiquity

---

[f] The older mischna says, " Priests
who have officiated in the Temple of
Onias cannot officiate in Jerusalem :
they are to be looked on as priests
who have infirmities (gebreche) ; they
may participate and eat of the offerings, but cannot offer." It appears
from this that the service in the Onias
Temple was not considered idolatry,
but as sacrifice in an unhallowed place.
A man who has vowed an offering, h
he offers in the Onias Temple has not
fulfilled his vow. See the rest of the
passage. Jost, i. 118.

as a nation, and reproached them with the servitude and base condition of their ancestors in Egypt, which they grossly exaggerated; the Greeks treated their national literature with contempt; the rigid Jews could not forgive their adoption of the Greek language and study of Greek letters. The strange legend about the origin of their version of the Scriptures, commonly called the Septuagint, evidently originated in their desire to gain a miraculous sanction for their sacred books, and thus to put them in some degree on the same footing with the original Hebrew Scriptures. This work, which probably was executed at different periods, by writers of various abilities and different styles, was reported by a certain Aristeas to have been the work of seventy-two translators, deputed by the grand Sanhedrin, at the desire of Ptolemy Philadelphus, who were shut up in separate cells, yet each rendered the whole work, word for word, in the same language.[s] The romantic history of the persecution of the Alexandrian Jews, sometimes called the third book of the Maccabees, was apparently compiled with a similar design, to show that they had been exposed, on account of their religion, to equal barbarities with their brethren, endured them with equal courage, and were delivered in a manner equally miraculous. Ptolemy Philopator (or Ptolemy Physcon, for it is not easy to fix a period for the legend) had determined on the extermination of the Jews, unless they would apostatise from their religion. Only 300 consented to this base compliance; the rest were shut up

---

[s] Philo distinctly asserts (and he is a trustworthy authority) that the translation *of the Law* was executed in the reign of Ptolemy Philadelphus. His account, though manifestly that of a Jew, giving the transaction the highest state and importance, has nothing incredible; and his assertion that an annual festival was kept in the island of Pharos to commemorate the event can hardly be called in question.—De Mose, pp. 138 et seqq

in the Hippodrome to be destroyed by elephants. The king being engaged in a drunken revel, the Jews remained a whole day expecting, yet boldly determined to endure, their miserable fate. When the elephants were let loose, they refused to assail the Jews, but turned all their fury on the spectators, on whom they committed frightful ravages.[h] We have mentioned these facts as illustrating the character of the Alexandrian Jews: we pass unwillingly over their controversies with the Egyptians and the Greeks, and the curious union of Grecian philosophy with the Jewish religion, which prevailed in their schools, as these subjects belong rather to the history of Jewish literature than to that of the Jewish people.[i] The Alexandrian Jews mingled in all the transactions and attained the highest honours of the state. Onias, who built the temple during the pontificate of Jonathan, filled the most eminent offices in the state and in the army; and at a later period we shall find Chelcias and Ananias, two Jews, commanding the armies of Cleopatra.

While Egypt and Syria were desolated by the crimes and the contentions of successive pretenders to their thrones, the state of Judæa enjoyed profound peace

---

[h] Herzfeld accepts this as history, stripping off, as is his wont, the marvellous or miraculous part. He assigns it to the reign of Philopator. He may be right. But the parallel story, the same in almost all its incidents, especially as to the elephants, is related by Josephus (contra Apion, ii. 5), and placed under Ptolemy Physcon.

Herzfeld dismisses the angels, said to have appeared, and supposes the elephants to have been frightened by the wild cry arising from thousands of Jews crowded together, and in terror of a most dreadful death.

[i] This subject would still require more ample space and wider investigation than this work can afford. Among the authors who have examined it with industry and success I wou'd name Gfrorer, and especially Dahne, Geschichtliche Darstellung der Jüdisch - Alexandrinischen Religions Philosophie. Halle, 1834.

under the rigorous administration of Hyrcanus. Having
destroyed Sichem, he next turned his forces against
Idumea, subjugated the country, compelled the ancient
rivals of his subjects to submit to circumcision, and to
adopt the Jewish religion; and so completely incorporated the two nations, that the name of Idumea
appears no more in history as a separate kingdom.
Hyrcanus maintained a strict alliance with the Romans,
and renewed a treaty, offensive and defensive, against
their common enemies.[k] In the twenty-sixth year of
his reign he determined to reduce the province and city
of Samaria to his authority. He entrusted the command
of his army to his sons, Aristobulus and Antigonus.
The Samaritans implored the protection of Antiochus
Cyzicenus, then king of Damascus, who marched to
their relief, but suffered a total defeat by the brothers.
In conjunction with 6000 Egyptian allies, Antiochus
made a second attempt to rescue this province from the
power of the Jews, but with no better success. Samaria
fell after an obstinate resistance of a whole year; one of
the Syrian generals betrayed Scythopolis and other
towns to the Jews. Thus Hyrcanus became master
of all Samaria and Galilee. The city of Samaria was
razed, trenches dug (the hill on which it stood being
full of springs), and the whole site of the detested city
flooded and made a pool of water.

---

[k] For the reign of Hyrcanus, Joseph.
Ant. xiii. 10. Justin writes: "Quorum
(Judæorum) vires tantæ fuere, ut post
hunc (Antiochum) nullum Macedo-
nium regem tulerunt, domesticisque
imperiis usi Syriam magnis bellis in-
festaverunt."—Justin, xxxvi. 1.

Justin proceeds to give the view of
the Jews and of their history popular
among the Greeks : a singular confusion of the true and the erroneous.
The expression of wonder at the union
of the temporal with the religious
law under the Priest-Kings (whom he
carries up to Moses and Aaron) is
striking. "Semperque exinde hic mos
apud Judæos fuit, ut eosdem reges et
sacerdotes haberent; quorum justitia
religione permixta, incredibile quantum coaluere."

But though thus triumphant abroad, Hyrcanus, at the end of his reign, was troubled by serious dissensions at home. Two great religious and political factions divided the state—those of the Pharisees and Sadducees. No question in Jewish history is more obscure than the origin and growth of these two parties. The Maccabees had greatly owed their success to the Chasidim, or righteous. The zeal, and even the fanaticism of this party, had been admirable qualities in the hour of trial and exertion. Austerity is a good discipline for the privations and hardships of war. Undaunted courage, daring enterprise, contempt of death, fortitude in suffering, arose directly out of the leading religious principles of this party—the assurance of Divine protection, and the certainty of another life. Their faith, if it led them to believe too much, and induced them to receive the traditions of their fathers as of equal authority with the written law and authentic history, made them believe only with the stronger fervour and sincerity all the wonders and glories of their early annals; wonders and glories which they trusted the same Power, in whose cause, and under whose sanction, they fought, would renew in their persons. Even their belief in angels, celestial, unseen beings, who ever environed them, to assist their arms, and discomfit their enemies, contributed to their confidence and resolution. In this great conflict the hero and the religious enthusiast were one and the same. But those qualities and principles which made them such valiant and active soldiers in war, when the pride of success and conscious possession of power were added, tended to make them turbulent, intractable, and domineering subjects in peace. Those who are most forward in asserting their liberty do not always know how to enjoy it, still less how to concede

it to others.   Their zeal turned into another channel—
the maintenance and propagation of their religious
opinions—and flowed as fiercely and violently as before.
Themselves austere, they despised all who did not practise the same austerities; earnest in their belief, not
only in the law, but in every traditional observance,
they branded as free-thinkers all whose creed was of
greater latitude than their own; and considered it their
duty to enforce the same rigid attention, not merely to
every letter of the law, but likewise to all their own
peculiar observances, which they themselves regarded
as necessary, and most scrupulously performed.   In
every thing, as they were the only faithful servants, so
they were the delegates and interpreters of God.   As
God had conquered by them, so he ruled by them ; and
all their opponents were the enemies of the national
constitution, the national religion, and the national
Deity.   Thus the generous and self-devoted Assideans,
or Chasidim, degenerated into the haughty, tyrannical,
and censorious Pharisees, the Separatists of the Jewish
religion, from *Pharez*, the Hebrew word for " to separate,"
or stand aloof.   The better order among the opponents
of the Pharisees were the Karaites, strict adherents to
the letter of the law, but decidedly rejecting all traditions. The great strength of the party consisted, however, of the Sadducees.[1]   The religious doctrines of the

---

[1] " Daraus ergab sich für alle die-
jenigen welche nach dieser Richtung
hin ihre Ansicht von Judenthum dar-
legten, indem sie jene Berührung des
Unreinen sorgfältig mieden, und schon
dadurch vom Volke und von geselligen
Verkehr sich sonderten, die Benen-
nung *Parusch*, Abgesonderten, sie
mögen solche selbst angenommen oder
von Andern erhalten haben.'   Jost,
Jud. i. 200.
    There is a very remarkable chapter
on the origin of the Sadducees and
Pharisees in Geiger, Urschrift und
Übersetzungen der Bibel, p. 101 et
seqq. He derives the name Sadducee
from Zadok.   The hierarchical families, the descendants of the High Priest

Sadducees, it is well known, were directly opposite to those of the Pharisees. The Pharisees were moderate Predestinarians: the Sadducees asserted Free Will. The Pharisees believed in the immortality of the soul, and the existence of angels, though their creed on both these subjects was strongly tinged with Orientalism: the Sadducees denied both. The Pharisees received not merely the Prophets, but the traditional Law likewise, as of equal authority with the book of Moses. The Sadducees, if they did not reject, considered the Prophets greatly inferior to the Law. The Sadducees are commonly said to have derived their doctrine from Sadoc, the successor of Antigonus Socho in the presidency of the great Sanhedrin.[m] Antigonus taught the lofty doctrine of pure and disinterested love and obedience to God,

---

Zadok, were obliged to cede the High Priesthood first to the Asmoneans, the Maccabees, then to the High Priests appointed by Herod and his successors and by the Romans. But they remained as a priestly aristocracy, proud of their descent, and administering many priestly functions; but gradually shrunk into a sect. "Die Zadokiter hatten so mit aufgehört die Regenten zu sein, sie waren nicht mehr die Melkhisedek 'die Könige der Gerechligkeit' nicht mehr die Zaddikim, 'die Gerechter,' sie standen nicht mehr über dem Volke; die Sadducäer, in welchen die Zadokiten den kern bildeten, waren nun eine Partei im Volke, eine abgeschlossene aristokratische, welche in ihre Exclusivetät den Zudrang der Mässe von sich abwehrte, aber durch als adlige, durch alter des Geschlechts, durch Priesterheiligkeit oder durch neu erworbene Ansehn den bedeutendensten Einfluss hatte, eine kleine aber machtige Partei." The Pharisees, though separatists, were the popular, the democratic faction. Geiger adds with characteristic Germanism:—"Sie sind um eine Analogie aus neuerer Zeit anzwenden, die Independenten gegenuber den Episcopalen." Geiger refers, as an illustration of his views, to the remarkable passage, Acts iv. 1-4.

[m] They were by most accounts two kindred, but to a certain degree conflicting sects, the Sadducees and Boethusians, derived from Sadoc and Boethus. The latter, however, are but dimly traced, and either died away or melted into the cognate Sadducees. Jost asserts that the earliest distinct account of the origin of the Sadducees is in a late Rabbinical work, the Aboth of R. Nathan: but both names are found in the older Mischna; and Josephus is full concerning them.

without regard to punishment or reward. Sadoc is
said to have denied the latter, without maintaining the
higher doctrine on which it was founded. Still the
Sadducees were far from what they are sometimes
represented, the teachers of a loose and indulgent
Epicureanism; they inculcated the belief in Divine
Providence, and the just and certain administration of
temporal rewards and punishments. The Pharisees had
the multitude, ever led away by extravagant religious
pretensions, entirely at their disposal: Sadduceeism
spread chiefly among the higher orders.[n] It would be
unjust to the Sadducees to confound them with that
unpatriotic and Hellenized party, which, during the
whole of the noble struggles of the Maccabees, sided
with the Syrian oppressors, for these are denounced as
avowed apostates from Judaism; yet probably, after
the establishment of the independent government, the
latter might make common cause, and become gradually
mingled up with the Sadducean party, as exposed alike
to the severities of the Pharisaic administration.[o] During

---

[a] I have no doubt that in one of
the noblest books among those called
the Apocryphal we have the work of a
Sadducee, or rather, for it is a manifest fusion of several books, a full
declaration of the views of the higher
Sadducaic anti-traditional party. In
the book of Ecclesiasticus there are
magnificent descriptions of God's crea-
tive power, of His all-comprehending
providence, of His chastisement of un-
righteousness, of His rewards of godli-
ness; the most beautiful precepts of
moral and social virtue, of worldly
wisdom and sagacity, of chastity, temperance, justice, beneficence—*but of a
life after death not one word.* Not only

this (and silence on such a subject is
conclusive), but there is what amounts
to a direct abnegation of such doctrine.
" For all things cannot be in men,
because the son of man is not immortal," (xvii. 30.) In sorrow for the
dead, too, there is no word of consolation from the hope of another life,
xxii. 11 ; xxxviii. 17 ; xl. (and xli.) So
as to angels: in the whole book there is
no word recognising any intermediate
beings between God and man. I can
find no passage which might not have
been written by a highly religious Sadducee ; and that such Sadducees there
were, there can be no doubt.
[o] Jost has a curious chapter on the

the rest of the Jewish history we shall find these parties
as violently opposed to each other, and sometimes
causing as fierce and dangerous dissensions, as those
which rent the commonwealths of Greece and Rome, or
the republican states of modern Italy.

It was at the close of his reign that Hyrcanus broke
with the Pharisaic party, and openly joined the opposite
faction—a measure of which the disastrous consequences
were not entirely felt till the reign of his son Alexander.
The cause of this rupture is singularly characteristic of
Jewish manners.   During a banquet, at which the chief
of the ruling sect were present, Hyrcanus demanded
their judgement on his general conduct and administration of affairs, which he professed to have regulated by
the great principles of justice, and by strict adherence
to the tenets of their sect.   The Pharisees, with general
acclamation, testified their approval of all his proceedings;—one voice alone, that of Eleazar, interrupted the
general harmony.   "If you are a just man, abandon
the High-priesthood, for which you are disqualified by
the illegitimacy of your birth."   The mother of Hyrcanus had formerly, it was said, though, according to
Josephus, falsely, been taken captive, and thus exposed
to the polluting embraces of a heathen master.   The
indignant Hyrcanus demanded the trial of Eleazar for
defamation.   By the influence of the Pharisees he was
shielded, and escaped with scourging and imprisonment.
Hyrcanus, enraged at this unexpected hostility, listened
to the representations of Jonathan, a Sadducee, who
accused the rival faction of a conspiracy to overawe the
sovereign power; and from that time he entirely

differences between the Pharisees and
Sadducees in their interpretation of
the Law, as to some points of the
daily or other sacrifices, and as to some
of the ordinary usages of life, even of
inheritance. c. ix. p. 216.

alienated himself from the Pharisaic council. This
able prince reigned for twenty-nine years; he built the
castle of Baris on a rock within the fortifications which
surrounded the hill of the Temple, on the north-west
corner of which it stood. It afterwards became the
Antonia of Herod.

Aristobulus, the son of Hyrcanus, succeeded: his reign,
though brief, was long enough for much crime and
much misery. His mother, by the will of Hyrcanus,
claimed the sovereignty; he threw her into a dungeon,
and starved her to death. The fate of his brother
Antigonus (the one of his brothers whom he loved)
will immediately appear: the other three of his brethren
were kept in close imprisonment. Soon after he had
assumed the diadem, the new king made a successful
expedition and subdued Iturea, a district at the foot of
Anti-Libanus, afterwards called Auranitis. He returned,
suffering under a dangerous malady. His brother
Antigonus, a short time after, having completed the
conquest, as he entered Jerusalem, hastened, all armed
as he was, with his soldiers, to pay his devotions in the
Temple; to utter his thanksgiving prayers, it is added,
for his brother's recovery.[p] This innocent act was misre-
presented by the queen and the harem of Aristobulus as
covering a treacherous design. Aristobulus sent to sum-
mon his brother to attend him unarmed. The treacherous
enemies of Antigonus, instead of this message, delivered
one commanding him to come with some very splendid
armour, which his brother wished to see. The guards
were posted; and Antigonus, appearing in arms, was
assassinated in the subterranean gallery which led from
the Temple to the palace of Baris. Aristobulus, seized

---

[p] Joseph. Ant. xiii. 11.

with agonizing compunction for his crime, vomited blood. The slave who bore the vessel away, happened to stumble on the very spot where Antigonus had been slain, and the blood of the two brothers mingled on the pavement. A cry of horror ran through the palace. The king, having extorted from the reluctant attendants the dreadful cause, was seized with such an agony of remorse and horror, that he expired.[q]

Alexander Jannæus, the next in succession, assumed the throne; a feeble attempt was made by his younger brother to usurp his place, but the rebel was seized and put to death.[r] Alexander was an enterprising rather than a successful prince; and it was perhaps fortunate for the kingdom of Judæa that the adjacent states were weakened by dissension and mutual hostility. Egypt was governed by Cleopatra, widow of Ptolemy Physcon; Cyprus by Ptolemy Lathyrus, her eldest son, and most deadly enemy. The Syrian monarchy was shared by Antiochus Grypus and Antiochus Cyzicenus: one held his court at Antioch, the other at Damascus. The Jews possessed the whole region of Palestine, except the noble port of Ptolemais; Dora and the Tower of Straton were in the hands of Zoilus, who owned a sort of allegiance to Syria. Gaza was likewise independent of the Jewish government. The first object of Alexander was to reduce all these cities. He formed the siege of Ptolemais. The inhabitants sent to demand relief from Ptolemy Lathyrus, but after the Cyprian king had levied an army of 30,000 men, dreading the loss of their independence, the Ptolemaites refused to admit him into their gates.

---

[q] All this was said to have been foreshown by an Essenian prophet. Perhaps the life of Aristobulus was darkened by religious animosity: he was called by the unpopular name φιλέλλην.

[r] Joseph. Ant. xiii. 12.

D 2

Ptolemy turned on the dominions of Zoilus, and on Gaza. Alexander entered into negotiations with Ptolemy for the friendly surrender of those places, and at the same time with Cleopatra for a large force to expel the king of Cyprus from Palestine. Ptolemy, detecting the double intrigue, marched into Judæa, took Asochis near the Jordan on the Sabbath, ravaged the country, and (by the assistance of an expert tactician, Philostephanus) totally defeated Alexander, with the loss of 30,000 men, pursued his ravages, and, to spread the terror of his name, is said to have practised most abominable cruelties.[a] Having surprised a village full of women and children, he ordered them to be hewn in pieces, and cast into caldrons, as if to be boiled; so that the horror of this invasion of cannibals spread throughout the whole country. The kingdom of Judæa was lost but for a great army of Egyptians under the command of Chelcias and Ananias, two Alexandrian Jews.[b] Lathyrus retreated into Cœlesyria: part of Cleopatra's army pursued him, part formed the siege of Ptolemais. Lathyrus determined on the bold measure of marching into Egypt: he was repelled, and retreated to Gaza. Ptolemais fell; and Alexander came to congratulate the Queen of Egypt on her victory. Cleopatra was strongly urged to seize the prince, and thus make herself mistress of Judæa: the remonstrances of Ananias, the Jew, dissuaded her from this breach of faith.

The Cypriot and Egyptian armies being withdrawn, Alexander resumed his sovereignty; but his restless disposition involved him in new wars, with no better success. He invaded the country east of the Jordan, took Gadara, but was totally defeated before Amathus,

---

[a] Joseph. Ant. xiii. 12. 5, 6   [b] Joseph. Ant. xiii. 13. 1.

which he had plundered of the treasures of Theodorus, prince of Philadelphia.   The indefatigable Prince Priest next fell upon the territory of Gaza, took Raphia and Anthedon, and, although constrained to raise the siege of Gaza by a descent of Lathyrus, he formed it again the next year.   Gaza made an obstinate resistance.   At one time the besieger had nearly lost his whole army by a desperate sally of the besieged; at length, however, the commander of the garrison, Apollodotus, having been slain by treachery, Gaza surrendered.   Alexander at first seemed inclined to mercy, but, before long, let loose his troops to revenge themselves on the town.   The inhabitants took up arms; yet, after a considerable loss, the conqueror succeeded in totally dismantling and destroying this ancient city, and left it a heap of ruins.

But the most dangerous enemies of Alexander were at home.   The Pharisaic faction had the populace at their command; and at the feast of Tabernacles, while he was officiating as king and High Priest, a mutiny broke out.   The mob pelted him with citrons, reproached him with the baseness of his descent, and denied his right to the priesthood.   Alexander commanded his troops to fall on the unarmed multitude, and slew 6000.   To prevent these insults in future, Alexander raised a wooden partition between the court of the priests and that of the people; and, to awe the insurgents, enrolled a body guard of foreign mercenaries, chiefly Pisidians and Cilicians.   He then, a second time, invaded the country east of Jordan, reduced it to pay tribute, took Amathus, but again suffered a total defeat by Orodes, king of Arabia.   The Jews seized the opportunity to rise in rebellion, and for six years the country suffered all the horrors of civil war.   Alexander at first met with great success; but when he endeavoured to bring the mutineers to terms, they cried out with one voice, that they would yield only on one condition, that he would put himself to death. At length, pressed on all sides, the insurgents demanded the assistance of Demetrius Euchærus, one of the kings of Syria. Alexander, always unfortunate in battle, was routed, with the loss of all his 6000 mercenaries and many other of his troops. He fled to the mountains; but a sudden revulsion of popular feeling took place in his favour, and he found himself at the head of 60,000 men. Demetrius retreated, and Alexander, master of the whole country, besieged his enemies in Bethome, took the city, and marched to Jerusalem in triumph. His vengeance was signal and terrible. During a banquet, in the midst of his concubines, he publicly crucified 800 men, and slew their wives and children before their faces. From this atrocity he was named the Thracian. Of the disaffected, 8000 abandoned the city; but, under his iron sway, the whole country remained in awed submission, though not unharassed with wars against the Syrians and Arabians, during the rest of his reign. His foreign policy at this period was equally vigorous. The kingdom of the Jews at his death comprehended the coast from the Tower of Straton to Rhinocorura, Idumea, Samaria, and considerable provinces to the east of the Jordan. In the fourth year after his triumph over the insurgents, Alexander Jannæus was seized with a mortal malady. A disturbed and rebellious kingdom, and newly conquered provinces, were not likely to submit to the feeble authority of women and children.[u] The dying

---

[u] Ptolemy Lathyrus had established Demetrius on the throne of Damascus. His brother Philip reigned in Antioch. Joseph. Ant. xiii. 14.

It is to all this period of Jewish history that Tacitus appears vaguely to allude :—" Dum Assyrios penes Medosque et Persas Oriens fuit despec-

king summoned his wife Alexandra, and strongly urged, as the only means of preserving the kingdom, that on his death she should throw herself into the arms of the Pharisaic party, powerful on account of their numbers and turbulence, and still more from having the people entirely under their direction. Thus, after an unquiet and eventful reign of twenty-seven years, Alexander Jannæus died.[x] His widow Alexandra immediately adopted the policy which he had suggested, and threw the administration into the hands of the Pharisees. The change was instant; the greatest honours were paid to the remains of the unpopular Jannæus, and the High-priesthood was conferred on his eldest son, Hyrcanus II.

During the whole reign of Alexandra, the wisdom, or rather the imperious necessity of her husband's dying admonition, became more manifest; the throne stood secure, the whole land, says Josephus, was at rest, except the Pharisees, who began to execute dreadful reprisals upon their former adversaries. Having strengthened their party by a general release of prisoners and recall of exiles, they began their attack on Diogenes, a favourite of the late king. They next demanded public justice

---

tissima pars servientium: postquam Macedones præpotuêre rex Antiochus demere superstitionem et mores Græcorum dare adnixus, quominus teterrimam gentem in melius mutaret, Parthorum bello prohibitus est: nam eâ tempestate Arsaces desciverat. Tum Judæi, Macedonibus invalidis, Parthis nondum adultis (et Romani procul erant), sibi ipsi reges imposuere; qui mobilitate vulgi expulsi, resumpta per arma dominatione, fugas civium, urbium eversiones, fratrum, conjugum, parentum, neces, aliaque solita regibus ausi, superstitionem fovebant: quia honor sacerdotii firmamentum potentiæ adsumebatur." Hist. v. 8. Strabo, after a strange, loose account of Moses and the earlier history of the Jews, jumps to this period—Ἤδη δὲ δυν φανερῶς τυραννουμένης τῆς Ιουδιας, πρῶτος ἀνθ' ἱερέως ἀνεδειξεν ἑαυτον βασίλεα 'Αλέξανδρος. Lib. xvi. p. 762.

[x] Joseph. Ant. xii. 16.

on all who had been accessory to the execution of the
800 who were crucified.[y]   Alexandra, unable to resist,
was compelled to submit; but her second son, Aristobulus, a man of daring ambition and intrigue, seized the
opportunity of placing himself at the head of the party,
which, though now oppressed, was still powerful. They
appealed to the justice as well as to the mercy of the
queen, and remonstrated on the ingratitude of abandoning the faithful adherents of her husband to the vengeance of their enemies. She adopted a measure intended to secure them, without offending the Pharisees;
they were allowed to leave Jerusalem, and were enrolled
as the garrisons of the frontier cities. To employ the

---

[y] According to Rabbinical authorities (Jost, i. 241), the administration of justice rested during the reign
of Alexandra with Simon b. Schetach
and Judah b. Tabbai, both Pharisees.
One of the great points in dispute
between the two sects was as to the
punishment to be inflicted on false
witnesses in capital cases. The Sadducees maintained that the false witnesses were not to be executed unless
the accused had suffered death through
their perjury. Ben Tabbai put to death
certain false witnesses where the accused
had not lost his life. "As I hope for
comfort," he said, "to confute the lying
doctrine of the Sadducees." "As I
hope for comfort," said B. Schetach,
"you have done wrong : false witnesses
incur neither death nor stripes, unless
they are all convicted of false witness."
Ben Tabbai declared that he would never
again deliver a judgment without con-
sulting Ben Schetach. Every day he
prostrated himself on the grave of
them whom he had executed, and implored pardon. But Ben Schetach
hung up eighty women, near Ascalon,
for witches, having himself been the
only witness of their dark proceedings
in a cave. In revenge for this, his son
was accused of a capital crime. The
son was condemned to death. As he
was carried to execution the witnesses
declared that they had sworn falsely.
Ben Schetach ordered his son to be
released. "Father, if thou wishest
for the welfare of Israel, let me die."
Some suppose that the cool-blooded
youth wished to ensure the death of
his perjured enemies. But whether
he was actually put to death does not
appear. Jost, Jud., 244. This is a
curious illustration of the hatred of
the two parties, both zealous for the
written law, but sacrificing their own
lives and those of others for their own
interpretation of it.

Simon ben Schetach, says Jost, was
the soul of the new Pharisaic legisla-
tion.

restless mind of her son Aristobulus, she sent him, with a considerable army, under the pretence of checking the depredations of Ptolemy, who ruled a small independent kingdom at Chalcis, but with the secret design of seizing Damascus. Aristobulus succeeded both in the object contemplated by his mother and in his own; he got possession of Damascus, and strongly attached the army to his person. After a prosperous reign of nine years, Alexandra fell sick and died; a woman of masculine understanding and energy of character. Before her decease, Aristobulus secretly fled from Jerusalem, put himself at the head of the army, summoned all the frontier garrisons, which were composed of his own party, to his assistance, and immediately, upon the death of his mother, advanced rapidly towards Jerusalem. The Pharisaic party, with Hyrcanus at their head, seized as hostages the wife and children of Aristobulus, and hastily raising their forces, met the invader at Jericho. But the affections of the army were centered in the bold and enterprising Aristobulus; a great part deserted, the rest were discomfited, the younger brother entered Jerusalem, the elder was besieged in the palace of Baris; till at length the mild and indolent Hyrcanus consented to yield up the sovereignty, and retire perhaps to the happier station of a private man. The blow was fatal to the Pharisaic party.

But an enemy remained, whose descendants were to be more dangerous opponents to the Asmonean house even than the Pharisees. Antipater, the father of Herod, an Idumean of noble birth, was the son of Antipas, who had been governor of that province under Alexander Jannæus. Antipater had acquired great influence over the feeble mind of Hyrcanus as his chief minister. He had every prospect of enjoying all but the name of a sovereign. He ill brooked the annihilation of his ambitious hopes by the conquest of Aristobulus. At length, after long working on the fears of Hyrcanus, as if his life were in danger, Antipater persuaded him to fly to Aretas, the King of Arabia. This kingdom had silently grown up to considerable power. Petra, its capital, had become the great emporium of the commerce through the Red Sea and Persian Gulf. Aretas marched an host of 50,000 men against Aristobulus. The capricious army of the Jews wavered. Aristobulus suffered a defeat, and fled to Jerusalem. There, abandoned likewise by the people, he shut himself up in the Temple, where the priests prepared for defence. He was vigorously pressed by Aretas, Antipater, and Hyrcanus. During this siege two characteristic circumstances took place. An old man, named Onias, had the fame of having prayed for rain during a drought, and rain had immediately fallen. The party of Hyrcanus brought him out to employ his powerful prayers against Aristobulus. The patriotic old man knelt down, and uttered these words:—"O God, the King of the Universe, since on one side are thy people, on the other thy priests, I beseech thee hear not the prayers of either to the detriment of the other." The cruel and infatuated populace stoned him to death. The second occurrence was as follows:—The Passover drew near, and there were no victims in the Temple for sacrifice. The besieged entered into an agreement that, on payment of a certain price, lambs should be furnished for the great national offering. They let baskets down the walls, but the perfidious besiegers took the money and sent up the baskets empty, or, as the Rabbins relate with the deepest horror, loaded with swine.

An unexpected deliverer at length appeared: a mili-

tary officer of that haughty republic which had been
steadily pursuing its way to universal dominion; and
now, having trampled under foot the pride and strength
of the great Asiatic monarchies, assumed a right of interfering in the affairs of every independent kingdom.
Rome, who had up to this time been content to awe
Asia and the East with the remote thunders of menace
and admonition, to establish alliances, and to hold herself up as the protector of those weak states who implored her aid, and whom it was politic (of justice she
thought not) to support against powerful oppressors, now
appeared in the persons of her consuls and their subordinate officers. Scaurus, the lieutenant of Pompey, had
seized Damascus; the competitors for the Jewish throne
endeavoured to outbid each other for his protection.[s]
Aristobulus offered 400 talents—Hyrcanus the same.
The rapacious Roman hesitated; but Aristobulus was in
possession of the public treasures of the Temple, and
therefore most likely to make good his terms. Scaurus
sent an order to Aretas to break up the siege; the
Arabian complied. The enterprising Aristobulus, hastily
collecting troops, fell unexpectedly on his rear, and gave
him a signal defeat.

In a short time, Pompey himself arrived at Damascus.
Kings crowded from all sides to pay homage and to conciliate, with splendid presents, the greatest subject of the
republic. The present of the king of Egypt was a gold
crown, worth 4000 pieces of gold; that of Aristobulus a
golden vine, worth 500 talents.[a] After a short absence
in Pontus and Armenia, Pompey returned to Syria,

---

[s] Joseph. Ant. xiv. 2. In the account, B. J. 1. 6, the bribes were
offered only by Aristobulus.

[a] Strabo, according to Josephus,
had seen this precious and beautiful
piece of workmanship: it was called

and the ambassadors of Hyrcanus and Aristobulus
appeared before the tribunal of their master; the wily
Antipater on the part of Hyrcanus—on that of Aristobulus a certain Nicodemus, who had so little address
as to complain of the extortions of the Roman commanders, Scaurus and Gabinius.   Pompey appointed a
solemn hearing of the cause for the next spring at Damascus, and accordingly, at that time the ambassadors of
Hyrcanus, of Aristobulus, and of the Jewish people,
stood before the tribunal of the Roman.   The people
began the charge against both the brothers: they had
usurped (it was urged) an authority which belonged
solely to the High Priests, introduced a kingly despotism,
and reduced a free people to servitude.   The ambassador
of Hyrcanus pleaded his superior title as the elder born;
accused Aristobulus not merely of usurping the throne
of his brother, and degrading him to a private station,
but of committing wanton depredations by land and
piracies by sea, on all the neighbouring states.   The
cause of Hyrcanus was supported by more than a thousand of the most illustrious of the Jews, suborned by
Antipater.   On the part of Aristobulus, the total incapacity of Hyrcanus was strongly pressed; his own pretensions to power were limited to that enjoyed by his
father Alexander.   On his behalf appeared a troop of
insolent youths, splendidly arrayed in purple, with flowing hair, and rich armour, who carried themselves as if
they were the true nobles of the land.   But Pompey
had a greater object in view than the settlement of

---

the Delight (τερπώλη). Joseph. Ant.
xiv. 3, 1.   Tacitus suggests a strange
conclusion from this vine, found, as
he says, in the Temple—that the Jews
were worshippers of Bacchus. " It was

not true," says he; " for the worship
of Bacchus is glad and gay, that of the
Jews absurd and sordid." , Was this
vine of Greek workmanship?   Tac.
Hist. v. 5.

Judæa—the subjugation of Arabia, with the seizure of
Petra and its trade. He dismissed both parties with
great civility, particularly Aristobulus, who had the
power of impeding his designs. Aristobulus, suspecting
the goodness of his own cause, endeavoured to put the
country in a state of defence; but Pompey, on his return
from Arabia, began to assume a higher tone. He collected his forces, and marched directly into Judæa. He
found Aristobulus shut up in a strong citadel on a rock,
called Alexandrion. Aristobulus attempted to negotiate; twice he descended from his place of security
to hold a conference with Pompey; the third time
Pompey forced him to sign written orders for the surrender of all his fortresses. The bold and enterprising
spirit of Aristobulus could not brook the disgrace of
submission; too high-minded to yield, too weak to
resist, his conduct shows a degree of irresolution and
vacillation which it is more just to attribute to the difficulty of his situation than to want of vigour in his
character. He fled to Jerusalem, and prepared for resistance.

Pompey advanced to Jericho, where the Romans were
struck with admiration at the beautiful palm-groves
and gardens of balsam-shrubs, which, originally the
growth of Arabia, flourished in that district with great
luxuriance: their produce had become an important
article of trade.[b] As he approached Jerusalem, Aristobulus, who found the city too much divided to make
effectual resistance, met him, and offered a large sum of
money, and the surrender of the capital. Gabinius was

---

[b] "Opes genti ex vectigalibus opo-
balsami crevere, quod in his tantum
regionibus gignitur." Justin, xxxv. 3.
Florus uses these remarkable expressions :—"Damascumque transgressus
per nemora alta odorata, per thuris et
balsami sylvas, Romana circumtulit
signa." Hist. vi. 2.

sent forward to take possession of the city, but the
bolder party, meantime, had gained the ascendancy,
and he found the gates closed and the walls manned.
Indignant at this apparent treachery, Pompey threw the
king into chains, and advanced in person on Jerusalem.[c]
The party of Hyrcanus were superior in the city, and
immediately received the invader with open arms. The
soldiery of Aristobulus took possession of the Temple,
and, with the priesthood, cut off all the bridges and
causeways which communicated with the town, and prepared for an obstinate defence. The hill of the Temple,
precipitous on three sides, was impregnable, except from
the north. On that side Pompey made his approaches,
where, nevertheless, there was a rapid descent, flanked
by lofty towers. Notwithstanding the arrival of military
engines from Tyre, this holy citadel held out for three
months, and was only lost through the superstitious observance of the Sabbath. The Maccabean relaxation of
this law only provided for actual self-defence ; the
Romans soon perceived that they might carry on their
works without disturbance on that day. They regularly,
therefore, suspended their assault, but employed the
time in drawing the engines near the walls, filling up
the trenches, and in other labours, which they carried
on without the least impediment. At the end of the
three months, one of the battering engines threw down
the largest of the towers. Cornelius Faustus, a son of
Sylla, mounted the breach, and, after an obstinate

---

[c] This view of the proceedings
reconciles the somewhat conflicting
accounts in Josephus and in Dion
Cassius, lib. xxxvii. 15. According
to the latter, Aristobulus was a prisoner in chains in the camp of Pompey
on his advance.

Dion Cassius writes of the Jews—
καὶ ἔστι παρὰ τοῖς Ῥωμαίοις τὸ γένος
τοῦτο, κολουσθὲν μὲν πολλάκις,
αὐξηθὲν δὲ ἐπὶ πλεῖστον, ὥστε καὶ ἐν
παρρησίαν τῆς νομίσεως ἐκνικῆσαι.

resistance and great loss of life, the Romans remained masters of the Temple.[d]   During the assault, the priests had been employed in the daily sacrifice: unmoved by the terror, and confusion, and carnage around, they calmly continued their office. Many of them were slain, many of the more zealous defenders of the Temple threw themselves headlong down the precipices.   The conduct of the Roman general excited at once the horror and the admiration of the Jews.   He entered the Temple, surveyed every part, and even penetrated and profaned with his heathen presence the Holy of Holies, into which the High Priest entered only once a year.   Great was his astonishment to find this mysterious sanctuary entirely empty, with no statue, or form or symbol of the Deity, to whom it was consecrated.   In the other parts he found immense riches—the golden table and candlesticks, a great store of precious frankincense, and two thousand talents in the treasury.   All these with gene-

---

[d] Josephus quotes as his Roman authorities for the taking of Jerusalem by Pompey, Strabo, Nicolaus of Damascus, and Titus Livius. Cicero pro Flacco writes thus :—" At Cn. Pompeius, captis Hierosolymis, victor ex illo fano nihil attigit. In primis hoc, ut multa alia, sapienter, quod in tam *suspiciosa ac maledica civitate* locum sermoni obtrectatorum non reliquit, non enim, credo, religionem et Judæorum et hostium impedimento præstantissimo imperatori, sed pudorem fuisse." c. 28. Compare Tac. Hist. v. 5. The account in Dion Cassius is so singularly coincident with that of Josephus, that it may have been taken from it. Compare Strabo, xvi.; Appian, Syriac. 1.; Mithridat. çvi., cxvii. In the inscription re-

lating the names of the captive kings subdued by Pompey appears the King of the Nabathæans, not the King of the Jews. See the quotation above from Dion Cassius ; he proceeds :—καὶ μάλισθ' ὅτι τῶν μὲν ἄλλων θεῶν οὐδένα τιμῶσιν, ἕνα δέ τινα ἰσχυρῶς σέβουσι. 'Οὐδ' ἄγαλμα οὐδὲν ἐν αυτοῖς ποτε τοῖς Ἱεροσολύμοις ἔσχον· ἄρρητον δὲ δὴ καὶ ἀειδῆ αὐτὸν νομίζοντες εἶναι, περισσότατα ἀνθρώπων θρησκεύουσι. Dion goes on to admire the splendour of the Temple.

Cicero in one place writes of Pompey as "noster Hierosolymarius"—thus seeming to attach great importance to the occupation of Jerusalem even among the splendid services of Pompey. The passage is in the oration pro Flacco.

rosity not less noble because it was politic, he left
untouched—commanded the Temple to be purified from
the carnage of his soldiers—nominated Hyrcanus to the
priesthood, though without the royal diadem. Then,
having appointed the stipulated tribute which the
country was to pay—demolished the walls of the city—
and limited the dominions of Hyrcanus to Judæa—
he departed, carrying with him Aristobulus, his two
sons and two daughters, as prisoners to Rome. Alexander, the elder son, on the journey, made his escape;
but the Jewish king and his second son adorned the
splendid triumph of the conqueror. The magnanimity
of Pompey, in respecting the treasures of the Temple,
could not obliterate the deeper impression of hatred excited by his profanation of the sacred precincts. The
Jews beheld with satisfaction the decline of Pompey's
fortune, which commenced from this period, and attributed it entirely to his sacrilegious impiety. Throughout
the world they embraced the party of Cæsar, fortunate,
inasmuch as the course they followed from blind passion
conduced eventually to their real interests, and obtained
for them important privileges and protection from the
imperial house.

Alexander, the son of Aristobulus, inherited the
daring and active courage of his father; he soon gathered
a considerable force, and garrisoned Machaerus, Hyrcania, and the strong fort of Alexandrion. Hyrcanus
hastily summoned the Romans to his assistance. Gabinius entered Judæa, and, having defeated Alexander,
for the Jews could make no great stand in the open
field, besieged him in Alexandrion. While the siege
lasted, to secure the affections of the provinces, Gabinius
commanded many of the cities which the Asmoneans
had destroyed, to be rebuilt—Samaria, Dora, Scytho-

polis, Gaza, and other towns. In the mean time, the mother of Alexander, who had always espoused the Roman party, by her interest with Gabinius brought about a treaty, in which Alexander received an amnesty for his insurrection, on condition of surrendering his fortresses. No sooner was he subdued, than Aristobulus himself and his younger son, having escaped from Rome, raised again the standard of revolt, but with worse fortune; for, though many of the Jews deserted to his banner, and he had time to refortify Alexandrion, he was taken, after being severely wounded, and sent back in chains to Rome. The interest of the mother procured the intercession of Gabinius for the release of her son Antigonus, which was granted by the senate. Aristobulus remained a prisoner. Gabinius, in the interval between these insurrections, reorganized the whole government of the country; he deprived the High Priest of the royal authority, and established five independent senates or sanhedrins, according to the form of the great Sanhedrin of seventy-one, which perhaps had existed from the Captivity. The places where the sanhedrins sat, were Jerusalem, Jericho, Gadara, Amathus, and Sepphoris. This form of government lasted till Julius Cæsar re-invested Hyrcanus with the supreme dignity. Gabinius, with Mark Antony, who had signalized his valour during three campaigns, as his master of the horse,[*] now determined on the conquest of Egypt; but scarcely had he drawn off his troops from Syria, when the restless Alexander appeared again in arms, and drove the few remaining Romans into a strong position on Mount Gerizim, where he besieged them. On the return of Gabinius, Alexander had the courage to meet him, at

---

* Plutarch, Vit. Antonii.

the head of 80,000 men, in the open field, near Mount
Tabor; but the irresistible Roman discipline bore all
before it, and the Jewish prince was obliged to take
flight.

It was singular, and the fact strongly tended to confirm the Jews in their conviction that they were under
the especial protection of the Almighty, that the worst
enemies of their nation seemed marked for disaster and
disgrace. Gabinius no sooner returned to Rome, than
he was ignominiously banished for his rapacity and mal-
versations. The fate of Crassus in Parthia followed
almost immediately on his sacrilegious plunder of the
Jewish Temple. When the rapacious triumvir entered
Jerusalem on his way to that fatal expedition, the High
Priest, Eleazar, attempted to appease his avarice by the
surrender of a bar of gold of immense value, concealed
within a hollow beam of wood, known to none but himself.
This offering only whetted the appetite of Crassus; he
pillaged without remorse all that Pompey had spared,
even the sacred treasures, and all that had since accu-
mulated;—for the Jews, now spread throughout almost
all the world, made it a part of religion to send an
annual contribution for the service of the Temple. This
sum was so large, even in Italy, that Cicero, in his
oration in defence of Flaccus, seems to urge the wisdom
of a similar measure to that adopted by his client in
Asia Minor, a prohibition of the practice, as draining
the Roman provinces of their wealth.[f] Hence the plunder

---

[f] "Cum aurum, Judæorum nomine, quotannis ex Italiâ, et ex omnibus provinciis, Hierosolyma exportari soleret, Flaccus sanxit edicto, ne ex Asiâ exportari liceret. Quis est Judices, qui hoc non verè laudare possit? Exportari aurum non oportere, cum sæpe antea senatus, tum, me consule, gravissimè judicavit. Huic autem barbaræ superstitioni resistere, severitatis; multitudinem Judæorum, flagrantem nonnunquam in concionibus, pro republicâ contemnere, gravitatis summæ fuit." This very remarkable passage

of Crassus from the Temple of Jerusalem, estimated at
ten thousand talents, according to Prideaux, near two
millions of money, though perhaps exaggerated, may not
be so remote from truth.

During the great civil war, the fate of Judæa, like
that of the world, hung in trembling suspense. Cæsar,
master of Rome, sent Aristobulus an order to create a
diversion in the province of Palestine. The partisans of
Pompey contrived to poison the ill-fated monarch; and
Scipio publicly executed his gallant son Alexander at
Antioch. Thus Hyrcanus, or rather Antipater under his
name, retained the sovereignty.[s] After the death of
Pompey, in that romantic war which Cæsar, delaying to
assume the empire of the universe, waged in Egypt in
favour of Cleopatra, the prudent Antipater rendered
him essential service. He facilitated the march of
Mithridates, king of Pergamus, Cæsar's ally, to his
relief, and contributed to the reduction of Pelusium;
conciliated the Egyptian Jews, who had espoused the
opposite party, and greatly distinguished himself in an
important battle. His reward was the full re-establishment of Hyrcanus in the High-priesthood; for himself,

---

(see the conclusion above) shows,
curiously enough, the Jews as already
exporters of gold, though but religious
offerings, yet affecting the markets of
the world; their great numbers, and
clamour in the public assemblies in
the cities of Asia Minor; the astonishment that Pompey had the moderation,
for which Cicero is perplexed to account, not to plunder the Temple, and
was unwilling to expose himself to the
reproaches of a people so likely to be
heard as the Jews.

According to Appian there were
Jewish as well as Syrian and Phœnician troops in the army of Pompey at
Pharsalia (B. C. ii. 71). They were
probably forced levies.

[s] Joseph. Ant. xiv. 8, 1. Josephus
had quoted a passage in Strabo in
which the geographer asserts that a
large part of Alexandria was assigned
to the Jews, and that they formed a
fourth part, or class, of the inhabitants
of the Cyrenaica (xiv. 7, 3).

the rights of Roman citizenship, and the appointment
of Procurator over the whole of Judæa.[h] The first care
of the new government was to rebuild the walls of Jerusalem, prostrate since the siege by Pompey; but before
long, Antipater, still further presuming on the incapacity
of Hyrcanus and the protection of the Romans, appointed his elder son Phasael to the government of Jerusalem, and the younger, Herod, to that of Galilee. Herod,
though but fifteen years old, according to Josephus,[i]
began immediately to develop his natural decision and
severity of character. He seized a notorious captain of
banditti, Hezekiah, who had been the terror of all the
country, and put him to death, with almost the whole of
his band. The leading Jews, jealous of the Idumean influence, persuaded the feeble Hyrcanus that the execution
of these robbers without trial was an infringement of the
law. Herod was summoned to Jerusalem, to answer for
his offence. He appeared in arms before the affrighted
Sanhedrin; not a voice was raised against him, till at last
Sameas,[k] a man of high integrity, rose and rebuked him
for appearing, not in the humble garb of a criminal, but
thus clad in purple and armour. To the honour of
Herod, when subsequently he slew the whole Sanhedrin,
he spared the life of Sameas. The timid Hyrcanus ad-
journed the trial, and sent secret intimation to Herod to

---

[h] Josephus inserts the treaty of
peace decreed by the Senate with a
decree of the Athenians highly favourable to the Jews. Ant. xiv. 8.

[i] Josephus says that Herod at this
time was only 15, but in the year 47
B.C. he must have been at least from
20 to 25. He lived 70 years according to Josephus, reigned 34, reckoning from the siege by Agrippa and

Gallus, B.C. 37 to A.C. 4.

[k] This is the Shammai of the Rabbins, who, with Pollion (Abtaleon),
were the great Rabbins of this period.
See below, p. 61.

According to Salvador this Sameas
and Pollio, also mentioned about this
time, were Schammai and Hillel.
Salvador, Domination Romaine en
Judée, i. 281.

escape. He took refuge at Damascus with Sextus Cæsar, in whose favour he rose with great rapidity, and obtained, by means of a bribe, the military command of Cœlesyria. He then advanced against Jerusalem, but on the intervention of his father Antipater, withdrew his forces.

After the death of Cæsar, the great protector of Hyrcanus and of the Jews,[m] Cassius assumed the administration of Syria. Judæa was heavily oppressed by his rapacity. Though Antipater and his sons undertook, with Malichus, a powerful Jew, the collection of the tribute, so severe were the exactions (the Roman exacted the enormous sum of 700 talents), that the whole population of some towns were sold as slaves, and Malichus himself would not have escaped the resentment of Cassius, had not Hyrcanus defrayed the deficiency in his accounts. The dexterous Herod had contrived to insinuate himself into the favour of Cassius by prompt and profuse payments; but Malichus, head of the Jewish faction, seized the opportunity to undermine the Idumean influence in Jerusalem. He contrived to poison Antipater, who is said to have saved his life by his intercession with Cæsar, and at the same time to exculpate himself from all participation in the crime.[n] By the advice of his cautious brother, Phasael, Herod dissembled his vengeance; till, at length, after much subtle intrigue on both sides, he got Malichus into his power, and caused him to be murdered. The

---

[l] It seems that he was in correspondence with Sextus Cæsar, and had ensured his powerful protection :— Σέξτος μέντοι, ὁ τῆς Συρίας ἡγεμὼν, γράφει παρακαλῶν Ὑρκανὸν ἀπολῦσαι τὸν Ἡρώδην. Joseph. Ant. xiv. 9. 4.

[m] Josephus inserts a number of edicts of Cæsar and the Senate in favour of the Jews, granting to Hyrcanus and to them, among various immunities, the city of Joppa, and the privilege of observing the Sabbath and the Sabbatical Year (xiv. 10).

[n] Joseph. Ant. xiv. 11. 4.

feeble Hyrcanus witnessed the bloody deed, and fainted away : but when Herod asserted that the assassination was by the order of Cassius, he humbly acquiesced, and declared Malichus a wicked enemy of his country. Cassius had protected Herod; but no sooner had he left Syria, than the adverse faction rallied, Felix, the Roman commander in Jerusalem, taking their side. They were suppressed by the vigour of Phasael. A new enemy arose in the person of Antigonus, the surviving son of Aristobulus, who, with his brother-in-law the king of Chalcis, advanced into Galilee. They were repulsed and defeated by Herod.

In the mean time, the fate of the world was decided at Philippi.[c] Herod, ever a dexterous worshipper of the rising sun, hastened to render his allegiance to the conqueror, and, knowing the character of the man, made acceptable offerings, in the shape of large sums of money, to the victorious Mark Antony. Henceforth the Roman was deaf to the complaints of Herod's enemies. He issued several edicts favourable to Hyrcanus and the nation in general, particularly commanding the liberation of those Jews whom Cassius had sold for slaves, but appointed Phasael and Herod tetrarchs of the province.

An unexpected power advanced upon the scene. Judæa was again to be the prize and the victim of the strife for empire between the East and the West; as of old between Babylon and Egypt, between the Seleucidæ and the Ptolemies, so now between Rome and Parthia. Two years after, the Parthians under Pacorus, the king's

---

[c] See in Josephus the proclamation which alludes to the battle of Philippi, the defeat of the enemies of gods and men. The sun refused to behold the murder of Cæsar. δι ἃ καὶ τὸν ἥλιον ἀπεστράφθαι δοκοῦμεν, ὃς καὶ αὐτὸς ἀηδῶς ἐκεῖδε τὸ ἐπὶ Καίσαρι μύσος. (xiv. 12, 3.)

son, entered Syria and Asia Minor, and overran the
whole region. A part of their army, under Barzapharnes,
took possession of Cœlesyria. Antigonus, the last remaining branch of the Asmonean race, determined to
risk his fortune on the desperate hazard of Parthian protection; he offered 1000 talents and 500 Jewish women
of the noblest families—a strange Oriental compact—as
the price of his restoration to the Jewish kingdom.
Antigonus, himself, raised a considerable native force,
and entered Judæa, followed by Pacorus, the cup-bearer
of the king, who had the same name with the king's son.
Antigonus fought his way to Jerusalem, and by means
of his party entered the city. Of the ambassadors of the
adverse party, some he allowed Herod, some his own
soldiers, to massacre. Herod being received with mutiny
in Jerusalem, he put to death those whom he had imprisoned. Jerusalem was torn asunder by the contending factions; and the multitudes who came up at the
feast of Pentecost, adopting different parties, added to
the fierce hostility and mutual slaughter. The Anti-
gonians held the Temple, the Hyrcanians the palace;
and, daily contests taking place, the streets ran with
blood. Antigonus at length invidiously proposed to
submit their mutual differences to the arbitration of
Pacorus, the Parthian general. Phasael weakly consented, and Pacorus, admitted within the town, prevailed on the infatuated Phasael to undertake a journey
with Hyrcanus, and to submit the cause to Barzapharnes, the commander-in-chief. He set forth on this
ill fated expedition, and was at first received with
courtesy: the plan of the Parthians being to abstain
from violence till they had seized Herod, who, having
vainly remonstrated with his brother on his imprudence,
remained in the city. But the crafty Herod, receiving

warning from his brother, whose suspicions had been
too late awakened. fled towards Masada. He took with
him the female part of the family, his mother, his sister,
and his betrothed wife Mariamne, of the Asmonean
house, and her mother, the daughter of Hyrcanus. The
journey was extremely dangerous, and at one time Herod
in despair had almost attempted his own life. At Masada,
a strong fortress on the western shore of the Dead Sea,
he received succours brought by his brother Joseph
from Idumea. Him he left in command at Masada,
and retired himself into Arabia; from thence to Egypt,
and at length to Rome. In the mean time Hyrcanus
and Phasael had been made prisoners; the former,
Antigonus not wishing to put him to death, was in-
capacitated for ever from the office of High Priest,
by the mutilation of his ears. Phasael anticipated the
executioner by beating his brains out against the wall of
his prison.[p]

Notwithstanding their alliance with Antigonus, who
assumed the sovereignty, the Parthians plundered the
city, and ravaged the country. Herod, however, pros-
pered in Rome beyond his most ambitious hopes; his
design had been to set up the claim of Aristobulus, the
brother of the beautiful Mariamne, to whom he was betrothed. This youth united the titles both of Hyrcanus
and Aristobulus, being the son of Alexander, the elder
son of Aristobulus by the daughter of Hyrcanus.[q] But

---

[p] It was reported, no doubt to make
the Parthians more odious, and the report was naturally adopted by the historians in the party of Herod, that the
wound inflicted on himself by Phasael
was not mortal, but that physicians
were sent who poisoned the wound.

Jos. Ant. xiv. 13. 10.

[q] Ewald, not without ground,
doubts Josephus's account of this.
"Dann hätte er eben kein Herodes
gewesen sein müssen." That Herod
was in earnest in this proposal, or did
it from any motives of loyalty, or from

Augustus and Antony united in conferring the crown of Judæa on Herod himself. Herod was not a man to decline, or not to make the most of the favours of fortune; he wasted no time in the courtly circle, or in the luxuries of Rome. In seven days he despatched all his business, returned to his ships at Brundusium, and after an absence of scarcely three months, landed at Ptolemais. The fortress of Masada,[r] in which his brother and his beautiful bride were shut up, was his first object; the Parthians had broken up on the advance of the Roman general Ventidius and left Antigonus to defend himself as well as he could. Antigonus had almost reduced Masada, which, but for a timely rain which filled the water-tanks, was reduced to the greatest extremity from drought. Herod speedily raised a force, united with some Roman auxiliaries under Silo, took Joppa, overran Galilee, relieved Masada, and sat down before Jerusalem. Silo was a man equally perfidious and rapacious; by assisting both parties, he enriched himself. Hitherto he had befriended Herod: now, under pretext of a mutiny among his soldiers for want of provisions, he broke up the siege of Jerusalem, pillaged Jericho, where Herod had laid up ample stores for both armies, and retired into winter quarters.[s] Herod, unable with his own forces to undertake the invasion of Judæa, fixed his head quarters at Samaria, and employed his time in reducing Galilee, then infested by bands of daring robbers, who dwelt in caves among the wild and craggy mountainous districts of Upper Galilee. A great number he drove beyond Jordan, the

---

any other motive but policy, may assuredly be doubted. Ewald, p. 466, note.

[r] Masada will assume still further importance as the history proceeds.

[s] Joseph. Ant. xiv. 15. 3.

rest he surprised in their dens.   Chests full of armed
men were let down by windlasses from the precipices
above the caves; when they were thus landed at the
mouths of the caves, the soldiers transfixed those they
could reach with harpoons, and finally set fire to the
caves.   One desperate old man slew his wife and
children, threw them down the precipice, and dashed
himself after them.

The next year the campaign against Antigonus was
renewed. The Roman auxiliaries, two legions and 1000
horse, were under the command of Machæras. Silo had
been called away by Ventidius to aid him in putting an
end to the Parthian war, and Machæras, on the defeat
and death of Pacorus, sent to support the cause of
Herod.[t] Machæras being repulsed from the walls of
Jerusalem, revenged the affront on the Jewish followers
of Herod, who retreated to Samaria, and from thence
departed to Samosata, to pay his homage and lodge his
complaints before Antony, who was engaged in the
siege of that city. Antony commanded Sosius to march
to the aid of Herod; two legions were sent forward, Sosius followed with a much larger army. Joseph,
his brother, was left in command in Judæa, with strict
injunctions not to risk a battle; he disobeyed, was
routed and slain. Herod, on his return, revenged his
death by the total discomfiture of Pappus, the general
of Antigonus.   Antigonus had ordered the head of
Joseph to be cut off; Herod sent the head of Pappus to
his brother Pheroras.[u] In the spring of the next year
Herod formed the regular siege of Jerusalem; during
the siege he returned to Samaria to consummate his
marriage with Mariamne, and having thus formed an

---

       [t] Joseph. Ant. xiv. 15.   [u] Joseph. Ant. xiv. 16.

intimate connexion with the line of the Asmonean princes, he hastened to secure his throne by the conquest of the capital. Jerusalem held out for above half-a-year; it was a Sabbatical year, and they were hard pressed by famine. The Romans under Sosius, furious at the obstinate resistance, after the capture gave loose to all their revengeful cruelty and rapaciousness. It was only through the interference of Herod, who bitterly expostulated on the indignity of leaving him king not of a noble city, but of a desert, that the whole town escaped destruction.[x] Herod exerted himself with no less energy and success in preventing the heathen soldiers from penetrating into the Holy places; with his characteristic sagacity, never overlooking an opportunity of working either on the popular feeling, or on that of his Roman confederates, for his own advantage. Antigonus craved his life in a mean and abject manner from Sosius, to whom he had surrendered. The stern Roman treated his unmanly weakness with contempt, called him by the feminine name Antigone, not Antigonus, and sent him in chains to Antony. There, at the solicitation of Herod, he was put to death by the barbarous and insulting stroke of the common lictor.[y]

---

[x] Dion Cassius (xlviii. 22) writes of this siege:—πολλὰ μὲν δὴ καὶ οἱ Ἰουδαῖοι τοὺς Ῥωμαίους ἔδρασαν (τὸ γάρ γένος αὐτῶν θυμωθὲν, πικρότατόν ἐστι) πολλῷ δὲ δὴ πλείω αὐτοὶ ἔπαθον. He adds that Jerusalem was taken on the Sabbath: ἐν τῇ τοῦ Κρόνου καὶ τότε ἡμέρᾳ ὠνομασμένῃ; and that the prisoners taken by Sosius entreated permission to go up to the Temple to be present at the accustomed rites.

[y] Let us hear another, a modern Jewish view of this:—"Mais en admettant ces larmes pour vraies, toute la conduite précédente d'Antigone et ces combats attestent qu'à cette heure solennelle il n'était pas ému du seul danger de sa propre vie. Il pleurait la nationalité si chère à ses aïeux, qui venait d'être frappée dans sa racine; il pleurait l'héroïque race des Maccabées, qui tombait définitivement devant l'audace et l'intrigue d'un

homme que l'indignation du prince qualifiait depuis longtemps de misérable Iduméen." Salvador, i. p. 300.

Plutarch (Vit. Antonii) and Dion Cassius observe that this was the first king thus put to death by the Roman lictor. Dion adds that he was first scourged—the usual preliminary of Roman decapitation. I agree with Salvador in indignation at the want of indignation in Josephus, who represents the death of Antigonus as the just reward of his pusillanimity.

BOOK XL

HEROD.

Accession — Battle of Actium — Death of Mariamne — Magnificence
of Herod — Sebaste built — Rebuilding of the Temple — Cæsarea
— Sons of Mariamne — Death of Antipater — Death of Herod.

THUS Herod the Great, the last independent sovereign
of Palestine, became master of his dominions. So far
his career had been marked with uncommon ability;
nor had it been disgraced by unusual atrocity. With
signal penetration he had eluded the arts, by the rapidity and decision of his measures triumphed over the
open hostilities, of his antagonists : by his knowledge of
the Roman character, and that of the successive extraordinary men who had held the destiny of the world at
their command, he had secured not merely their protection, but their friendship.[a] Still his situation was
difficult and precarious ; it demanded his utmost dexterity and vigour, and unhappily gave him the. tyrant's
plea of necessity for the most relentless cruelties. The
mass of the people were still ardently attached to the
great Asmonean family ; the faction of Antigonus was
strong in Jerusalem. Against the latter he proceeded
without scruple, put to death forty-five of the chiefs, and
confiscated all their property. The whole Sanhedrin
fell victims to his vengeance, excepting Sameas (Sche-
majah) and Pollio (Abtaleon).[b] The two latter, during

---

[a] Joseph. Ant. xv. 1, 2.
[b] These two great Rabbins were sons of proselytes.

the siege, had endeavoured to persuade the city to capitulate. The rest had raised the popular cry—" The Temple of the Lord! the Temple of the Lord!" and excited a strong enthusiasm against the alien from the blood of Israel.[c] The appointment to the office of High Priest caused the greatest embarrassment. The nation would never have endured the usurpation of that dignity by an Idumean stranger. Hyrcanus, the old patron of the Herodian family, returned from his honourable captivity in Parthia; he was received with every mark of outward respect by Herod, but the mutilation of his ears by Antigonus disqualified him for reinstatement in his function. Herod invited Ananel, an obscure man, of the lineage of the High Priest, from Babylon.[d] Alexandra, the widow of that gallant Alexander, the son of Aristobulus, who was executed by Scipio, beheld this choice with secret indignation. She was a high-minded and ambitious woman: the marriage of her daughter, Mariamne, to Herod, aggravated, rather than palliated, the indignity of excluding her son, the rightful heir of both the Asmonean families, from the priesthood. Unscrupulous as to her means of vengeance, she sent the pictures of her two children, a son and her daughter the wife of Herod, both of exquisite beauty, to Antony, in order, by this unnatural and odious scheme, to work on the passions of the voluptuous triumvir.[e] Herod

---

[c] Compare Jost, Jud. i. 253.

Jost distinguishes between Shemajah (so he renders Sameas) and Schamnai, the colleague and rival of the famous Hillel. These two schools began five or six years after the accession of Herod.

[d] It is well to observe that Josephus takes the opportunity of saying that

many myriads of Jews were settled in Babylonia. Ant. xv. 3. 1.

[e] I must leave in Greek as much as I may of the repulsive part of this transaction, too characteristic of the Romans, and especially of Antony, and too striking an illustration of the insolence of the Romans, and of the fanaticism of Jewish faction, and, alas!

was seized with apprehension, changed at once his policy, displaced Ananel, and instead of sending him, as desired, to Antony, installed the young Aristobulus in the pontificate.   But mistrust and hatred had taken too deep root.   Alexandra was detected in a secret correspondence with Cleopatra ; and a plan which she had formed to fly with her son to the court of Egypt was only disconcerted by the excessive vigilance of Herod.ᶠ Worse than all this, when the lovely boy of seventeen, the heir of their rightful princes, appeared before the assembled nation at the Feast of Tabernacles, in the splendid costume of the High Priest, and performing his solemn office with the most perfect grace, the popular feeling was too evident to be mistaken.   Herod saw that his own suspicions were sadly verified ; he had raised up a dangerous rival to his power in the young Asmonean.   He dissembled his jealousy, and joined in the general admiration ; but, contriving shortly after to remove the youth to Jericho, he caused him to be drowned by his companions while bathing in a tank.ᵍ   He assumed great grief on the melancholy event, and attempted to divert the popular indignation by a splendid funeral.   But the people were

---

of their profound corruption by Greek manners. ἐπέστελλε δὲ πέμπειν τὸν παῖδα σὺν εὐπρεπείᾳ; προστιθείς, ἐι μὴ βαρὺ δοκοίη· τουτῶν ἀπενεχθέντων πρὸς Ἡρώδην, οὐκ ἀσφαλὲς εκρινεν, ὥρᾳ τε καλλιστον ὄντα, ἐκκαιδεκαέτης γὰρ ὢν ἐτύγχανε..
... Ant. xv. 6. Herod's only fear was the influence which the youth might obtain over the Triumvir, and that the throne of Judæa might be the reward of his shame.   Dellius, the agent of Antony in this foul intrigue,

is the "moriture Delli" in the beautiful ode of Horace (Lib. ii. 3). Antony would not send for Mariamne, because she was the *wife of Herod*, and because he was afraid of exciting the jealousy of *Cleopatra*.

ᶠ The plot was betrayed by one Sabbia, who was eager to obtain forgiveness from Herod for his suspected complicity in the poisoning of Herod's father, Antipater.

ᵍ Ant. xv. 3. 3.

not deceived, still less the heart of the bereaved and wretched parent. Alexandra sent intelligence of the murder to Cleopatra, who espoused her cause with the warmest interest of a woman and a mother; not without some secret suggestion from her ambition, which already began to look towards Judæa as a valuable province of Egypt. Antony was at the height of his devotion to the luxurious queen: the ruin of Herod seemed inevitable. With his characteristic boldness he determined to try the effect of his personal presence, which might awaken early friendship and give weight to those more powerful arguments, the immense bribes, with which he hoped to secure his cause. He obeyed the summons of Antony to appear before him at Laodicea. He left Jerusalem under the government of his uncle Joseph; he entrusted to his care not merely his interests, but his incomparable Mariamne. He went, certainly, to danger, perhaps to death; and, with a strange jealousy, he could not endure that any one should possess his wife, even after his.death, least of all the licentious Antony. He left a secret charge with Joseph, that if he should fail in his mission, Mariamne was to be immediately put to death. During his absence, the incautious Joseph betrayed this secret order to Mariamne. Her mother excited her to revenge. A sudden rumour spread abroad that Herod had been slain by Antony. Alexandra and Mariamne began to take immediate measures for securing the royal authority,[h] but intelligence of an opposite nature frustrated their plans. Not merely had Antony contemptuously, notwithstanding the adverse influence of Cleopatra, dismissed the

---

[h] Alexandra had hopes that if Antony saw Mariamne, their cause was safe. No one, least of all the Triumvir, could resist her irresistible beauty.

charges against Herod; he had seated the Jewish king
beside his throne, invited him to his luxurious banquets,
added the province of Cœlesyria to his dominions. On
the return of Herod, his sister, Salome, wounded at the
haughtiness with which she had ever been treated by
the proud Asmonean princess, endeavoured to poison
his mind with suspicions of his wife. She accused her
of too intimate correspondence with Joseph, the governor, her own husband. Yet the beauty of Mariamne,
once seen, overpowered every emotion but that of unbounded love. Unhappily, in the transport of tender
reconciliation, Mariamne asked, whether, if he had
really loved her, he would have given that fatal order
for her death. Herod sprang from her arms in fury.
The betrayal of this secret warranted his worst suspicions; it could not have been yielded up but at the
price of her honour. He would have slain her on the
spot, but her loveliness, even then, disarmed him; his
whole vengeance fell on Joseph and Alexandra. The
first he executed, the second he imprisoned with every
mark of insult. Cleopatra, in the mean time, having
been unable to extort the gift of Judæa from her para-
mour, was obliged to content herself with the balsam
gardens near Jericho. On her return from accompa-
nying Antony in his campaign to the Euphrates, she
entered Jerusalem, and Herod was in as great danger
from her love as from her hate. Whether from prudence or dislike, he repelled the advances of Cleopatra,
and even entertained some thoughts of delivering himself from a dangerous neighbour, and Antony from a
fatal and imperious mistress, by her assassination. His
friends dissuaded him from the hazardous measure. A
short time after, he found himself engaged in a war,
which he entered into with the ostensible design of

enforcing Cleopatra's right of tribute over Malchus, king of Arabia. By complying with the wishes of Antony on this point, the dexterous politician escaped taking any prominent part in the great war between the Eastern and Western world, which was to award the empire to Antony or to Octavius. In his first invasion of Arabia Herod was successful; but afterwards, through the treachery of Athenion, who commanded the troops of Cleopatra, met with so signal a defeat, that he was constrained to change the war into one of sudden irruptions into the border of the enemy, without risking a battle. A more tremendous blow fell on Judæa—an earthquake, which threw down many cities, and destroyed 30,000 lives. Though the army of Herod, encamped in the open air, escaped the frightful effects of the earthquake, the Arabs seized the opportunity of this disaster, and put the Jewish ambassadors to death. But this conduct enabled Herod to rouse the national spirit, and the Arabians, defeated with the loss of 5000 men, were besieged in their camp. Many surrendered from want of water; the rest made a desperate but fatal sally, in which 7000 more perished.

Still, though not personally engaged in the battle of Actium, Herod had reason to apprehend the triumph of Octavius Cæsar. Having secured every thing at home, he determined to meet the youthful conqueror at Rhodes.[1] While one remnant of the Asmonean race survived, his throne was less secure; and the old Hyrcanus, now eighty years of age, at length paid the last penalty for having unhappily been born to a lofty station for which he was unfit. The documents in the

---

[1] Josephus is here seized with an unhappy ambition of rivalling Thucydides and the great Greek historians, and inserts a long oration of Herod (xv. 5. 4).

royal archives of Herod accused the poor old man of
having been persuaded, by his intriguing daughter,
Alexandra, into a treasonable correspondence with the
Arabian king; other accounts ascribe the invention of
the plot to Herod.   At all events, it was fatal to Hyrcanus, who thus closed a life of extraordinary vicissitude, borne with constitutional indolence, by a violent
death.   This done, Herod committed the government
to his brother, Pheroras; sent his mother, sister, and
children to Masada ; and committed Mariamne and
her mother to the charge of his own faithful partisans,
Soëmus (the Iturean) and Joseph (his steward), in the
fortress of Alexandrion. They had the same extraordinary
injunctions which he had before left, that, in case of his
death, Mariamne should be despatched.   He then set
sail for Rhodes.   He appeared before the conqueror,
without the diadem, but with all the dignity of an independent sovereign.   He addressed Octavius in a speech,
which, disdaining apology, enlarged on his obligations,
and avowed his attachment to Antony.   He declared
that, as a friend, he had given him the best advice;
such advice as might have made him again formidable
to Cæsar; he had begged him to put Cleopatra to death,
and vigorously resume the war.   "Antony," he pursued,
" adopted a counsel more fatal to himself, more advanta-
geous to you.   If, then, attachment to Antony be a
crime, I plead guilty; but if, having thus seen how
steady and faithful I am in my friendships, you determine to bind me to your fortunes by gratitude, depend
on the same firmness and fidelity." This lofty tone
and generous sentiment won the kindred heart of the
arbiter of the world's destinies.   Cæsar commanded the
dignified suppliant to resume the diadem, treated him
with great distinction, and Herod returned to Judæa, to

the admiration of his partisans, and the terror of his enemies, thus constantly breaking forth with greater splendour from every transient cloud of danger. Cæsar passed from Rhodes to Asia Minor; thence through Syria to Egypt. Herod met him at Ptolemais, made him a present of eight hundred talents, and, by the splendour of his entertainment, and the provisions with which he furnished his army, still further conciliated his favour. After the conquest of Egypt, Octavius restored to him the part of his own territory formerly bestowed on Cleopatra, with Gadara, Hippo, Samaria, and the maritime towns of Joppa, Anthedon, Gaza, and the Tower of Straton.

Thus, abroad, success seemed to wait on all the designs of Herod: the neighbouring kings might admire and envy the good fortune, or rather the consummate ability, with which he extricated himself from all his difficulties, and continued advancing in the career of prosperity and power; but at home, the most miserable peasant might compassionate the wretchedness which filled his palace with dissension, crime, and bloodshed. The magnificence of Herod's public life is strangely contrasted with the dark tragedy of his domestic history. Mariamne had again extorted the fatal charge entrusted to Soëmus; and indignant at the jealous determination of her husband that she should not survive him, she met him on his return with repulsive indifference, and even with undissembled dislike; she listened without joy to the recital of his perilous escape and his wonderful success; she hardly disguised her grief. Herod struggled between his love and his indignation; till one day, instead of submitting to his caresses, in the height of her passion she reproached him, in terms of the utmost bitterness, with his barbarous

conduct to her relations. The envious Salome watched
every opportunity of inflaming the resentment of her
brother; and suborned his cup-bearer to accuse Mariamne of having bribed him to administer a poisonous
philtre, or love-potion, to his master. Herod commanded
her favourite eunuch, to whom all her secrets were entrusted, to be put to the rack. The tortured man denied
all knowledge of the poison, but exclaimed that the
conduct of his mistress was entirely owing to the information she had received from Soëmus. Furious at this
new proof of her infidelity, he ordered Soëmus to be
despatched at once, and summoned Mariamne before
a tribunal of judges who were too much in dread of his
power not to pass the sentence of death. Still Herod
hesitated; he had no immediate intention of proceeding
further than imprisonment; but his mother and sister
so worked on his moody and violent temper, that he at
length issued the fatal orders for her execution. To the
horror of the spectators, her mother Alexandra assailed
the wretched Mariamne, as she went to death, with a
violent invective against her ingratitude to so gentle
and affectionate a husband, loudly declaring that she
deserved the fate she was about to suffer. The queen
passed on in silence with the dignity of conscious
virtue. Though deeply wounded at this disgraceful and
hypocritical conduct of her mother, who thus sought to
avert the suspicions of Herod from herself, and to save
her own life at the sacrifice of her daughter's honour,
she would not condescend to betray her emotion. She
met her death with the calm intrepidity of innocence,
and died worthy of the noble house of which the last
blood flowed in her veins.[k] She was a woman of unri-

---

[k] Joseph. Ant. xv. 7. 5.

valled beauty and a haughty spirit: unhappy in being the
object of passionate attachment, which bordered on
frenzy, to a man who had more or less concern in the
murder of her grandfather, father, brother, and uncle,
and who had twice commanded her death in case of his
own. Strange conflict of duties! who shall decide what
ought to have been her feelings and her conduct?

All the passions which filled the stormy mind of
Herod were alike without bound; from violent love,
and violent resentment, he sank into as violent remorse
and despair. Everywhere, by day and night, he was
haunted by the image of the murdered Mariamne; he
called upon her name; he perpetually burst into passionate tears; he ordered his servants to bring Mariamne
to him as though she were yet alive. In vain he tried
every diversion,—banquets, revels, the excitement of
society. A sudden pestilence broke out, to which many
of the noblest of his court and of his own personal friends
fell a sacrifice; he recognised and trembled beneath the
hand of the avenging Deity. On pretence of hunting, he
sought out the most melancholy solitude, till the disorder of his mind brought on disorder of body, and he
was seized with violent inflammation and pains in the
back of his head, which led to temporary derangement.
In this state he lay at Samaria. The restless Alexandra
immediately began to renew her intrigues; but Herod's
partisans sent intelligence to him, and she was at
length consigned to execution.

Herod slowly recovered from his malady, but it left
an indelible gloom upon his mind; and his stern temper,
instead of being softened by calamity, seemed to have
acquired a fierce and insatiable propensity to cruelty
and bloodshed. His next victim was Costobaras, an
Idumean, the husband of his sister Salome, whom she, in

defiance of the law, had divorced;[1] and, through her machinations, the unfortunate man was involved in the guilt
of a pretended conspiracy, and convicted of the concealment of some of the Asmonean partisans. He was put
to death with many other men of rank and distinction.

From these horrible scenes we may turn with satisfaction to the peace and happiness of the country,
and the liberality and magnificence of Herod's public
administration.   Yet Herod either did not understand,
or more probably suspected as adverse to his interests,
the strong and distinctive principles of the national
character.   Outwardly professing the utmost respect for
the religion of his subjects, he introduced public exhibitions and spectacles of every kind, as if to reconcile the
people by degrees to foreign usages, and so break down
the wall of partition which separated them from other
nations.   He built a theatre within the walls of Jerusalem, an amphitheatre of immense size without.   He
celebrated quinquennial games on a scale of unrivalled
splendour; invited the most distinguished proficients in
every kind of gymnastic exercise, in chariot racing,
boxing, and every kind of musical and poetic art;
offered the most costly prizes; and even introduced the
barbarous spectacles of the Romans, fights of wild
beasts, and combats of wild beasts with gladiators.   The
zealous Jews looked on in amazement and with praiseworthy though silent abhorrence at these sanguinary
exhibitions, so contrary to the mild genius of their great
lawgiver's institutions.   But when Herod proceeded to
adorn his theatre with representations of the victories of
Cæsar, and set up, as trophies around it, complete suits

---

[1] A man could serve a bill of divorce on his wife, not the wife on her
husband.

of armour which had been taken in his wars, the people broke out into a violent tumult, supposing that images were concealed within these panoplies. To appease the general dissatisfaction, Herod commanded one of them to be taken to pieces in the sight of all the people ; and when a bare peg of wood appeared within, their discontent and anger turned to laughter and ridicule.

But still a stern and dangerous enthusiasm prevailed among all who were zealously attached to the institutions of their ancestors. Ten men bound themselves by a solemn vow to assassinate the innovator in the scene of his delinquency : one of them was blind, yet, though he could not assist in the execution, he was determined to share in the peril of the enterprise. They entered the theatre with daggers under their cloaks ; but the vigilant police of Herod were on their guard : he received intimation, and returned into the palace. The men were apprehended, and instead of denying, boldly avowed and justified their design. They endured the most ignominious torture, but died firm and undaunted to the last. The informer, being discovered, was torn to pieces by the populace ; and though Herod with incredible pains detected and punished the ringleaders in this affray, he felt the insecurity of his government, and even of his life, particularly in Jerusalem. Actuated by his fears as well as the magnificence of his disposition, he built a strong and splendid palace on the hill of Sion, rebuilt as a fortress the palace of Baris, which commanded the Temple, and called it Antonia. Still further to secure himself against the turbulent disposition of the capital he determined to found other cities which might be more at his devotion. They would serve the double purpose of controlling the country as strong military posts, and affording him a retreat, on an emergency, from the dis-

affected metropolis. With this view he built citadels, at
Gaba in Galilee, and Heshbon in Peræa. The strongest
measure was the rebuilding of Samaria, which he did on
a scale of great magnificence and strength, and peopled
it partly with his soldiers, partly with the descendants of
the old Samaritans, who hoped to see their temple likewise restored. But Herod did not neglect more noble
and kingly means of regaining the lost affections of his
subjects. A long drought, followed by unproductive
seasons, involved not merely Judæa but the neighbouring countries likewise in all the horrors of famine, and
its usual consequence—a dreadful epidemic pestilence.
The little corn that remained, rotted, so that there was
not enough seed to crop the ground. Herod instantly
opened his treasures, secured a vast importation of grain
from Egypt, and made constant distributions, both of
food and of clothing. 50,000 persons are said to have
been maintained at his sole expense, and he even furnished corn for seed to the neighbouring inhabitants of
Syria; so that the fame of his munificence not merely
caused a strong reaction in his favour among his own
subjects, but secured him a high degree of popularity
with all the bordering states. This great expenditure
seems by no means to have exhausted the revenues of
Herod. He still indulged in his sumptuous passion for
building. Having married a second Mariamne, the
daughter of Simon, an obscure person of priestly lineage,
whom he appointed High Priest, he chose the spot on
which he had defeated Antigonus, about seven miles
from Jerusalem, as the site of a new fortified palace in
his usual style of architecture. It stood on the gentle
slope of a mound raised by human industry. The ascent
was by a hundred steps to an enclosure of circular towers,
within which were courts, ascending to the palace, which

stood like a citadel above the rest. A town rapidly
grew around the base of the hill. Water was brought by
costly aqueducts from a great distance.

Thus, terrible to his adversaries, generally courteous,
affable, and bounteous to his countrymen and to
strangers, securing his interests with Rome and its rulers
by the most costly adulation, Herod steadily pursued his
policy of counterbalancing, by a strong Grecian party,
the turbulent and exclusive spirit of his Jewish subjects.
More completely to secure this object, he determined to
found a powerful city, chiefly colonized with Grecians,
and dedicated to the name of his great Roman protector.
Samaria he had already called Sebaste (the August); the
new city was to take the name of Cæsarea. He chose a
maritime situation, for the advantage of commerce, and
may have thought of uniting in his new city the wealth
of ancient Tyre with the greatness of Jerusalem. There
was a small town called the Tower of Straton, mid-way
between Joppa and Dora. It possessed a haven, like all
the rest on that coast, dangerous on account of the violent south-western winds, against which they had no
protection. He first formed a strong mole or break-
water, by sinking stones fifty feet long, eighteen wide,
and nine deep. On this arose a pier two hundred feet
wide, defended by a wall and towers. The entrance to
this great artificial haven was from the north, and a vast
fleet could thus ride in perfect safety in a sort of double
harbour. All round ran a noble quay or esplanade,
and, probably under this, were arched buildings for the
entertainment and residence of mariners. Above, the
city rose like an amphitheatre in a uniform line of
sumptuous palaces. The subterranean arches, for drain-
age and other purposes, were on so great a scale, that
Josephus says there was as much building below ground

as above.   In the centre stood a great temple dedicated
to Cæsar, with two colossal statues, one of Rome, the
other of Cæsar.   A theatre and amphitheatre, the customary ornaments of a Grecian city, were not forgotten.
Cæsarea was twelve years before it was completed.

Thus Judæa was fast sinking into a province of the
Roman empire ; and Herod, instead of head of the
Hebrew religious republic, became more and more on a
level with the other vassal kings of Rome.   His elder
sons by Mariamne, Alexander and Aristobulus, were not
brought up in Jewish tenets or customs, but sent to
Rome for their education, where they were received into
the palace of Augustus, and treated with great care and
distinction.   Nothing could exceed the estimation in
which Herod stood, both with the Emperor and with his
favourite, Agrippa.   Cæsar was said to assign to Herod the
next place in his favour to Agrippa ; Agrippa to esteem
Herod higher than any of his friends, except Augustus.
Whenever either visited the eastern provinces, Herod
was the first to pay his homage.   To see Agrippa he
sailed to Mitylene, and afterwards entertained Augustus
himself in Syria.   On one occasion, when Agrippa was
engaged in war near the Bosphorus, Herod suddenly
appeared with a large fleet, and through all the campaign assisted him with his personal support and advice.
Herod took advantage of this alliance to enlarge his
dominions.   A district to the east of the sea of Gennesaret was farmed by a certain Zenodorus.   This man
maintained a suspicious connexion with the freebooters
who dwelt in the mountain caves of Trachonitis.   The
whole province was made over to Herod, who, with his
customary rigour and severity, suppressed and hunted
down the robbers.   Zenodorus, and some of the Gada-
renes, who complained of oppression, laid their grievances

first before Agrippa, afterwards before Augustus himself; but found their ears closed against all representations to the disadvantage of Herod. Part of this district was created into a Tetrarchate for his brother Pheroras. At Paneas, near the fountains of the Jordan, where Cæsarea Philippi afterwards stood, was built a temple of white marble to the honour of Cæsar.

But the higher Herod advanced in the good graces of the Romans by these costly and enduring marks of his adulation, the lower he sank in the good-will of his jealous Jewish subjects. They suspected him, not without reason, of a fixed design to heathenize their nation and country.[m] Neither his munificence in diminishing their annual tax one-third, nor his severities, could suppress their deep though secret murmurs. He exercised a stern and vigilant police, interdicted all fraternities and assemblies, occasionally surprised the most disaffected and hurried them to the Hyrcania (his Bastile), whence they never returned. He was even said to walk the streets in disguise, so to detect secret conspiracies, and form a judgment of the popular feeling. At one time he had determined to exact a general oath of allegiance; but the stricter and more powerful of the Pharisees and the Essenes, an ascetic fraternity, openly refusing compliance, he thought it better to urge the matter no further.

At length he determined on a measure which he hoped would at the same time employ the people and

---

[m] There is a curious instance of the jealous religious feeling of the people. Herod issued an edict that burglars (τειχώρυχοι) might be sold as slaves beyond the borders of the Holy Land to strangers. It was objected that the religion of these ruffians might be endangered by their being compelled to follow heathen usages. The Law, it was said, permitted their sale, but not to Gentiles. Ant. xvi. 1. 1.

ingratiate himself with all classes—the rebuilding the
Temple in its former pride and magnificence. The lapse
of five hundred years, and the sieges which it had undergone, as it was the great military post of the nation, had
much dilapidated the structure of Zorobabel. But the
suspicious Jews beheld the work of demolition commence
with the utmost jealousy and apprehension, lest, under
pretence of repairing, the king should destroy entirely
the sanctuary of their God. The prudence of Herod
calmed their fears; he made immense preparations
before he threw down the old building: the work proceeded with the greatest regularity, and the nation saw,
with the utmost pride, a new fabric of more regular and
stately architecture crowning the brow of Moriah with
its glittering masses of white marble and pinnacles
of gold.[a] Yet even while the Temple was proceeding,
Herod maintained his double character; he presided at
the Olympic games, made magnificent donations for
their support, and the Jewish monarch was nominated
perpetual president of this solemn festival of Greece.
On the other hand, Agrippa, on an excursion into Judæa,
during which Herod showed him all his great works,
offered one hundred oxen in the Temple and feasted the
whole people.

But the declining days of Herod were to be darkened
with a domestic tragedy as melancholy and awful as

---

[a] According to Josephus (Ant. xv.
11. 3) he destroyed the ancient foundations and enlarged the building to the
length of a hundred cubits: ἀνελὼν δὲ
τοὺς ἀρχαίους θεμελίους καὶ καταβα-
λόμενος ἑτέρους, ἐπ’ αὐτῶν τὸν ναὸν
ἤγειρε, μήκει μὲν ἑκατὸν ὄντα πη-
χῶν. These foundations I take to be
those of Zorobabel's Temple; and that

the vast substructions of Solomon still
remained, and subsist to the present
day. The height, Josephus says, was
120 cubits, but from a subsidence or
settlement in the time of Nero they
were reduced to 100. This reads very
strangely: τὸ δ’ ὕψος εἴκοσι περιττοῖς,
οὓς τῷ χρόνῳ συνιζησάντων τῶν
θεμελίων ὑπέβη.

those of his earlier life. His sumptuous palaces were
again to resound with strife, mourning, and murder.
Never was an instance in which the heathen might
recognize so distinctly their avenging Nemesis; or those
of purer faith the providence of a just and holy God,
making cruelty its own avenger, and leaving crime to
work its late, though natural consequences, horror, ruin,
and desolation. It might have seemed that the spirit of
the injured Mariamne hovered over the devoted house,
and, involving the innocent as well as the guilty in the
common ruin, designated the dwelling of her murderous
husband as the perpetual scene of misery and bloodshed.
On the return of Alexander and Aristobulus, the two
sons of Mariamne, to Jerusalem, whom, after a visit to
Rome, Herod brought back from the court of Cæsar,
they were received, notwithstanding their Roman education, with general enthusiasm. The grace and beauty
of their persons, their affable manners, above all, the
blood of the ancient Asmonean princes, which flowed in
their veins, rendered them objects of the deepest interest
to the whole Hebrew nation. Herod married them,
Alexander to Glaphyra, the daughter of Archelaus, king
of Cappadocia; Aristobulus to Mariamne, the daughter
of Salome. Notwithstanding this, the envious mind of
Salome, the sister of Herod, sickened at their praises.
Her own conscience, and that of her brother Pheroras,
reproached them with their share in the murder of
Mariamne; they apprehended condign vengeance on
the accession of the young princes. The youths themselves, perhaps, spoke without much discretion or reserve
about their mother's fate; and rumours, aggravated by
Salome and her party, began to spread abroad, that
they announced themselves as her future avengers. For
three years these insinuations made no deep impression

on the mind of Herod, who was justly proud of the popularity of his sons; but while he was absent with Agrippa,
in his war near the Bosphorus, during which period he obtained for the Jews of Asia Minor a ratification of all their
privileges, which the Greeks had endeavoured to wrest
from them,° these sinister reports began to obtain much
strength and consistency, and consequently more credit
with the suspicious father.   Herod resorted to a most
dangerous measure in order to subdue the pride of his
sons, and make them more entirely subservient to his
will.   He sent for his elder son, Antipater, borne
to him by Doris, the wife whom he divorced to marry
Mariamne, and set him up as a sort of counterpoise
to the popularity and hopes of Alexander and Aristobulus.   The dark, designing, and unscrupulously ambitious Antipater entered into all the plots of Salome
and Pheroras; and, as Herod had permission from Rome
to bequeath his crown to whichever of his sons he chose,
Antipater lost no opportunity of alienating his father's
affections from the sons of Mariamne.   Herod, to place
him more on a level with his rivals, introduced him to
Agrippa, and sent him in the suite of his powerful friend
to Rome.   From Rome the artful youth stedfastly pursued, by means of letters, his insidious designs, till the
mind of Herod was so inflamed, that he determined to
accuse his sons before the tribunal of Augustus.   The
king of Judæa and the two royal youths appeared before
the Emperor at Aquileia.   Herod opened the charge by
accusing them of unnatural obstinacy and disobedience,

° The long oration of Nicolaus, appointed by Herod to plead the cause
of the Jews of Asia Minor before the
tribunal of Agrippa, furnishes curious
evidence of the numbers, wealth, and
importance of the Jewish communities
in those regions. Ant. xvi. 4. This
was the celebrated historian Nicolaus of
Damascus. Compare also the edicts,
xvi. 6.

and of entering into criminal practices against his life.
Shocked at this dreadful charge, the youths stood silent,
unable to exculpate themselves without criminating
their jealous and cruel father.   Their situation, and still
more their silence, and the modest defence upon which
they at length entered,[p] excited the deepest interest in
their favour ; and Augustus, with that temperance and
moderation which distinguished all his actions after he
became Emperor, succeeded in reconciling the father to
his children.   Herod returned with them to Jerusalem.
Still, however, infatuated in favour of Antipater, he declared him heir to the throne ; in default of Antipater's
issue, the succession was to pass to the sons of Mariamne.
A short and deceitful peace ensued, during which Herod,
having finished his splendid city of Cæsarea, solemnly
dedicated it, at a great festival, to the Emperor, and instituted quinquennial games to his honour.   He founded
at the same time the towns of Antipatris, Cypron, and
Phasaelis ; and built a lofty tower in Jerusalem, called
likewise after the name of his elder brother Phasael.
Before long, the domestic dissensions broke out anew with
greater violence. Antipater, sometimes insidiously exculpating, sometimes artfully accusing his brothers, kept
the mind of Herod in a continued fever of suspicious
excitement.   The king's own favourite brother, Pheroras,
increased his wretchedness.   Pheroras had become so
infatuated with the love of a female slave, as to refuse

[p] Josephus has taxed his eloquence, or rather his rhetoric, in the composition of a speech which he attributes to Alexander, the eldest of the sons. Ant. xvi. 4, 3.

It is perhaps right to state that Nicolaus of Damascus took the part of Herod, asserted the guilt of Mariamne and the wicked intrigues of her sons against their father.   But Nicolaus, according to Josephus, and there is no reason to doubt his judgment, was an unscrupulous partisan of Herod. Ant. xvi. 7. 1.

the hand of one of Herod's daughters.   Not long after, on the offer of another daughter, Pheroras consented to break off his connexion with the slave.   But before the espousals, he again changed his mind, and refused to conclude the marriage.   Pheroras was a still worse enemy to the peace of Herod.   He instilled into the mind of Alexander, that his father secretly cherished a guilty passion for his wife Glaphyra.[q]   Alexander boldly questioned Herod about this scandalous imputation. Pheroras, to avoid the fury of his justly offended brother, laid the plot to the instigation of Salome, who vindicated herself with great energy.   Yet these two dangerous inmates for some time lost their influence in the court. But the wily Antipater still remained; the sons of Mariamne were every day accused of new plots; sometimes with perverting the eunuchs who held the chief offices about the royal person, from whom they were said to have discovered the secret and feminine artifices which Herod used, to disguise the advance of old age; sometimes with designing the death of their father; or with a design of flying to Rome, or as accusing their father at Rome of entering into treasonable correspondence with the Parthians.   Night and day these charges were repeated; the whole court became a scene of gloom, suspicion, and distrust.   Friend shrank from friend; every society swarmed with spies; men accused each other, from personal and private grounds of animosity.   Sometimes their evil practices recoiled on their own heads; when the evidence was insufficient, Herod, disappointed of his victims, wreaked his vengeance on

---

q There was jealousy, as it were, wheel within wheel. Glaphyra hated Berenice, the daughter of Salome, married to her husband's brother Aristobulus, and who therefore affected equality if not superiority over her, a king's daughter (xvi. 7. 2).

the accusers. Those who frequented the presence of the sovereign were suspected of sinister designs; those who stood aloof were self-convicted of disloyalty. Whoever had at any time shown marks of favour or attachment to the suspected sons of Mariamne, though his own most firm and stedfast friends, fell into disgrace. At length, all the confidential slaves of Alexander having been put to the rack, some kind of evidence was wrung from their extorted confessions, and the unhappy youth committed to prison and loaded with chains. Here he adopted a strange and desperate measure; he sent four papers to his father, filled with the most extravagant and improbable treasons, in all of which he avowed his participation, but implicated Salome, Pheroras, and all the most influential and faithful ministers of the king. Herod was worked up to a pitch of frenzy, persons of all ranks were daily seized, and either put to the torture, or executed at once.[r]

At length Archelaus, king of Cappadocia, the father-in-law of Alexander, arrived at the court of Jerusalem. By first dexterously humouring the frenzy of Herod, and pretending to enter into his suspicions; afterwards by arguing dispassionately the improbability of the accusations, he succeeded in reconciling the father and son, and Alexander was reinstated in freedom and favour.

At this period Herod was not without anxiety arising from foreign disturbances. With all his vigour and severity he had never entirely suppressed the banditti of the Trachonitis. Encouraged by the secret protection of the Arabs, this lawless race commenced new depredations. Obodes was at that time king of Arabia Petrea, but all the authority was in the hands of Syllæus. This

---

[r] Joseph. Ant. xvi. 8, 5.

Syllæus had formerly proposed to marry Salome, the sister of Herod; but the abjuration of his religion being demanded as the price of the connexion, he broke off the match, declaring that he should be stoned by the Arabians for such a compliance. The troops of Herod pursued the banditti into the dominions of Obodes, destroyed Repta, their stronghold, and discomfited an Arabian force which espoused their party. This was represented by Syllæus, at Rome, as a wanton and unprovoked aggression upon the kingdom of Arabia. The credit of Herod began to waver; but he immediately despatched the eloquent Nicolaus of Damascus (the historian whose contemporary biography of Herod is unfortunately lost) to the Roman Court, and through his address the cause assumed a better aspect, and was finally settled not only to the exculpation of Herod, but to his honour. Augustus had even determined to confer on Herod the kingdom of the Nabathæan Arabians: but the dreadful dissensions in his family, which had again broken out with greater fury than ever, induced the cautious Emperor at least to delay his munificent intention. It is difficult to trace, it were interminable to relate, the dark intrigues, the briberies, the extortions, the calumnies, which filled the miserable court in which figure eunuchs (for to this Oriental pomp and luxury had Herod attained), now in high favour, now on the rack; and strangers, especially one Eurycles, a Spartan by birth, with nothing of the Spartan in character. Antipater, Salome, and Pheroras, had again obtained the ear of Herod; hating each other with the bitterest cordiality, as seemed to be the doom of the family of Herod, they hated Alexander and Aristobulus with a more deadly hatred.

Herod wrote to Rome the most dreadful charges against the sons of Mariamne; and Augustus, after en-

deavouring to soothe the maddened spirit of the father,
consented that the sons should be brought to trial at
Berytus. Saturninus and Volumnius, the governors of
Syria, presided in the court. The only fact which was
clearly proved against them was a design of flying beyond the power of their suspicious father; but so heavy
were the charges, and so vehement the exertions of
Herod, who acted as his own advocate, examining
witnesses, and reading documents with the strongest and
most violent emphasis, that a verdict of condemnation
was at length extorted from a majority of the council.
The unhappy youths, who had not been permitted to
make their defence, nor produced before the court, in
which 150 persons sate as assessors, but were kept in
custody in the neighbourhood, awaited their doom in
silence. Still Herod wanted courage to execute his
own barbarous design. He had dared to appeal to the
law of Moses, according to which the son who should
curse his father or mother was to be put to death by
stoning; but he shrank from carrying this terrible statute
into effect. The whole people, particularly the army,
looked on in deep but suppressed interest, till one
Teron, a gallant soldier, openly expressed the general
feeling in the presence of the monarch. His interference
turned out, eventually, fatal to himself and to the sons
of Mariamne. Teron was accused of having tampered
with the barber of Herod against his life; and Alexander
was implicated as privy to the crime. The son of Teron,
a youth, an intimate associate of Alexander, to save his
father's life, confirmed the accusation. Teron was put
to death on the spot, and the final order issued that
Alexander and his brother should be strangled at Sebaste.
Either on this or on some similar occasion, his imperial
protector, Augustus, uttered this bitter sarcasm—that

he had rather be one of Herod's swine than one of his
sons.

The crime did not remain long unavenged; it recoiled
with dreadful force against almost all who were implicated.   The low-born wife of Pheroras had connected herself with the Pharisaic party ; and when, on the refusal of
7000 of that faction to take an oath of allegiance to
Augustus and to Herod, they were heavily fined, she
discharged the whole of the mulct.   Rumours began to
spread abroad of prophecies, which declared that God
intended to transfer the government of his people from
the line of Herod to that of Pheroras.   Pheroras was
commanded to separate himself from his wife, to whom
all these intrigues were attributed.   He refused, and lost
all the favour with which he had been once regarded by
his brother and benefactor.   Yet, when a short time
after Pheroras fell ill, and lay on his death-bed, the kindly
feelings of Herod revived, and he visited his brother with
fraternal tenderness.   On the death of Pheroras suspicions began to arise that his malady was not in the
course of nature: two of his freedmen openly charged
his wife with having poisoned him.   Herod ordered a
strict investigation of the transaction : in the process a
darker and more horrible secret came to light.   Antipater, the beloved son, for whom he had imbrued his
hands in the blood of his own children—Antipater, the
heir of his kingdom, was clearly proved to have conspired with Pheroras to poison his old and doting father,
and thus to secure and accelerate his own succession.
The wife of Pheroras acknowledged the whole plot, and
declared that the affectionate conduct of Herod to Pheroras on his death-bed, had melted the heart of the fratricide, who had commanded her to throw into the fire the
subtle poison which had already been prepared.   Herod's

wife, Mariamne, daughter of Simon the High Priest, was implicated in the conspiracy: Herod repudiated her immediately, deposed her father, and appointed Mattathias to the High-priesthood. Antipater was at Rome; and the horror-stricken Herod dissembled his detection of the conspiracy: yet still obscure intimations spread abroad, which, however, did not reach the ears of Antipater. Josephus accounts for the extraordinary fact, that of these events which spread over seven months not a rumour transpired in Rome, by the care and vigilance with which all the roads were watched, and the universal hatred of Antipater. Triumphing in the success of his intrigues, and the unbounded promises of support which he had purchased at Rome—confident in his speedy, if not immediate, inheritance of the throne —in all the pride of successful guilt, and the malignant assurance that his rivals were entirely removed by death, Antipater landed at Cæsarea.[s] The once-crowded port seemed a solitude; no acclamations rose around him, no deputations waited upon him at his landing: the few people who met turned aloof, or looked on as if they now dared to hate him undisguisedly; every one seemed in possession of some fearful secret, of which he alone was ignorant. It was too late to fly: he was constrained to dissemble his terrors, and proceed to Jerusalem. There he was immediately summoned before the tribunal of Herod, who sat with Varus, the Roman governor of Syria, for his assessor. The proofs of his guilt were full and conclusive: an artful defence which told with some effect on the judges, was refuted by the eloquent Nicolaus of Damascus. The poison was produced; a criminal

---

[s] At Celenderis in Cilicia he heard of his mother's repudiation, and began to have some misgivings, which were overruled. Ant. xvii. 5. 1.

condemned to death made to swallow it; he fell dead
before the judges. Antipater was then condemned without the least hesitation. Herod, already afflicted by his
last mortal malady, delayed the execution, but in the
mean time made his final alterations in his will. He
bequeathed the kingdom to Antipas, passing over Archelaus and Philip, who were supposed to be implicated in
the conspiracy of Antipater. He left splendid bequests
to Cæsar, to Cæsar's wife Julia, to her sons, to his friends,
and even to his freedman. Thus the great and magnificent Herod lay, afflicted in body by the most painful and
loathsome malady, tormented in mind by the ingratitude
of his favourite son—perhaps with remorse for the
murder of those of Mariamne. His last hours were still
further embittered by the turbulence and disaffection of
his subjects.[t]

Among the innovations of Herod nothing offended
the eyes of the zealous Jews more than a large golden
eagle, which he had placed over the great gate of the
Temple. Some daring and enthusiastic youths, instigated
by two celebrated teachers, named Judas and Matthias,
conspired to tear down the offensive emblem. On a
rumour of Herod's death, they put their design in execution. Being apprehended, they boldly justified their
conduct. Herod at first assumed something like moderation: he assembled the chiefs of the people, reproached
them with the ungrateful return which they made for
his munificence in rebuilding the Temple, which the

---

[t] Antipater had accomplices and influence at Rome; and in the Palace of
Cæsar, a certain Acme, a Jewish slave,
in high favour with the Empress
Julia, was concerned in the plot
against Herod. On the conviction of
Antipater, and the ratification of that
conviction at Rome, Acme was put to
death. Ant. xvii. 7. 1.

Asmonean princes had left in decay; and only displaced Mattathias, the High Priest, who was suspected of having encouraged the enterprise. The most criminal of the actual assailants and their teachers were burnt alive.

But now the disorder of the king made sensible progress; a slow fire seemed creeping through all his vital parts: he had a rabid appetite, which he dared not gratify on account of internal ulcers and dreadful pains, particularly in the colon. Dropsical symptoms appeared in his feet, which were swollen, and exuded. Ulcers, which bred worms, preyed on the lower region of his belly and the adjacent parts. His breathing was difficult; and violent spasms, which seemed to give him unnatural strength, convulsed his frame. He sought relief from the warm bituminous baths of Callirhoe, but returned to Jericho without improvement. There the frenzy of his malady working on the natural sternness of his disposition, he is said to have imagined a kind of testamentary cruelty, almost too horrible to be believed: he determined to extort a universal mourning for his death from the reluctant people. He commanded some of all the chief families in Judæa to be seized, shut up in the Hippodrome, and strictly enjoined his sister Salome that, immediately he expired, the guards should be let loose, and an unsparing massacre commence. Thus a wide, and general, and heartfelt wailing would spread throughout all the land with the news of his death. But the dying requests of kings proverbially fail of their accomplishment, and, happily for human nature, this sanguinary injunction was disregarded.

Among these atrocities of the latter days of Herod, what is called the Massacre of the Innocents (which took place late in the year before, or early in the same year with, the death of Herod, four years before the vulgar æra of Christ) passed away unnoticed. The murder of a few children, in a small village near Jerusalem, would excite little sensation among such a succession of dreadful events, except among the immediate sufferers. The jealousy of Herod against any one who should be born as *a King in Judæa*—the dread that the high religious spirit of the people might be re-excited by the hope of a real Messiah—as well as the summary manner in which he endeavoured to rid himself of the object of his fears, are strictly in accordance with the relentlessness and decision of his character.

At length, just before his death, the ratification of the sentence against Antipater arrived from Rome. It found Herod in a paroxysm of torment so great that he had attempted to lay violent hands on himself. The rumour of his death induced Antipater to make a desperate attempt to bribe the keeper of his prison. This last offence was fatal. Herod just raised himself up in his bed to give the mandate for his execution, and then fell back—had only time once more to remodel his will; and thus, dispensing death on one hand, and kingdoms on the other, expired!

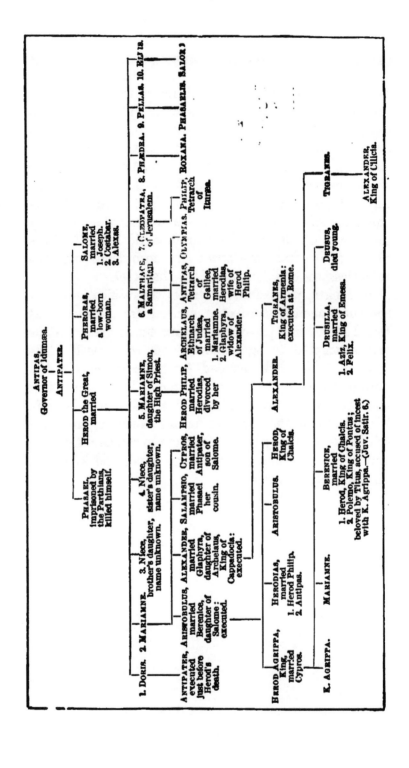

BOOK XII.

THE HERODIAN FAMILY.

Archelaus — Roman Governors — Pontius Pilate — Herod Antipas
— Philip — Accession of Caligula — Agrippa — Persecutions in
Alexandria — Philo — Babylonian Jews — Agrippa King.

THE history of the Jews after the death of Herod, not
rightly named the Great,[a] and the birth of Jesus, sepa-
rates itself into two streams: one narrow at first, and
hardly to be traced in its secret windings into the world,
but with the light of heaven upon it, and gradually widen-
ing till it embraces a large part of Asia, part of Africa,
the whole of Europe, and becomes a mighty, irresistible
river,—a river with many branches—gladdening and
fertilising mankind, and bearing civilization, as well as
holiness and happiness, in its course; the other at first
as expansive, but gradually shrinking into obscurity,
lost in deep, almost impenetrable, ravines: sullen apparently and lonely, yet not without its peculiar majesty
in its continuous, inexhaustible, irrepressible flow, and
not without its own peculiar influence as an under-
current on the general life and progress of mankind.
The broader and brighter stream I have attempted to
trace in its early course, and in one of its branches,[b] so

---

[a] Ewald observes that Herod is not
called the Great in any contemporary
document. There are inscriptions
which call him the Great King, as
the ὁ μεγὰς βασιλεῦς, and the Maha-
Rajah in India; but this is an epithet
of the office or a title, not an appellation of the man.

[b] The History of Latin Christianity.

strong, so broad, as to appear the one all-permeating tide. I return to the humbler and more obscure and less noble stream, too often attempted to be cruelly dried up by violent means, or turned into blood, yet still emerging when seeming almost lost, and flowing on as it still flows, and seems destined to flow. Though the Jewish and Christian history have much in common, they may be kept (as it is my design for obvious reasons to keep them) almost entirely distinct. As in Jewish history I shall touch but rarely and occasionally on that of Christianity, so in Christianity the history of the Jews sometimes forces itself upon the attention.

The executioner had made frightful ravages in the family of Herod; but still a powerful, if united, race survived. Ten wives of Herod are mentioned in history.[c] The *first*, Doris, the mother of Antipater, the last and the only unpitied victim of his vengeance.[d] The *second*, Mariamne, the Asmonean princess, the mother of the unfortunate Aristobulus and Alexander, and of two daughters, Salampsio and Cypros. Aristobulus, by Berenice, his cousin, left four children—1, Herod Agrippa, who became distinguished at a later period.—2, Herodias, infamous for her divorce of her first husband her uncle Philip, and her incestuous marriage with Herod Antipas.—3, Aristobulus.—4, Herod. The *third* wife of Herod the Great was Mariamne, daughter of Simon the High Priest, the mother of Herod Philip. The name

---

[c] Josephus observes on the polygamy of Herod: πάτριον γὰρ ἐν ταυτῷ πλείοσιν ἡμῖν συνοικεῖν. Ant. xvii. 1, 2. I suspect that it was rather an Oriental than a modern Jewish privilege in which Herod indulged.

[d] Doris was alive at the time of the detection of Antipater's conspiracy, and as a suspected accomplice despoiled of her wealth, which amounted to many talents. Ant. xvii. 4, 2.

of Herod Philip was effaced from the will of his father, on account of his mother's supposed connexion with the conspiracy against his life. The *fourth*, a niece by the brother's side; the *fifth*, a niece by the sister's side, whose names do not appear, and who had no issue. The *sixth*, Malthace, a Samaritan, the mother of—1, Archelaus—2, Herod Antipas—3, Olympias. It was among this family that his dominions were chiefly divided. The *seventh*, Cleopatra of Jerusalem, mother of—1, Herod—2, Philip, tetrarch of Trachonitis. The *eighth*, Pellas, the mother of Phasaelis. The *ninth*, Phædra, mother of Roxana. The *tenth*, Elpis, the mother of Salome.

The will of Herod had designated the sons of Malthace as his successors. To Herod Antipas were assigned Galilee and Peræa—to Archelaus, Idumæa, Samaria, and Judæa. Though the will of Herod could not be held valid until ratified at Rome, yet Archelaus, amid the acclamations of the army, at once assumed the direction of affairs in Jerusalem. The funeral of his father was the first object of his care. The lifeless remains of Herod seemed to retain his characteristic magnificence. The body was borne aloft on a bier, which was adorned with costly precious stones. The linen was of the richest dye; the winding-sheet of purple. It still wore the diadem, and, above that, the golden crown of royalty: the sceptre was in its hand. The sons and relatives of Herod attended the bier. All the military force followed, distributed according to their nations. First, his bodyguard—then his foreign mercenaries, Thracians, Germans, Gauls—then the rest of the army, in war array. Last, came five hundred of his court-officers, bearing sweet spices, with which the Jews embalmed the dead. In this pomp the procession passed on, by slow stages, to the Herodium, a fortified palace, about twenty-five miles from Jericho.[e]

Archelaus, according to Jewish usage, mourned for seven days ; but rumours were industriously propagated by his enemies, that, while he wore the decent garb of sorrow during the day-time, his nights were abandoned to revelry, and to the most undisguised rejoicing among his own private friends. At the end of this time, he gave a splendid funeral banquet to the whole people, and then entered the Temple in great pomp, amid general acclamations; and, taking his seat on a golden throne, delivered an address to the multitude. His speech was conciliatory and temperate. He alluded to his father's oppressions—thanked the. people for their loyal reception—promised to reward their good conduct, but declined to assume the royal diadem till his father's testament should be ratified at Rome.[f] The people vied with each other in the vehemence of their applause ; but their acclamations were mingled with demands by no means so acceptable to the royal ear. Some called for a diminution of the public burthen ; others for the release of the prisoners, with whom Herod had crowded the dungeons; some more specifically for the entire abandonment of the taxes on the sale of commodities in the markets, which had been levied with the utmost rigour. Archelaus listened with great affability, promised largely, and, having performed sacrifice, retired.

While he was preparing for his voyage, the zealous party which had been concerned in the demolition of

---

[e] The Antiquities state, ἦσαν δὲ ἐπὶ Ἡρωδιόυ στάδια ὀκτώ. This must have been the first stage, as according to the B. J. the Herodium (near Masada) was 200 stadia distant from Jericho. Compare Aldrich's note on the B. J. i., last page in Cardwell's Josephus.

[f] B. J. ii. i. 1.

the Eagle, collected their strength. They bewailed, with frantic outcries, the death of Matthias, the teacher, and his seditious pupils, who had even been deprived of the rites of burial by the unrelenting rigour of Herod: and no unintelligible execrations against the deceased monarch were mingled with their lamentations. They demanded the summary punishment of all who had been employed in the recent executions, the expulsion of the High Priest, and the substitution of one more legally appointed. Archelaus attempted to allay the tumult by conciliatory measures. He sent officer after officer to soothe, to expostulate, to admonish, to threaten. Argument and menace were alike unavailing. The clamorous multitude would listen to nothing, and the sedition grew every day more alarming. The danger was more urgent on account of the approaching Passover, which assembled the Jews from all quarters of the country, and even strangers from the most remote parts of the world. If it was difficult at any time to keep the fanatical multitude of Jerusalem in check, it was still more so when this formidable addition was made to their numbers. The leaders of the faction held their meetings in the Temple itself, where they were abundantly supplied with provisions by their friends, who did not scruple to beg in their behalf. It was high time to interfere, and Archelaus sent a centurion with a band of soldiers to disperse the multitude, to apprehend the ringleaders, and bring them before his tribunal. They arrived while the sacrifice was offering. The zealots inflamed the multitude, who attacked the soldiers, many of whom were stoned; the rest, with the centurion, made their escape, but with great difficulty, and dreadfully maimed. This done, the sacrifice quietly proceeded. Archelaus found it necessary, if he would not at once throw up all his authority, to act with greater vigour. He gave orders for a large body of troops to advance. The cavalry cut off the strangers from the provinces who were encamped without the city, from the zealots who occupied the Temple. The multitude fled on all sides; those of Jerusalem dispersed; the strangers retreated to the mountains; 3000 were slain. Archelaus issued a proclamation, commanding all the strangers to return to their homes; they obeyed with reluctance, and, to the universal horror, the great national festival, thus interrupted, was not concluded.

Archelaus set out for Rome, accompanied by Nicolaus of Damascus, and many of his relatives, all with the ostensible purpose of supporting his claim to the throne, some with the secret design of thwarting his advancement. Among the latter was Salome, the false and intriguing sister of Herod. At Cæsarea he met Sabinus, the procurator of Syria, who was hastening to Judæa, in order to make himself master of the treasures left by Herod, and to obtain military possession of the country by seizing the fortresses which the king had built. Through the interference of Varus, the prefect of Syria, Sabinus agreed to suspend his march, to leave Archelaus in possession of the treasures, and to undertake no measure till the arrival of an edict from Rome. But no sooner had Archelaus set sail and Varus returned to Antioch, than Sabinus marched to Jerusalem, seized the palace, summoned the keepers of the treasures to render up their accounts, and the military officers to cede the fortresses. All, however, remained faithful to their charge, and refused to comply without direct orders from Rome.

Archelaus had to encounter a formidable opposition to his attainment of the royal dignity, not merely from the

caprice or pride of the Emperor, but from intrigues set
on foot in his own family.   His younger brother, Herod
Antipas, arrived in Rome to maintain his own pretensions to the crown, grounded on a former will of Herod,
made, as his party asserted, when his father was in a
saner state of mind than at his decease, and in which Antipas was named first.   His mother Malthace, Salome
his aunt, Ptolemy the brother of Nicolaus of Damascus,
who had been a great favourite with his father, and
Irenæus, a man of remarkable eloquence and ability,
espoused the party of Antipas.   Augustus appointed a
solemn hearing of the cause, and in that haughty spirit
which delighted in displaying kings publicly pleading
for their thrones before the footstool of Roman subjects, appointed Caius the son of Agrippa and his own
daughter Julia, afterwards noted for her profligacy, to
preside on the occasion.   Antipater, the son of Salome,
conducted the cause of Herod Antipas.   He insisted on
the former will of Herod—accused Archelaus of assuming the crown without the sanction of the Emperor—of
unseemly rejoicings at the death of his father—and of
wanton acts of tyranny against the people—urging and
aggravating the dreadful slaughter during the tumult of
the Passover.   The eloquent Nicolaus of Damascus
maintained the cause of Archelaus with his accustomed
ability. - The Emperor took time to deliberate on his
judgment.

While these affairs were pending at Rome, intelligence arrived that Judæa was in a state of insurrection.
The rapacity and insolence of Sabinus had exasperated
the people, already in a state of tumultuary excitement.
Varus advanced to Jerusalem, seized the ringleaders,
and re-established order—but unfortunately left Sabinus
behind him to maintain the peace.   The sole object of

this unscrupulous commander was to find an opportunity
and excuse for seizing the tempting treasures of this
opulent city, as well those left by Herod, as the more
inestimable riches contained in the Temple. All his acts
tended to goad the people to insurrection.

The Pentecost drew on, and the Jews gathered together from all quarters with the deliberate intention of
wreaking their vengeance on Sabinus. From both the
Galilees, from Idumæa, from Jericho, and from the provinces beyond Jordan, vast multitudes came crowding
into the city. One party encamped in the circus to the
south, one occupied a position to the north, another to
the west of the Temple; and thus shut up the single
legion of Varus in the palace. Sabinus sent pressing
messages to Varus for relief. In the mean time he himself,—for with more than Roman rapacity he does not
seem to have possessed Roman valour,—ascending the
lofty tower of Phasaelis, gave orders to his troops to
make a desperate sally, and force their way to the
Temple. The Jews, though repelled by the disciplined
valour of the legionaries, fought with courage, and,
mounting on the roofs of the cloisters or porticoes which
surrounded the outer court of the Temple, annoyed the
assailants with stones, javelins, and other missiles. The
Romans at length set fire to the cloisters, the roofs of
which were made of wood, cemented with pitch and
wax; and the whole magnificent range became one immense conflagration: the gilding melted, the columns
fell, and all the Jews upon the roof were either crushed
to death among the blazing ruins, or lay victims to the
unrelenting fury of the enemy: some of the more desperate fell on their own swords: not one escaped. But
the flames could not repress the daring rapacity of the
Roman soldiery: they broke into the Temple, plundered

on all sides, and even seized the sacred treasures, from which Sabinus secured the greater part of 400 talents; the rest was secreted by the pillagers.   Maddened with this outrage, the bravest of the Jews assembled from all quarters, besieged the palace, but offered Sabinus his life if he and his legion would evacuate the city.   Many of Herod's soldiers deserted to the Jews; but, on the other hand, two distinguished officers, Rufus, the commander of Herod's cavalry, and Gratus, the captain of his infantry, with 3000 Samaritan troops, joined Sabinus. The Jews pressed the siege with vigour, and began to mine the palace; at the same time urging Sabinus to quit the city, and leave them to their own government; but Sabinus would not trust their faith.

The whole country was in the same dreadful state of anarchy.   The severe military police of Herod was now withdrawn or suspended, on account of the uncertainty of the succession.   The Romans exercised all the oppression without affording the protection of despotic sovereignty: and at the period when the nation was in the highest state of excitement—some looking forward, with sober patriotism, to the restoration of their national independence—others, of more ardent zeal, to the fulfilment of their national prophecies in the person of some mighty conqueror, the fame of whose destined birth at this period prevailed, according to the expression of the Roman historian, throughout all the East,—the whole country was without any regular government.   Adventurer after adventurer sprang up in every quarter, not one of whom was too base or too desperate not to assemble a number, either of daring robbers or deluded fanatics, around his standard.   Two thousand of Herod's troops having been dismissed, spread over Judæa, subsisted on plunder, and besieged Achiab, a cousin of Herod, who

took refuge in the mountains.[g] One Judas, son of
Hezekias, a noted captain of banditti, surprised Sepphoris, seized the treasures, and plundered the armoury,
from which he supplied his followers, who became the
terror of the district. Simon, a slave of Herod, a man
of great personal strength and beauty, had the audacity
to assume the diadem. He plundered the palace in
Jericho, and several other of the royal residences; his
followers burnt that of Betharamptha, near the Jordan.
He was at length attacked by Gratus, taken in a ravine,
and beheaded. Another adventurer, Athronges, a common shepherd, with his four brothers, men of extraordinary personal strength and courage, collected a predatory
band, and waged open war both against the Romans and
the royal party. Athronges also assumed the diadem.
He had the boldness to attack a Roman cohort, which
was escorting a convoy of provisions and arms, near
Emmaus. One centurion and 400 men were killed; the
rest escaped with difficulty, leaving the dead on the field
of battle. Nothing could exceed the rapacity and cruelty
of this band. They were not subdued till long after,
when one brother having been slain in battle by Gratus,
the other in a conflict against Ptolemy, and the eldest
taken, the youngest, who survived, broken in spirit, and
finding his troops dispersed, surrendered to Archelaus.

In consequence of urgent entreaties from Sabinus,
and dreading the peril in which his legion was placed,
Varus, the prefect of Syria, assembled at Ptolemais the
two legions remaining in Syria, and four troops of horse,
with some allies from Berytus, and some Arabian bands.
Part of these went forward into Galilee; they recovered and
burnt Sepphoris, and subdued the whole district. With

---

[g] Ant. xvii. 10.

the rest he advanced in person to Samaria, which he
spared as having taken no part in the late insurrections.
His Arabian allies committed dreadful depredations,
burning and ravaging on all sides: he himself gave
orders for the burning of Emmaus, in revenge for the
loss of the cohort defeated by Athronges. On his approach to Jerusalem, the forces from the country broke
up their siege of Sabinus and dispersed: the inhabitants
submitted, and laid the whole blame of the insurrection
on the strangers. Sabinus, ashamed of meeting Varus,
stole away to the coast, and took ship for Rome. Varus
spread his troops over the country, and seized the notorious ringleaders in the recent tumults; 2000 were
crucified, the rest pardoned. Finding, however, that the
rapacity of his soldiers, particularly his Arabian allies,
from their hatred of Herod, increased the mischief, he
dismissed the latter, and advanced only with his own
force on a body of 10,000 men, which appeared in arms
on the borders of Idumæa. These insurgents were persuaded by Achiab to surrender: the leaders were sent to
Rome for trial; a general amnesty was granted to the
rest. Augustus treated the criminals with lenity, excepting those who were related to the house of Herod,
whom he ordered to be put to death for their unnatural
hostility to the head of their own family.

In the mean time the great decision which was to
award the dominions of Herod remained in suspense. A
deputation of 500 Jews arrived at Rome, to petition for
the re-establishment of their ancient constitution, and
the total suppression of the kingly government. They
were joined by 8000 of their countrymen resident in
Rome. An audience was granted, in which they enlarged on the oppressions, cruelties, debaucheries, summary executions, and enormous taxations of the elder

'Herod.[h] The whole Herodian family now found it expedient to give up their dissensions; and to unite their
common interest. Herod Philip arrived at the same
time to support his own claims.

At length the imperial edict appeared: it confirmed
for the most part the will of Herod. Archelaus was appointed to the sovereignty of Judæa, Idumæa, and
Samaria, under the title of Ethnarch; that of King was
reserved as a reward for future good conduct. Herod
Antipas obtained Galilee and Peræa ; Philip—Auranitis,
Trachonitis, Paneas, and Batanea. The Samaritans were
rewarded for their peaceable behaviour by the reduction
of one quarter of their tribute. The chief cities of
Archelaus were Jerusalem, Sebaste (Samaria), Cæsarea,
and Joppa. Gaza, Gadara, and Hippo, as Greek towns,
were added to the prefecture of Syria. The annual
revenue of Archelaus was 600 talents. The bequests of
Herod to Salome were confirmed; and in addition she
obtained the towns of Jamnia, Azotus, and Phasaelis,
and a palace in Ascalon : her yearly revenue was sixty
talents. The wealth left to Augustus, he distributed,
chiefly as a dower to two unmarried daughters of Herod,
whom he united to two sons of Pheroras. He retained
nothing except some magnificent plate, as a memorial of
his friend.

At this juncture an impostor made his appearance,
who assumed the name of Alexander, the murdered son
of Mariamne.[1] So like was he in person to that ill-fated
youth, and so well had he been tutored by an unprincipled adventurer, who was intimately acquainted with

---

[h] Παρθένων μέντοι φθοράς, καὶ
γυναικῶν αἰσχύνας, ὁπόσας ἐπὶ πα-
ροινίᾳ καὶ ἀπανθρωπίᾳ δρωμενας σι-
γᾶν διὰ τὸ ἡδονὴν ἔιναι τοῖς πεπον-
θόσι τοῦ μὴ γεγόνεναι, τὴν ἐκ τοῦ
ἀνέκπυστα ἀυτὰ ἔιναι. Ant. xvii.
11. 2.

[1] Ant. xvii. 12.

the court of Herod, that wherever he went, in Crete and
Melos, where a number of Jews resided, he was received with all the attachment which the nation felt to
the race of their Asmonean princes: he was liberally
furnished with money, and boldly set out for Rome to
demand his inheritance. The Jews crowded forth to
meet him, and escorted him into the city with loud acclamations. Celadus, one of the Emperor's freedmen, who
had been familiarly acquainted with the sons of Mariamne, was sent to investigate the case; he was imposed
upon like the rest. Not so Augustus, who, on sending
for the false Alexander, observed that his hands were
hard and horny, and that his whole person wanted the
delicacy and softness of the royal youth. Still both he
and his tutor supported a strict cross-examination, till at
length Augustus himself led the youth aside, and promised to him a free pardon if he would confess the im-
posture. The youth, either supposing himself detected,
or awed by the imperial presence, acknowledged the
deception; and Cæsar, seeing that he was of a strong
and muscular make, ordered him as a rower to his
galleys. His instructor was put to death.

Archelaus (B.C. 3[1]) assumed the dominion of Judæa,
and governed with great injustice and cruelty. Such is
the unanimous report of all historians, confirmed by his
condemnation, after a solemn hearing before Augustus.
Yet few facts have transpired by which posterity may
judge of the equity of the sentence. He displaced
Joazar from the pontificate, and substituted his brother
Eleazar. Eleazar in his turn was supplanted by Jesus,
son of Siva. The unlawful marriage of the Ethnarch
with Glaphyra, the daughter of Archelaus, king of Cap-

---

[1] Before the Vulgar Æra, now generally acknowledged to be erroneous by
about four years.

padocia, the widow of his brother Alexander, and his divorce of his own wife, Mariamne, gave great offence to his zealous subjects.[k] He repaired the palace of Jericho with great magnificence, and paid much attention to the cultivation of the palm-trees in the neighbourhood. Such are the barren incidents of a reign of nine years; at the end of which Archelaus, while sitting at a banquet, was hastily summoned to Rome. His cause was formally heard, his brothers as well as his subjects being his accusers. He was banished to Vienne, in Gaul; his estates were confiscated, and Judæa reduced to a Roman province. Thus the sceptre finally departed from Judah; the kingdom of David and Solomon, of the Asmonean princes and of Herod, sank into a district, dependent on the prefecture of Syria, though administered by its own governor, a man usually of the equestrian order.

At this period of the Jewish history, when the last semblance of independence passed away, and Judæa became part of a Roman province, it may be well to cast a rapid view over the state of the people, and their more important existing institutions.

The supreme judicial authority was exercised by the Sanhedrin, the great ecclesiastical and civil council. The origin of this famous court is involved in much obscurity. The Jews, it has been observed, took pride in deducing its lineal descent from that established by Moses in the wilderness. The silence of the whole intervening history to the Captivity has been considered fatal to these lofty pretensions. Others date its origin

---

[k] The history of Glaphyra is curious. Between her two marriages with the two Jewish princes, she was married to an African prince of Libya, as Josephus calls him—Juba. On the death of Juba, she had returned to her father's court in Cappadocia. Ant. xvii. 13. 4.

from the Captivity: others again from the re-organiza-
tion of the Jewish polity by the Maccabees.[1]   The Sanhedrin consisted of seventy-one persons, partly priests,
partly Levites, partly elders.   The High Priest, whether
of right or not is much disputed, usually sate as president: he was entitled Nasi, or prince. At his right hand
sate the Ab-beth-Din, the father of the council, or vice-
president: on his left, the Wise Man, perhaps the most
learned among the doctors of the law.   The constitution
of the rest of the council, and their mode of election,
remain in the same obscurity.   The qualifications for
members of this court, as stated by the Jewish writers,
are curious.   They must be religious, and learned in
arts and languages.   Some added, in their fanciful
attachment to the number seventy, that they must understand seventy languages!   They must have some
skill in physic, arithmetic, astronomy, astrology, and be
acquainted with what belonged to magic, sorcery, and
idolatry, that they may know how to judge of them.
They must be without maim or blemish of body; men
of years, but not extremely old, because such are commonly of too great severity; and *they must be fathers of
children, that they might be acquainted with tenderness and
compassion.*

The council sate in the form of a semicircle round the
president, whose place was between the Ab-beth-Din
and the Wise Man.   At each end was a secretary; one
registered the votes of acquittal—the other of condemnation.

[1] Ewald inclines to the opinion that
it was founded by Ezra (p. 193), but
for once Ewald is not positive. Jost
would date it from the time of Simon
the Maccabee. I think this the most
probable date. The number was very
likely taken from the assembly of
Moses. Jost adds, "Von deren Wahl
und Geschäftskreiss ist nichts bekannt
geworden, weil *beides* sich jedenfalls
nur nach dem Herkommen verhielt."
i. p. 124.

At first the Sanhedrin sate in a room in the cloister of the court of the Israelites, called Gazith. They afterwards removed successively to other places. The proper period of sitting was the whole time between the morning and evening service. The Sanhedrin was the great court of judicature : it judged of all capital offences against the law : it had the power of inflicting punishment by scourging and by death. Criminals capitally condemned were executed in four different ways, by strangling, burning, slaying with the sword, and by stoning.

The Great Sanhedrin was a court of appeal from the inferior Sanhedrins of twenty-three judges, established in the other towns.

The Sanhedrin was probably confined to its judicial duties—it was a plenary court of justice, and no more— during the reigns of the later Asmonean princes, and during those of Herod the Great and his son Archelaus.[m] To the despotism of the two latter there was no check, except an appeal to Rome. When Judæa became a Roman province, the Sanhedrin either, as is more likely, assumed for the first time, or recovered its station as a kind of senate or representative body of the nation ; possessed itself of such of the subordinate functions of the government as were not actually admi-

[m] This is confirmed by Jost, p. 273, note. " Alles was Mischnah und Thalmud von Synedrion sagen, bezieht sich nur auf *Gerichtsbarkeit*, nicht aus Lehramt wie Maim. will. Nirgends wird gesagt, dass das Synedrion sich mit der Lehre beschäftigt. Es entscheidet nur über Anfragen oder richtet selbst wo ihm Klagen vorgebracht werden."

According to Jost the full Sanhedrin determined on great affairs, such as false prophets, charges against the High Priest, the extension of the hallowed limits of Jerusalem, some say the election of a king or a chief priest. Minor courts or committees of 31 had the power of passing capital sentences for certain offences. For smaller crimes, theft, robbery, injury, unchastity, which were punished with stripes, a court of three gave judgement.

nistered by the Roman procurator; and probably, on account of the frequent changes in the person of the High Priest, usurped, in some degree, upon his authority. At all events, they seem to have been the channel of intercourse between the Roman rulers and the body of the people. It is the Sanhedrin, under the name of the chief priests, scribes, and elders of the people, who take the lead in all the transactions recorded in the Gospels. Jesus Christ was led before the Sanhedrin, and by them denounced before the tribunal of Pilate.[n] Whether they had lost or retained the power of inflicting capital punishment, has been debated with the utmost erudition; and, like similar questions, is still in a high degree uncertain.[o]

---

[n] This is denied distinctly by Jost, who asserts this assembly to have been a tumultuary and irregular meeting of the enemies of Jesus. I fear that the historian must pronounce against Jost, though the Christian would allow him and his modern brethren the full benefit of the disclaimer. I fear that this too has influenced Jost's notion as to the discontinuance of the regular Sanhedrin for the century from the time of Simon ben Schetach till the establishment of Christianity. p. 279.

[o] This question mainly depends on the true meaning of the sentence in St. John's Gospel, xviii. 31: *It is not lawful for us to put any man to death.* The Jewish Tract Sanhedrin, 7, 1, lays down the law: "Quatuor supplicia capitalia senatui tradita sunt, lapidatio, ustio, interemtio quæ fit gladio, strangulatio." Ibid. 7, 4: "lapidantur autem, profanator Sabbati, qui ad apostasiam impellit magus," &c. The stoning of St. Stephen, in the Acts, seems to have been a judicial, not a tumultuary proceeding. The older Christian writers were perplexed with this difficulty. Theophylact thinks its meaning to be that they had no power to put to death by crucifixion; others that they had no power to put to death for treason; and the crime of which Jesus was accused was treason against the Roman authority. Augustine and Chrysostom, that it was not lawful to put a man to death on a holy day, as the Preparation for the Passover. I am inclined to adhere to the opinion adopted in the History of Christianity, vol. i. p. 342, that at this time, during the transition from the national government under the Herodian family to the direct government of the Romans, the authority of the Sanhedrin was altogether undefined; that they did not know whether the Romans would permit them to execute capital punishment, especially on a criminal accused of rebellion. There were ter-

The body of the people, at least all above the lowest order, seem to have addicted themselves to one or other of the two great prevailing sects—the Pharisees and the Sadducees. The multitude, though not actually enrolled among the former, were entirely under their sway, and zealously adhered to their faction. In all places of public resort the Pharisees were always seen with their phylacteries or broad slips of parchment, inscribed with sentences of the Law, displayed on their foreheads and the hems of their garments: even in the corners of the public streets they would kneel to pray; and in the Temple or synagogues they chose the most conspicuous stations, that their long devotions might excite the admiration of their followers. They fasted rigorously, observed the Sabbath with the most scrupulous punctuality, and paid tithes even upon the cheapest herbs.[p] In private societies they assumed the superiority to which their religious distinction seemed to entitle them; they always took the highest places. But their morals,[q] according to the unerring authority of Jesus Christ, were far below their pretensions: they violated the main principles of the Law, the justice and humanity of the Mosaic institutions, while they rigidly adhered to the most minute particulars, not merely

---

rible and recent reminiscences how Herod, and even Archelaus, had possessed and executed the power of life and death. Had the Romans appropriated to themselves that power, or would they permit the Law to be put in force by its ancient and ordinary administrators?

[p] Read the curious passage about the subtle distinctions as to the payment of tithes in Jost, Jud., i. 201—a

remarkable comment on the sentence in the Gospel about tithing mint, anise, and cummin.

[q] Josephus, himself a Pharisee, displays the brighter side of the Pharisaic character. He denies that they were absolute fatalists: πράσσεσθαι τε εἱμαρμένῃ τὰ πάντα ἀξιοῦντες, οὐδὲ τοῦ ἀνθρωπείου τὸ βουλόμενον τῆς ἐπ' αὐτοῖς ὁρμῆς ἀφαιροῦνται. Ant. xviii. 1, 2.

of the Law itself, but of tradition likewise. Still they
were the idols of the people, who reverenced them as
the great teachers and models of virtue and holiness.
The Sadducees were less numerous and less influential: [q]
for, besides the want of this popular display of religion,
they were notoriously severe in the execution of the national statutes. Denying all punishment for crime in
a future life, their only way to discourage delinquency
was by the immediate terrors of the law; and this they
put in force, perhaps with the greater rigour, because
their disbelief of future rewards and punishments was
represented by their enemies as leading necessarily
to the utmost laxity of morals. This effect it would
probably have on many of the weak or licentious;
but the doctrine of the Sadducees, which fully recognised the certain punishment of guilt in this world
by Divine Providence, is not justly chargeable with
these consequences. It is singular that this notorious
severity in the administration of the law is strongly
exemplified in the Christian history. The first persecution of the Apostles took place when the Sadducees
were in possession of the High-priesthood, and probably
formed a majority of the Sanhedrin; [r] and the High
Priest who put Saint James to death, was, in all probability, of that sect.

Besides these two great sects, there was a considerable party attached to the persons of the Herodian
family; who probably thought it the best interest of the

---

[q] εἰς ὀλίγους τε ἄνδρας οὗτος ὁ
λόγος ἀφίκετο, τοὺς μέντοι πρώτους
τοῖς αξιωμασι. This accounts for the
comparative silence about them in the
Gospels. There were probably few or
none of them in the villages of Galilee;
in Jerusalem they would hardly fall in
the way of a popular teacher. They
dwelt aloof in their palaces, and were
less frequently in places of common
resort.

[r] Acts v. 17.

country to remain quietly under the government of native princes and the protection of the Roman emperors. This faction most likely comprehended what may be called the Grecian party; rather inclined to Grecian habits and customs, than strongly attached to the national institutes and usages.

At a considerable distance from the metropolis, in some highly cultivated oases amid the wilderness on the shores of the Dead Sea, were situated the chief of the large agricultural villages of the Essenes.[s] According to Josephus, their number was about 4000.[t] Almost in every respect, both in their rules and in the patient industry with which they introduced the richest cultivation into the barren waste, the Essenes were the monastic order of the Jews. Among groves of palm-trees of which, according to the picturesque expression of Pliny, they were the companions, and amid fertile fields won from the barren wilderness, they passed their rigid and ascetic lives. They avoided populous cities, not from hatred of mankind, but from dread of their vices. In general, no woman was admitted within their do-

---

[s] There is no certain derivation for the word Essene. It is used by Philo and Josephus, but occurs neither in the Apocryphal books nor in the New Testament, nor, according to Jost, in the Rabbinical writings. This is to me a convincing proof that they were not found, as some, even Ewald, suppose them to have been, in the cities, but were strictly confined to their own monastic settlements. Why, Jost pertinently asks, did Josephus retire for three years into the Desert, to acquaint himself with their tenets, if he could study them in Jerusalem or other towns? The Essenes were the monks of Judaism, and monachism seems to be the natural and necessary offspring of all, especially Eastern religions; and even of philosophies, as with the Pythagoreans, so long as philosophy has not set itself apart from religion. Herzfeld's notion that they arose in Egypt, and were really Pythagorean in their origin, appears to me in itself utterly improbable; and the few Pythagorean maxims which they held are common to all Asiatics.

[t] Ant. xviii. 11. 5.

mains. Some of the inferior communities allowed
marriage, but only associated with their wives for the
procreation of children; the higher and more esteemed
societies practised the most rigid celibacy, and entirely
forswore all communication with the other sex.[u] Wonderful nation, says the Roman naturalist, which endures
for centuries, but in which no child is ever born![x] They
were recruited by voluntary proselytes, or by children
whom they adopted when very young, and educated in
their discipline. Among the Essenes all pleasure was forbidden as sin: the entire extinction of the passions of the
body was the only real virtue. An absolute community of
goods was established in their settlements: even a man's
house was not his own; another person might enter and
remain in it as long as he pleased. The desire of riches
was proscribed; every lucrative employment, commerce,
traffic, and navigation were forbidden. They neither
bought nor sold: all they had was thrown into a common fund, from which each received the necessaries of
life; but for charity, or for the assistance of the poor or
the stranger, they might draw as largely as they would
on this general revenue. They were all clothed alike
in white garments, which they did not change till they
were worn out: they abhorred the use of oil; if any
one were anointed against his will, he scrupulously
cleansed himself. Their lives were regulated by the
strictest forms; they rose before the sun, but were forbidden to speak of any worldly business, and devoted all
the time till break of day to offering up certain ancient
prayers that the sun might shine upon them. After
this they received their orders from the superior, and
went to work, according to his commands, at the la-

---

[u] Joseph. Ant. xviii. 1. 5.   [x] Pliny, Hist. Nat.

bour or craft in which they were skilled; but their artisans might only work on articles used in peace, by no means on swords, arrows, or military weapons; though they carried arms, when they travelled, to defend themselves against robbers. Having worked till the fifth hour, eleven o'clock, they assembled for refreshment. First, however, they washed and put on a linen garment; they then went into a room which no one might enter into who was not of their sect. After that they entered the common refectory as if it were a sacred place; there in silence waited till grace was said; then each received his portion from the baker and the cook, of bread, salt, and hyssop. They abstained from animal food, by which they were distinguished from all their Jewish brethren. To them the law of clean and unclean meat was superfluous. Another grace closed the meal: then, putting off their sacred garment, they returned to their toil till evening, when they again assembled to supper. No noise or tumult was heard; they spoke only by permission and in turn: on other occasions, if ten were met, one could not speak without the consent of the nine. In company they were to avoid spitting either before them or to the right hand. They observed the Sabbath with the strictest precision, not even lighting a fire, or performing the necessities of nature. At all other times they concealed their excrements with scrupulous care, digging a pit a foot deep, lest the holy light should be defiled. They then washed themselves with the utmost nicety. On the Sabbath they all met in their synagogues, where the elders interpreted the sacred writings, explaining them chiefly by parables.

In their religious opinions they differed from their countrymen; though they sent their gifts to the Temple,

they offered no sacrifices there.[y]   They were strict predestinarians. They believed that the body was mortal, the
soul immortal: that the soul, emanating out of the noblest
and purest air, is imprisoned in the body, where it is subjected to severe trials: when released from its corporeal
bonds, it escapes as it were a long servitude, and soars
back rejoicing to its native element. They believed,
with the Greeks, in a delightful region beyond the
ocean, in which the souls of the good dwelt for ever.
There rain, and snow, and parching heat were unknown,
but the air was continually refreshed with balmy and
gentle breezes from the sea. The souls of the wicked
were doomed to a cold and gloomy place of everlasting
punishment. They were great students of their sacred
books, and especially of the prophetic writings. Many
were endowed, according to Josephus, with that gift.
They studied likewise the nature and cure of diseases,
and the medicinal properties of herbs and minerals.
Their morals were rigid in every respect. They were
bound, by solemn vows, to worship God and to be just
to men; to keep inviolable faith; if entrusted with
authority, to abstain from all wrong and from splendid
apparel; to love truth and hate liars; to communicate
only to the members of the society the tenets of the
sect; to preserve their sacred doctrinal books, and the
names of the angels. They paid the highest veneration
to age: many of them, from their temperate habits,
lived to more than 100 years. They abstained from all

---

[y] It does not seem, as some have
asserted, that they offered their own
sacrifices, or any sacrifices at all. I
suspect that they had a Buddhist aversion to take away life. Philo says
distinctly—ὀυ ζῶα καταθύοντες, αλλ'
ἱεροπρεπεῖς, τὰς ἑαυτῶν διανοίας
κατασκευάζειν ἀξιοῦντες.   By this
the passage in Josephus must be interpreted.   No doubt they quoted the
Prophets, that "the best sacrifice is a
broken and a contrite heart."

oaths, considering an oath as bad as perjury. They
abhorred slavery, as an infringement of the natural
liberty of men. In their civil constitution they were
all equal as regards their rights, but were divided into
four classes; of which the superior class looked down
so much on those beneath them, that if touched by
one of a lower order, they were defiled, and washed
themselves.

There were stewards who managed the common
stock, and officers who took care of all strangers who
might enter their towns. No one was admitted into
the society without the strictest probation; the proselyte received a small pick-axe, linen garments, and a
white dress, and so commenced his year of noviciate.
After having given satisfactory proof of continence
and temperance for that period, he was admitted to
closer intimacy, and to wash in the holy water: yet for
two years longer he remained on trial, and only at the
end of that time was admitted to the common refectory.
Whoever was guilty of any great crime was expelled
from the society—a fearful doom! for having sworn
that he would receive no food but from his own sect, the
outcast fed, like a beast, on the grass of the field, till at
length he perished with hunger. Sometimes, if at the
last extremity the criminal showed sincere repentance,
he was readmitted, from compassion, within the society.
But this awful fate was inflicted with great reluctance;
for justice was administered with the utmost care; and
no verdict could be given unless a hundred were present;
it was then usually irrevocable.

The Essenes were cruelly persecuted by the Romans,
who probably entered their country after the capture of
Jericho. They were tortured, racked, had their bones
broken on the wheel, in order to compel them to blas-

pheme their lawgiver, or eat forbidden meats.   They did not attempt to appease their tormentors; they uttered no cry, they shed no tear; and even smiled in the worst agony of torment; and in stedfast reliance on the immortality of their souls, departed, rejoicing, from life.   These were usually called practical Essenes; there was another class in Egypt, called the Therapeutæ or Contemplative.   These were mystics; they have been claimed by some Roman Catholic writers as primitive Christian monks, but, though doubtless the prototypes of the monastic or eremitical life, they were as certainly Jews.

The origin of this singular people, the Essenes, is involved in obscurity.   Some have deduced them from very high antiquity, but without the slightest ground for their opinion: others derive them from the Rechabites, mentioned in the latter period of the monarchy.   In certain respects they may seem to have been formed in imitation of the schools of the Prophets, some of which, if not all, bound themselves to a severe and abstemious life; and not only does Josephus inform us that many of the Essenes pretended to the gift of prophecy, but we meet with Essene prophets in several parts of the later Jewish history.   The main principles of their tenets seem evidently grounded on that widespread Oriental philosophy, which, supposing matter either the creation of the Evil Being, or itself the Evil Being, considered all the appetites and propensities of the *material* body in themselves evil, and therefore esteemed the most severe mortification the perfection of virtue.   The reverence for the names of the angels points to the same source, and there is one ambiguous expression in the account of Josephus, which, taken literally, would imply that they worshipped the sun.

On the complete alteration in the civil state of Judæa, P. Sulpicius Quirinius, who had passed through all the offices of the Roman magistracy, and attained the consulate, was appointed to the prefecture of Syria. The subordinate administration of Judæa was entrusted to Coponius, a man of equestrian rank. Quirinius is by some supposed to have acted formerly as coadjutor to the Syrian prefect, Saturninus, having been appointed for the special purpose of conducting the general census of the population in this region. This is what is incorrectly called the general taxation, in our common translation of St. Luke's Gospel, which, in fact, was only a registry. Quirinius had now the more invidious office of taking a second census, of property as well as of persons, in order to regulate the taxation exacted by the Roman government from the subject provinces.ˣ The proud spirit of the Jews submitted in sullen reluctance to this last mark of subjection. The prudence of Joazar, who, in what manner it is unknown, had resumed the office of High Priest, repressed all dangerous indications of discontent; but the fiercer spirits found a leader in Judas, called the Galilean, though born in Gamala, a city of Gaulonitis. He was a man of eloquence, which he employed on the popular subjects—the sovereignty of God over his chosen people—the degradation of subjection to a foreign yoke—the unlawfulness of paying

---

ˣ This census, which first enregistered the Jews as subjects of Rome, not subjects to a king vassal to Rome, was one of the great revolutions in their history. It was this against which Judas the Gaulonite proclaimed his rebellious protest—it was the act of the enslavement of the people. τὴν δὲ ἀποτίμησιν οὐδὲν ἄλλο ἤ ἄντικρυς δουλείαν ἐπιφέρειν. It is singularly in accordance with the whole spirit of the Gospel, that the first (if it may be so said) unconscious act of the unborn Jesus was the quiet recognition of the Roman sovereignty, an anticipation of the giving *to Cæsar the things that were Cæsar's*, and a preannouncement that his kingdom was not of this world

tribute.   Multitudes crowded around him: the highspirited—the adventurous—those who were full of burning zeal for their country and their law—unhappily
also the fierce and licentious.   With his confederate,
Sadoc, a Pharisee, Judas formed a fourth sect, in addition to those of the Pharisees, Sadducees, and Essenes.
The watchword of his party was—We have no lord and
master but God.   But the days were passed when a
similar war-cry had rallied the whole nation under the
banner of the Maccabees, and won the independence of
Judæa at the point of the sword.   The circumstances of
the times were widely different; the national character
was altered for the worse; the power of the oppressor,
who wielded all the forces of the Western world with
Roman vigour and ability, irresistible; and the God, in
whose name and under whose protection they had been
accustomed to triumph, was now about to withdraw his
presence.   A kingdom, *not of this world*, was to rise out
of the ruins of the temporal sovereignty, which had so
long remained among the heirs and successors of David.
Judas himself perished—his followers were dispersed;
but to the influence of their tenets, in support of which
numbers endured the most horrible tortures and death
with the martyr's fortitude, Josephus attributes all the
subsequent insurrections, and the final ruin of the city
and the Temple.   The Gaulonites were the doctrinal
ancestors of the Zealots and Assassins (Sicarii) of later
days.   The sons of Judas were true to their father's
precepts, and, as we shall see hereafter, shared his
fate.

Quirinius, having completed the sale of the confiscated
goods which belonged to Archelaus—deposed Joazar,
who had become unpopular, from the pontificate, and
substituted Ananus, the son of Seth—retired to Syria

Coponius remained as governor of the province. No
other incident of his administration is related, but a
singular story of a wanton profanation of the Temple by
some Samaritans, who stole in on one of the nights during
the Passover, and strewed the sacred pavement with
dead men's bones.[a]

Coponius was succeeded by M. Ambivius, during
whose government died Salome, the sister of Herod,
leaving Jamnia and her other territorial possessions to
Livia, the wife of Augustus. M. Ambivius was followed
by Annius Rufus. This rapid succession of provincial
governors took place at the close of the reign of Augustus ; his successor, Tiberius, pursued a different policy. During his reign of twenty-three years, Judæa had
only two rulers, Valerius Gratus (A.C. 16), and Pontius
Pilate (A.C. 27). This was avowedly done by Tiberius
on principles of humanity, and implied a bitter sarcasm on
the rapacity of Roman prefects. "A rapid succession of
rulers," observed the shrewd tyrant, "only increases the
oppressions and exactions of the provinces. The governor
who anticipates but a short harvest, makes the most of
his time, and extorts as much as he is able in the
shortest possible period. A governor who expects to
remain longer in office, pillages on a more gradual,
and therefore less oppressive system—it is even possible that his avarice may be satiated."[b]   He compared a Roman province to the poor wounded man in
the fable, who lay by the wayside covered with flies;
and when a kind-hearted traveller offered to drive them
away, declined his service, as those were already glutted,
and would only be replaced by a more hungry swarm.
As if the governors of Judæa had exemplified the justice

---

[a] Joseph. Ant. xviii. 2. 2.   [b] Joseph. Ant. xviii. 6. 5.

of the Imperial pleasantry, the Jews petitioned Tiberius for a diminution of the burthens by which they were overwhelmed. The decision was left to Germanicus, who was then in the East; but whether any inquiry took place is uncertain. The government of Gratus is remarkable only for the perpetual changes which he made in the appointment to the High-priesthood. He deposed Ananus, and substituted Ismael, son of Fabi— then Eleazar, son of Ananus—then Simon, son of Camith—and lastly, Joseph Caiaphas, the son-in-law of Ananus.

During this period Judæa enjoyed tranquillity, but the Jews of Rome were exposed to a dreadful calamity. The rapid progress of foreign superstitions, as they were called, particularly among the women of high rank, alarmed the vigilance of the government. A young libertine, Decius Mundus, had bribed the priests of the Egyptian Isis, and by their means, in the character and habit of the god Anubis, had debauched the wife of Saturninus, Paullina, a woman of rank and virtue, but strangely infatuated by her attachment to the Egyptian religion.[c] Mundus boasting of the success of his profligacy, the affair was detected. Mundus was banished, the priests crucified, the temple razed, and the statue of Isis thrown into the Tiber. Just at this juncture, some Jews were discovered to have obtained so great an ascendancy over the mind of Fulvia, a noble matron, as not only to have made her a proselyte, but to have extorted from her large sums of money, as offerings to the Temple, which they had converted to their own use. The Jews were involved in the same sentence with the Egyptians; they were expelled from Rome, perhaps

---

[c] Joseph. Ant. xviii. 3.

from Italy; 4000 were drafted into the army, and sent to Sardinia, where the greater part fell victims to the unwholesome climate. Philo attributes this persecution to the intrigues of Sejanus, who apprehended that the attachment of the Jews to the person of the Emperor might stand in the way of his daring designs; and adds, that Tiberius, having discovered this after the death of Sejanus, issued an edict more favourable to that people.[d]

Up to this period the Roman prætor seems to have resided in Cæsarea, and avoided all collision between his troops and the turbulent zealots of the capital. Pontius Pilate determined to transfer the winter quarters of his army from Samaria to Jerusalem. The Romans had hitherto so far respected the prejudices of their subjects, as not to introduce their standards, on which appeared not only the offensive *image* of the eagle, but likewise that of Cæsar, within the walls of the city. The troops entered the gates by night, and in the morning the people were shocked and surprised at beholding the effigy of the Emperor publicly displayed in their streets. They abstained from all violence, but a numerous deputation set out to Cæsarea, and for many days entreated Pilate to remove the standards. Pilate treated the affair as an insult on the Emperor, and, weary of their importunity, concealed some troops, with which he surrounded and hoped to disperse them. When the soldiers appeared, the Jews with one accord fell on the

---

[d] Tac. Ann. ii. 85; Suet. in Tib. xxxvi. The Jews even then inhabited the Vatican in great numbers; they were chiefly freedmen. Augustus had treated them with extraordinary favour; indulged them in perfect freedom of worship; gave them their full share in the largesses of corn; and when the distribution took place on their sabbath, permitted it to be reserved for the next day. Compare on this Joseph. Ant. xviii. 3, with the letter of Agrippa in Philo de Legatione, p. 590.

ground, declaring that they were ready to die rather than sanction the infringement of their law. Pilate had the prudence to withdraw the obnoxious emblems.[e]

The refractory spirit of Jerusalem broke out on other occasions.[f] Pilate seized some of the revenue of the Temple, and applied it to the useful and magnificent design of building an aqueduct, which was to bring a supply of water to the city from the distance of 200 stadia—about 25 miles. The populace rose, and interrupted the workmen. Pilate, having dressed some of his soldiers in the common garb of the country, with their swords concealed, commanded them to mingle with the people, and when they began their usual obstruction to his works, to fall upon and disperse them. The soldiers executed their commission with greater cruelty than Pilate had intended, and committed dreadful havoc among the unarmed multitude.[g]

Such was the man, not naturally disposed to unnecessary bloodshed, but, when the peace of his province appeared in danger, stern, decided, and reckless of human life—on all other occasions by no means regardless of ingratiating himself in the popular favour, before whose tribunal Jesus Christ was led. Pilate was awed perhaps by the tranquil dignity of Jesus, or at least saw no reason to apprehend any danger to the Roman sovereignty from a person of such peaceful demeanour. He probably detected the malice, though he might not clearly com-

---

[e] It is difficult to decide whether the account given by Philo, of the hanging up certain bucklers in Herod's palace, is a version of the same story or a different one. The question is discussed by Lardner, i. p. 184; by Mangey in his note on the passage in Philo, ii. p. 591; and by Valesius ad Euseb., H. E. ii. 6. Compare on the subject of images, as permitted by the Jews, a sensible note of Aldrich in Cardwell's Josephus, ii. p. 498.

[f] B. J. ii. 9. 3.

[g] B. J. ii. 9. 4.

prehend the motive, of the accusation brought forward
by the priests and populace. Still, however, he shrank
from the imputation of not being "Cæsar's friend," and
could not think the life of one man, however innocent,
of much importance in comparison with the peace of the
country, and his own favour at Rome. In this dilemma
he naturally endeavours to avoid the responsibility of
decision, by transferring the criminal to the tribunal of
Herod, to whose jurisdiction Christ, as a Galilean, belonged, and who happened to be at Jerusalem for the
celebration of the Passover. At length, however, finding
the uproar increasing, he yields without much further
scruple, and the Roman soldiery are permitted to become the willing instruments of the Jewish priesthood,
in the crucifixion of that man in whom Pilate himself
could find no fault. We leave to the Christian historian
the description of this event, and all its consequences—
inestimable in their importance to mankind, but which
produced hardly any *immediate* effect on the affairs of
the Jewish nation. Yet, our history will have shown
that the state of the public mind in Judæa, as well as
the character of Pilate, the chief agent in the transaction, harmonize in the most remarkable manner with
the narrative of the Evangelists. The general expectation of the Messiah—the impatience of the Roman
sovereignty, fostered by the bold and turbulent doctrines
of Judas the Galilean—the extraordinary excitement of
the more fanatical part of the people, which led them to
crowd round the banner of each successive adventurer,
who either assumed or might assume that character—
the rigid prudence of the chief priests, lest the slightest
indication of revolt should compromise the safety of the
city and the Temple, and expose the whole nation to the
jealous resentment of the Roman governor—these cir-

cumstances of the times sufficiently account for the reception which such a teacher as Jesus of Nazareth met with in Jerusalem. Appearing, as he did, with doctrines so alarming to the authority of the priesthood —so full of disappointment to the fanatic populace—so repugnant to the national pride, as implying the dissolution of the Mosaic constitution, and the establishment of a new and more comprehensive faith—and, above all, openly assuming the mysterious title, the Son of God —it excites less astonishment than sorrow and commiseration, that the passions of such a people should at once take arms, and proceed to the most awful violence against a Teacher, whose tenets were so much too pure and spiritual for their comprehension, whose character was so remote from their preconceived notions of the expected Messiah.

St. Luke relates another characteristic act of violence committed during the administration of Pilate, of which the Jewish records take no notice,—the massacre of certain Galileans while they were offering sacrifice. Some have supposed that these might be followers of Judas the Gaulonite.

An act which displayed the same vigilant jealousy of popular commotion, and the same reckless disregard of human life, led to the recall and the disgrace of Pilate. The Samaritans had, hitherto, remained in peaceful submission to the Roman government; they are stated occasionally to have shown their old enmity against the Jews, by waylaying those of the northern provinces who were travelling on their way to the Passover at Jerusalem. Now, however, the whole province was thrown into a state of excitement by an impostor, who promised to discover certain vessels, according to his statement (grounded, doubtless, upon some old tradition), buried by Moses on

Mount Gerizim. Multitudes appeared in arms at a village named Tirabatha, at the foot of the mountain. Pilate, with his usual vigilance and decision, ordered some troops to station themselves on the road, attacked the village, slew the leaders, and dispersed the rest.

The Samaritan senate carried their complaints before Vitellius, the president of Syria, the father of that Vitellius who afterwards obtained the empire. Vitellius sent immediate orders to Pilate to withdraw to Rome, and there answer to the charges which were made against him.[b]

Vitellius then, in person, visited Jerusalem; he was received with great magnificence, and was present during the celebration of the Passover. He remitted the tax on the sale of the fruits of the earth. He likewise conferred a benefit on the nation, which was considered of signal importance. By a remarkable accident, the custody of the High Priest's robes of office had passed into the hands of the Romans. Hyrcanus had been accustomed to lay them up in the Baris, the castle near the Temple. This usage was continued by his successors. Herod having converted the Baris into the strong fortress called Antonia, it afterwards became the chief place of arms to the Roman garrison. The Jews, tenacious of ancient customs, did not think of removing these important vestments. They thus fell into the power of the foreign rulers, who, as the High Priest could not officiate without them, might impede or prevent the performance of the Temple ceremonies. They were kept in a stone building, and sealed by the seal of the High

---

[b] Tacitus gives this character of Vitellius:—" Regendis provinciis priscâ virtute egit: unde regressus . . . . turpe in servitium mutatus exemplar apud posteros adulatorii dedecoris habetur: cesseruntque prima postremis, et bona juventæ senectus flagitiosa obliteravit." Ann. vi. 32.

Priest, from whence they were taken with great ceremony, seven days before the feast, and purified; after
they had been used, they were replaced with the same
care.   Vitellius gave up the robes to the High Priest,
and they were transferred to a treasury within the
Temple.   Vitellius degraded Caiaphas from the High-
priesthood, and substituted Jonathan, son of Ananus, or
Annas.   He then returned to Antioch.

During this period, the two other sons of Herod had
reigned in peace over their respective provinces: Herod
Antipas, as Tetrarch of Galilee, in Sepphoris, his capital;
Philip in the district beyond the Jordan.   Both had endeavoured to ingratiate themselves with the reigning
Emperor by the costly flattery of founding or ornament-
ing cities to be called after his name.   Philip called
Paneas, Cæsarea; and Bethsaida, Julias. Antipas called
Betharamptha, Julias, after the wife of the Emperor, and
founded Tiberias on the lake of Gennesaret.   The city
having been built over an ancient cemetery, Herod was
obliged to use force and bribes to induce the people to
settle there.   Philip was a prince of great justice and
humanity; wherever he went, the divan of justice followed him; and directly any appeal was made to his
tribunal, a court was formed, and the cause decided.
He died about this time, without issue; his territory
was annexed to the province of Syria.[1]

Herod had seduced and married Herodias his niece,
the wife of Herod Philip (not Philip the Tetrarch, but a
son of Herod the Great by Mariamne, daughter of
Simon the High Priest).   It was on her account that he
put to death John the Baptist.   This marriage led him
into danger, as well as into crime.   His repudiated wife

---

[1] Joseph. Ant. xviii. 4. 6.

was a daughter of Aretas, king of Arabia. This prince
took arms, to avenge the wrong and insult offered to his
daughter, and in a great battle, the whole army of
Herod was cut off. Herod sent to intreat the interference of Tiberius, who gave orders to Vitellius to
chastise the insolence of Aretas. Vitellius set his troops
in motion to advance on Petra, the Arabian capital. His
march lay through Judæa, but the heads of the people
sent an earnest request that he would not display his
standards, which were adorned with images, within their
territory. Vitellius complied; he sent his army across
the Jordan, and himself, with Herod and his friends,
went up a second time, to witness the Passover at Jerusalem. He deposed the High Priest, Jonathan, and
substituted his brother Theophilus. On the fourth day
of the festival, intelligence arrived of the death of
Tiberius, and the accession of Caligula. Vitellius dismissed his troops to their quarters, and returned to
Antioch.[k]

The accession of Caligula was an event of the greatest
importance to another branch of the Herodian family—
Agrippa, the son of Aristobulus, one of the two unfortunate princes, the sons of Herod the Great by Mariamne the Asmonean. The early life of Agrippa had
been a strange course of adventure and vicissitude. On
his father's execution, he was sent to Rome, where he
enjoyed the favour of Antonia, the widow of the elder
Drusus, the brother of Tiberius. Antonia entertained a
sincere friendship for Berenice, the mother of Agrippa,
and under her protection the young Idumæan prince
attached himself to the person of Drusus, the son of
Tiberius. Agrippa inherited the profusion, but not the

---

k Joseph. Ant. xviii. 5. 3.

wealth, of the Herodian race. On his mother's death, he speedily dissipated his whole property, and found himself overwhelmed with debts. His associate and friend, Drusus, died; and Tiberius issued orders that none of the youth's intimate companions should be admitted into his presence, lest they should awaken the melancholy recollection of his beloved son. Agrippa, in the utmost distress, retreated to his native land, and took up his residence at Malatha, an insignificant village in Idumæa. There he was in such a state of destitution that he began to entertain designs of ridding himself of his miserable life by suicide. His affectionate wife Cypros consoled him in his despair, and gave him excellent counsel. According to this at length he had recourse to his sister Herodias, the incestuous wife of Herod Antipas. Through her interest, he obtained a welcome reception at Sepphoris, where the Ethnarch of Galilee held his court. From Antipas he obtained a yearly allowance, and the government of Tiberias. But Herod, during the conviviality of a banquet, having cast some reflection on his pensioner, the indignant Agrippa withdrew from Galilee, and retired to the protection of Pomponius Flaccus, the Prefect of Syria, into whose good graces he insinuated himself with hereditary address. At Antioch he met his step-brother, Aristobulus, but there was not much fraternal amity between them, and Aristobulus seized the opportunity of supplanting his rival in the favour of the Roman Prefect. Agrippa received a bribe, to secure his interest with Flaccus, from the inhabitants of Damascus, who were engaged in a dispute about their borders with the Sidonians. Detected in this discreditable transaction through the jealous vigilance of his brother, he was forced to leave Antioch in disgrace, and retired to Ptolemais in a state

of the lowest indigence. There, through his freedman,
Marsyas, he tried in vain all the money-lenders, for he
had neither bondsman nor security to offer, till at last, a
freed slave of his mother lent him 17,500 drachms on a
promissory bond for 20,000. With this sum he got to
Anthedon, intending to sail for Rome. But he was suddenly arrested by Herennius Capito, Prefect of Jamnia,
for a debt of 300,000 drachms, which he had borrowed
at Rome of the Imperial exchequer. Agrippa promised
to settle the debt, but his vessel slipping her cables by
night, he escaped to Alexandria. There his wife, Cypros,
prevailed on the Jewish Alabarch to lend him 200,000
drachms. The prudent Alabarch, however, advanced
only five talents, promising that the rest should be forth-
coming on his arrival in Italy. With this money, having
sent his wife back to Palestine, Agrippa set sail for
Rome. On his landing at Puteoli, he despatched a
letter to Tiberius, then at Capreæ. The Emperor sent
to congratulate him on his arrival, invited him to
Capreæ, and entertained him with great courtesy, till a
despatch arrived from Herennius Capito, relating to his
dishonourable evasion from Anthedon. He was forbidden
the Imperial presence, and retired in disgrace to Rome.
But his mother's friend, Antonia, still protected him.
She lent him a sum sufficient to discharge his debt to
the Imperial treasury, and Agrippa was reinstated in the
favour of Tiberius. The Emperor recommended him to
attach himself to the person of his grandson, the
younger Tiberius; but the Jewish prince, with better
fortune or judgement, preferred that of Caius Caligula.
In this state of advancement, he borrowed a million
drachms of Thallus, a Samaritan freedman of Cæsar,
and repaid his debt to Antonia. Unfortunately, one day
when he was riding with Caligula in a chariot, he ex-

pressed aloud his earnest petition to Providence, that
Tiberius might speedily be removed, in order to make
room for a more worthy successor.   The speech was
overheard by Eutychus, a freedman, the driver of the
chariot.   Eutychus, punished for a theft, hastened to
revenge himself by laying a charge against his master.
The dilatory Tiberius, according to his custom, post-
poned the examination of the accuser, who remained
in prison; till Agrippa, imprudently, or having forgotten the whole affair, urged on the inquiry, and the
fact was clearly proved.   Tiberius was already offended
at the court paid by Agrippa to the young Caius; and
suddenly, in the public circus, commanded Macron, the
captain of his guard, "to put that man in chains."
Macron, surprised at the sudden change, delayed the
execution of the command; till, Tiberius returning to
the same spot, he inquired against whom the order was
directed.   The Emperor sternly pointed to Agrippa, and,
notwithstanding his humble supplications, the heir of
the Asmonean princes, clad as he was in the royal
purple, was put in fetters like a common malefactor.
The day was excessively sultry, and a slave of Caligula
passing by with a vessel of water, Agrippa entreated for
a draught.   The slave complied, and Agrippa promised
that when he should be released from his chains, he
would repay the kindness through his interest with Caligula—a promise which, to his honour, he faithfully kept.
Even in this fallen condition, Antonia did not desert the
son of her friend Berenice; she obtained for him some
mitigation of the discomforts and privations of his
prison.   At length after six months' imprisonment,
during which the historian relates a wild tale of the
augury of a German fellow-captive, from an owl on a
tree above them, of the liberation and future greatness

of Agrippa, his release arrived. The tyrant of Capreæ
expired. Immediately on the death of Tiberius, Marsyas, his faithful freed-slave, hastened to his master's
dungeon, and communicated the joyful intelligence,
saying in the Hebrew language, "The lion is dead."
The centurion on guard inquired the cause of their rejoicing; and when he had extorted the information from
Agrippa, anxious to propitiate the favour of a prisoner
whose advancement he foresaw, he ordered his chains to
be struck off, and invited him to supper. While they
were at table, a rumour reached the prison that Tiberius
was still living. The affrighted centurion bitterly reproached Agrippa with betraying him into so serious a
breach of discipline, and ordered the prisoner immediately
to be reloaded with his chains. That night Agrippa passed
in the most anxious state of suspense and apprehension.
With the morning the news was confirmed, and shortly
after Caligula entered Rome in imperial state. On the
very day of his entry, but for the prudence of Antonia,
he would have commanded the release of his friend. A
short time after he sent the order for his liberation,
received him at his court, and conferred on him the
vacant Tetrarchate of Philip, with the title of king.
He presented him likewise with a chain of gold, of the
same weight with that of iron with which he had been
fettered.[1]

Agrippa remained that year in Rome; during the
next, the second of Caligula's reign, he arrived in Pales-

---

[1] This story is related more at
length, as illustrating the relation of
the Jews, even of the royal race, to
the Romans; the contemptuous superiority with which they were at
one time treated with high honour,
the next with the utmost ignominy;
now as princes, now as miserable
debtors; now in purple, now in a dungeon—at the caprice of the Emperor or
his favourites.

tine with royal pomp, to take possession of his dignity. But if the good fortune of Agrippa excited the general wonder, it aroused the bitterest jealousy in the mind of Herodias, the wife of Herod, the tetrarch of Galilee. She saw the splendour of her husband eclipsed by the beggarly spendthrift, who, although her own brother, had been dependent on their charity. The evil passions of this woman were as fatal to the prosperity as to the virtue of Herod. Her insatiable and envious ambition would not allow him to rest till he had obtained a royal title which should set him on a level with the upstart Agrippa. Herod, whose character is described as cool and crafty (he is designated in the Gospel "as that fox Herod"), was carried away by her perpetual urgency, and, in an inauspicious hour, he undertook a journey to Rome, in order to solicit the title of king. Agrippa instantly despatched a messenger to counterwork the intrigues and outbid the bribery of Herod. The messenger made such good speed as to arrive at Baiæ before the Tetrarch. Agrippa's letter to Caligula accused Herod of former intrigues with Sejanus, and secret intelligence with the Parthians. It charged him particularly with having laid up a great store of arms, in case of a revolt. Directly Herod appeared, the Emperor closely questioned him upon the plain fact, whether he had furnished his palace with large quantities of warlike stores. The Tetrarch could not deny the charge, and Caligula immediately deprived him of the ethnarchate, which he added to the dominions of Agrippa, and ordered him into banishment.[m] Lyons, in Gaul, was the place of his exile ; and thus, in the same remote province, two sons of the magnificent Herod were condemned to waste their in-

---

[m] Joseph. Ant. xviii. 7.

glorious lives by the summary sentence of the Roman Emperor.

On account of her relationship to Agrippa, Caligula was inclined to exempt Herodias from the disgrace of her husband; he offered to restore her to all the possessions which she could claim as her own. In a nobler spirit than could have been expected from such a woman, Herodias rejected his mercy, and determined to share the fortunes of her banished husband.

Up to the reign of Caligula, the Jews had enjoyed, without any serious interruption, the universal toleration which Roman policy permitted to the religion of the subject states. If the religion had suffered a temporary proscription at Rome under Tiberius, it was as a foreign superstition, supposed, from the misconduct of individuals, to be dangerous to the public morals in the metropolis. Judaism remained undisturbed in the rest of the empire; and, although the occasional insolence of the Roman governors in Judæa might display itself in acts offensive to the religious feelings of the natives, yet the wiser and more liberal, like Vitellius, studiously avoided all interference with that superstition which they respected or despised. But the insane vanity of Caligula made him attempt to enforce from the whole empire those divine honours which his predecessors condescended to receive from the willing adulation of their subjects. Every where statues were raised and temples built in honour of the deified Emperor. The Jews could not submit to the mandate without violating the first principle of their religion, nor resist it without exposing their whole nation to the resentment of their masters.[n]

---

[n] Compare throughout the two very curious tracts by Philo, adversus Flaccum, et de Legatione, the chief or rather the only valuable authorities for these events.

The storm began to lower around them: its first violence broke upon the Jews in Alexandria, where, however, the collision with the ruling authorities first originated in the animosities of the Greek and Jewish factions, which divided the city. This great and populous capital, besides strangers from all quarters, was inhabited by three distinct races, the native Egyptians, Jews, and Greeks. The native Egyptians were generally avoided as of an inferior class; but the Jews boasted of edicts from the founder of the city, and from other monarchs of Egypt, which entitled them to equal rank and estimation with the descendants of the Macedonian settlers. They were numerous: Philo calculates that in Egypt they amounted to a million of souls.[o] They were opulent, and among the most active traders of that great commercial metropolis. It is probable that they were turbulent, and not the peaceful and unoffending people described by their advocate Philo—at all events they were odious to the Greek population. The Roman pre-

---

[o] This included the Jews in Alexandria, and scattered settlers up to the borders of Ethiopia (p. 523).

Tradition thus speaks of the Synagogue in Alexandria:—"He who has never seen the Double Hall of Alexandria has never beheld the majesty of Israel. It rose like a great Palace (Basilica); there was colonnade within colonnade; at times a throng of people filled the building twice as great as that which went out of Egypt with Moses. There were seventy golden thrones within, inlaid with precious stones and pearls, according to the number of the seventy elders of the Sanhedrin. Each of these cost 25 millions of gold denarii. In the midst arose an *Alhamra* of wood, on which stood the choir leader of the Synagogue. When any one rose to read in the Law, the President waved a linen banner, and the people answered 'Amen.' At every benediction which the President spoke, he waved the banner, and the people answered 'Amen.' They did not sit promiscuously, but each separate with his guild, so that strangers who entered might join their guild, and every man find his own trade."

This remarkable illustration of the traditions of the Egyptian settlement of the Jews, which we are surprised to find in the Talmud, is quoted from the Suka, in Delitsch, Geschichte der Judischen Poesie, p. 26.

fect at this period was Flaccus Aquilius. For the five last years Flaccus had administered the affairs of this important province, and the municipal government of this unruly city, with equal vigour and discretion. His attention to business; his perfect acquaintance with the usages, interests, and factions of the whole country; his dignity on the tribunal of justice; his prudence in suppressing all clubs and assemblies of the lower orders, which were held under the pretence of religion, but were acknowledged to be dangerous to the public peace, excited universal admiration. He had introduced a system of good and equal laws into the city, while by constant reviews of the military forces he had both improved the discipline of the army, and overawed the turbulent and disaffected by the display of his power. The death of Tiberius, according to Philo, wrought a total change in this wise and upright character. Flaccus had attached himself to the party of the younger Tiberius, and apprehended the resentment of the new Emperor. He became careless of business, remiss in all the great duties of his station, his vigorous mind seemed paralysed. The death of his friend Macro, who alone repressed the violence of Caligula, deprived him of his last hope of maintaining himself in the Imperial favour. He determined, therefore, to ingratiate himself with the people of Alexandria, in order that their good report might plead his cause, and commend the wisdom of his government with the Emperor. With this view he relaxed the sternness of his police, and allowed the Grecian party to proceed to every outrage and insult on the hated Jewish population.[p] The accidental arrival of king

---

[p] Philo describes the Greeks who got the ear of Flaccus and exasperated him against the Jews, as διονύσιοι, δημοκόποι, Λάμπωνες, γραμματοκύφωνες, Ἰσίδωροι, στασιάρχαι, φιλοπράγμονες, κακῶν εὑρεταί, ταοα

Agrippa was the signal for this collision of the two factions.   On his way to Palestine, where he was going to take possession of his kingdom, Agrippa, to avail himself of the Etesian winds, sailed direct to Alexandria. He arrived unexpectedly in the evening, and landed in the night, that he might avoid all unnecessary display. According to Philo, the sight of a Jew honoured with a royal title, and surrounded by guards, whose armour glittered with gold and silver, exasperated the envious Alexandrians.   They insulted him; wrote pasquinades against him, probably alluding to the beggarly condition in which he had before appeared in Alexandria; brought him on the stage, and even proceeded to a more offensive practical jest.

There was a poor idiot named Carabas, who used to wander naked about the streets, the butt of idle and mischievous boys.   Him they seized, and placed on a lofty seat near the Gymnasium, dressed him in an old mat for a robe, put a paper crown on his head, and a cane in his hand for a sceptre.   Boys, with sticks for halberds, went before him to represent his body-guard; and, to complete the parody on the royal state of Agrippa, some did him homage, some presented petitions, some addressed him on affairs of state, and called him by a word which signified "Lord" in the Syrian language. Flaccus, though outwardly he showed all possible respect to Agrippa, secretly connived at their insulting proceedings, and even fomented them.   This, however, is the most improbable part of Philo's story; for if it was the main object of Flaccus to secure the favour of Ca-

---

ξιπόλιδες. Lampon and Isidore were famous libellers, perhaps also Dionysius. Philo, edit. Mang., ii. p. 520.
  He speaks afterwards about the παλαιὰν, καὶ τρόπον τινα γεγεννημένην πρὸς Ἰουδαίους ἀπέχθειαν: p. 521—the almost innate hatred.

ligula, no man of his prudence would unnecessarily have offended his acknowledged friend and favourite. Agrippa, probably, soon withdrew from the inhospitable city, bearing with him a decree of the Jews, in which they offered to Caligula all the honours compatible with their law. This decree Flaccus had promised to forward, but had treacherously withholden from the knowledge of the Emperor. Encouraged by the apparent connivance of the prefect, the Greek faction assembled in the theatre, and demanded, with loud cries, that the statue of the Emperor should be placed in all the Jewish Proseuchæ, their oratories or places of prayer. They then proceeded to carry their own demands into execution; they cut down the trees which surrounded those picturesque places of worship, burned some, and profaned the rest by erecting images within them; in the most considerable they determined to place a great statue in a chariot drawn by four horses. Not having a chariot ready, they seized an old one which had formerly belonged to Cleopatra, an ancestress of the celebrated Egyptian queen of that name. A few days after their oratories had thus been violated,[q] Flaccus issued an edict, in which the Jews were called strangers, thus depriving them at once of their boasted rights of citizenship. Philo would persuade us that the Jews had not given the slightest provocation, and bore all these repeated outrages with the utmost meekness.[r] This is not probable; and the next measure of the governor seems as if it had been intended to separate the two conflicting parties, and so secure the peace of the distracted city. Alexandria was divided

---

[q] Philo uses a singular argument against this violation of the Proseuchæ: that the Jews being deprived of their houses of prayer, would be unable to propitiate heaven, as he assumes that they do most effectively, by supplications for the Augustan family. p. 524.

[r] De Legatione, p. 565.

into five quarters, named from the first five letters of
the alphabet. Two of these were entirely peopled by
Jews, and many of them dwelt scattered about in
the other three. They were ordered to retire into one
of these districts, which was so much too small to contain them, that they spread about upon the sea-shore
and in the cemeteries. The vacant houses in the quarter
from which they had retired were pillaged by the mob;
the magazines and shops, which were shut on account of
a general mourning for Drusilla, the Emperor's sister,
were broken open: the goods publicly shared in the
market-place. Philo complains that great distress was
caused by the pledges being taken away from the
brokers, whence it appears that the Jews had already
taken up the profession of money-lenders.[8] But this was
not the worst. Cooped up in one narrow quarter of
the city, they began to suffer dreadfully from the heat
and unwholesomeness of the air. Pestilential disorders
broke out, and though the year was plentiful, they suffered all the miseries of famine, for they were almost
besieged in their quarter. Those who ventured out into
the market were robbed, insulted, maltreated, pursued
with sticks and stones. Bloodshed soon ensued; many
were slain with the sword, others trampled to death;
some, even while alive, were dragged by their heels
through the streets. When dead, their bodies were still
dragged along till they were torn to pieces, or so dis-
figured that they could not be distinguished if at length
recovered by their friends. Those who strayed out of
the city to breathe the purer air of the country, or the
strangers who incautiously entered the walls to visit and
relieve their friends, were treated in the same way, and

---

[8] P. 525.

beaten with clubs till they were dead. The quays were watched, and on the landing of a Jewish vessel, the merchandise was plundered, the owners and their vessel burned. Their houses were likewise set on fire, and whole families, men, women, and children, burned alive. Yet even this was a merciful death compared with the sufferings of others. Sometimes, from want of wood, their persecutors could collect only a few wet sticks, and over these, stifled with smoke, and half consumed, the miserable victims slowly expired. Sometimes they would mock their sufferings by affected sorrow; but if any of their own relatives or friends betrayed the least emotion, they were seized, scourged, tortured, and even crucified.[t]

During all these horrible scenes, Flaccus, who could at once have put an end to the tumult, looked on in calm indifference. He now, according to his accuser, openly took part against them. He sent for the principal Jews, as if to mediate an accommodation, in reality only to find new pretexts for cruelty. The Jews had their Alabarch or chief magistrate, and their council or senate. Flaccus ordered thirty-eight of the most distinguished members of this body to be seized, bound them as criminals, and, although it was the Emperor's birth-day, a day of general rejoicing, they were brought into the theatre, and publicly scourged with such cruelty that many of them died instantly of the blows, others, shortly after, of the mischiefs they received. It was thought an aggravation of this cruelty, that as there were different kinds of flagellation, according to the rank of the criminal, these distinguished men were condemned to that usually inflicted on the basest. Those who escaped with life, were thrown into prison; others

---

[t] Compare the De Legat., p. 564, with the Adversus Flaccum.

of this miserable race were seized and crucified. It was the morning spectacle of the theatre to see the Jews scourged, tortured both with the rack and with pullies, and then led away to execution; and to this horrible tragedy immediately succeeded farces and dances and other theatrical amusements. Women were occasionally seized and exposed to the public view—sometimes female peasants were taken for Jewesses, when discovered they were let go; if any doubt remained, swine's flesh was brought and the women commanded to eat; those who complied were released; those who refused, treated with every kind of indignity.

As if to justify these cruelties by an apparent dread of insurrection, Flaccus sent a centurion, Castus, to search all the houses of the Jews for concealed arms. The search was conducted with the utmost rigour, even the women's apartments ransacked, but no weapon was found more dangerous than common knives used for domestic purposes.

At length the hour of retribution arrived; all the attempts of Flaccus to secure the favour of Caligula were unavailing. A centurion, Bassus, was sent to arrest him. Flaccus had kept back a loyal address from the Alexandrian Jews, which he had promised to transmit. It had reached Rome, however, through King Agrippa. Bassus proceeded, not with the boldness of a messenger armed with an imperial edict, but as if he had to surprise an independent sovereign in the midst of loyal subjects.[a] This seems to warrant a suspicion, either that Flaccus entertained some design of revolting, or at least, that his popularity at Alexandria was so great as

---

[a] ἐκ τοῦ σφόδρα εὐδοκιμεῖν παρὰ τῷ πλείστῳ μέρει τῆς πόλεως ἕνεκα τοῦ μὴ προαισθόμενον Φλάκκον καὶ βουλευσάμενόν τι νεώτερον ἄπρακτον αὐτῷ τὴν ὑπηρεσίαν ἐργάσαοθαι. p. 333.

to render his capture difficult and dangerous. Bassus
arrived at night, landed secretly, and found that Flaccus
was abroad, at a banquet given by one Stephanio, a
freedman of Tiberius. One of his followers mingled
with the guests, and finding that the governor was only
attended by eight or ten slaves, Bassus surrounded the
chamber with his soldiers, and displayed the Imperial
edict. Flaccus at once saw his fate, and was led away
without resistance. It was the feast of Tabernacles:
but the sad and persecuted Jews had little inclination
for the usual joy and merriment of the season. When
the rumour of the apprehension of Flaccus spread abroad,
they supposed it to be a deception intended to tempt
them to rejoicings which would be cruelly revenged.
When the intelligence was confirmed, they began, not
to rejoice over the ruin of their enemy, for that was forbidden in their humane law,[v] but to praise God; and
during the whole night the people were occupied in
hymns and songs of thanksgiving. The wrath of heaven,
as they believed, now pursued the miserable Flaccus;
he had a tempestuous voyage; on his arrival at Rome
he was accused by Lampon and Isidore, two men of the
basest character;[x] his property was confiscated, and he
himself banished first to Gyara, an island in the Ægean
Sea, proverbial for the hard fate of those who were
exiled to its shores. By the interest of Lepidus he
obtained a commutation of this punishment, and was sent
to Andros, where he arrived after a disastrous voyage,
and after having been an object of contempt or commise-

---

[v] The words of Philo : 'Ουκ ἐφησδό-
μεθα . . ὦ δέσποτα, τιμωρίαις ἐχθροῦ,
δεδιδάγμενοι πρὸς τῶν ἱερῶν νόμων
ἀνθρωποπαθεῖν. p. 334.

[x] The lives of these two consummate

villains as painted, darkly enough no
doubt, by Philo, are curious studies of
Roman and provincial manners and
morals at this period.

ration in the various towns through which he passed. Philo asserts that he was haunted by bitter remorse for his cruelties towards the Jews. He was soon after put to death in a horrible manner by order of Caligula.[x]

Thus Philo describes the persecutions of the Jews in Alexandria, and the conduct of Flaccus; but it may be justly suspected that both the sufferings and the peaceful disposition of his countrymen are highly coloured; and in the character and motives of Flaccus there appears so much inconsistency as perpetually to remind us that we are reduced to follow the narrative of an advocate, not that of a dispassionate historian.

A deputation from each of the parties in Alexandria arrived in Rome, to lay the whole history of the late disturbances before the Emperor. At the head of the Grecian party was Apion, a man of eloquence, and a determined enemy to the Jews; on the other side appeared Philo, the author from whose writings the recent account has been extracted, a person of rank, for he was the brother of the Alabarch, and of unquestioned ability. The reception which the Jewish party met with at first was apparently flattering; Philo alone apprehended an unfavourable event. They presented a memorial, which the Emperor seemed to receive with gaiety and urbanity. They then followed the court to Puteoli: their great object was to obtain the security of their Proseuchæ from being desecrated by images. These oratories they possessed in every city where they resided.

---

[x] I am afraid that the manifest satisfaction with which Philo relates the horrible execution of Flaccus shows that he was not very deeply imbued with the humanity which he boasts of as inculcated by his legislator.

Read the frightful scene: he ends— τοιαῦτα καὶ Φλάκκος ἔπαθε, γενόμενος ἀψευδοτάτη πίστις τοῦ μὴ ὑπεροράσθαι τῶν Ἰουδαίων ἔθνος ἐπικουρίας τῆς ἐκ Θεοῦ. p. 544.

While they were discussing their hopes of succeeding in this great object of their mission, suddenly a man rushed in with a pale and disordered countenance, and communicated the dreadful intelligence, that an edict had been issued to place the statue of the Emperor within the Temple of Jerusalem.[y]

The mad vanity of Caligula had been irritated by the resistance of the Jews in Alexandria; other circumstances, combined with evil counsellors, made him determine to triumph over what he considered the disloyal obstinacy of this self-willed people. Capito, a receiver of revenue in Judæa, at first a very poor man, had grown rich in his employment, and apprehended that complaints of his exactions might reach the ear of the Emperor. He determined, therefore, that his accusers should appear in an unfavourable light, and, to this end, he persuaded certain Greeks, who lived mingled with the native population in Jamnia, to build a miserable altar of brick in honour of Caius. The Jews, as he expected, rose and demolished the altar; they then carried their complaints before Capito himself, who seized the opportunity of representing the affair in Rome as an act of wanton and unprovoked sedition.

The evil counsellors of Caligula were Helicon, an Egyptian, a slave by birth, a buffoon by occupation, and Apelles,[z] a tragic actor, of Ascalon, in Syria. Both

---

[y] This divine worship demanded by Caligula was more unexpected and offensive from the extreme reluctance with which Augustus usually accepted, and the prudence, almost reverential, with which Tiberius usually declined, such honours. " Nihil deorum honoribus relictum cum se templis et effigie numinum, per flamines et sacer- dotes coli vellent." Tac. Ann. i. 10: of Augustus. Compare De Legatione, p. 568.

[z] If Apelles was instrumental in this transaction, he met with just though horrible retribution. Suetonius relates, that as he was standing with Caligula near a statue of Jupiter, the Emperor suddenly asked him which

these men were born and brought up in hostility to the
Jewish race. By their advice the fatal mandate was
issued, that a gilded colossal statue of Caligula should
be placed in the Holy of Holies, and that the Temple
should be dedicated to Caius, the present and younger
Jupiter. The execution of the edict was intrusted to
P. Petronius, who was appointed to succeed Vitellius as
prefect of Syria. But before we describe the attempt
to enforce this edict in Palestine, it may be well to anticipate the fate of the Alexandrian deputation, which
is related by Philo, and is curiously characteristic both
of the Emperor and of the estimation in which the Jews
were generally held. After a long and wearisome attendance, the deputies were summoned to a final audience.
To judge so grave a cause, as Philo complains with
great solemnity, the Emperor did not appear in a public
court, encircled by the wisest of his senators; the embassy was received in the apartments of two contiguous
villas in the neighbourhood of Rome, called after Lamia
and Mæcenas. The bailiffs of these villas were commanded at the same time to have all the rooms thrown
open for the Emperor's inspection. The Jews entered,
made a profound obeisance, and saluted Caligula, as
Augustus and Emperor—but the sarcastic smile on the
face of Caius gave them little hope of success.* "You
are then," he said, showing his teeth as he spoke, "those
enemies of the gods who alone refuse to acknowledge
my divinity, but worship a deity whose name you dare
not pronounce"—and here, to the horror of the Jews,

---

of the two was the greater. Apelles
hesitated, and Caligula ordered him to
be scourged with the utmost violence,
praising the sweetness of his voice all

the time that he was shrieking in his
agony.

* σαρκάζων γὰρ ἅμα καὶ σεσηρὸς
p. 597.

he uttered the awful name.[b]   The Greek deputies from
Alexandria, who were present, thought themselves certain of their triumph, and began to show their exultation
by insulting gestures; and Isidore, one of the accusers of
Flaccus, came forward to aggravate the disobedience of
the Jews.   He accused them of being the only nation
who had refused to sacrifice for the Emperor.   The Jews
with one voice disclaimed the calumny, and asserted
that they had three times offered sacrifice for the welfare
of the Emperor—and indeed had been the first to do so
on his accession.   "Be it so," rejoined the Emperor,
"ye have sacrificed *for* me, but not *to* me."   The Jews
stood aghast, and trembling.   On a sudden, Caius began
to run all over the house, up stairs and down stairs; in-
specting the men's and the women's apartments; finding
fault, and giving orders, while the poor Jews followed
him from room to room, amid the mockery of the attendants.   After he had given his orders, the Emperor
suddenly turned round to them: "Why is it that you
do not eat pork?"   The whole court burst into peals of
laughter.   The Jews temperately replied, that different
nations have different usages: some persons would not
eat lamb.   "They are right," said the Emperor; "it is
an insipid meat."   After further trial of their patience, he
demanded, with his usual abruptness, on what they
grounded their right of citizenship.   They began a long
and grave legal argument; but they had not proceeded
far when Caius began to run up and down the great
hall, and to order that some blinds, of a kind of trans-
parent stone, like glass, which admitted the light and

---

[b] τὸν ἀκατονόμαστον . . καὶ ἀνα-
τείνας τὰς χεῖρας ἐς τὸν οὐρανὸν,
ἐπεφήμιζε πρόσρησιν, ἣν οὐδὲ ἀκου-
ειν θεμιτὸν, οὐχ ὅτι διερμηνεύειν
αὐτολεξεί. Ibid.

excluded the heat and air, should be put up against the windows.[c] As he left that room, he asked the Jews, with a more courteous air, if they had anything to say to him ; they began again their harangue, in the middle of which he started away into another chamber, to see some old paintings. The ambassadors of the Jews at length were glad to retreat, and felt happy to escape with their lives. Caius gave them their dismissal in these words : " Well, after all, they do not seem so bad ; but rather a poor foolish people, who cannot believe that I am a god."[d]

The instructions to Petronius, appointed governor of Syria, were distinct and precise ; he was to place the statue of Caligula in the Temple of Jerusalem at all hazards.[e] He was to withdraw, if necessary, the two legions which were usually stationed on the Euphrates. Yet he was too prudent and humane not to hesitate ; he called a council, where the bigoted attachment of the Jews to their Temple, and their formidable numbers, both in Judæa and other countries, were discussed. But it was unanimously agreed that the mandate of the Emperor was imperative ; and Petronius issued out orders to the Sidonian workmen to make the statue. He then collected his troops, and went into winter-quarters at Ptolemais. He had made known to the priests and rulers of the Jews the designs of the Emperor ; but no

---

[c] τοῖς ὑάλῳ λευκῇ παραπλησίοις διαφανέσι λίθοις.

[d] Philo relates some curious acts of Caligula's self-deification (we must remember that it is a Jew who writes ; but nothing seems to have been too wild for this mad youth): his assuming the attributes first of deities of the second order, then those of the first ; dressing himself like Hercules, and Bacchus, and the Dioscuri ; then calling himself Hermes, Apollo, and Mars. Philo well calls it τὴν ἀθεωτάτην ἐκθείωσιν. p. 557.

[e] Compare throughout Joseph. Ant. xviii. 8, with Philo de Legatione. In the Syrian transactions I am more inclined to follow Josephus.

sooner had the intelligence spread, than many thousands of the people assembled from all quarters, without distinction of rank, age, or sex. They covered the country for a great distance like a vast cloud; they were unarmed and defenceless; many of them were clad in sackcloth, and had ashes on their heads, and every mark of the deepest mourning. All with one voice declared their steadfast and deliberate resolution to sacrifice their lives, rather than consent to the profanation of their Temple. Petronius sternly rebuked them, and insisted on his own obligation to fulfil the positive commands of his sovereign. They answered, that they were as much bound to respect the ordinances of their God—that no fear of death would induce them to the violation of their Law—that they dreaded the wrath of their God more than that of the Emperor.

Petronius shrank from the horrible task of commencing a war of massacre and extermination for such an object; and in order to obtain more certain information on the state of the country, he left his troops at Ptolemais, and himself, with some of his more distinguished officers, moved to Tiberias. Here many of the rulers, and the people by thousands, crowded again into his presence. Once more Petronius urged the power of the Romans, the positive mandate of the Emperor, and the uniform obedience of all other nations. The Jews replied with entreaties and supplications, that he would not think of violating their sanctuary with the images of man. "Are ye resolved, then," said the Roman, "to wage war against your Emperor?" "We have no thought of war," they replied unanimously; "but we will submit to be massacred rather than infringe our Law"—and at once the whole body fell with their faces to the earth, and declared that they were ready to offer their throats to the swords of the soldiery.

For forty days this scene lasted : it was the time for sowing;[f] and the whole land remained uncultivated. Aristobulus, the brother of Agrippa—Helcias, called the Great—and others of the most distinguished men of the nation—appeared before Petronius, and remonstrated with him on the impolicy of reducing a flourishing province to a desert, from which no tribute could be drawn. The people, they urged, were obstinately determined not to till the soil, and would betake themselves to robbery; so that it was impossible to calculate the dreadful results of his persisting in the odious measure. They entreated that he would forward their representations to Caligula, in hopes that the Emperor might yet be persuaded to relent.

The humane Petronius, after holding a council with his friends, resolved to risk the wrath of the Emperor, rather than deluge the whole country with blood.[g] According to one account, he determined not to forward the petition of the Jews, but to delay, under the pretence of allowing time for the statue to be finished; and to represent the inconvenience of permitting the province to remain uncultivated, more particularly as the Emperor and the court were about to visit Alexandria.

---

[f] Joseph. Ant. xviii. 8, 4. According to Philo, of gathering in the harvest.

[g] According to Philo, Petronius had some glimmerings of what Philo calls Jewish philosophy : ἀλλ ἐιχέ τινα καὶ αὐτὸς, ὡς ἔοικεν, ἐναύσματα τῆς Ἰουδαϊκῆς φιλοσοφίας ἅμα καὶ εὐσεβείας· εἴτε καὶ πάλαι προμαθὼν ἕνεκα τῆς περὶ παιδείαν σπουδῆς, εἴτε καὶ αφ' ὃυ τῶν χωρῶν ἐπιτρό-πευσεν, ἐν ὅις Ἰουδαῖοι καθ' ἑκάστην πόλιν ἐισὶ παμπληθεῖς Ἀσίας τε καὶ Συρίας· εἴτε καὶ τὴν ψυχὴν ὄυτω διατεθείς, αὐτηκόῳ καὶ αὐτοκελεύστῳ καὶ αυτομάθει τινι πρὸς τὰ σπουδῆς ἄξια φύσει. This is a curious passage, as if a knowledge of the Jewish religion was a part of good education.

But whatever turn he gave to the affair in his despatches to Rome, he assembled the people at Tiberias; declared his determination to suspend the execution of the decree till he should receive further instructions; and promised that he would use all his interest to obtain the total repeal of the edict. He well knew the danger to which he exposed himself by his disobedience to the Imperial decree; but he was willing to stand the hazard in order to preserve the Jewish people from the horrors of war. He exhorted them in the mean time to disperse peaceably, and betake themselves to their usual occupations and to the tillage of their lands. The season had been uncommonly sultry; the customary rains had not fallen. But scarcely had Petronius ended his speech, than the day, which had been till then serene, became overcast, and the showers began to fall. The people saw the mark of the Divine approbation with unmingled satisfaction; Petronius himself is said to have been greatly struck by this singular coincidence.

The Jews, however, owed their security rather to the interest of their king with the Emperor, than to the humanity of the prefect. Throughout the history of the whole preceding transaction, our two authorities, Philo and Josephus, have differed in many most important particulars. It is scarcely possible to reconcile their narrative of the conduct of Agrippa. According to the former, the despatches of Petronius threw Caligula into one of his most violent paroxysms of fury. Before he had recovered, Agrippa entered, and from the Emperor's fiery eye and disordered countenance, apprehended that something was wrong. Caligula suddenly turned upon him, and broke out into the bitterest reproaches against his countrymen for their obstinate resistance to his will. The Jewish prince was so appalled, that he trembled in

every limb; he fainted away; and would have fallen to
the ground, but that his attendants caught him, and
removed him from the Imperial presence. Till the next
evening he remained without giving signs of life and
consciousness. At length he opened his eyes, and then
fainted again. The third day he came to himself, and
inquired with a shudder whether he was still in the
dreaded presence of the Emperor. His attendants
urged him to rise, to bathe and take refreshment; he
refused all sustenance, except some flour and pure
water. He then sat down, and wrote a long letter to
Caius; but that which is extant in Philo's work displays too much of the Alexandrian orator to induce us
to suppose it genuine.[h] Such is the narrative of Philo—
that of Josephus is more creditable to the character of
the king. Agrippa having entertained Caligula at a
banquet so sumptuous as to excite astonishment even
in that age of prodigal luxury and magnificence, the
Emperor offered to grant any request that he might
make. Agrippa, with a feeling worthy of one who had
the blood of the Asmoneans in his veins, instead of
demanding an accession of wealth or territory, immediately petitioned for the repeal of the fatal edict.
The wounded pride of Caligula struggled hard with his
attachment to Agrippa, and with the shame of for-
feiting the Imperial word, which he had given with so
much publicity. At last, however, he relented, and the
fatal decree was suspended. At the same time the disobedience of Petronius was not to be pardoned. A letter

---

[h] This letter, even if the declama-
tory work of Philo, is curious as illustrating the position which the Jews
supposed themselves to hold in the
empire; as not merely the people of
the Holy Land, but as settled in all
parts of the Eastern world, in Asia
Minor, Greece, Libya.

was written, in which he was accused of having preferred the bribes of the Jews to his allegiance to his sovereign; and he was commanded to prepare himself, as about to undergo the most exemplary punishment. But this letter was accidentally delayed, and the news of Caligula's death reached Petronius first. If Philo is to be credited, this event was equally fortunate for the Jewish nation; for Caligula, with his customary irresolution, repented of his lenity, and ordered a colossal statue of bronze to be cast, which he intended, when he should arrive at Alexandria, where he was to be solemnly inaugurated as a god, to have placed by stealth in the Temple of Jerusalem.[1]

It might seem as if the skirts of that tremendous tempest, which was slowly gathering over the native country and the metropolis of the Jewish nation, broke, and discharged their heavy clouds of ruin and desolation successively over each of the more considerable, though remote, settlements of the devoted people. The Jews of Babylonia had now their turn. There is something very remarkable in the history of this race, for the most part descendants of those families which had refused to listen to the summons of Zorobabel, Ezra, and Nehemiah, and to return to the possession of their native country. It was, perhaps, natural that men born in a foreign region, and knowing the lovely land of their ancestors only by tradition, or by the half-forgotten descriptions of their departed parents, should hesitate to abandon their houses, their fields, and their posses-

---

[1] Jost observes that of all this affair there is hardly an obscure trace in the Rabbinical writings—"Was noch seltsamer erscheint, die rabbinische Ueberlieferung hat kaum eine dunkele Erinnerung von den ganzen Vorfalle." Jud. i. p. 360.

sions, in the hospitable country to which their fathers
had been transported by force, but where they themselves had become naturalized. But the singular part
of their history is this, that though willing aliens from
their native Palestine, they remained Jews in character
and religion; they continued to be a separate people, and
refused to mingle themselves with the population of the
country in which they were domiciliated. While those
who returned to the Holy Land were in danger of
forming a mixed race, by intermarriages with the neighbouring tribes, which it required all the sternest exercise
of authority in their rulers to prevent, the Babylonian
Jews were still as distinct a people as the whole race of
Israel has been since the final dispersion. They adhered together, though wanting as well the bond of persecution, as the deep religious hope of restoration to the
promised land in more than their ancient glory; for
this hope was obviously not strong enough to induce
them to avail themselves of the present opportunity of
return, at the price of their possessions in the Median
dominions. Nor did they, like the Jews of Alexandria,
become in any degree independent of the great place of
national worship; they were as rigid Jews as if they
had grown up within sight of the Temple. They still
looked to the Holy of Holies at Jerusalem as the centre
of their faith: they regularly sent their contributions to
its support. The passionate attachment to their native
country gave place to a more remote, though still
profound, attachment to the religious capital of their
people. The Temple became what the Caaba of Mecca
is to the Mohammedans, the object of the profoundest
reverence, and sometimes of a pious pilgrimage; but
the land of their fathers had lost its hold on their affections: they had no desire to exchange the level plains

of Babylonia for the rich pastures, the golden cornfields, or the rocky vineyards of Galilee and Judæa.
This Babylonian settlement was so numerous and
flourishing, that Philo more than once intimates the
possibility of their marching in such force to the assistance of their brethren in Palestine, in case the Roman
oppression was carried to excess, as to make the fate of
the war very doubtful.[k] Their chief city, Nearda, was
strongly situated in a bend of the river Euphrates,
which almost surrounded the town. Here, in a place
impregnable to the Parthian robbers, the Jews of Mesopotamia had made a sort of treasury, in which they laid
up the tribute of two drachms a head, which was re-

---

[k] Ἐφόβουν δὲ αὐτὸν (Petronium)
καὶ ἀι πέραν Εὐφράτου δυνάμεις·
ἤδει γὰρ Βαβυλῶνα καὶ πολλὰς
ἄλλας τῶν Σατραπειῶν ὑπὸ Ἰουδαίων
κατεχομένας . . . . He dreaded a
general insurrection of the Jews from
all lands, who, gathering on every
side, might hem him in, and crush
him before aid could arrive. p. 578.

Agrippa in his letter says:—Καὶ
σιωπῶ τὰς περαν Εὐφράτου. Πᾶσαι
γὰρ ἔξω μέρους βραχέος (Βαβυλῶνος
καὶ τῶν ἄλλων Σατραπειῶν ἀι ἀρε-
τῶσαν ἔχουσι τὴν ἐν κύκλῳ γῆν)
Ἰουδαίους ἔχουσιν δικήτορας. p. 387.
The whole of this affair, related by
Josephus, gives a notion of the
formidable numbers of the Jews iu
these regions. Josephus expressly says
that the Jews hoped that all their
countrymen beyond the Euphrates
would join in the insurrection. ἐπειδὴ
Ἰουδαιῶν μὲν ἅπαν τὸ ὑπὲρ Εὐφράτην
ὁμόφυλον συνεπαρθήσεσθαι σφίσιν
ἤλπισαν. B. J., i. 2.
This Babyloniau settlement is of

great importance in Jewish history,
not less perhaps in Christian. I have
long held and more than once expressed a strong opinion that the
Babylon from which St. Peter's Epistle
was dated is this Babylonian settlement. What more likely than that
the Apostle of the Circumcision should
place himself in the midst of his brethren in that quarter, and address
as it were a pastoral letter to the
conterminous settlements in Asia ?

It must have been for these Jews,
dwelling among the ἄνω βαρβάρους,
that Josephus wrote the first version
of his 'Jewish War' in their native
tongue (Aramaic). It shows their importance at the period immediately
after the Jewish war, even to a man
so entirely Romanised as Josephus. ἃ
τοῖς ἄνω βαρβάροις τῃ πατρίῳ φώνῃ
συντάξας ἀνεπεμψα πρότερον. It
must have been addressed to his countrymen, who spoke their own language
in those regions.

ceived for the service of the Temple, and at stated
intervals transferred to Jerusalem. In this city were
two orphans, named Asinai and Anilai, who had been
bred up as weavers, probably of those rich stuffs for
which Babylonia was so long celebrated. On some ill-
usage from the master-manufacturer, they fled to a low
district between two branches of the river, where there
were rich meadows, and a place where the shepherds
used to lay up their stores for the winter. There a
number of indigent and discontented youths gathered
around them, and they became the captains of a formidable band of robbers. They built a strong fortress,
secured by the marshes around, and levied tribute on
the shepherds, whom, however, they defended from all
other assailants. The Satrap of Babylon determined to
suppress them, and seized the favourable opportunity of
the Sabbath for his attack. Asinai happened to be
reposing among a number of his followers, whose arms
lay scattered around: he suddenly exclaimed, "I hear
the trampling of horses; it must be more than a troop
of wild ones in their pastures, for I hear likewise the
jingling of the bridles." Spies were sent out, and the
whole band determined to sacrifice their respect for the
Sabbath to their self-preservation. They attacked and
defeated their assailants with great slaughter. Artabanus, the King of Parthia, heard with admiration of
their extraordinary valour, and sent to offer terms of
accommodation. Anilai was sent to the court, where
the king pledging his personal honour for their security,
Asinai was persuaded to follow him. The king received
them with great courtesy, admired their singular cor-
poral strength and activity, and refused all the secret
solicitations of his officers to rid himself by treachery of
such dangerous men. He even appointed Asinai to the

supreme command in Babylonia, with strict injunctions
to suppress all robbers. Asinai conducted himself with
equal vigour and prudence, and rose to the highest
degree of wealth and power. But wealth and power
led to their usual consequences, insolence and injustice.
Anilai became enamoured of the wife of a Parthian
chieftain, whom he excited to hostilities, and slew.
This woman, to the great offence of the Jews, adhered
to the Parthian religion. The Jews strongly urged
on the brother, Asinai, the imperative necessity of
preventing this breach of the law in his own family.
Asinai at length strongly remonstrated with his brother,
and insisted on the dismissal of the woman. His
remonstrances were fatal to himself; for the Parthian
woman, apprehending some further exercise of authority,
poisoned Asinai ; and thus the supreme authority passed
into the hands of Anilai. Anilai, with equal bravery,
but far less prudence and virtue than his brother, attacked the territory of Mithridates, a Parthian chieftain of the highest rank and connected by marriage
with the king, surprised him by an unexpected attack
on the Sabbath, and took him prisoner. Contrary to the
advice of his more desperate associates, he refused to put
the captive to death, and released him. The royal wife
of Mithridates, furious at the disgrace, instigated her
husband to revenge ; and they assembled considerable
forces. Anilai, disdaining to rely on the strength of
his marshes, advanced a great way into the plains,
where his troops suffered grievously from want of water.
In this state they were attacked by Mithridates, and
totally defeated. But desperate adventurers flocked
from all quarters to the standard of Anilai; his losses
were speedily restored, and he waged a marauding war
and carried fire and sword into the Babylonian villages.

The Babylonians sent to Nearda, the chief settlement of the Jews, to demand the surrender of Anilai. Those in Nearda were unable or unwilling to comply with this order. At length the Babylonians surprised the camp of the robber, when his soldiers were sunk in debauchery and sleep, slew the whole band, and Anilai himself.

The Babylonians were not content with vengeance against the offenders, but began to commit dreadful reprisals on the whole Jewish population. The Jews, unable to resist, fled in great numbers to Seleucia: six years after, many more took refuge from a pestilence in the same city. Seleucia happened to be divided into two factions; one of the Greeks, the other of the Syrians. The Jews threw themselves into the scale of the Syrians, who thus obtained a superiority, till the Greeks came to terms with the Syrians; and both parties agreed to fall upon the unhappy Jews. As many as 50,000 men were slain. The few who escaped fled to Ctesiphon. Even there the enmity of the Seleucians pursued them; and at length the survivors took refuge in their old quarters, Nearda and Nisibis.

The assassination of Caligula delivered the Jews within the Roman dominion from their immediate danger, and delayed the fatal hour which his madness seemed rapidly hastening. Agrippa was in Rome at that critical period, and, during the confusion which ensued, he sustained an important part. His conduct was honourable to his feelings, as well as to his address and influence. He alone paid the last honours to his murdered friend and Emperor. He then became mainly instrumental in the peaceful re-establishment of that order of things, which, however different from what an ardent lover of the old Roman liberty might have desired, was perhaps the best which the circumstances of the times would admit. He persuaded the Senate to abandon their unavailing resistance to the infuriated soldiery; reassured the weak and unambitious spirit of Claudius; and at the same time dissuaded him from taking those violent measures against the Senate, to which the army were urging him, and which would have deluged Rome with blood.[1]

His services were amply repaid by the grateful Emperor. Agrippa received the investiture of all the dominions which belonged to the Great Herod. Judæa and Samaria were re-united with Galilee, Peræa, and the provinces beyond Jordan, in one kingdom: Abilene, the district at the foot of Antilibanus, was added. Herod, his brother, received the kingdom of Chalcis. This donation of the Jewish kingdom was made with the utmost publicity: the edict which announced it contained a high eulogium on Agrippa; and the act was registered on a brass tablet, in the Capitol. A treaty was formally concluded between the Emperor and Agrippa, in the Forum.

The death of Caligula was the signal for new commotions in Alexandria. The Jews attempted to recover their former rights. Claudius issued a temperate edict, favourable to the Jewish inhabitants of that city, and confirming their privileges.[m] This was followed by a second general decree, which secured the freedom of

---

[1] This important part assumed by Agrippa in the restoration of the empire rests on the authority of Josephus, Ant. xix. 4, and B. J., ii. 11. 1, 4. The Roman historians are silent, except Dion, who says incidentally that Claudius made grants to Agrippa: συμπράξοντί δι τὴν ἡγεμο-velav, l. x. p. 670. The fact, however, that decrees so favourable to Agrippa and to the Jews were issued by Claudius, seems to confirm the supposition that Agrippa rendered valuable services to the Emperor on his accession.

[m] The two edicts in Joseph. Ant. xix. 5.

religious worship to the Jews throughout the empire ; at the same time they were admonished to behave with decency to the religions of other people.   Under this decree the inhabitants of Dora were condemned by Petronius, for wantonly insulting a Jewish synagogue by placing a statue of Claudius within its walls.

Agrippa returned to his kingdom in great splendour. He displayed the utmost respect for the national religion ; he hung up in the Temple the golden chain which Caligula had bestowed upon him, of equal weight with the iron one with which he had been bound as a prisoner, as a memorial of the rapid change of human fortune and of the protection of Almighty Providence. He observed the Mosaic law with great exactness ; offered sacrifice every day ; and abstained from every legal impurity.   In all other respects Agrippa aimed at popularity ; he remitted the house tax of the inhabitants of Jerusalem.[n]   Yet the sterner zealots looked on with jealousy ; and while he was absent at Cæsarea, one Simon assembled a number of the people ; accused him of violating the law, probably on account of his fondness

---

[n] The Rabbinical writings are tender to the memory of Agrippa: they dwell on the gentleness of his disposition.   On the eighth day of the Feast of Tabernacles, when the Torah was read, "Thou shalt set him king over thee whom the Lord shall choose. . . Thou mayest not set a stranger over thee, which is not thy brother" (Deut. xvii. 15), Agrippa burst into tears, for he was of foreign descent. But a cry arose, "Be not troubled, King Agrippa; thou art our brother." They thought no doubt of his kindred with the Asmonean family.   He had

great respect for the common usages. It was a custom that bridal processions should give way before the king.   Agrippa saw a bridal procession coming towards him, and turned into a side street to let it pass.   Jost, i. 420.

A more doubtful instance of his respect for the Law is recorded.   Instead of executing criminals condemned to death, he let them fight as gladiators in his splendid amphitheatre at Berytus, and kill each other. See next page.

for theatric exhibitions, and demanded his exclusion
from the Temple. Agrippa sent for Simon to Cæsarea;
placed him by his side in the public theatre, and mildly
inquired whether he saw anything contrary to the Law.
Simon was silent; upon which Agrippa dismissed him
without molestation.°

The conduct of Agrippa to Silas, one of his faithful
followers, though more severe, can scarcely be considered as an exception to the general mildness of his
disposition. Silas had steadfastly adhered to his fortunes, and received as a reward the command of his
forces. But presuming on his services, he was perpetually reminding the king of his former low condition.
His insolence, at last, provoked Agrippa to dismiss Silas
from his employment, and imprison him. Once he
relented; but the intractable Silas treated his overtures with the utmost arrogance; and Agrippa left
him in confinement. Agrippa exercised his supreme
authority in Jerusalem by continually displacing the
High Priest. He first deposed Theophilus, son of
Annas, and substituted Simon, named Cantherus, son of
Boethus. Afterwards he offered the dignity to Jonathan, son of Annas, who declined it, and his brother
Mathias was appointed. Before the close of his reign
he degraded Mathias, and substituted Elionæus, son of
Simon Cantherus.

Agrippa inherited the magnificent taste for building
which distinguished the elder Herod. At Berytus, a
city which he highly favoured, he built a splendid
theatre, where the most costly musical exhibitions were
displayed; and in an amphitheatre in the same city,
two troops of gladiators, malefactors, of 700 each, were

---

* Joseph. Ant. xix. 7. 4.

let loose upon each other; and thus horribly fulfilled the sentence of the law.

In Jerusalem he commenced a more useful work. To the north of the city, a new suburb, called Bezetha, had grown up: this he encircled with a wall; and was proceeding to strengthen the whole line of fortifications round the city.[p] But Vibius Marsus, who had succeeded Longinus as Prefect of Syria, beheld this proceeding with great suspicion; and, on account of his representations at Rome, Agrippa thought it prudent to desist from the work.

Marsus watched all the motions of the Jewish monarch with the same jealousy. Agrippa, probably with an innocent view of displaying his magnificence, assembled five kings at a great entertainment in Tiberias; Herod, king of Chalcis, his brother; Antiochus, king of Commagene; Cotys, king of the Lesser Armenia; Sampsigeranus, king of Emesa; and Polemon, king of Pontus. Marsus arrived at the same time; and Agrippa, out of respect, went forth to receive him: the imperious Roman sent orders to the several kings to withdraw themselves into their own territories. Agrippa was greatly offended; and sent a letter to Claudius, earnestly entreating the recall of Marsus.

Unhappily, besides his splendour, munificence, and conformity to the law, Agrippa sought other means of ingratiating himself with his Jewish subjects—the persecution of the unoffending Christians. He put to death James, the brother of St. John, and threw St. Peter into prison.[q]

---

[p] This wall, according to Josephus, would have rendered Jerusalem impregnable to the Romans. τηλικοῦτον γὰρ περιβάλλειν ἤρξατο τοῖς Ἱερυ- σολύμοις τεῖχος, ἥλικον ἂν τελεσθὲν ἀνήνυτον τὴν ἐν Ῥωμαίοις ἐποίησ πολιορκίαν. B. J., ii. 11. 6.

[q] Acts xii. 2.

Having completed a reign of three years over the whole of Palestine, Agrippa ordered a splendid festival at Cæsarea, in honour of the Emperor. Multitudes of the highest rank flocked together from all quarters. On the second day of the spectacle, at the early dawn, the king entered the theatre in a robe of silver, which glittered with the morning rays of the sun, so as to dazzle the eyes of the whole assembly, and excite general admiration. Some of his flatterers set up a shout—"A present god." Agrippa did not repress the impious adulation which spread through the theatre. At that moment he looked up, and saw an owl perched over his head, on a rope. The owl had once been to him a bird of good omen. While he was in chains at Rome, a fellow prisoner, a German, had augured, from the appearance of one of these birds, his future splendid fortune; but he had added this solemn warning, that when he saw that bird again, at the height of his fortune, he would die within five days. The fatal omen, proceeds Josephus, pierced the heart of the king; and with deep melancholy, he said, "Your god will soon suffer the common lot of mortality." He was immediately struck, in the language of the sacred volume, by an angel. He was seized with violent internal pains, and carried to his palace. There he lingered five days in extreme agony; being "eaten of worms," the cause of his intestine disorder.[r] He died in the forty-fourth year of his age, having reigned seven years over part of

---

[r] Joseph. Ant. xix. 8.

The account of the death of Herod in Acts xii. 21-23 shows the same event as seen from a Christian point of view. What ground has Jost for his suspicion of poison? — " vielleicht durch Vergiftung." p. 422.

To Agrippa's reign are attributed humane regulations concerning idolaters. The poor of them were to share in the gleanings; the poor idolater was to be aided with alms, the sick to be tended, the dead buried like the Israelites. Gittin, 61 a.

his dominions, and three over the whole of Palestine. He left one son, Agrippa; an elder, Drusus, had died in his infancy; and three daughters—Drusilla, married first to Aziz King of Emesa, then to Claudius Felix; Berenice, married to his brother Herod, king of Chalcis; and Mariamne.

The inhabitants of Sebaste and Cæsarea, probably the Greek party, and particularly his own soldiers, expressed the most brutal exultation at the death of Agrippa. They heaped his memory with reproaches, took the statues of his young daughters, carried them to brothels, and there placing them on the roof, treated them with every kind of indignity. They then made a great feast, to celebrate the *departure* of the king. Claudius heard with much indignation of this ungrateful conduct, and ordered the cohorts in Sebaste and Cæsarea to be removed into Pontus, and their place to be filled by draughts from the legions in Syria. Unhappily, this purpose was not executed. The troops remained with this sentence of disgrace rankling in their hearts, and exasperating them to still greater animosity towards the whole Jewish nation; a chief cause, Josephus adds, of the subsequent disasters.[a]

---

[a] δι καὶ ταῖς ἐπιοῦσι χρόνοις τῶν μεγίστων Ἰουδαίοις ἐγένετο συμφο- ρῶν ἀρχὴ, ~οῦ κατὰ Φλῶρον πολέμου σπέρματα βαλόντες. Ant. xix. 9. 2.

BOOK XIII.

THE ROMAN GOVERNORS.

Cuspius Fadus — Tiberius Alexander — Ventidius Cumanus — Felix
— Porcius Festus — Albinus — Gessius Florus — Commencement of the Revolt — The Zealots — Manahem — Massacre of
the Jews in the Provinces — Advance and Defeat of Cestius
Gallus.

At the decease of Herod Agrippa, his son, who bore the
same name, was seventeen years old. He was considered
too young to bear the burthen of royalty; and Judæa
relapsed into a Roman province.   Cassius Longinus was
appointed to the presidency of Syria; Cuspius Fadus
was sent as governor of Judæa.   Fadus administered his
office with firmness.   He found a civil war disturbing
the district beyond the Jordan.   The inhabitants of
Peræa, on some boundary dispute, had attacked the
Philadelphians.   Fadus seized three of the ringleaders;
executed one, named Hannibal, and banished the rest.
The easy yoke of Agrippa had permitted the robbers,
who perpetually rose up to waste this fertile country, to
gain head.   Fadus made them feel the vigour of the
Roman arm: he cleared the whole country of their
bands, and put to death Ptolemy, a noted captain, who
had committed great excesses against the Idumæans and
Arabians.   Apprehending, it may seem, that the High
Priest possessed too much independent authority, Fadus
proceeded to revoke the edict of Vitellius, by which the
custody of the pontifical robes had been surrendered.

He commanded that they should be replaced in the
garrison of Antonia; and Longinus himself appeared in
Jerusalem, with a considerable force to overawe all
resistance. The Jews appealed to the Emperor, who, at
the earnest entreaty of young Agrippa, issued an imperial mandate in favour of the Jews. At the same time
Herod, king of Chalcis, petitioned, and obtained the
sovereignty over the Temple, and the power of nomi-
nating the High Priest. He displaced Cantherus, who
had regained the office, and appointed Joseph, son of
Camith.

This was the second year of a grievous famine, which
for several years prevailed in Judæa. The metropolis
derived great advantage from the bounty of a royal
proselyte, Helena, the queen of Adiabene, a district
beyond the Tigris. She imported vast quantities of
corn from Alexandria and dried figs from Cyprus, which
she distributed among the lower orders. Her son,
Izates, who had likewise adopted the Jewish faith, sent
great sums to Jerusalem, for the same charitable purposes. Helena was both the wife and sister, according
to the ancient Persian usage, of Monobazus, king of
Adiabene. Izates was the favourite son of that monarch,
who, apprehensive of the jealousy with which he was
looked on by his brothers, sent him to Abenerig, king
of Characene (a district on the Persian Gulf), whose
daughter he married. In that commercial district there
was a Jew merchant, named Ananias, who was accustomed to have free ingress into the women's apartments,
probably for purposes of traffic, and there seized every
opportunity of teaching the religious tenets of the Jews.
Izates became a convert; and, by a singular coincidence,
his mother, Helena, at the same time adopted the same
opinions. On the return of Izates to Adiabene, his

M 2

father made him governor of a district named Carrhæ, in
which, according to tradition, the remains of Noah's ark
were still to be seen. On the death of his father, Helena
had the address to secure the succession to the throne
for Izates. His brother, Monobazus, assumed the crown
till Izates should arrive ; and the rest of the monarch's
sons, by different mothers, were thrown into prison, and
were even in danger of their lives. Immediately that
Izates appeared, Monobazus abdicated the sovereignty ;
Izates expressed great indignation at the imprisonment
of his brethren. Izates was so ardent a convert that
he insisted on undergoing circumcision. His prudent
preceptor, Ananias, from fear lest the unpopularity
of the measure should make the king odious to his subjects, and himself thus be exposed to personal danger,
dissuaded him from his design. But a more zealous
Galilean insisted that the honour of God was concerned ;
and the monarch immediately, to the great alarm of
Ananias, submitted to the rite. Izates was a king of
great prudence and resolution. By his moderation and
address he reinstated Artabanus, king of Parthia, on his
throne, from which he had been driven by his own
satraps ; and, afterwards, dissuaded his son, Bardanes,
from entering into a war with the Romans. Bardanes
immediately declared war on Izates ; but he was set
aside by his own subjects. The king's brother, Monobazus, and the chief satraps of the kingdom, endured for
some time, but with great reluctance, the yoke of a
sovereign who had apostatized from the national religion.
Monobazus conspired with Abiah, an Arabian king, to invade Adiabene ; but Abiah was defeated with great loss.
Afterwards they had recourse to Vologeses, king of
Parthia ; but his invasion was arrested by a rebellion
among his own dependants. On the death of Izates,

who wore the crown for twenty-four years, his remains, and those of his mother, Helena, were transported to Jerusalem, and buried in a splendid cemetery, which remained till the time of Jerome.

Before the recall of Fadus, the peace of the country was disturbed by an impostor, named Theudas, who gave himself out as a prophet, and gained a great number of proselytes. Multitudes thronged forth, with all their possessions, to the banks of the Jordan, which Theudas asserted that, like Joshua of old, he would divide in the midst, and carry them through in triumph. Fadus, with his usual vigilance, seized the impostor, cut off his head, and sent it to Jerusalem.

To Fadus succeeded Tiberius Alexander.[a] Alexander was an apostate Egyptian Jew. For, if in the remote East the worshippers of Jehovah gained royal proselytes, in the West they lost some of their own sons of high rank. Tiberius was the son of Alexander, the Alabarch of Alexandria, and the nephew of the celebrated Philo. The only act recorded of his short government was the crucifixion of James and Simon, two sons of Judas the Galilean, who had attempted to disseminate the dangerous doctrines of their father. Notwithstanding, however, the famine, by which the land was still afflicted—the seditious tenets of the Galilean rebels—and the government of an apostate, which must have been singularly odious

---

[a] Josephus says of Cuspius Fadus and Tiberius Alexander, ὅτι μηδὲν παρακινοῦντες τῶν πατρίων ἐθῶν, ἐν ἰρήνῃ τὸ ἔθνος διεφύλαξον. B. J. ii. 11. 6; see also Ant. xx. 5. 2.

Alexander in later times threw off this milder character as he had thrown off his religion. He was appointed procurator of Egypt by Nero, and slew 50,000 of his countrymen in an insurrection at Alexandria. He was the first procurator who dared to declare his allegiance to Vespasian; and was present during the siege and at the fall of Jerusalem. Compare B. J. ii. 1. 8. 7; iv. 10. 6; v. 1. 6; Suet. Vespas. vi.; Tacit. Hist. ii. 74. 79.

to the zealous Jews, the province continued in peace until the arrival of Ventidius Cumanus, to supersede Alexander.

At this time Herod, king of Chalcis, died, having once more changed the High Priest, and substituted Ananias, son of Nebid, for Joseph, the son of Camith. He left sons; particularly Aristobulus, afterwards appointed, by Nero, to the kingdom of Lesser Armenia; but the kingdom of Chalcis, and the sovereignty of the Temple, were assigned to young Agrippa, who assumed the title of king.

During the government of Cumanus, the low and sullen murmurs which announced the approaching eruption of the dark volcano, now gathering its strength in Palestine, became more distinct. The people and the Roman soldiery began to display mutual animosity. To preserve the peace during the crowded festivals in Jerusalem, the Romans mounted a guard in the Antonia, and in the adjacent cloister. One of these soldiers, to show his contempt for the religious rites and usages of the Jews, indecently exposed his person.[b] The furious populace not only vented their rage on the offender, but uttered the most violent reproaches against Cumanus himself. The governor immediately ordered his whole forces into the Antonia. The affrighted people fled; the narrow streets were choked; and 20,000 perished. The sacrifice was suspended, and the whole city given up to wailing and lamentation.

This disturbance was scarcely appeased, when another succeeded. Near Bethhoron, in the pass about twelve miles from Jerusalem, a party, half insurgents and half

---

[b] This is rather differently related in Ant. xx. 5. 3, and B. J. ii. 12. 1. | The best comment is Horat. Sat. i. 9. 70.

robbers, attacked, in the public road, Stephanas, a
slave of the Emperor, and plundered his baggage.   Cumanus sent a troop of soldiers to plunder the neighbouring villages, and seize the chief persons in them. During
this scene of pillage, a soldier found a copy of the Law of
Moses, and tore it to pieces, uttering the most offensive
blasphemies. The Jews sent a formal deputation before
Cumanus to complain of the insult ; Cumanus, by the
advice of his friends, ordered the soldier to execution.

The animosities of the populace and the Roman soldiery were not the only conflicting elements in this
distracted country ; the jealousies of the natives began
again to break out.   The road by which the Jews of
Galilee went up to the Temple, led through the territory
of Samaria.   The Samaritans waylaid and slew many of
them.   Cumanus, bribed by the Samaritans, refused to
take cognizance of any complaints. The Jews, headed
by two valiant robber chieftains, took up arms, and set fire
to some of the Samaritan villages.   Cumanus marched
against them ; and, with the aid of the Samaritans, defeated them.   Jerusalem was in an uproar, and, but for the
authority and influence of the chiefs, the whole people
would have risen in insurrection.   Clad in sackcloth,
and with ashes on their heads, the priests and rulers
passed through the streets, entreating the insurgents to
lay aside their arms, lest they should bring fire and sword
on the city, and ruin on the Temple. With difficulty the
tumult was allayed in Jerusalem.   But the whole country was in a state of confusion.   The Samaritans carried
their complaints before Ummidius Quadratus, prefect
of Syria.   The Jews pleaded the wanton aggression of
the Samaritans, and their bribery of Cumanus.   Quadratus deferred his judgement, till a short time after,
having investigated the affair on the spot, he condemned

the Samaritans; but put to death, as seditious persons, all the Jews taken by Cumanus. He then removed his tribunal to Lydda, where he received information that a certain Dortus and others had openly exhorted insurrection against the Romans. He ordered the four ringleaders to be crucified; and sent Ananias, the High Priest, with Annas, the captain of the Temple, in chains, for trial at Rome. At the same time Cumanus, and Celer, his military tribune, were also sent to Rome to answer for their conduct before the Emperor. From Lydda, Quadratus moved to Jerusalem, and finding peace entirely re-established, he returned to Antioch.

Great interest was made at Rome by Cumanus, Celer, and the Samaritan party; but the influence of Agrippa, then at Rome, predominated. Cumanus was banished; Celer sent to Jerusalem, to be dragged publicly through the streets and beheaded; the ringleaders of the Samaritans were put to death.

In evil hour for himself and for his country, Jonathan, who had succeeded to the High-priesthood, exerted his influence to obtain the appointment of governor of Judæa for Felix, brother of Pallas afterwards the freed slave and all-powerful favourite of the Emperor Nero. According to Tacitus, who is quite at variance with the Jewish historian, Felix was already in Palestine, as independent governor of Samaria, where he had inflamed the civil commotions, and ought to have appeared with Cumanus as a criminal before the tribunal of Quadratus; but Quadratus, dreading his interest at Rome, placed him by his own side on the seat of justice. Cumanus was condemned, and suffered the penalty of the crimes of Felix as well as of his own. Born a slave, Felix was magnificent in his profligacy. He had three wives, all of royal blood.

One of these was the beautiful Drusilla, the daughter of King Agrippa the First, whom, by the aid of Simon, a magician (by some, though improbably, supposed the Simon Magus of the Acts), he had seduced from her husband, Aziz, king of Emesa.[c] Aziz had carried his complacency so far as to submit to circumcision in order to obtain the hand of Drusilla, who now gave up her religion to marry Felix. Felix administered the province with the authority of a king, and the disposition of a slave. Supported by the interest of Pallas, says Tacitus, he thought he might commit all crimes with impunity. The land was full of armed robbers, who wasted the country. Felix at first proceeded with vigour and severity against them; but afterwards, for his private ends, entered into a confederacy with some of the most daring.[d] The High Priest, Jonathan, assuming the privilege of a friend, like the Christian Apostle, would reason with him *on temperance and righteousness.* His remonstrances, if at the time they produced the same effect, and *made Felix tremble,* were fatal to himself. Felix, weary with his importunity, entered into a

---

[c] These three daughters of Agrippa the First did little honour to their race or their religion; they vied with each other in profligacy. Drusilla was the eldest. The second, Berenice, was married to her uncle, Herod of Chalcis. On his death she remained a widow, but in bad repute, as living in incest with her brother. By her wealth she tempted Polemo, king of Cilicia, to take her to wife. Polemo, another royal proselyte, submitted to circumcision, and embraced Judaism with fervour and constancy. She left Polemo to live a life of free indulgence.

Mariamne, the third, having repudiated her husband Archelaus, married Demetrius, the Alabarch of Alexandria.

[d] " At non frater ejus, cognomento Felix, pari moderatione agebat, jampridem Judææ impositus, et cuncta malefacta sibi impunè ratus, tantâ potentiâ subnixus." Tac. Ann. xii. 54. Compare the whole passage.

" Antonius Felix, per omnem sævitiam et libidinem, jus regium servili ingenio exercuit, Drusillâ, Clecpatræ et Antonii nepte, in matrimonium acceptâ." Tac. Hist. v. 9. Compare Suet. Claudius, xxviii.

secret conspiracy with some of the Sicarii, or Assassins, the most extravagant of the school of Judas the Galilean.[e] These were men, some fanatics, some unprincipled desperadoes, who abused the precepts of the Mosaic law, as authorising the murder of all on whom they might affix the brand of hostility to their country and their God. Having bribed Doras, the intimate friend of Jonathan, through his means Felix sent a party of these wretches into the Temple. With their daggers under their cloaks, they mingled with the attendants of the High Priest. They pretended to join in the public worship, and suddenly struck dead the unsuspecting pontiff, who lay bleeding on the sacred pavement. From this period, says the indignant Josephus, God hated his guilty city, and disdaining any longer to dwell in his contaminated Temple, brought the Romans to purify with fire the sins of the nation.[f]

The crime remained unrevenged and unnoticed. The Assassins, emboldened by their impunity, carried on their dreadful work. No man was secure. Some from private enmity, others on account of their wealth, as they pursued their peaceful occupations, were struck dead by men who passed by, apparently unarmed and as peacefully disposed as themselves. Even the Temple was not a place of safety; the worshipper did not know but that the man who knelt by his side was preparing to plunge a dagger to his heart.

---

[e] Joseph. Ant., xx. 7. 3. Tac. Ann. xii. 54. See above.

The Mischna (Tract Sota, ix. 9) asserts that at the time when these Assassins, or Sicarii, multiplied, the sacrifice of a calf, which, according to the law, was made by the neighbouring city whenever the body of a murdered man was discovered, came to an end.

[f] καὶ τὸν Θεον .... Ρωμαίους ἐπαγαγεῖν ἡμῖν καὶ τῇ πόλει καθάρσιον πῦρ, καὶ δουλείαν ἐπιβαλεῖν σὺν γυναιξὶ καὶ τέκνοις, σωφρόνησαι ταῖς συμφοραῖς βουλόμενον ἡμᾶς. Ant. xx. 8. 5.

Such was the state of the city; the country was not much more secure. The robbers multiplied and grew more bold. Nor were these the worst. In every quarter arose impostors, and pretenders to magic, who, asserting their miraculous powers, led the people into desert places, and harangued them on the impiety of obedience to the Roman government. Felix in vain scoured the country with his horse; as fast as some were seized and crucified, others arose, and the fanatical spirit of the people constantly received new excitement. The most formidable of these men was a Jew of Egyptian birth. He assembled in the desert, probably that of Quarantania, between Jerusalem and Jericho, as many as 30,000 followers. He led them to the Mount of Olives, and pointing to the city below, assured them that its walls would fall down and admit his triumphal entrance. Felix marched out to attack him: the Egyptian escaped; but many of his followers were killed, many taken, the rest dispersed.[g]

In the mean time Claudius died, having promoted Agrippa from the kingdom of Chalcis to the more extensive dominion—the Tetrarchate of Philip, Gaulonitis, Trachonitis, Batanea, and Paneas, to which was afterwards added part of Galilee and Peræa. On the whole, the government of Claudius was favourable to the race of Israel; but rather as subjects of his friend Agrippa than as Jews. At one time he closed their synagogues, and expelled them from Rome—probably on account of some tumult caused by their persecutions of the Christians. Agrippa appointed Ismael, son of Fabi, to

---

[g] Compare Acts xxi. 38. The immediate followers of the Egyptian were probably 4000, as in the Acts. The rabble who joined him may have reached the larger and vaguer number. B. J. ii. 13.

the Pontificate, vacant since the death of Jonathan—
though in this interval, probably, a kind of illegitimate
authority had been resumed by that Ananias, son of
Nebid, who had been sent in chains to Rome by Quadratus, and had been released through the influence of
Agrippa. It was that Ananias who commanded St.
Paul to be smitten when he was addressing the people.
St. Paul either did not know or did not recognize his
doubtful title.[h]

Up to this period, according to the representation of
the Jewish annalist, the Pontificate had remained almost
entirely uncontaminated by the general licence and turbulence which distracted the nation. The priests were
in general moderate and upright men, who had endeavoured to maintain the peace of the city. Now the evil
penetrated into the sanctuary, and feuds rent the sacred
family of Levi. A furious schism broke out between
the chief priests and the, inferior priesthood. Each party
collected a band of ruffians, and assailed the other with
violent reproaches, and even with stones. No one interfered to repress the tumult; and the High Priests are
said to have sent their slaves to levy by force the tithes
which belonged to the inferior class, many of whom in
consequence perished with hunger. Even the worst
excesses of the dagger-men seem to have been author-
ised by the priesthood for their own purposes. The
forty men who, with the connivance of the priests, bound
themselves by a vow to assassinate St. Paul, if not of the
fraternity, recognised the principles of that sanguinary
crew.

It was in Cæsarea that the events took place which
led to the final rupture with Rome. This magnificent

---

[h] Acts xxiii. 3.

city had rapidly risen to a high degree of wealth and populousness. It was inhabited by two races—the Syrian Greeks, who were heathens, and the Jews. The two parties violently contended for the pre-eminence. The Jews insisted on the foundation of the city by Herod their king, and on its occupying the site of the old Jewish town called the Tower of Straton; the Greeks appealed to the statues and temples erected by Herod himself, which clearly proved that Cæsarea was intended for a Pagan city. The feud became gradually more fierce; tumults and bloodshed disturbed the streets. The more aged and prudent of the Jews could not restrain their followers. The Jews were the more wealthy; but the Roman soldiery, chiefly levied in Syria, took part with their countrymen. The officers attempted, but in vain, to keep the peace; and when Felix himself came forth to disperse a party of Jews, who had got the better in an affray, they treated his authority with contempt. Felix commanded his troops to charge them. The soldiery were too glad to avail themselves of the signal for licence; many of the Jews fell, many were seized, and some of the more opulent houses plundered. After the recall of Felix, a deputation of each party was sent to Rome, to lay the whole case before the Emperor. The Jews brought heavy charges against Felix; but the powerful protection of his brother Pallas, now in the highest favour with Nero, secured his impunity. The Greeks, by a large bribe to Burrhus, who had been the preceptor of Nero, obtained a decree which deprived the Jews of the rights of equal citizenship. This decree still further inflamed the contest. The Greeks became more and more insulting; the Jews more and more turbulent.

In the rest of the province the administration of the

rigid but upright Porcius Festus caused a short interval of comparative peace.   Festus kept down all the
bands, whether we are to call them robbers or insurgents,
and repressed the dagger-men.[1]   His soldiers put to
death an impostor who had led multitudes into the
desert.

At this period King Agrippa resided in Jerusalem, in
the palace of the Asmonean princes, which stood on the
cliff of Mount Sion, towards the Temple.   In front of
this was the Xystus, an open colonnade, which was connected by a bridge with the Temple.   Agrippa reared a
lofty building in this palace, which commanded a beautiful prospect of the whole city, particularly of the
Temple courts.   Reposing on his couch he might see the
whole course of the religious ceremonies.   The priesthood
were indignant at the intrusion, and hastily ran up a
wall, on the western side of their own court, by which
they intercepted not merely the view of the king, but
that of the Roman guard which was mounted in the
outer western portico.   Agrippa and Festus ordered the
demolition of this wall.   The Jews demanded permission to appeal to Nero ; Festus consented, and a deputation of ten, headed by Ismael, the High Priest, and
Hilkiah, the keeper of the treasury, set off to Rome.
There they obtained the interest of Poppæa, the profli-
gate empress of Nero, whom Josephus describes as *devout*,
as if she had been inclined to the Jewish religion : if so,
she was no very creditable proselyte.   Through her
interest the wall was permitted to stand, but the High
Priest and treasurer were detained at Rome.   Agrippa·
seized the opportunity of appointing another High Priest

---

[1] The Sicarn, so called from a kind
of sword or dagger which they carried,
about the size of the Persian acinace,
but curved like the Roman sica. Joseph. Ant. xx. 8. 10.

—Joseph, named Cabi, son of Simon Cantherus. Soon after, he degraded Joseph, and appointed Annas, the fifth son of Annas, in Jewish estimation the happiest of men, for he himself had been High Priest, and had seen his five sons and his son-in-law, Caiaphas, successively promoted to that dignity.[k] Annas united himself to the sect of the Sadducees, if he did not inherit those doctrines from his father. The Sadducees were noted for their rigid administration of the law; and while the place of the Roman governor was vacant, Annas seized the opportunity of putting to death James the Just, and others of the Christians, at the feast of the Passover.[l] But the act was unpopular, and Agrippa deprived him of the priesthood, and appointed Jesus, son of Damnai.

Unhappily for this devoted country the upright Festus died in Judæa, and Albinus arrived as his successor. With the rapacious Albinus, everything became venal. At first he proceeded with severity against the robbers, but in a short time began to extort enormous ransoms for their freedom. This was little better than to set a price on robbery and assassination. In the mean time the taxes were increased, and the wasted country groaned under the heaviest burthens. Two men alone grew rich amid the general distress, the Roman governor and Ananias, formerly High Priest, who, keeping both Albinus and the High Priest in pay, committed all kinds of outrages, seizing the tithes of the inferior priesthood, who were again so reduced that many of them died of famine. Ananias was too wealthy a prize to escape the robbers who infested the country. In the open day, and at the time of a festival, they seized the

---

[k] Joseph. Ant. xx. 9. 1.
[l] Ibid. This passage seems to be genuine.

scribe of Eleazar, captain of the guard, who was probably the son of Ananias, carried him off, and demanded
as a ransom the release of ten of their companions who
were in prison. Ananias persuaded Albinus, no doubt
by a great bribe, to comply. Encouraged by this success, whenever any one of the Assassins was taken, they
seized one of the dependants on Ananias, and demanded
an exchange.

Agrippa, as if he foresaw the approaching danger,
began to prepare a place of retreat. He enlarged the
city of Cæsarea Philippi (Paneas), and called it Neronias.
But his chief expenditure was made at Berytus, where
he built a theatre, and at great cost provided for the
most splendid exhibitions. He likewise distributed corn
and oil; collected a noble gallery of statues and copies
from the antique; in short, he transferred to that city
the chief splendour of his kingdom. This liberality to
a foreign city was highly unpopular at Jerusalem. The
degradation of Jesus, son of Damnai, and the appointment of Jesus, son of Gamaliel, increased the general discontent. Each of these rival High Priests had his party,
who attacked each other in the streets; in short, every
one who had wealth or power assembled his armed adherents. Ananias, as the richest, got together the
strongest band; and two relatives of Agrippa, Saül and
Costobar, appeared at the head of their own followers,
plundering on all sides without scruple. Albinus aggravated the mischief. Having heard of his intended
recall, he brought forth all the malefactors, who crowded
the prisons, executed the most notorious, but allowed the
rest to pay their ransoms. Thus the prisons were
empty, but the whole province filled with these desperate ruffians. The completion of the works in the
Temple added to the multitude of the idle and unem-

ployed—eighteen thousand workmen were discharged.
The more prudent of the people dreaded the letting
loose this vast number of persons, without employment,
on society; and with no less forethought they apprehended the accumulation of vast treasures in the Temple,
which had hitherto been for the most part profitably
employed on the public buildings, and would now serve
no purpose but to excite the rapacity of the Romans.
They petitioned that the eastern portico might be raised
to a greater degree of magnificence.   Agrippa, who
was entrusted by the Emperor with the command over
the Temple, refused their request, but permitted them
to pave the city with stone.   He afterwards deposed
Jesus, son of Gamaliel, and appointed Matthias, the
last legitimate High Priest of Jerusalem.

Nothing was wanting to fill the measure of calamity
which this fruitful and once happy land was to exhaust,
but the nomination of a governor, like Gessius Florus,
who made the people look back with regret to the administration of the rapacious Albinus.   Albinus at least
dissembled his cruelties and exactions.   Relying on the
protection of the Empress, who was attached to his wife
Cleopatra by long friendship and kindred disposition,
Florus made an ostentatious display of his oppressions.
Without compunction and without shame, as crafty as
he was cruel, he laid deliberate schemes of iniquity, by
which, at some distant period, he was to reap his harvest
of plunder.   He pillaged not only individuals, but even
communities, and seemed to grant a general indemnity
for spoliation, if he was only allowed his fair portion of
the plunder.   Many villages and towns were entirely
deserted; the inhabitants left their native country to fly
beyond the reach of his administration.   Cestius Gallus,
a man of a congenial spirit, commanded in Syria.   The

fear of Florus, as long as Cestius remained in Syria, prevented the Jews from appealing to his tribunal; they would not have been suffered to arrive there in safety. But when Cestius, during the days preceding the Passover, visited Jerusalem, three millions of suppliants, that is, the whole population assembled for the great annual feast, surrounded him, and entreated his interference. Florus stood by the side of Cestius, turning their complaints into ridicule. Cestius, however, promised that he would use his interest with Florus to treat them with greater moderation, and Florus, without further reproof, was permitted to escort his colleague in iniquity, on his way to Antioch, as far as Cæsarea.

In the mean time wild and awful prodigies, thus the Jewish annalist relates, had filled the timid with apprehensions of the approaching desolation. But the blind and desperate multitude neglected all these signs of Almighty wrath. A comet, which had the appearance of a sword, hung above the city for a whole year. While the people were assembled at the feast of unleavened bread, at the sixth hour of the night, a sudden light, as bright as day, shone about the altar and the Temple, and continued for nearly half an hour. A cow led forth to sacrifice, brought forth a calf. The inner gate on the side of the Temple looking eastward was of brass, and of such immense weight as to require twenty men to close it in the evening. It was fastened by strong iron bolts, let into the stone door-posts. Suddenly this gate flew open, and it was with much difficulty that all the assembled guard could reclose it. This the vulgar considered a good omen, as indicating that God had opened the gate of blessing: but the wise more sadly interpreted it as a manifest sign of the insecurity of the Temple, and that it prefigured the opening of the gate of the Holy Place to the enemy. A few days after this festival, a still more incredible circumstance occurred; such, says Josephus, as would appear a fable, had it not been attested by eye-witnesses, and justified by the subsequent events. Before sunset, chariots and armed squadrons were seen in the heavens; they mingled and formed in array, so as to seem to encircle the city in their rapid and terrific career. And on the Pentecost, when the priests on duty entered by night into the Temple, they said that they heard a movement and a noise, and presently the voice as it were of a great host, which said, "Let us depart hence." More alarming still! while the city was yet at peace and in prosperity, a countryman named Jesus, son of Ananus, began suddenly to cry aloud in the Temple—"*A voice from the east! a voice from the west! a voice from the four winds! a voice against Jerusalem and against the Temple! a voice against the bridegrooms and the brides! a voice against the whole people!*" Day and night in the narrow streets of the city he went along repeating these words with a loud voice. Some of the leaders seized him, and had him severely beaten. He uttered no remonstrance, no entreaty for mercy, he seemed entirely regardless about his own person, but still went on reiterating his fearful burthen. The magistrates then apprehended him, and led him before Albinus, the Roman governor; there he was scourged till his bones could be seen, he uttered neither shriek of pain, nor prayer for mercy, but raising his sad and broken voice as loud as he could, at every blow cried out, *Woe, woe to Jerusalem!* Albinus demanded who he was, and whence he came? he answered not a word. The Roman at length supposing that he was mad, let him go. All the four years that intervened before the war, the son of Ananus paid no attention to any one, and never spoke, excepting the same words, *Woe, woe to Jerusalem!* He neither cursed any one who struck him, nor thanked any one who gave him food. His only answer was the same melancholy presage. He was particularly active during the festivals, and then with greater frequency, and still deeper voice, he cried, *Woe, woe to the city and to the Temple!* At length, during the siege, he suddenly cried out, *Woe, woe to myself!* and was struck dead by a stone from a balista.

It is not improbable that the prophecies of the approaching ruin of Jerusalem disseminated by the Christians might add to the general apprehension. Mingled as they were with the mass of the people, their distinct assurances that their Divine Teacher had foretold the speedy dissolution of the state, could scarcely remain unknown, especially when, in obedience to the command of Christ, they abandoned Jerusalem in a body, and retreated to Pella, a town beyond the Jordan.

There was another sign, which might have given warning to the political sagacity or to the humanity of the Romans, upon the nature of the approaching contest, as showing how immense a population they were thus driving to desperation, and what horrible carnage would be necessary, before they could finally subdue the rebellious province. When Cestius Gallus was at Jerusalem, at the time of the Passover, he inquired the number of Jews present from all quarters. The priests counted the lambs sacrificed, and found 255,600. None but Jews, and those free from legal impurities, might sacrifice. Reckoning at a low average of ten to each lamb, the numbers were 2,556,000. Josephus supposes that three millions would not have been an immoderate calculation.[m]

---

[m] See on these numbers below.

The fatal flame finally broke out from the old feud at
Cæsarea.[a] The decree of Nero had assigned the magistracy
of that city to the Greeks.   It happened that the Jews
had a synagogue, the ground around which belonged to
a Greek.   For this spot the Jews offered a much higher
price than it was worth.   It was refused; and to annoy
them as much as possible, the owner set up some mean
shops and buildings upon it, and rendered the approach
to the synagogue as narrow and difficult as he could.
The more hot-headed of the Jewish youth interrupted
the workmen.   The men of greater wealth and influence,
and among them, John, a publican, collected the large
sum of eight talents, and sent it as a bribe to Florus,
that he might interfere and stop the building.   Florus
received the money, made great promises, and immediately set out from Cæsarea for Sebaste, in order to
leave full scope for the riot.   On the following day, a
sabbath, while the Jews were crowding to the synagogue,
a man overset an earthen vessel in the way, and began
to sacrifice birds upon it.   It has been conjectured that
this was a particularly offensive jest.   The heathens
generally represented the ancestors of the Jews to have
been expelled from Egypt, as a race of lepers; and since
birds were the first sacrifice appointed in cases of leprosy,
it was most likely meant to gall the old wound.[b]   However that may be, the more violent Jews, furious at the
affront, attacked the Greeks.   The Greeks were already
in arms, waiting this signal for the affray.   Jucundus,
the governor, attempted in vain to appease the tumult,
till at length the Jews, being worsted, took up the books

---

[a] B. J. ii. 14. 4.
[b] "Hac re lepra Judæis exprobratur
per mactationem avis supra vas fictile :
quod in leprosorum mundatione ex lege
Dei (Levit. xiv.) fieri debuit."   Reland,
quoted by Hudson in a note on the
passage in the B. J.

of their Law, and went away to Narbata, about 7½ miles distant. John the Publican, with twelve of the highest rank, went to Samaria to Florus, implored his assistance, and modestly reminded him of the eight talents he had received. Florus threw them into prison with every mark of indignity.

The news of this outrage and injustice spread to'Jerusalem. The city was in a state of violent excitement. It was the deliberate purpose of Florus to drive the people to insurrection, both that all inquiry into his former oppressions might be drowned by the din of war, and that he might have better opportunities for plunder. He seized this critical moment to demand seventeen talents from the sacred treasury under pretence of Cæsar's necessities. The people assembled around the Temple with the loudest outcries. The name of Florus was passed from one to another with every epithet of hatred and contempt. Some carried about a basket, entreating alms for the poor beggar, Florus. Neglecting entirely the tumult in Cæsarea, Florus advanced with all the force he could collect against Jerusalem. To his disappointment, the people, instead of maintaining their seditious demeanour, endeavoured to excite his clemency by the most submissive and humiliating conduct. They crowded forth, received his army with acclamations, and hailed the Procurator himself as a public benefactor. But Florus was too keen-sighted to be imposed upon by these unmerited marks of popularity. He chose to remember nothing but the insults and contumely with which his name had been treated. He sent forward Capito with fifty horse, commanding the people to disperse; they obeyed, and retreating to their houses, passed the night in trembling expectation of his vengeance.

Florus took up his quarters in the Palace.[p] In the morning his tribunal was erected before the gates. The High Priest and the leaders of the people (probably the Sanhedrin) were summoned to attend. Florus demanded the surrender of all those who had insulted his name, and added, if the heads of the people refused or delayed, he should proceed against them as responsible for the offence. The priests represented the general peaceable disposition of the city, and entreated his forbearance, throwing the blame on a few hot-headed youths, whom it was impossible to detect, as all had repented, and none would confess their guilt. At these words Florus broke out into the most violent fury; he gave the signal to his troops to plunder the upper market, and put to death all they met. The soldiery were but too ready instruments of his cruelty. They cleared the market, then broke into the houses, pillaged them, and put to death the inhabitants. The narrow streets were crowded with fugitives; many who escaped the sword were trampled to death. Unoffending citizens were seized, carried before Florus, scourged and crucified. Of men, women, and children, for neither age nor sex was spared, there fell that day 3600. Florus paid no regard to the sacred rights of Roman citizenship; some free-men of the first distinction, for many of the Jews had attained even the equestrian rank, were scourged and executed with their meaner countrymen.

Agrippa was absent in Egypt, but his sister Berenice was in Jerusalem, in pursuance of a religious vow. She sent repeated messages to Florus, imploring him to stay the fury of his soldiers; and even herself, in her penitential attire, with her hair shorn and with naked feet,

---

[p] B. J ii. 15.

stood before his tribunal. The Roman was deaf to her
entreaties; he had no ear but for the accounts of
wealth, which was brought in, every hour, in great
masses. Even in the presence of Berenice, her miserable countrymen were scourged and hewn down. She
herself was obliged to take refuge in one of the royal
residences, and dared not go to rest, lest the soldiers
should force their way through her feeble guard.

The next day multitudes assembled in the scene of
the massacre, the upper market-place; and among the
wailings for the dead were heard but half-suppressed
execrations and menaces against the cruel Florus. The
chief heads of the city with the priests were in the
greatest alarm; they tore their robes, rushed among
the people, addressed them individually with the most
earnest supplications not again to provoke the anger of
the governor. The populace, partly out of respect,
partly out of fear, quietly dispersed.

Florus and his satellites alone were grieved at this
pacification; he determined, if possible, to renew these
profitable tumults. He sent for the priests and leaders,
and commanded them, as the last proof of their submission, to go forth and receive, with the utmost cordiality,
two cohorts of troops who were advancing from Cæsarea.
The priests assembled the people in the Temple, made
known the orders of Florus, and exhorted them to obedience. The more turbulent did not disguise their seditious intentions. Then all the priesthood, the Levites,
the musicians and singers in their sacred vestments, fell
upon their knees and supplicated the people, that they
would not bring down certain ruin on the whole city, or
give excuse to the rapacious plunderer to profane the
Holy Place, and pillage the sacred treasures of God.
The priests of the highest rank, with robes rent and

ashes on their heads, went about, calling on the most
influential by name, and urging with the most solemn
vehemence, that however degrading the submission to
the commands of Florus, it was a trifling sacrifice, if it
might avert the desolation of the city, and all the
horrors of war: that it would be the height of madness
to allow themselves to be borne away by a few of the
factious or misguided populace, whom they, the rather,
ought to overawe with their authority.

They succeeded in allaying, for the time, the enraged
multitude; the more turbulent were silenced, as
menaces were mingled with entreaties; and the chief
priests led forth the whole populace in peaceful array.
The procession, in obedience to their admonitions, wel-
comed the cohorts with apparent gladness. The cohorts,
who had received their secret instructions from Florus,
advanced in sullen silence, not condescending to return
the greetings. The more violent Jews took fire, and
broke out into audible imprecations against Florus. The
troops turned upon them; struck them with their staves;
the horsemen rode over them, and trampled them
down; many were bruised, many wounded. At the
gates there was a violent rush to obtain entrance. Those
behind pressed on those before; the horsemen came
trampling on, and forcing their way through the dense
mass; numbers fell, pushed down by their own people,
or under the hoofs of the horses; their bodies were so
crushed and mangled, that when they were taken up
for burial, they could not be distinguished by their
friends.

The soldiery still kept on, advancing, and driving the
multitude before them, or riding over them, all through
the suburb of Bezetha. Their object was to press forward, and gain possession at the same time of the An-

tonia and the Temple. At this moment Florus sallied
from the Palace, and attempted to force his way to that
part of the castle which joined the Temple, but without
success: for the people blocked up the narrow streets,
so that his men could not cut their way through the
living masses, and were themselves beaten down by
stones and missiles from the roofs of the houses. They
retreated to their quarters. The insurgents, apprehending that the enemy might force their way from the
Antonia to the Temple, cut off the porticoes and galleries which connected them. This bold measure made
Florus despair of succeeding in his main object, the
plunder of the sacred treasury during the confusion.
He suspended the attack, sent for the chief priests and
rulers, and proposed to evacuate the city; but offered
to leave a guard of sufficient force to preserve the peace.
They entreated him to leave only one cohort, and that,
not the one which had been engaged against the people.
On these terms, Florus retired unmolested to Cæsarea.

But Florus did not yet despair of inflaming the province and commencing an open war on more advan-
tageous terms. He sent to his superior officer, Cestius
Gallus, an artful representation of the tumults, in which
all the blame was laid on the intractable and rebellious
spirit of the Jews, whose unprovoked and wanton insults
on the Roman authority had called for instant and exemplary justice. The Jews on their part were not
remiss. The Rulers and Berenice sent the most touching accounts of the terrible rapacity and cruelty of
Florus and his troops. Cestius summoned a council; in
which it was resolved that he should repair in person to
Jerusalem, to examine into the causes of the revolt, to
punish the guilty, and confirm the Roman party in their
allegiance.

In the mean time he sent forward Neopolitanus, a centurion, to prepare for his approach. At Jamnia, Neopolitanus met with Agrippa, then on his return from Egypt, and communicated to him the object of his mission. Before they left Jamnia, a deputation of the priesthood and heads of the people appeared, to congratulate Agrippa on his return. Agrippa artfully dissembled his compassion, and even affected to reprove the turbulent conduct of his countrymen. About seven or eight miles from Jerusalem, Neopolitanus and Agrippa were met by a more mournful procession. The people were preceded by the wives of those who had been slain. The women, with wild shrieks and outcries, called on Agrippa for protection; and recounted to Neopolitanus all the miseries they had undergone from the cruelty of Florus. On the entrance of the king and the Roman into the city, they were led to the ruined market-place, and shown the shops that had been plundered, and the desolate houses where the inhabitants had been massacred. Neopolitanus having passed through the whole city, and found it in profound peace, went up to the Temple, paid his adorations there in the court of the Gentiles, exhorted the people to maintain their loyal demeanour, and returned to Cestius.

Agrippa, on his part, declined to countenance an embassy which they proposed to send to Nero. He assembled the whole multitude before the Xystus, and taking his seat in a lofty part of the Palace, with Berenice by his side, commenced a long harangue. He enlarged on the prospect of a milder government than that which had recently afflicted them, when the real state of the province should reach the ears of the Emperor. He urged that their hopes of independence were vain: if they could not resist part of the Roman forces under

Pompey, how could they expect to make any effectual
struggle when the Romans wielded the power of the
whole universe? He adduced the example of all other
nations, Greeks, Germans, Gauls, Africans, Asiatics,
who were held in submission by a few Roman troops:
finally, he dwelt on the horrors of war, and the danger
of destruction which they would bring on the city and
the Holy Place. He ended in tears, and his sister wept
aloud. The people, with one voice, cried out, that they
had taken arms, not against the Romans, but against
Florus. Agrippa replied, that the refusal of tribute,
and the demolition of the galleries which united the
Antonia with the Temple, were overt acts of war against
Rome. He exhorted them forthwith to discharge their
tribute, and repair the buildings. The people obeyed.
The king and Berenice joined eagerly in urging forward the reconstruction of the porticoes. Chief persons were sent out to collect the arrears of tribute,
and forty talents were speedily brought in. The war
seemed at an end; and Agrippa might entertain the
lofty satisfaction of having by his influence averted
inevitable ruin from his country, profanation and sacrilege from the Temple of his God. The cornfields and
vineyards of Judæa might yet escape the trampling
havoc of armed squadrons; the city at its festivals receive its gay and cheerful inhabitants; the Temple
resound with the uninterrupted music and psalmody of
the whole united nation. Vain hope! the fire was only
smothered, not extinct. In an evil moment, Agrippa
attempted to persuade the people to render the usual
allegiance to Florus, until the Emperor should send
another governor in his place. At the sound of that
name, all influence and authority fell, as it were by
magic, from the person of Agrippa. The populace rose,

began to assail him, first with insulting language, afterwards with stones; they even ordered him to leave the city. Despairing, at the same time, of being of any farther use, and indignant at this treatment, Agrippa, having sent certain of the leaders to Florus, in order that he might nominate some of them to collect the tribute, retreated to his own kingdom, and left the ungrateful city to its fate.

Still the more prudent of the higher orders entertained hopes of quelling the tumult, and averting the storm. But every day the breach became more inevitable. The important fortress named Masada stood on the brow of a hill, at no great distance from the Dead Sea, near the fertile spot called the gardens of Engeddi. It was a place of great strength, originally built by Jonathan the Maccabean, and fortified at great expense by Herod. Some of the bolder and more zealous of the war party contrived to obtain entrance into this post, put the Roman garrison to the sword, and openly unfolded the banner of revolt. In the city a still more decisive measure was taken. It had been the custom to receive the gifts and sacrifices of foreign potentates in the Temple; and since the time of Julius Cæsar, according to the policy of Rome, offerings had been regularly made, in the name of the Emperor, to the national God of the Hebrews. Eleazar, the son of Ananias, the chief priest, who then commanded the guard in the Temple, had the ambition of becoming the head of the war faction. He persuaded the lower orders of the officiating priests to reject the Imperial offerings, and to make a regulation that from that time no foreigner should be allowed to sacrifice in the Temple. This was a direct renunciation of allegiance. The Roman party, or rather that party which was anxious to preserve

peace, made a strong but unavailing effort. The chief
priests, joined by the heads of the Pharisees, who as yet
had maintained great influence over the populace, met
in frequent council. They agreed to assemble the people
in the quadrangle of the Temple, which was before the
great brazen gate which looked to the east: this was
called also the Gate of Nicanor.�q They addressed them in
strong language, representing the honour and wealth
that the Temple had long obtained by the splendid donations of foreigners. They urged that this act amounted
to an open declaration of war; that it was not merely
inhospitable, but impious, to preclude strangers from
offering victims, and kneeling in worship before God;
that they would consider such a decree an act of
inhumanity against an individual; how much greater
then must it be against the Emperor and the whole Roman people! Above all, the Jews must take heed lest,
by prohibiting others to sacrifice, they bring upon themselves the same prohibition; and thus, having as it
were outlawed the rest of the world, be themselves condemned to a more fatal outlawry. They then brought
forward those who were thought best acquainted with
the precedents and customs of the Temple worship.
The learned in the law unanimously declared that it was
the ancient and immemorial usage to receive the offerings
of strangers. The violent faction paid not the least

---

q πρὸ τῆς χαλκῆς πύλης . . . .
ἥτις ἦν τοῦ ἔνδον ἱεροῦ τετραμμένη
πρὸς ἀνατόλην ἡλίου. B. J., ii. 17. 3.

Some of the later Jewish writers
make much of this assembly. Their
great object is to show that during all
this period, including the crucifixion
of Christ and the persecution of his
followers, there was no legitimate

Sanhedrin, no representative body,
whose acts could fairly be held as
national. I am not convinced by their
arguments. They add that throughout
there was a struggle between the two
great schools of Jewish teaching, the
milder and more yielding school of Hillel,
the sterner and bolder school of Schammai.

attention to argument or remonstrance; the lower order
of priests openly refused to officiate.   The pacific party
made one effort more.   They sent one deputation,
headed by Simon, son of Ananias, to Florus; another to
Agrippa, headed by his relatives, Saul, Antipas, and
Costobar, entreating them to march instantly on Jerusalem, or all would be lost.   These were glad tidings to
Florus, who saw, in quiet and ferocious delight, the progress of the mutiny.   He did not condescend to reply.
Agrippa, still anxious to preserve the city and Temple,
sent immediately 3000 horse from Auranitis, Batanea,
and Trachonitis, commanded by Darius and Philip the
son of Jacimus.

On the arrival of these troops, the chiefs of the people
made themselves masters of the upper city.   The insurgents, under Eleazar, who now appeared openly at the
head of the war faction, occupied Acra and the Temple.
The two parties began to assail each other with missiles
and slings.   Bands occasionally met and fought hand to
hand.   The royal troops had the advantage in discipline,
the insurgents in courage.   The Temple was the great
object of the struggle.   For seven days affairs remained
in this state, neither party obtaining any positive advantage.   The following day was the festival of wood-carry-
ing, in which it was the custom for every individual
among the Jews to contribute a certain supply of wood
for the fire of the altar, which was never allowed to go
out.   The insurgents refused to admit the more distinguished of the opposite party; while they themselves
received a great accession of strength.   With the meaner
people who were permitted to enter the Temple, stole in
a great number of the Zealots, called the Assassins.
These desperadoes infused new daring as well as
strength.   They made a vigorous attack on the upper

city, the royal troops gave way; the victorious insurgents set fire to the house of Ananias, the chief priest, to the palaces of Agrippa and Berenice, and to the public archives, in which the bonds of the debtors were registered. In this proceeding all the debtors eagerly took their side, and assisted in cancelling their debts by destroying the records. This measure was as politic as it was daring; it annihilated at one blow the influence of the wealthy, who being generally their creditors, had before this the poorer people entirely in their power. Some of the priests and heads of the people concealed themselves in the sewers; others, for the time more fortunate, secured the upper towers of the Palace, and closed the gates. Among the latter were Ananias and his brother, Hezekiah, and those who were obnoxious, as having been deputed to Agrippa. Flushed with their victory, the insurgents retired to rest.

The next day they attempted a much more daring enterprise. A feeble garrison still held the important fortress, the Antonia, which, if better manned, might long have resisted the attacks of undisciplined soldiers. In two days the insurgents carried this citadel, put the garrison to the sword, and burnt the keep. They then turned against the Palace, where the miserable remains of the royal party had taken refuge. They divided themselves into four troops, and made a simultaneous attempt to scale the walls. The few defenders, distracted by these separate attacks, dared not venture on a sally, but contented themselves with striking down the assailants as they climbed singly up the battlements. Many of the insurgents fell. Night and day the conflict lasted; the besiegers expecting that the royal troops would speedily be reduced by famine—the besieged, that their tumultuary assailants would grow weary of the attack.

In the mean time a new leader arose, who had hereditary claims on the ardent attachment of the Zealots. Judas the Galilean had been the first who had openly declared the impiety of owning any king but God, and had denounced the payment of tribute to Cæsar, and all acknowledgment of foreign authority, as treason against the principles of the Mosaic constitution. These doctrines, after having long fermented in secret, and only betrayed themselves in local tumults or temporary insurrections, were now espoused, as it were, by the whole nation. Judas himself, not long after his outset on his career, and his two elder sons, during the government of Tiberius Alexander, had fallen martyrs to their opinions. All eyes were now turned on Manahem,[r] a younger son, who they hoped would maintain the lofty principles of his father with better success. Manahem suddenly appeared in the conquered fortress of Masada, plundered the armoury of Herod, and, girt with a resolute and confident band, approached Jerusalem. The gates flew open, and he entered the city in royal pomp; he was admitted at once as the captain of their forces, and gave orders to press the siege of the palace. The palace still bravely held out; the assailants had no battering engines; and, when they attempted to mine the walls, they were beaten down by stones and javelins from above. They began, therefore, a mine at a considerable distance, and when they got under one of the towers, they carried in a great quantity of wood, and set it on fire. The flames caught the timbers of the foundations, and the tower fell with a tremendous crash.

---

[r] Josephus calls him ὁ σοφιστής.

The insurgents were already rushing to the assault,
when they found themselves checked by a second wall,
which the besieged had built within. During this consternation of the assailants, the garrison sent to demand
terms. The insurgents readily granted safe passage to
the troops of Agrippa and to the Jews, who marched
out, leaving the few Roman soldiers in the most desperate condition, without a hope of cutting their way
through the countless multitudes of their assailants, and,
even if they should submit to the disgrace of surrendering on conditions, almost certain that those conditions
would not be kept. They retreated to the three strong
towers which Herod had built, and called Hippicos,
Phasaelis, and Mariamne. Manahem and his followers
broke into the palace, slew the few who had not made
good their retreat, plundered the baggage, and set fire
to their encampment.

The following morning Ananias was discovered, with
his brother, Hezekiah, in an aqueduct leading to the
palace: they were put to death without remorse. The
towers were surrounded, so as to prevent any chance of
escape. Manahem grew intoxicated with success; he
already assumed all the state of a king, and maintained
his authority with the most unsparing bloodshed. The
death of Ananias was an unpopular measure; yet probably this, as well as other sanguinary acts, might have
been pardoned. But Eleazar did not patiently endure
that the supreme authority, for which he had so subtly
plotted and so resolutely dared, should thus be wrested
at once from his hands. His partisans began to murmur, that they had only changed a Roman tyrant for
one home-born: that Manahem, though he had no
claim or title to this superiority, had insolently gone up
to worship in the Temple, in royal attire, and surrounded

by his guards. The populace rose on the side of Eleazar, and began to stone the adherents of Manahem. His followers fled. Many were slain outright, many in places of concealment. A few with Eleazar, the son of Jair, a relation of Manahem, made good their retreat to Masada. Manahem himself was taken, having fled to a part of the city called Ophlas; he was dragged forth, and put to death with great cruelty. Many of his partisans, one Absalon in particular, shared his fate. Thus fell Manahem, who, if he had united discretion with his courage, might have given the insurgents what they felt the want of during the whole war—an acknowledged leader, who might have concentred the resources and consolidated the strength of the revolt.

Many of the populace had taken part against Manahem, in hopes that by his death the tumult might be suppressed; but this was not the intention of Eleazar and his party. They pressed vigorously the siege of the towers. At length Metilius, the Roman commander, found himself constrained to demand terms. The garrison offered to surrender on condition that their lives were spared; their arms and every thing else were to be at the mercy of the conquerors. The treaty was accepted, and solemnly ratified. Gorion, son of Nicomedes—Ananias, son of Sadoc—and Judas, son of Jonathan, on the part of the insurgents—swore to the execution of the conditions. Metilius led out his soldiers. While they retained their arms, no movement was made; directly they had piled their swords and bucklers, the followers of Eleazar fell upon them and slew them, unresisting, and wildly appealing to the faith of the treaty. All fell, except Metilius, who had the un-Roman baseness (the word may be excused) to supplicate for mercy, and even agreed to submit to circum·

cision. After this treacherous and horrid deed, the last
faint hope of accommodation was quenched, as it were,
in blood. The more moderate foresaw the inevitable
ruin; they did not conceal their profound sorrow; the
whole city, instead of resounding with triumph, was
silent, dejected, and melancholy. It was an aggravation of the general terror and depression, that this atrocious massacre was perpetrated on a Sabbath!

On that very day and hour, by a coincidence which
Josephus considered providential,[*] a dreadful retribution
for the crimes of their countrymen was, as it were, pre-
exacted from the Jews of Cæsarea. The Greeks, now
tolerably certain that to satiate their own animosity
would be to please rather than offend the Romans, or,
perhaps, under secret instructions from Florus, suddenly rose, and massacred the Jews almost to a man—
in one hour, 20,000, an incredible number! were said
to be killed. Not a Jew appeared in Cæsarea. The
few who fled were seized by Florus, and sent to the
galleys.

By this act the whole nation was driven to madness.
Committed by the enormities of their brethren in Jerusalem—thus apparently proscribed every where else for
slaughter—they determined, if mankind thus declared
war upon them, to wage unrelenting war upon mankind.
They rose, surprised, and laid waste all around the cities
of Syria, around Philadelphia, Sebonitis, Gerasa, Pella
(where probably as yet the Christians had not taken
refuge), and Scythopolis. They made a sudden descent
upon Gadara, Hippo, and Gaulonitis; burnt and destroyed many places, and advanced boldly against
Cedasa, a Tyrian town, and the important places of

---

[*] ὥσπερ ἐκ δαιμονίου προνοίας. B. J. ii. 18. 1.

Ptolemais and Gaba, and even against Cæsarea itself.
Sebaste and Ascalon offered no resistance—at least to
the inroad on their territory; Anthedon and Gaza they
razed to the ground. The hamlets around these cities
were pillaged, with immense slaughter.

The Syrians took the alarm; and either for security,
or out of old animosity, committed dreadful havoc on
the Jewish inhabitants of their towns. Every city was,
as it were, divided into two hostile camps. The great
object was to anticipate the work of carnage. The days
were passed in mutual slaughter, the nights in mutual
dread. All agreed that the Jews were to be put to the
sword without mercy—but how to treat the numerous
proselytes to Judaism? Should they respect their
Syrian blood, or punish their conformity to the Jewish
faith? The fatal wealth of the Jews even then, as in
after ages, was at once their pride and their ruin. Many
were put to death from the basest motives of plunder;
and he who could display the greatest heap of Jewish
spoil was considered a hero. The streets were strewn
with unburied bodies—aged men and infants—women
with the last covering of modesty torn off; the whole
province was bewailing the present calamities, and
trembling with foreboding apprehensions of still worse.

So far the Jews had confined their attacks to foreign
troops or settlers; but making an inroad into the domain of Scythopolis, they met with unexpected resistance from the Jewish inhabitants, who had taken arms
with those of Syrian race, and united with them in
defence of their common territory. But the Scythopolitans mistrusted their fidelity, and, dreading lest they
should make common cause with the assailants during
the attack, desired them to retire with their families
into an adjacent grove. Suspecting no danger, the

Jews at once complied, and for two days they remained in quiet, encamped under the trees. The third night the perfidious Scythopolitans attacked them unawares, put them all to the sword, and seized all their property. Thirteen thousand perished. This barbarous act clearly proved to all the Jews, that no course remained but to unite hand and heart with their revolted countrymen. A particular incident which occurred during this massacre was well suited to spread from mouth to mouth, as a tale which might excite the revengeful spirit of the most lukewarm, and drive the most cautious to insurrection, as his last hope. There was a certain Simon, the son of Saul, a Jew of distinction in Scythopolis, who, during the Jewish attack upon the city, had fought against his countrymen with the most consummate bravery. He had slain many, and broken squadrons by his single strength. On that fatal night when the Scythopolitans surrounded their Jewish brethren, he saw that all resistance to such numbers was vain. He cried aloud—"Men of Scythopolis, I acknowledge the justice of the penalty I am about to pay for having wielded arms against my countrymen, and put my trust in you. The blood of my own brethren calls for vengeance. It shall be satisfied; but no enemy, like you, shall boast of my death, or insult my fall." He then with wild and glaring eyes looked round on his family. He had a wife, children, and aged parents. He first seized his father by the hoary hair, and pierced him with his sword; his mother next willingly bared her bosom to the blow. Then fell his wife and children, who crowded round him, eager to die by his hand rather than by that of the enemy. Last of all, he mounted upon their bodies, so as to make himself as conspicuous as possible, and drove his sword into his own entrails.

The rest of the Grecian cities followed the example
of Scythopolis.   In Ascalon 2500 were put to the
sword, in Ptolemais 2000, and as many thrown into
prison.   In Tyre many were killed; in Hippo and
Gadara they put to death the most dangerous, and
threw the rest whom they suspected into prison.   Of
the Syrian cities, Antioch, Sidon, and Apamea alone
showed real humanity, and forbade the death, or even
the imprisonment, of their Jewish fellow-citizens.   In
these towns, indeed, the Jews were less numerous, and
therefore less formidable ; yet the exception is not the
less honourable to the inhabitants.   The citizens of
Gerasa not merely abstained from injuring those who
remained in their city, but escorted those who chose to
leave it into the mountains.   The dominions of Agrippa
were not without disturbance.   Agrippa himself had
gone to Antioch to Cestius Gallus, and left the administration of his kingdom to Varus, a relation of Sohemus,
the Tetrarch of the district about Lebanon.   It happened
that Philip, the son of Jacimus, the commander of
Agrippa's troops in Jerusalem, had escaped the massacre committed by the partisans of Manahem.   He was
concealed for four days by some relatives, Babylonian
Jews, then at Jerusalem.   On the fifth, by putting on
false hair, he escaped, and arrived at length at a village
of his own near the fortress of Gamala.   There, while
he was thinking of summoning his friends, he was seized
with a fever, and as he lay ill, he sent letters to the
children of Agrippa and to Berenice, announcing his
escape.   Varus was jealous of the influence of Philip
with Agrippa.   He accused the bearer of forgery, and
declared that Philip had certainly perished at Jerusalem.
A second messenger arrived, and him also Varus made
away with ; for a report had reached him from Cæsarea

that Agrippa had been put to death by the Romans, on account of the revolt of his countrymen, and Varus began to entertain hopes, being of royal blood, that he might secure to himself the vacant kingdom. He intercepted, therefore, all communication from Philip, and, to ingratiate himself with the Cæsareans, he put to death many Jews.[t] He then determined to make an attack on Ecbatana, or Bathura—a town probably in Batanea. With this view he sent twelve Jews of Cæsarea to accuse them of meditating an insurrection against Agrippa, and to demand seventy of the chief citizens to answer the charge. The Cæsarean Jews found the town perfectly quiet, and the seventy citizens were sent with the utmost readiness. Varus, without trial, ordered them all to be put to death, and advanced upon the town. One, however, had escaped, and gave the alarm. The inhabitants immediately seized their arms, leaving their great possessions in flocks and herds, and fled to the fortress of Gamala. Thence they sent to Philip, entreating him to come to their assistance. On his arrival, there was a general outcry that he should put himself at their head, and instantly lead them to battle against Varus and the Greeks of Cæsarea. The more prudent Philip restrained their impetuosity, and by his influence preserved the peace of Gamala, and kept the whole district faithful to the Romans till the commencement of the war. Agrippa sent to supersede Varus; his great connexions rendered it dangerous to inflict a more severe punishment

---

[t] Josephi Vita, ii. This is passed over in the B. J. Instead of it appears a peaceful embassy of seventy of the chief inhabitants of Batanea to demand forces to keep the peace in the district. These Varus surprised and put to death. Also the seizure of the fort Cypros above Jericho, and of Machærus, which the Romans surrendered. B. J. ii. 18. 6.

The Alexandrian Jews were not exempt from the general calamities of the nation: but they are less worthy of compassion, as they seem in a great degree, by their turbulence and rashness, to have brought the persecution upon their own heads. At a public assembly of the Alexandrians, to despatch an embassy to Nero, many of the Jews, whether to maintain a contested right or not, thronged into the amphitheatre with the Greeks. An outcry immediately arose against the intruders, as enemies and spies. They were attacked; some were killed in their flight; others were taken, and dragged along as if to be burnt alive. The whole Jewish population rose, and at first assailed the Greeks with stones. They then surrounded the amphitheatre with lighted torches, and threatened to burn the spectators to a man. They would have executed their purpose, but for the immediate intervention of Tiberius Alexander, the governor—the same who had before governed in Judæa, and who was by birth a Jew—the nephew of Philo. Alexander acted with humane consideration; he sent for the more influential of the Jews, ordered them to put an end to the affray, and warned them against bringing the Roman soldiery upon their heads. The more seditious mocked at his admonitions, and heaped personal abuse upon his name.

Alexander instantly ordered out his troops; besides his two legions, he had 5000 soldiers, recently come from Libya. He gave them leave not merely to kill, but also to pillage and to burn houses. The troops immediately forced the Delta, the quarter in which the Jews lived. The Jews made resistance; but once routed, the slaughter was horrible. The houses were stripped, or set on fire full of inhabitants, who had taken refuge in them; neither age nor sex was spared: the

whole place was like a pool of blood : 50,000 bodies
were heaped up for burial. The few who remained sued
for mercy.   Alexander gave the signal for the cessation
of the carnage ; and such was the influence of the commander and the discipline of the troops, that he was
instantly obeyed by the soldiery.   The more vindictive
animosity of the Alexandrian populace was not so easily
arrested ; they could only be dragged by force from the
dead bodies.[a]

In Palestine one thing only was wanting to plunge the
whole nation headlong into the revolt. They had already
to stimulate them, on one hand, the remembrance of the
galling oppression of their successive governors—the
desperate conviction that they were already committed
by the events in Jerusalem—the horrible proofs that in
every city every man's hand was armed against them,
and every heart steeled against their sufferings : on the
other, the bold and lofty tenets of Judas the Galilean,
in whose sense their older sacred scriptures might be
made to speak without much violence of interpretation
—the universal belief in the immediate coming of the
triumphant Messiah, which was so widely diffused as to be
mentioned by Suetonius and by Tacitus[x] as a great cause
of the war,—all these motives could not but operate in
a most powerful manner.   That which was wanting, was
a bright gleam of success, to break the gloom that
lowered all round the horizon, and animate the timid
and desponding with the hope of possible victory.   This
was given by the imbecility of Cestius Gallus, the prefect of Syria.   Cestius had under his command the 12th
legion, complete in its numbers, about 4200 strong : besides these he had 2000 picked men ; six cohorts of

---

[a] B. J ii. 18. 7.   [x] Tac. Hist. v. 13 ; Suet. Vespas.

foot, about 2500; and four troops of horse, about 1200.
Of allies he had from Antiochus, king of Commagene,[7]
2000 horse and 3000 foot, all archers: from Agrippa as
many horse, but less than 2000 foot; Sohemus followed
with 4000 more, a third of which were horse, the rest
archers. With this army of nearly 10,000 Roman
troops, and 13,000 allies, Cestius advanced to Ptolemais. Many volunteers crowded forth from the Syrian
cities, and Agrippa and Sohemus attended on his march.
His first exploit was against the town of Zebulon, called
Andron, which divided the territory of Ptolemais from
the Jewish province of Upper Galilee. The inhabitants
fled to the mountains. The city, in which was abundance of wealth and provision, was pillaged by the soldiers; and its noble buildings, said to be as handsome
as those of Tyre, Sidon, or Berytus, were burned to the
ground. After having wasted the adjacent district,
Cestius returned to Ptolemais. The Syrians, particularly those of Berytus, lingering behind to plunder, the
Jews rose upon them, and cut off about 2000.

Cestius advanced to Cæsarea: from thence he sent
forward part of his army to Joppa, with orders, if they
could take the city, to garrison it; if the inhabitants
were prepared for resistance, to await the arrival of the
rest of the army. Part marched inland, part by the sea
coast. They found the city open; the inhabitants
neither attempted to fly nor to resist. They put them
all to the sword, and pillaged the town. The number
slain was 8500. With the same savage cruelty the
cavalry wasted Narbatene, a district near Cæsarea; killing, and plundering, and burning on all sides.

---

[7] Antiochus is mentioned with
Agrippa as among the vassals and
allies of Rome. Tac. Ann. xiii. 7.
See also Hist. ii. 81. Suet. Caligula,
16. Dio. lix. 8.

Cestius sent Gallus, the commander of the twelfth legion, into Galilee, with sufficient force to subjugate that province. Sepphoris opened its gates: the other cities followed the example of the capital. The insurgents fled to a mountain opposite to Sepphoris, called Asamon. There, favoured by the ground, they at first made a gallant resistance, and killed 200 of Gallus's men: at length the Romans gaining the upper ground, and surrounding them, they were broken and dispersed: 2000 were slain. Gallus, having subdued the province, returned to Cæsarea.

Cestius advanced to Antipatris, dispersed a small band at the tower of Aphek, and burned their camp. From Antipatris he marched to Lydda, which was deserted, the inhabitants having gone up to Jerusalem for the Feast of Tabernacles. Fifty men, who came forth to meet him, were put to death; the city was burned. He then ascended the hills near Bethhoron, and encamped at Gabao, fifty stadia, rather more than six miles, from Jerusalem. No sooner did the Jews hear that the war was approaching their gates, than they flew to arms; they broke off the festival; they paid no more respect to the Sabbath.[a] It is possible that they called to mind that it was near this very place, in the passes about Bethhoron, in the days of old, the *Lord cast down great stones* on the Canaanites, when, as their histories declared, the sun stayed his course at the command of Joshua. In the same mountain country Judas the Maccabee had discomfited the immense army of Nicanor. Now they poured forth by thousands; they fell upon the Roman van; broke it; and rushing in, began so great a slaughter, that if the horse and some

---

[a] B. J. ii. 19.

light troops had not made a circuit, and charged them
in the rear, the whole army of Cestius might have been
destroyed.   Notwithstanding this advantage, they drew
back; having killed 515, of which 400 were horsemen.
Their own loss was but twenty-two.   Their most distinguished men in this battle were strangers: Monobazus
and Cenedæus, relations of the King of Adiabene;
Niger, of Peræa; and Silas, a Babylonian, who had
quitted the service of Agrippa.   The Jews made good
their retreat; and as the Romans ascended the hill of
Bethhoron, Simon, son of Gioras, a man who will afterwards make an eminent figure in the history, hung on
their rear, and cut off their stragglers and beasts of
burthen, many of which he carried safe to the city.
Cestius remained quiet for three days, the Jews keeping
watch on the hills, waiting for his troops to move.

At this juncture, Agrippa determined to make a last
effort to avert the war.   He sent a deputation to persuade his countrymen to surrender, offering, in the name
of Cestius, an amnesty for all that had passed.   The
leading insurgents dreaded the effect of these proposals
on the people.   They suddenly attacked the deputation;
slew one, named Phœbus, wounded the other, Borcæus,
with sticks and stones; and drove back those who appeared to take any interest in their fate.   Cestius seized
the opportunity of this dissension to advance on Jerusalem: he encamped at Scopos, within seven stadia, not
quite a mile, to the north of the walls.   Three days he
suspended his attack, in hopes of receiving an offer of
surrender: in the mean time his horse scoured the villages around for provision and forage: on the fourth the
Romans advanced to the attack.   The insurgents had not
only to repel the enemy, they had also to watch a formidable party within the walls, whom they suspected of being

but lukewarm in the cause. They were struck with
consternation at the order and discipline of the Roman
army as it came slowly on to the attack. They abandoned the outer walls, and fled into the Temple and the
other fortified places within the city. Cestius passed
through the new suburb of Bezetha, and burned it as he
proceeded: he then advanced against the upper city,
and encamped opposite to the palace. Had he then
rushed at once to the assault, the city would have fallen.
But, as Josephus asserts, with no great probability, the
general, Tyrannius Priscus, and several of the commanders of cavalry, bribed by Florus to prolong the
war, dissuaded him from the attack.[a]

It is more probable that Cestius entertained hopes of
the surrender of the city by means of a powerful party
within the walls; for many of the chief persons, at the
persuasion of Ananus, the son of Jonathan, invited the
Roman to continue the attack, and promised to open
the gates. But the irresolute Cestius, either from anger
or mistrust, delayed and lost time. The conspiracy was
detected by the insurgents; Ananus and his followers
were thrown headlong from the walls: the rest were
assailed with stones, and driven to their houses. The
war faction manned all the towers, and beat down with
missiles all who approached the walls. For five days
the Romans made only uncombined and desultory
attacks: on the following, Cestius, with the flower of
nis army and his archers, made a vigorous assault on
the north side of the Temple. The Jews defended themselves from the cloisters with the most resolute valour;
continually repulsed the enemy; till at length, galled
by the showers of missiles, the Romans recoiled. But

---

[a] B. J. ii. 19. 4.

they retreated to make a more dangerous attack. They formed what was called a testudo: those in the van fixed their shields firmly against the wall; the next rank joined theirs in succession, till the shields, fitting over each other like the shell of a tortoise, formed an iron pent-house over their heads, under which the soldiers began to mine the walls, and attempted to set fire to the gates.

The besieged were in the most dreadful consternation; many endeavoured secretly to make their escape from the devoted city. The peaceful party took courage, and began to muster in considerable force, in order to open the gates, and admit Cestius as their deliverer. A short time, an hour or less, might have made the Romans masters of the city: "but God, I conceive," says the Jewish historian, "on account of our sins, abhorring his own sanctuary, would not permit the war to end thus."[b]

Cestius, ignorant of the state of affairs within the town, both of the despondency of the insurgents and the strength of the Roman party, suddenly called off his troops, and, to the universal surprise, retreated entirely from the city. The insurgents passed at once from the lowest depression to the wildest courage: they sallied from all quarters, and cut off many stragglers, both horse and foot. Cestius passed the night in his former en-campment, at Scopos (the watch-tower). On the follow-ing day he continued to retire. The further he retreated, the more bold became the enemy: they harassed his rear: coming along cross roads, they took his files in flank. The Romans dared not turn to make head; for they thought that countless multitudes were pouring be-hind them; and while the heavily-accoutred legionaries

---

[b] ἀλλ' οἶμαι διὰ τοὺς πονηροὺς ἀπεστραμμένος ὁ Θεὸς ἤδη καὶ τὰ ἅγια, τέλος λαβεῖν ἐπ' ἐκείνης τῆς ἡμέρας ἐκώλυσε τὸν πόλεμον. B. J. ii. 19. 6.

continued their slow and sullen march, the light-armed Jews flew about with the utmost rapidity; assaulting, retreating; now on one side, now on the other; dashing down where they saw an opening, and starting off when they met resistance. The road was strewn with the dead; every one who, for an instant, quitted the ranks, was cut off. Nor did the loss fall only on the common soldiers. Priscus, the captain of the sixth legion; Longinus, a tribune, and Æmilius, a prefect of horse, were slain; till at length, with great loss of men, and still more of baggage and munitions, the army reached its former quarters at Gabao. There, with his usual irresolution, Cestius lost two days in inactivity: the third, when he saw the whole country in arms, and the Jews swarming on all the heights, he determined on retreat.

That he might retire with greater expedition, he commanded the soldiers to throw away every thing that might impede their march. All the mules and beasts of burthen were killed, except those which bore arrows and the military engines; the latter he would have saved for future use, and dreaded lest they should fall into the hands of the enemy. The Romans then entered the fatal pass down to Bethhoron. The Jews, who had preserved some respect for their close and serried ranks while they were in the open plain, no sooner saw them entangled in the defile, than they attacked them on all sides: some hastened to block up the outlet of the pass; some from behind drove them headlong down the ravine: and at the end of the defile, incalculable multitudes showered darts upon them, till the whole squadron seemed clouded over with missiles. The legionaries stood wavering, uncertain how to act. The cavalry were in a still more perilous condition: they could not form in ranks; the steep sheer sides of the mountains were impracticable for their horses. At one moment they found themselves on the verge of frightful precipices, hanging over rugged, and, it seemed, bottomless ravines. Flight and resistance were alike hopeless: they began to utter wild cries of despair, and to groan aloud in the agony of their hearts: the shrill battle-cry of the Jews answered; their savage shouts of exultation and fury rang from rock to rock. The whole Roman army must have fallen, had not night come on, which enabled the greater part to make its way to Bethhoron. The Jews crowned every hill, and blocked up every pass around.

Cestius, despairing of being able openly to force his way, began to think of securing his personal safety by flight. He selected four hundred of his bravest men, distributed them about the defences of the camp, with orders to mount guard; and in the morning to display all their ensigns, that the Jews might suppose the whole army was still stationary. He then retreated in silence thirty stadia, not quite four miles. At the break of day, the Jews discovered that the camp was deserted: enraged at the manœuvre, they rushed to the assault, and slew the four hundred to a man. They then pursued Cestius with the utmost rapidity. The Romans, who had got the start of several hours during the night, hastened their retreat, which bore every appearance of a rout. All the military engines, the catapults, battering-rams used in besieging cities, were abandoned, and fell into the hands of the Jews, who afterwards employed them with dreadful effect against their former masters. The conquerors continued the pursuit as far as Antipatris; and at length, finding that they could not overtake the fugitives, they turned back to secure the engines, strip the dead, and collect their immense booty. With hymns

of victory they re-entered the capital; having suffered
hardly any loss on their own part, and having slain of
the Romans and their allies 5300 foot, and 380 horse.[c]
The Roman arms had not received so disgraceful an
affront, nor suffered so great loss, since the defeat of
Varus in the forests of Germany; and this not by a
fierce and unconquered people among woods and mo-
rasses never before penetrated by civilized man, but in
a province which had long patiently endured the Roman
yoke, and had received for its sovereigns either native
kings or foreign prefects, with the humblest submission
to the Imperial will.

---

[c] Suetonius adds that an eagle was taken. " Judæi, legatum insuper Syriæ consularem suppetias ferentem, captâ aquilâ, fugaverunt." In Vesp. iv.

BOOK XIV.

PREPARATIONS FOR THE WAR.[a]

Vespasian — Josephus — Affairs of Galilee — John of Gischala —
Affairs of Jerusalem — Ananus the Chief Priest — Simon, son of
Gioras — Battles near Ascalon.

JUDÆA was now in open rebellion against Rome. It
was a mad and desperate revolt, for to declare war
against Rome was to defy the whole force of the civil-

---

[a] On the whole of this period Josephus is almost the only trustworthy authority. The traditions in the Talmud may be described as chiefly anecdotes, of the desultory and uncertain nature which belongs to such stories usually related for the description or embellishment of character. The few condensed and pregnant chapters of Tacitus rarely add to or contradict Josephus.

Josephus, comparing himself, of course to his own advantage, with his enemy the rival historian, Justus of Tiberias, adduces testimonies in favour of his own fidelity and accuracy, which to the historian of our times may rather call his impartiality in question. "Why," demands Josephus, "was not the History of Justus published during the life-time of those who were the eyewitnesses and chief actors in these events—Vespasian, Titus, and King Agrippa?" Josephus on the other hand had presented his History both to Vespasian and to Titus, and had freely communicated on the subject with King Agrippa and some of his relatives. The Emperor Titus, it appears, refused to certify to the accuracy of Josephus, and would only give the sanction of his authority to what may be called the published official despatches. ὁ μὲν γὰρ αὐτοκράτωρ Τίτος ὄντως εκ μόνων αὐτῶν ἐβουλήθη τὴν γνῶσιν τοῖς ἀνθρώποις παραδοῦναι τῶν πραξέων, ὥστε χαράξας τῇ ἑαυτοῦ χειρὶ τὰ βιβλία δημοσιεύσεσθαι προσέταξεν. Josephus had, however, sixty-two letters of Agrippa, all bearing witness to his veracity. He subjoins two: in one of these Agrippa writes in modern phrase:—"I have read your work with pleasure. You seem to me to have drawn up your History with greater diligence and accuracy than any other writers. Send me the rest." In the second Agrippa is equally laudatory:—"In general you have no need of further information on events with which you are so fully acquainted; but

P 2

ized world. The insurgents neither had, nor could hope for allies ; the rest of the Roman provinces were in profound peace, and little likely to answer the call or follow the example of a people they despised, in assertion of their independence.[b] In Europe the only unsubdued enemies of the Romans were the wild tribes in the north of Britain, or in the marshes of Germany. In Asia, the only independent kingdom, the Parthian, was not in a state to make a war of aggression. Philo, in his oratorical invective against Caligula, throws out hints of the formidable numbers of his countrymen in Babylonia, and of the multitudes who were scattered throughout almost all the cities in the Eastern dominions of Rome.[c] But the foreign Jews in the Roman dominions, though, as Josephus hints in one place, solicited by ambassadors, either took no interest in the fate of their countrymen, or were too sadly occupied in averting the storm ol public detestation from their own heads, or in bewailing its consequences in the unprovoked carnage of their own friends and families.[d] They were trembling in the

---

when we meet I shall be able to instruct you on some points of which perhaps you are ignorant." Agrippa, Josephus says further, when his History was finished, not out of flattery or dissimulation, bore witness to his truth. Vit. c. 65.

[b] Tacitus no doubt expresses the Roman sentiment of wonder and indignation, that this single nation, insignificant in extent of territory and numbers, should alone dare to resist the Roman supremacy. " Augebat iras, quod soli Judæi non cessissent." Hist. v. i.

[c] Josephus asserts that they expected a general insurrection throughout the empire, and powerful aid from their Trans-Euphratic brethren. He dwells

too in his first chapter on the state of the world, the commotions in Gaul, and the confusion which followed on the death of Nero. But this flourishing preface is belied by his tone throughout the History. See Proemium to the B. J. c. 2.

[d] Immediately on the defeat of Cestius, the inhabitants of Damascus hastened to wreak their vengeance on the Jewish residents. They were obliged to proceed with caution, for fear of their wives, who *were almost all attached to the Jewish religion!* At last they contrived to take them at advantage, in some confined space, and, attacking them unarmed, massacred 10,000. B. J. ii. 20. 2.

agony of personal apprehension, or gathering up for burial the bodies of their murdered countrymen.

The state of the country offered scarcely better grounds for any reasonable hope of permanent resistance. The fortified places were not all in the power of the insurgents; they had no organized or disciplined force; no warlike engines, except those captured from the enemy; no provisions of any kind for a long war. Worse than all, they were divided among themselves. In every city there was an interested, or a timid, or a prudent party, anxious to purchase peace at any cost. They had no acknowledged leader. The representative of the Herodian house, Agrippa, openly espoused the Roman party. The rest were either undistinguished as soldiers, or strangers, and robber chieftains. Their only trust was in their own stubborn patience and daring valour, in the stern fanaticism with which they looked upon themselves as the soldiers of their God, and in the wild hope that Heaven would work some miraculous revolution in their favour.

Yet, however frantic and desperate the insurrection, why should the Jews alone be excluded from that generous sympathy which is always awakened by the history of a people throwing off the galling yoke of oppression, and manfully resisting to the utmost, in assertion of their freedom? Surely if ever people were justified in risking the peace of their country for liberty, the grinding tyranny of the successive Roman Procurators, and the deliberate and systematic cruelties of Florus, were enough to have maddened a less highspirited and intractable race into revolt. It is true that the war was carried on with unexampled atrocity; but on the other hand insurrectionary warfare is not the best school for the humaner virtues; and horrible oppression is apt to awaken the fiercer and more savage, not the loftier and nobler passions of our nature. And it must be borne in mind, that we have the history of the war, only on the authority of some brief passages in the Roman authors, and the narrative of one to whom, notwithstanding our respect for his abilities and virtues, it is impossible not to assign the appellation of renegade. Josephus, writing to conciliate the Romans, both to his own person and to the miserable remnant of his people, must be received with some mistrust. He uniformly calls the more obstinate insurgents, who continued desperately faithful to that cause which he deserted, by the odious name of robbers; but it may be remembered that the Spanish guerrillas, who were called patriots in London, were brigands in Paris. It is true that the resistance of many was the result of the wildest fanaticism. But we must not forget in what religious and historical recollections the Jews had been nurtured. To say nothing of the earlier and miraculous period of their history, what precedents of hope were offered by the more recent legends of the daring and triumphant Maccabees! It is, moreover, true that the Son of Man had prophesied the destruction of Jerusalem, and that the New Testament appears to intimate that the measure of wickedness in the Jewish people having been filled up in the rejection of Christ, they were doomed from that time to inevitable ruin. But we must avoid the perilous notion of confounding the Divine foreknowledge with the necessary causation of events. According to the first principles of the Mosaic constitution, national guilt led to national ruin. But still the motives which actuated many in the fatal struggle that led to the accomplishment of the Divine predictions, may have been noble and generous. It was

the national rejection of Christ, not the resistance to
Rome, which was culpable.   The Jew, though guilty of
refusing to be a Christian, might still be a high-minded
and self-devoted patriot.   Although we lament that the
gentle and pacific virtues of Christianity did not spread
more generally through the lovely and fertile region
of Palestine, yet this is no reason why we should refuse
our admiration to the bravery, or our deepest pity to the
sufferings, of the Jewish people.   Let us not read the
fate of the Holy City in that unchristian temper which
prevailed during the dark ages, when every Jew was considered a personal enemy of Christ, and therefore a legitimate object of hatred and persecution, but rather in the
spirit of Him who, when he looked forward with prophetic foreknowledge to its desolation, nevertheless was
seen "to weep over Jerusalem."

The astonishment of the Romans at the revolt of this
comparatively small province, and at the news of the
total defeat of a Roman prefect at the head of his legionaries, was not unmingled with consternation.   The Emperor Nero was then in Achaia.   The first intelligence
of the affair was brought by Costobar and Saul, two
brothers related to the Herodian family, who, with
Philip, the son of Jacimus, the general of Agrippa, had
made their escape from Jerusalem.[d]   The two former
were despatched, at their own request, to the Emperor
by Cestius, who instructed them to lay the whole blame

---

[d] Is it impossible that this intelligence conveyed to Rome may have
had some connexion with the renewed
persecution of the Christians, in which
St. Paul certainly, and St. Peter, according to those who believe him to
have died at Rome, suffered martyrdom?   The cruel and base-born
Helius, who ruled during that year
in Nero's name in Rome, may have
thought to show his zeal by putting to
death men suspected of some strangely
dangerous views, and guilty at least of
Jewish descent.   The martyrdom of
St. Paul certainly took place this year,
A.D. 66.

of the war on Florus. Nero, according to Josephus, affected to treat the affair lightly. He expressed great contempt for the revolt, but great anger at the misconduct of Cestius; yet he could not help betraying visible marks of disturbance and terror. The importance really attached to the affair may be judged by the selection of the most able and distinguished military commander in the empire. Vespasian had been bred to arms from his youth; he had served with great fame in the German wars; had reduced the unknown island of Britain into a Roman province, and obtained the honours of a triumph for the Emperor Claudius, without his own personal exertion or danger. Nero repressed his resentment against Vespasian, who was in disgrace for not having sufficiently admired the fine voice and style of singing of the theatrical Emperor. He committed the province of Syria to his charge. With his characteristic despatch, Vespasian immediately sent his son, Titus, to Alexandria, to conduct the fifth and tenth legions to Palestine: he himself travelled, with all speed, by land to Syria, and collected all the Roman troops, and forces from the neighbouring tributary kings.[*]

In the mean time the insurgents were not inactive. Some of the more prudent hastened, as Josephus says, to desert the sinking ship. Those who still *Romanized* were brought over, some by persuasion, some by force. They called a general assembly in the Temple, and proceeded to elect their governors and commanders. Their choice fell on Joseph, the son of Gorion, and Ananus, the chief priest, who were invested with unlimited authority in the city. Eleazar, the son of Simon, who had taken so active a part in originating and conducting the first

---

[*] B. J. iii. 1. 1. 2.

insurrection, and in the death of Manahem, was passed over. He was suspected, not without grounds, of aiming at kingly power, for he went about attended by a body-guard of Zealots. But Eleazar, probably as commanding within the Temple, had made himself master of the spoil taken from the Romans, the military chest of Cestius, and a great part of the public treasures. In a short time, the want of money, and his extreme subtlety, won over the multitude, and all the real authority fell into the hands of Eleazar. To the other districts they sent the men whom they could best trust for courage, and fidelity to their cause. To Idumæa, Jesus, son of Saphus, one of the chief priests, and Eleazar, the son of Ananias, also a chief priest. Niger of Peræa, who had hitherto commanded in that district, was directed to receive his orders from them. To Jericho was sent Joseph, son of Simon; to Peræa, Manasseh; to Thamna, John the Essene: for even among these peaceful hermits were found men who would fight for their freedom. The toparchies of Lydda, Joppa, and Emmaus were added to his command. John, the son of Ananias, had the toparchies of Gophni and Acrabatene. Joseph, the son of Mathias, was entrusted with the command of Upper and Lower Galilee, with particular charge of the strong city of Gamala. Almost all, if not all these leaders, were of the more moderate, at least not of the Zealot party.[r]

---

[r] The question which divided the war party among the Jews, the more furious and more moderate, is well stated by Salvador:—" Il s'agissait de savoir d'après quel esprit de conduite on se règlerait à l'avenir. Fallait-il seulement faire à l'étranger une guerre de transaction ou de redressement de tort, comme les hommes prudens et politiques le voulaient, une guerre qui fût dirigée plutôt contre la tyrannie personnelle des procurateurs Romains que contre le nom de César, contre l'Empereur lui-même ? Ou bien, fallait-il se jeter dans une lutte à outrance comme l'entendait la partie a

Galilee was the province on which the storm would
first break, and the confidence of the insurgents in the
ability and zeal of Joseph, the son of Mathias, may be
fairly estimated from their committing this important
frontier to his charge. As long as the passes and hill
fortresses of Galilee were defended, the southern region,
and Jerusalem itself, might have time to organize their
forces, and fortify their strongholds. Joseph, the son
of Mathias, is better known as the celebrated Josephus,
the historian. He was a man of illustrious race, lineally
descended from a priestly family, from the first of the
twenty-four courses—an eminent distinction! By his
mother's side he traced his genealogy up to the Asmonean princes. His father, Mathias, was of upright
character, as well as of noble birth ; he resided in Jerusalem, where the young Joseph grew up with a brother,
named Mathias, with great reputation for early intelligence and memory. At fourteen years old (he is his own
biographer) he was so fond of letters that the chief
priests used to meet at his father's house to put to him difficult questions of the law.[g] At sixteen he determined to
acquaint himself with the three prevailing sects, those
of the Pharisees, Sadducees, and Essenes. For though
he had led·for some time a hardy, diligent, and studious
life, he did not consider himself yet sufficiently acquainted with the character of each sect to decide which
he should follow. Having heard that a certain Essene,
named Banus, was living in the desert the life of a
hermit, making his raiment from the trees, and his

---

plus ardente des zélateurs, dans une
lutte qui imposât pour première loi
d'exciter les colères religieuses et politiques de la nation, de creuser un
abîme infranchissable entre les Juifs et
les Romains ?"   ii. p. 8.

[g] The curious analogy of this incident
with what is related of Jesus (at the
age of twelve) " among the doctors '
cannot but strike every reader.

food from the wild fruits of the earth, practising cold
ablutions at all seasons, and, in short, using every
means of mortification to increase his sanctity ; Josephus, ambitious of emulating the fame of such an example of holy seclusion, joined Banus in his cell.   But
three years of this ascetic life tamed his zealous ambition.   He grew weary of the desert, abandoned his great
example of painful devotion, and returned to the city at
the age of nineteen.   There he joined the sect of the
Pharisees.   In his twenty-sixth year he undertook a
voyage to Rome, in order to make interest in favour of
certain priests who had been sent there, to answer some
unimportant charge, by Felix.   They were friends of
Josephus, and his zeal in their favour was heightened
by hearing that, with religious attachment to the law,
they refused, when in prison, to eat any unclean food,
but lived on figs and nuts.   On his voyage he was ship-
wrecked, like St. Paul, and in great danger.   His ship
foundered in the Adriatic, six hundred of the crew and
passengers were cast into the sea, eighty contrived to
swim, and were taken up by a ship from Cyrene.   They
arrived at Dicæarchia (Puteoli), the usual landing-place ;
and Joseph, making acquaintance with one Aliturus, an
actor, a Jew by birth, and, from his profession, in high
credit with the empress Poppæa, he obtained the release
of the prisoners, as well as valuable presents from
Poppæa, and returned home.   During all this time he
had studied diligently, and made himself master of the
Greek language, which few of his countrymen could
write, still fewer speak with a correct pronunciation.

On his return to Jerusalem, he found affairs in the
utmost confusion ; great preparations were making for
the war, and the insurgents were in high spirits.   He
united himself to the party who were for peace, and

strongly urged the rashness and peril of the war. Apprehensive that these unpopular doctrines had made him an object of suspicion to the more violent, and dreading lest he might be seized and put to death, he retired, after the capture of the Antonia, into the Inner Temple. After the murder of Manahem, he stole forth from thence, and joined himself to a considerable body of the chief priests and leading Pharisees, who pretended to enter into the insurrectionary measures that they might save the lives of those who capitulated in the palace, yet looked with anxious eagerness for the advance of Cestius, who, it was expected, would easily suppress the revolt.[h]

On the disastrous retreat of Cestius, and the barbarous massacre of the Jews in Sepphoris and the Syrian cities, many of the more peaceful party joined heart and hand with the insurgents, others pursued a more temporizing policy, and outwardly uniting in defensive measures, still cherished a secret inclination to submission. To which of these parties Joseph the son of Mathias belonged, it is not quite so easy to decide: without his having acquired some confidence with the war faction, he would scarcely have been entrusted with the command in Galilee; yet he undertook that post with the approbation and at the request of the more moderate.[i] Josephus, with his two coadjutors, Joazar and Judas, hastened to their government.

---

[h] Josephus attributes the war chiefly to these risings and the massacres of their countrymen, which compelled the more peaceful to join in the common cause, as now become simply and therefore unavoidably defensive. νυν δ' αὐτῶν ἐτεμνήσθην, βουλόμενος παραστῆσαι τοῖς ἀναγινώσκουσιν ὅτι ὀυ προδίρεσις ἐγένετο τοῦ πολέμου πρὸς Ῥωμαίους Ἰουδαίοις, ἀλλὰ τὸ πλέον ἀνάγκη. Vit. c. 6.

[i] In the Life creeps out another view of the object for which he was appointed by the prudent party to the

The province of Galilee was divided into two districts, called Upper and Lower Galilee; it contained all the territory which had belonged to the northern tribes of Napthali, Zebulun, Issachar, and half Manasseh, reaching to the district of Ptolemais on the north, and Samaria on the south. The Jordan was the eastern limit. The people were a bold, hardy, and warlike race; considered somewhat barbarous by the inhabitants of the metropolis, and speaking a harsh and guttural dialect of the Syro-Chaldaic language, now the vernacular tongue of Palestine. The country was remarkably rich, abounding in pasture, corn land, and fruit-trees of every description. The population was very great. They lived in cities, which were numerous and large, and in great open villages, the least of which, says Josephus, contained 15,000 inhabitants. In many of these cities there was a mingled population of Syrians and Jews, rarely on an amicable footing, often forming fierce and hostile factions. Sepphoris was the capital, but that rank was disputed by Tiberias on the Sea of Galilee.

The measures of Josephus were prudent and conciliatory, yet by no means wanting in vigour and decision. He remained in sole command. His priestly colleagues, having collected a great quantity of tithes, determined to return home; they delayed for a short time, at the earnest request of Josephus.[k] The object of Josephus was to promote union, and to organize the

---

command in Galilee—to disarm the Zealots, to transfer their arms and power to the *better* orders, and to remain quiet till they saw the course which the Romans would pursue. τείσοντας τοὺς πονηροὺς καταθέσθαι τὰ ὅπλα, καὶ διδάξοντας, ὡς ἐστιν ἄμεινον τοῖς κρατίστοις τοῦ ἔθνους αὐτὰ τηρεῖσθαι. Ἔγνωστο δὲ τούτοις ἀεὶ μὲν ἔχειν τὰ ὅπλα τοὺς τὸ μέλλον ἕτοιμα, περιμένειν δὲ, τί πράξουσιν Ῥωμαῖοι μαθεῖν. c. 7.

[k] Vit. c. 12.

whole country on one regular system.　He endeavoured
to acquire the confidence and attachment of the people.
In order to interest and pledge all ranks to the common
cause, as well as to secure the public peace, he appointed
a sort of Sanhedrin of seventy, and seven judges in each
city; all less important causes were to come before the
latter tribunal; cases of murder before himself and the
Sanhedrin.[l]　Yet he acknowledges that he kept the
seventy about his person as a kind of hostages.[m]　In all
respects he endeavoured to maintain the strictest character for probity and justice, particularly laboured in
those lawless times to protect the chastity of the females
from insult or outrage, refused all presents for the administration of justice, and declined all opportunities of
enriching himself, though he confesses that he secured
a considerable share in the confiscated property of the
Syrian inhabitants in the cities, when they were expelled or massacred by the Jews, which he sent to his
friends at Jerusalem.[n]　As he could not suppress the
robbers, he obliged them, as far as he could, to give up
their profession, and enroll themselves as regular troops.
Having thus provided that the war, if commenced, should
be that of an orderly and united people, not the desultory conflict of insurgents and robbers, he proceeded to
fortify, with the greatest strength and expedition, the
most defensible towns, among many others, Jotapata,
Tarichea, Tiberias, Itabyrium on Mount Tabor, and
certain caves near the lake of Gennesaret.[o]　To the
wealthy inhabitants of Sepphoris, who seemed to enter
zealously into the cause, he granted the privilege of
building their own fortifications, and gave permission to

---

[l] B. J. ii. 20. 5.　　[m] Vit. 15.

[m] Vit. c. 14.　　[o] B. J. ii. 20. 6. 7

John, the son of Levi, afterwards the celebrated John of Gischala, to strengthen that city. The others he superintended in person. He then raised an army of 100,000 men, armed them with weapons obtained from all quarters, and proceeded to introduce the Roman discipline. He appointed centurions and decurions, regularly exercised the whole force in military manœuvres, and thus organized an effective army of 60,000 foot, and, according to the text of Josephus, from which probably a number has fallen, 250 horse. Besides these he had 4500 mercenaries, on whom he placed his chief reliance, and a body guard of 600.

Such were the general results of the administration of Josephus; but all these vigorous and prudent measures were perpetually interrupted and rendered abortive, partly by the internal dissensions of the province, but chiefly by the machinations of his subtle enemy, John of Gischala. While Josephus invariably represents himself as the most upright, incorruptible, and patriotic of men, no colours are too dark for the character of his antagonist. John of Gischala surpassed all men of high rank in craft and deceit, all of every class in wickedness. He was at first a poor adventurer, his poverty stood in the way of his advancement, but by his readiness in falsehood, and by the singular skill with which he glozed over his falsehoods, so as to make all men believe them, he deceived his nearest friends; affecting humanity, yet most sanguinary for the slightest advantage; lofty in his ambition, but stooping to the basest means to obtain his end. He began as a single robber, but gradually collected a powerful and select banditti, for he would only admit men distinguished either for strength, bravery, or warlike skill. His force at length amounted to 4000, and with these he long wasted Galilee. Such was the man who counterworked all the measures of Josephus, and inflamed the dissensions of the province, already too little disposed to lasting union.[p]

For though the cities of Galilee seem generally to have submitted to the administration of Joseph and his coadjutors, so as to permit their walls to be put in a state of defence, yet each had its separate interests and inclinations, and was distracted by violent factions. Sepphoris, though entrusted with building its own walls, and, as Josephus says in one place, hearty in the cause, yet inclined to the Roman party: the inhabitants had sworn fealty, and given hostages from the chief families of the city to Cestius; these were still at Cæsarea. On the arrival of Josephus in his province, he found the territory of Sepphoris threatened with an attack by the rest of the Galileans on account of their dealings with the Romans. This danger was averted by Josephus, and the Sepphorites united, as was before said, in the common cause. Tiberias was distracted by three factions. This city belonged to Agrippa, and one faction, consisting of the more opulent and respectable burghers, headed by Julius Capellus, was desirous of preserving their allegiance to the king. A second of the lowest class, headed by Jesus, son of Saphia, was clamorous for war. A third was headed by Justus, who afterwards wrote a History of the war. Justus, according to his rival Josephus, only regarded his own interests. He had endeavoured to excite a feud between Tiberias and Sepphoris, asserting that on account of the manifest defection of the latter to the Roman party, Tiberias might justly be considered the capital of Galilee.[q] He had meditated

---

[p] Josephus acknowledges that John had a singular power of attaching men to his person. B. J. iv. 7. 1.

[q] Vit. c. 63.

an attack on the Sepphorite district, but as yet had only carried his plundering bands into the lands of Gadara and Hippos. Josephus, after settling affairs at Sepphoris, went to Bethmäus, within half a mile of Tiberias. He sent for the senate, who came readily to parley with him; he opened his commission from the Sanhedrin at Jerusalem, and demanded the demolition of a palace built by Herod the Tetrarch, and adorned with "graven images" of living creatures. The party of Agrippa opposed this measure; but the war faction, headed by Jesus son of Saphia, were ready for any work of destruction. Besides, they were not a little tempted by the hope of plunder, for the roof of the palace was gilded. They proceeded to plunder the furniture, and then to burn the palace to the ground. Flushed with their success, they rose on the Syrians, massacred all they could find, and at the same time seized the opportunity of revenging themselves on all their fellow-citizens who had been their enemies before the war.

Josephus seems to have been anxious to remain in amity with Agrippa. He assumed great indignation at the plunder of the palace, of which he had authorized the demolition, gathered up the wrecks of the furniture, consisting of candlesticks of Corinthian brass, royal tables, and uncoined silver, and committed them to the custody of Capellus, the head of Agrippa's party. Josephus then proceeded to Gischala. At the commencement of the insurrection, John had rather inclined to the Roman faction. Upon this the inhabitants of Gadara, Gebara, Sogana, and other towns, had assaulted and burnt Gischala. John, however, had rallied his forces, recovered the town, and fortified it more strongly than before. As yet, John and Josephus were on good terms. Josephus admired the activity of John, and

John was anxious to obtain every possible advantage
from the governor of the province. He first proposed
to Josephus that he might be permitted to carry off
large quantities of corn stored up by the Romans in
Upper Galilee; the sale of this, he stated, would enable
him to complete his fortifications. Josephus answered,
that he should keep that corn either for the Romans,
the owners, (a suspicious answer!) or for the use of the
province entrusted to him by the Sanhedrin of Jerusalem.[r] John then demanded and obtained a monopoly
of oil sold in Syria. For the Jews in the Syrian towns
would not use the unclean oil prepared by the heathen,
and were obliged to obtain it from their own country.
John drove a thriving trade; for four Attic drachms he
bought four measures of oil, which he sold again at the
same sum for half a measure. This money he employed
in undermining the power of Josephus, and industriously
propagated reports, which accused him of intending to
betray the province to the Romans. Whether or not
the suspicions of John had any substantial grounds,
strong circumstances combined to throw a shade on the
popularity of Josephus. Certain youths of a village
called Dabarittæ, in the great plain, waylaid and plundered Ptolemy, the agent of king Agrippa. With
their spoils, consisting of embroidered robes, silver vessels, and six hundred pieces of gold, they went to Josephus, then at Tarichea.[s] Josephus rebuked them for
the robbery, and committed the property to the custody

---

[r] Vit. 13. At Gischala he allowed
his colleagues, who had been bribed by
John, as he says, to take that side, to
retire to Jerusalem. Vit. 14.

[s] B. J. ii. 21. 3. Compare Vit. c.
26. In the Life it is the wife of
Ptolemy, four mule loads of rich
stuffs and silver vessels, 500 pieces of
gold. Ptolemy was of the same tribe
with himself (Vit. 26). He told the
robbers that he reserved the plunder
to rebuild the walls of Jerusalem.

of one of the chief citizens of Tarichea, to be restored to
the owners.   The robbers, deprived of their booty,
raised loud outcries against the governor, whom they
accused of being in a treasonable league with the king.
One hundred thousand armed men assembled (Josephus
is prone to large numbers) and thronged the circus of
Tarichea ; some cried out to depose, some to burn him.
With this intent, they surrounded his house ; all his
friends, except four, fled : Josephus suddenly awoke
from sleep ; he was neither confounded by the noise of
his assailants, nor by the desertion of his friends.   He
rent his robes, poured ashes on his head ; with his hands
behind him, and his sword suspended around his neck,
he went out to face the tumult.   The Taricheans were
moved with compassion : the ruder countrymen continued their clamour, ordered him to bring forth the
plunder, and confess his treasons.   Josephus answered
with an effrontery and readiness of falsehood which
might have done credit to his mendacious rival, John of
Gischala.   "Men of Tarichea, ye are quite in error if
ye suppose that I retain these treasures with any design
of restoring them to king Agrippa.   The fact is, that
seeing the walls of your town in a ruinous and dismantled state, I have kept them to be spent in fortifying
your loyal city."   This bold address threw the Taricheans, to the number of 40,000, on his side.   The
strangers, particularly those of Tiberias, continued the
tumult for some time, but at length sullenly withdrew,
with the exception of 2000 (600) of the most desperate.
These men, when Josephus retired again to rest, surrounded his house, and threatened to break down the
doors.   Josephus had recourse to a stratagem still more
daring.   He mounted the roof of the house, and making
a sign that he wished to address them, he began with

saying that from the height he could not distinguish their demands, but if they would depute some of their leaders, he was ready to treat with them. No sooner were those few admitted, than he ordered them to be dragged into the inner part of the house, and scourged till their bowels were laid open. The mob began to grow impatient, when the doors were opened, and their leaders were turned out among them in this bloody and mangled state. The mob, supposing that he would not have ventured on such a step without a great force concealed, dispersed in consternation.[t] The secret enemy of Josephus, John of Gischala, had prompted this outrage; but as there was no open breach between them, John, pretending to be ill, sent to demand permission to visit Tiberias, for the benefit of the warm baths in that city.[n] There, partly by persuasion, partly by bribes, he induced the inhabitants to renounce their allegiance to the governor. Silas, who commanded in the city under Josephus, sent immediate intelligence of the state of affairs. Josephus travelled night and day, and suddenly appeared in Tiberias. John, pretending that he was

---

[t] This transaction, as indeed the whole narrative of his administration in Galilee, is related with such extraordinary variations in the Life of Josephus, and in the History of the Jewish War, as to leave a very unfavourable impression, if not of the writer's veracity, at least (Vit. 30; B. J. ii. 21. 5) of his accuracy. It is impossible to keep the same order of events, and in this affair the War gives the number of armed men at 2000, the Life at 600. In the former, those admitted into the house are called the more distinguished and the rulers, and are sent in to treat on terms of agreement; in the other, some of the men are sent in to receive the money, which he was accused of appropriating. In the one, all those admitted are scourged; in the other, one ringleader, who has his hand cut off and hung about his neck.

[n] e. g. in the Vit. The feigned sickness of John, and the affair at Tiberias, precede the robbery committed by the Dabarittæ and the scene at Tarichea; in the B. J. the plot of John and the peril of Tiberias is the δευτέρα ἐπιβουλή. ii. 21. 6.

confined to his bed, excused himself from paying his respects to the governor.   Josephus assembled the people of Tiberias in the circus.   He had begun to address them, when he was suddenly interrupted by a loud outcry from the spectators; turning round, he saw a band of armed men, with their swords drawn, who were placed by John to assassinate him; he leaped from his rostrum, which was about six feet high, rushed to the beach, seized a boat, and, with two of his followers, pushed out into the lake and escaped.

His soldiers, in the mean time, attacked the band of John; but Josephus, apprehensive of a civil war, sent orders to his troops to abstain from bloodshed, and resisted all the urgent entreaties of his other Galilean friends, who were eager to make an example of the treacherous city.   John fled to Gischala, where Josephus did not think it prudent to attack him, but contented himself with expelling those who espoused John's party from every city in Galilee.

During these events Sepphoris began again to waver. The inhabitants sent to Jesus, who commanded a noted troop of banditti, 800 strong, on the borders of Ptolemais, offering him a large sum to make war on Josephus.   Jesus thought it more prudent to earn his wages by stratagem than by open force.   He sent to request an interview with Josephus, that he might salute him, and then instantly began his march with his whole troop.   One of his followers, however, deserted, and put Josephus on his guard.   Thus forewarned, Josephus proceeded to the interview, having occupied all the roads with his own forces, and gave orders that Jesus alone, and his followers, should be admitted within the gates, which were to be closed immediately on their entrance. Jesus entered boldly, but Josephus instantly ordered him to throw down his arms, or he was a dead man. Trembling, Jesus obeyed. Josephus took him apart, informed him that he was aware of his treacherous designs but offered him pardon if he would repent and swear to be faithful to him in future. Jesus complied, and Josephus having severely threatened the Sepphorites, departed to quell new disturbances. On his way he encountered two officers of the king, from Trachonitis, who wished to join him with some horse; these men the Jews would have forced to submit to circumcision. Josephus interfered, and asserted the right of every man to worship God according to his conscience.

Gamala now demanded the presence of the indefatigable governor. After the departure of Philip, Agrippa's general, a certain Joseph, son of a female physician, had persuaded the people to revolt. They forced some to enter into their views, others they put to death. They fortified the city, with the approbation of Josephus; and all Gaulonitis, a district which skirted Upper Galilee, followed their example. Gamala was now threatened by Æquicolus Modius; at the same time, Neapolitanus, with some Roman troops, pushed towards Tiberias, and Æbutius, a decurion, advanced against Josephus, who lay at Simonias. Æbutius endeavoured to draw him down to the plain, where his cavalry would have given him an advantage. Josephus continued on the hills, and Æbutius withdrew with some loss. Josephus then, in his turn, made an attack on some magazines of corn, which he carried off, quietly loading his camels and asses, in the sight of Æbutius, who was fairly out-generalled. Æquicolus Modius failed in his attempt on Gamala.

John of Gischala, all this time, remained quiet in his citadel, but it was only because he was laying a train from a greater distance, which was to explode under the

feet of his enemy.[x] He sent his brother Simon, and
Jonathan, son of Sisenna, to Simon, son of Gamaliel, at
Jerusalem, to persuade the people that Josephus was
forming a dangerous power in Galilee, and to demand
his recall. Simon was a man of great character and
weight, but ill-disposed to Josephus, and closely allied
with John. By bribes they brought Ananus, the chief
priest, who, at first, espoused the cause of Josephus, and
Jesus, the son of Gamala, into their party.[y] They determined to act with caution, lest Josephus should advance
with his numerous and devoted army against Jerusalem.
Jonathan and Ananias, two learned and influential Pharisees, and Joazar and Simon, priests, were sent, gradually to alienate the Galileans from their attachment
to Josephus, and then, either to put him to death, or
bring him alive to Jerusalem. They had troops with
them ; John of Gischala received orders to render them
every support; and Sepphoris, Gabara, and Tiberias
were to hold their troops in readiness at the command of
John. Josephus got intelligence of the plot through
his father, and also, as he relates, through a remarkable
dream, which warned him that he should remain in
Galilee, and fight against the Romans. In compliance
with the earnest supplications of all the Galileans, who
entreated him not to abandon them, he gave up his intention of submitting to the mandate and withdrawing
to Jerusalem. With 8000 foot and 80 horse, he posted

---

[x] Vit. 38.

[y] This is utterly inconsistent with
the high character, given by Josephus
himself, of Ananus. Jost uses strong
language : — " Wenn aber der Ge-
schichtschreiber Josephus ihm beschul-
digt, ohne Mitwissen des Kriegesaus-
schusses Boten nach Galiläa gesendet
zu haben, um ihn (Josephus) nach
Jerusalem zu locken, oder allenfalls zu
tödten.—So ist das eine der dreisten
Unwahrheiten, ersonnen· aus persön-
licher Feindschaft, die er selbst offen
bekennt." p. 443.

himself at Chabolo, on the frontier of Ptolemais, under
the pretext of making head against Placidus, who had
begun to waste Galilee. Four cities, Sepphoris, Gamala,
Gischala, and Tiberias, acknowledged the authority of
the deputation from Jerusalem. The deputies, who had
travelled secretly and with expedition, in order to come
on Josephus unawares, finding him on his guard, still
attempted to proceed by craft rather than by force.
They sent a friendly letter informing him that they were
come to punish the subtle proceedings of his enemy
John, and to force him to obedience. Josephus kept the
letter unopened to the evening, when he had a great
banquet of his friends, to which he invited the messenger. He then secretly made himself master of its
contents, and sealed it up again. He ordered the messenger 20 drachms, as a reward for having brought welcome intelligence. The messenger was delighted. He
then plied him with wine, and offered him a drachm
with every cup, till the man betrayed the whole plot.
Josephus wrote back a friendly answer, excusing himself
from attendance, on account of the necessity of watching
Placidus. The deputies, who passed from place to place
and found almost every town in favour of Josephus and
enraged against John,[1] sent a more peremptory message,
requiring his attendance at Gabara, to make good his
charge against John of Gischala. Josephus expressed
his readiness to wait upon them, but not at Gabara or
Gischala, where he apprehended treachery.[2] They determined to send messengers throughout Galilee to excite
the malcontents. Josephus waylaid the roads from
Gabara, seized the messengers, and made himself master

---

[1] He names Japha, the largest village (κώμη) in Galilee; Sepphoris,
which Romanised, and was indifferent as
to Josephus; Asochis, and others. c. 45.

[2] ἡ μὲν γὰρ πατρίς ἐστιν Ἰωάννου,
ἡ δὲ σύμμαχος καὶ φίλη.   c. 45.

of all the letters. Upon this he surrounded Gabara with his own Galileans, and boldly entered the town. He first went to repose at an inn; his enemies seized the opportunity to raise the people against him, but failed. Josephus soon after made his appearance in the assembly.[b] The Galileans surrounded the hall with loud acclamations. John and his friends endeavoured in vain to make their escape. Josephus publicly read the letters which he had intercepted, the deputies were confounded, the people unanimous in their applause. The mob would willingly have fallen on the whole assembly, who were saved only by the merciful intervention of Josephus. The governor then took horse and rode away to Sogana. From thence he despatched an embassy of 100 men of distinction, escorted by an armed guard of 500, to Jerusalem.

The discomfited deputies retired to Tiberias, John to Gischala. At Tiberias they expected the city to declare in their favour, but Josephus suddenly made his appearance there. They received him with hypocritical courtesy, but requested him to withdraw, on account of the approaching Sabbath, lest there should be a disturbance. He retired to Tarichea; new scenes of trickery followed; the deputies, with Jesus and Justus, the turbulent leaders of Tiberias, endeavoured to raise the town. Josephus again appeared with his soldiers; they got rid of him by a false alarm of Roman troops seen in the neighbourhood. Josephus counteracted this by another plot. They appointed a general fast, during which no one was to appear armed at the Proseuchæ.

---

[b] They called him to account about twenty pieces of gold taken from the public treasury. This Josephus had expended on his counter deputation to Jerusalem. They became ashamed of this pitiful charge, and accused Josephus of setting up a tyranny. c. 60.

Josephus and his friends concealed their daggers and breastplates under their robes, and when the enemy expected to find them defenceless, they brandished their weapons. The deputation of Josephus, in the meantime, returned from Jerusalem with a favourable answer, confirming him in the government. He summoned an assembly of the Galileans, who, in the same spirit, declared their ready and cheerful submission to his command. Emboldened by this, he began to act with greater vigour; he chastised the unruly inhabitants of Tiberias, got the deputies into his power, and sent them back to Jerusalem.

Tiberias attempted again to revolt, and to surrender the city to the troops of Agrippa. Not having his forces in readiness, Josephus had recourse, as usual, to one of his stratagems. He seized 240 vessels, put not above four sailors in each, and commanded them to take their station in sight of the town; and he then advanced boldly to the gates. The citizens supposing the ships full of soldiers, surrendered at discretion. Josephus got the senators to the number of 600, and 2000 of the people, within his power, and sent them to Tarichea. They denounced one Clitus as the ringleader; he was carried to the shore to have his hands cut off; on his earnest supplication, one was spared; the left, which he was induced himself to cut off to save the other; the rest of the malcontents were pardoned.[c] After this, Josephus surprised Gischala, and gave it up to pillage. Sepphoris admitted the troops of Gallus into their city. Josephus, with his forces, scaled the walls, but was beaten back, and afterwards defeated in the open plain. The troops of Agrippa soon after made their appearance under the

---

[c] B. J. ii. 21. 10; Vit. 67. 68.

command of Sylla ; they were posted near Julias. Josephus endeavoured, by a feigned flight, to betray them
into an ambush, and might have succeeded, but his
horse unfortunately plunged into a morass, and he was
severely hurt in the wrist, and carried to Cepharnome.
From thence, feverish symptoms appearing, he was removed to Tarichea.[d]

Thus we have endeavoured to wind our weary way
through the intricate politics of Galilee. It is difficult
to conceive how all these intrigues, as well as all the
masterly and effective warlike preparations of Josephus,
could be carried on simultaneously, more particularly if
all these transactions must be crowded into the winter
of one year, 66-7.[e] Besides the details of armies raised,

---

[d] Vit. 72.

[e] In the "Jewish War." it is not difficult to trace a certain order of these
events, if not strictly chronological,
yet of historical arrangement. Josephus first relates his reception in Galilee and the measures which he took for
the organization of the province, the
levying and disciplining of his army,
the defensive fortification of the chief
cities. He then passes to his strife
with John of Gischala, and the long
and obstinate struggle in Galilee and
in Jerusalem with this noted rival.
This may account for some transposi-
tion of events, and some discrepancy
with the Life.

Vit. c. 15.

The "Life" was written much later,
after the death of Vespasian and
Titus, long after the publication of the
"Jewish War," and after the publication
of the "History" of Justus of Tiberias,
against whom Josephus writes in a
spirit of bitter controversy. The whole

"Life" is almost occupied with the
events between his arrival in Galilee and
the siege of Jotapata: out of 76 chapters
only six relate to his early life, three
to the period after his capture in
Jotapata. It has, it must be acknowledged, a strongly romantic cast; it
is an undisguised panegyric on his
own valour, enterprise, activity, craft,
promptitude, wisdom; it is full of
strange hair-breadth escapes, and
stirring adventures. Yet vanity can
hardly have been the sole motive for
its composition. It was avowedly
written to vindicate himself from the
calumnies of Justus of Tiberias, his old
enemy in that city, who had written a
History of the Jewish war, long unhappily lost. The work of Justus
compelled Josephus to utter things
which he had so long kept in silence.
ἀπολογήσεσθαι γὰρ νῦν ἀνάγκην
ἔχω, καταψευδομαρτυρούμενος, ἐρῶ
τὰ μέχρι νῦν σεσιωπημένα. c. 65.
The heaviest part of the misrepresenta-

armed, and exercised; cities fortified and strengthened;
the civil administration set on a regular footing; by his
own statement, Josephus twice took Sepphoris, four
times Tiberias, once Gadara, perhaps Gischala; counteracted the plots, defeated the troops, took and pardoned
his subtle antagonist John. Yet we must either, adher-
ing to the usual chronology, admit this improbability, or
throw back the whole events of the year which ended
in the defeat of Cestius Gallus, into the year 65; and
adopt almost as incredible a supposition, that, with most
unusual inactivity, the Romans left the defeat of Cestius
unrevenged, and allowed the Jews a whole year to organize their revolt, and strengthen their territory against
invasion.

During this time the insurgents in Jerusalem continued to press their preparations for war, with as great
activity and less interruption than those in Galilee. For
though the timid and moderate groaned in heart to hear
the din of war, the clattering of arms, the gymnasia
echoing with the trampling march of all the youth in
military exercise; and sadly foreboded the miseries and
ruin to which the joyous city, the place of national festival, the rich, the beautiful, the holy city of Sion was
thus self-devoted; though they could not utter their
prayers in the Temple, nor make their offerings on the
altar of Jehovah without awful misgivings that before
long the worship might be proscribed, and fire and sword

---

tions of Justus, which he seeks to confute, is that he (Josephus) was the first
great rebel against Rome, the author
of the revolt of Galilee. He retorts on
Justus as a turbulent fellow who before this had raised Tiberias in insurrection; in short, that Justus was an
earlier and more daring rebel than
himself, and only escaped by singular
good fortune the just punishment for
his offences. Throughout the work is
that of a man advanced in years relating the deeds of his youth from
memory—a constant struggle between
his vanity and his fear of offending
his Imperial patrons at Rome.

lay waste the courts of the Lord's house : yet they were constrained to suppress or conceal the unpopular weakness, and trembled lest the fierce eye of the Zealot or the Assassin should detect the dangerous or unpatriotic emotion.[f]

In the city, Ananus the chief priest took the lead; arms were fabricated with the greatest activity ; the walls strengthened, military engines made, and stores of every kind laid in with the utmost care and expedition.   The timid and moderate were not the only enemies with whom Ananus had to contend.   The fierce Simon, the son of Gioras, has already appeared, at the head of his daring bandits, rendering good service during the retreat of Cestius.   In the toparchy of Acrabatene,[g] he had betaken himself, not to the regular defence of the country, but to the most lawless ravage.   He broke open and pillaged the houses of the opulent; and even inflicted personal violence, scourging and maltreating all who opposed him.   Already men began to forebode both his daring ambition, which would not be content with less than the highest station, and his cruelty, which would scruple at no means of obtaining or securing advancement.   Ananus sent some troops against him : Simon took refuge with men of a kindred spirit, who held Masada; and from thence he pursued his ravages in Idumæa, till the magistrates of that district were constrained to raise an army, and set a guard in every village.

It was probably not long after the defeat of Cestius, that an unsuccessful expedition was attempted against

---

[f] B. J. ii. 22.

[g] There were two Acrabatenes, which cause great confusion : one,
according to Jerome, between Neapolis, Sichem, and Jericho ; the other in the south of Judæa, bordering on Idumæa.

Ascalon. That strong city, situated about sixty-five
miles from Jerusalem, was weakly garrisoned by one
cohort of foot and one troop of horse, under a commander named Antonius. The Jews marched out in
great force under Niger of Peræa, Silas the Babylonian,
and John the Essene. Antonius, undismayed by the
number and the daring of the enemy, led out his horse.
The Jewish soldiers were all infantry, undisciplined and
unused to war. The first furious charge of the cavalry
broke their van, which fell back on their main body,
threw it into confusion, and the whole army was scattered in small squadrons over the field. The active
Roman horse attacked first one band, then another,
charging and riding round them,—their mounted archers
making dreadful havock. Numbers were of no avail,
or rather stood in the way of effective defence. The
vast and confused multitude could not fight, and would
not fly. Night put an end to the battle, or rather to
the carnage. 10,000 men, with Judas and Silas, fell:
Niger escaped with the rest to a small tower named
Sallæ.[h] The Jews were not cast down by this signal defeat. In the shortest time, not enough for the wounded
to get healed, they assembled all their forces, and in
still greater pride and indignation again marched out
against Ascalon. They had learned as little prudence
as humility. Antonius occupied the passes with an ambush, and suddenly surrounding the Jewish army with
his horse, after scarcely any resistance cut down 8000
of them. Niger, who showed great courage in the retreat, again escaped, and got possession of a strong
tower in a village called Bezedel. The Romans, who
had not time for a regular siege, and yet were unwilling

---

[h] B. J. iii. 2. 1. 2.

to allow so formidable a leader to escape, set fire to the wall. Having seen the tower in flames, they retreated in triumph. Niger, however, leaped down into a deep cavern, which was under the tower; and when his sorrowing companions came, three days after, to find his body, that they might bury it, they heard his feeble voice calling them from below. The Jews were full of joy, and looked on the escape of their champion as little less than a miraculous proof of divine favour.

BOOK XV.

THE WAR.

Vespasian — Siege of Jotapata — Fall of Japha — Mount Gerizim — Capture of Jotapata — Josephus — Surrender of Tiberias — Fall of Tarichea — Massacre — Siege of Gamala — Fall of Itabyrium — Taking of Gamala — of Gischala — Flight of John -- Feuds in Jerusalem.

WITH the early spring Vespasian appeared at Antioch,[a] at the head of his powerful army. There Agrippa met him with all his forces. Vespasian advanced to Ptolemais : he was met by a deputation from Sepphoris. The metropolis of Galilee, notwithstanding the authority and the threats of Josephus, again made overtures to join the invader. Vespasian received the deputies with great courtesy, and sent them back with a strong body of 1000 horse and 6000 foot, to defend their city against any attack of the Jews.[b] These troops, under the command of Placidus, took up their position towards the great plain, the foot within the city, the cavalry encamped without the walls. From these quarters they ravaged the surrounding country. Josephus made one strong effort to recover the capital of Galilee, but was repulsed, and only the more exasperated the Romans,

----

[a] Josephus says that Antioch was incontestably (ἀδηρίτως) the third city in the Roman Empire. This is important in Jewish as well as in Christian history. Compare Strabo, xvi. p. 1089. According to Strabo the other two were Seleucia on the Tigris, and Alexandria. Of course Rome is excluded.

[b] B. J. iii. 4. 1.

who spread fire and sword over the whole region; they slew all who were able to bear arms, the rest they carried off as slaves.

Titus, with expedition unusual during the winter season, sailed from Achaia to Alexandria. From thence he shipped his troops for Ptolemais, and joined his father. Vespasian was now at the head of three of the most distinguished legions of the Roman army,—the fifth, tenth, and fifteenth. Besides these, he had twenty-three cohorts, five of them from Cæsarea. Ten of these cohorts mustered 1000 men; the rest 600, with 150 horse each.[c] The allied force consisted of 2000 foot, all archers, and 1000 horse furnished by Antiochus, Agrippa, and Sohemus. Malchus, king of Arabia, sent 1000 horse and 5000 foot, the greatest part archers. The whole army amounted to 60,000 regulars, horse and foot, besides followers of the camp, who were also accustomed to military service, and could fight on occasion.[d]

The campaign was now formally opened: the forces of Placidus overspread the whole country. Josephus attempted no resistance in the open field. The inhabitants had been directed to fly to the fortified cities; all who were not expeditious or fortunate enough to escape were cut off or seized. But these were the unwarlike part of the people: the more active and courageous had all crowded into the cities. The strongest of all these was Jotapata, where Josephus commanded in person. Placidus concluded that if, by an unexpected attack, he could make himself master of that important post, the blow would so terrify the rest, that they would

---

[c] "Additis igitur ad copias duabus legionibus, octo alis, cohortibus decem, atque inter Legatos majore filio assumto." Suet. Vesp. iv. "Bellum Judaicum Flavius Vespasianus . . . tribus legionibus administrabat." Tacit. Hist. i. 10.

[d] B. J. iii. 4, 2.

immediately fall. He marched rapidly against Jotapata ;
but the garrison had received timely information. They
anticipated the assault by a daring sally, for which
the Romans were entirely unprepared. The troops of
Placidus were repulsed ; many wounded, but only seven
killed ; for the legionaries retreated in good order, and
being entirely covered with their defensive armour, sel-
dom received mortal wounds. The Jews were only
light-armed troops, who rarely ventured to fight hand to
hand, but annoyed the enemy at a distance with their
javelins. It was an inspiriting commencement of the
campaign.

At length the vast army of Vespasian began to move.
Josephus describes the order of march with the accuracy
of an eye-witness.[e] He must, indeed, have watched its
stern and regular advance with the trembling curiosity
of the sailor, who sees the tempest slowly gathering,
which is about to burst, and perhaps wreck his weak and
ill-appointed bark. The van was preceded by the light-
armed allies and their archers, who scattered over the
plain to observe any unexpected attack of the enemy,
and to examine all the woods or thickets that might
conceal an ambuscade. Then came part of the heavy-
armed cavalry and infantry, followed by ten of each
centenary, carrying the furniture and vessels of the
camp. After these the pioneers, who were to straighten
the winding roads, level the hills, or cut down the woods
which might impede the march of the main army.
Then came the baggage of the general and his officers,
strongly guarded by cavalry. Next rode the general,
with a picked troop of foot, horse, and lancers. After
him the horse of his own legion, for to each legion there

---

[e] B. J. iii. 6. 2.

were 120 cavalry attached. Then the mules which carried
the military engines, and the besieging train. The lieu-
tenant-generals, the commanders of cohorts, and the
tribunes followed, each with a chosen band of men.
Then the eagles, of which each legion had one. The
standards were followed by the trumpeters. Behind
came the phalanx itself, in files of six deep. A centurion, whose business it was to keep order, brought up
the rear. Behind them were the servants with the baggage, on mules and other beasts of burthen. After the
Romans marched the mercenaries; a strong rear-guard
of light and heavy-armed foot, and many horse, closed
the procession. The host passed on in its awful magnificence. Vespasian halted on the frontier of Galilee, as
if to give the revolted province time for repentance,
or to strike terror into the more obstinate insurgents.
The measure was not without effect. No sooner did the
army of Josephus, which was encamped at Garis, not far
from Sepphoris, hear of this tremendous invasion, than,
before they had seen the enemy, they dispersed on all
sides; and Josephus, left almost alone, began to despair
of the war.[f] It was idle to think of opposing such an
enemy with a few dispirited troops; he gathered, therefore, the wreck of his army, and fled to Tiberias.

Vespasian marched against Gabara;[g] the city was
ungarrisoned, and the stern Roman proceeded to make
a terrible example, and to wipe out the affront of Cestius with the blood of the enemy. The youth were put
to the sword,—not a man escaped; the city, with every
village and hamlet in the neighbourhood, was burned to
the ground; the few villagers, whose lives were spared,

---

[f] B. J. iii. 6. 3.
[g] This must be the right reading.

Gadara was on the eastern side of the
Sea of Galilee.

were seized as slaves.   The retreat of Josephus to Tiberias filled the city with consternation ; they naturally construed it into a proof that he despaired of success. They were not wrong, for the manner in which the war was conducted made him consider resistance hopeless.   Yet, though by his own account he could immediately have made terms with the Romans, he determined not to abandon the cause.   He sent despatches to Jerusalem, strongly worded, in which he exhorted the people to make their immediate option, either of capitulating at once, or sending a powerful and effective army into the field.

Jotapata [h] was the city in which the greater part, and those the bravest, of the Galilean warriors, had taken refuge.   It was strongly situated in a rugged, mountainous district.   The roads were scarcely practicable for infantry, quite impassable for horse.   In four days the pioneers of Vespasian cut a practicable road right through the mountains, and, on the fifth, Jotapata lay open to the army.   Josephus contrived to throw himself into the city.   This was made known to Vespasian by a deserter ; and he became the more eager for the capture of the town, when he heard that the general-in-chief was within the walls.   It seemed as though the most prudent of the enemy had surrendered himself, as into a prison.   Placidus and Æbutius, decurions of great merit, in whom Vespasian had the highest confidence, were sent with 1000 horse to surround the walls, and to cut off all possibility of escape.

The next day, May 15th, Vespasian advanced in per-

---

[h] Jotapata, of which Robinson is silent, seems first to have been discovered by Schulz: there are ruins on a jagged cliff called Dschebel Dschifat, which answers to the situation and description of Jotapata.   Ritter, Erdkunde, viii. ii. p. 764.

son with his whole army. During all the day, till late in the evening, the defenders of Jotapata saw, from their lofty battlements, the slow and endless files emerging from the straight and level road which led to the city walls. It was on the strength of their position, amidst their rugged and precipitous mountains and their dark and impenetrable forests, that they had relied for their security. To their consternation they saw the woods falling before the axe of the pioneer, like grain before the sickle of the reaper; the lofty crests of their mountains, as it were, bowing down their heads before the resistless invader; and Nature herself giving up the custody of her unprotected fortress. Vespasian drew up his whole army on a hill, less than a mile to the north of the city; his object was to strike terror into the defenders by the display of his whole force, which lay encamped on the slope. He was not mistaken in the effect which it produced: the garrison cowered behind their walls; not a man ventured forth. The army, weary with their long march, did not advance to an immediate assault: they proceeded to draw a triple line of circumvallation round the city; and thus every chance of escape was cut off. This, however, instead of striking terror, drove the whole garrison to despair. They felt themselves cooped up like wild beasts in their lair; they had no course left but to fight gallantly to the utmost; and their first consternation gave place to the fiercest valour and most stubborn resolution.

The next day the attack began. The Jews, disdaining to be pent up within their walls, pitched their camp before the trenches, and went boldly forth to meet the enemy. Vespasian ordered the bowmen and slingers to gall them with their missiles, and himself with the infantry began to ascend a declivity which led to the

least defensible part of the wall. Josephus saw the
danger, and with the whole strength of the garrison
made a resolute sally, and drove the assailants down the
hill. Great valour was displayed by both parties. On
one side fought desperation; on the other the haughty
shame of being defeated by such a foe: the Romans had
skill in the use of their weapons; the Jews made up
what they wanted in practice and experience with reckless bravery. Night separated the combatants, yet the
slaughter was not great on either side. The Romans
had lost thirteen killed, and many wounded; the Jews
seventeen killed, but six hundred wounded.

On the following day they again attacked the Romans.
They had become more resolute, since they found they
could make head against their formidable enemies.
Every morning added to the fury of the contest; for
five days the Romans continued to make their assaults,
and the Jews to sally forth or fight from the walls, with
equal courage. The Jews had now lost all their terror
of the Roman prowess; while the Romans, with their
obstinate bravery, persisted in forcing their way to the
walls.

Jotapata stood on the summit of a lofty hill, on three
sides rising abruptly from the deep and impassable ravines which surrounded it. Looking down from the top
of the walls the eye could not discover the bottom of
these frightful chasms. It was so embosomed in lofty
mountains, that it could not be seen till it was actually
approached. It could only be entered on the north,
where the end of the ridge sloped more gradually down;
on this declivity the city was built; and Josephus had
fortified this part with a very strong wall. Vespasian
called a council of war. It was determined to raise an
embankment (agger) against the most practicable part

of the wall. The whole army was sent out to provide materials. The neighbouring mountains furnished vast quantities of stone and timber. In order to cover themselves from the javelins and arrows of the garrison, the assailants stretched a kind of roof, made with wattles of wicker-work, over their palisades; under this penthouse they laboured securely at their embankment. They worked in three divisions, one bringing earth, the others stone, or wood. The Jews were not idle; they hurled down immense stones and every kind of missile upon the workmen, which, although they did not do much damage, came thundering down over their heads with appalling noise, and caused some interruption to their labours.

Vespasian brought out his military engines, of which he had 160, in order to clear the walls of these troublesome assailants. The catapults began to discharge their hissing javelins, the balistas heaved huge stones of enormous weight, and balls of fire and blazing arrows fell in showers. The Arab archers, the javelin men, and the slingers, at the same time, plied their terrible weapons, so that a considerable space of the wall was entirely cleared: not a man dared approach the battlements. But the Jews, who could not fight from above, began to attack from below. They stole out in small bands, like robbers, came secretly on the workmen, pulled down their breastworks, and struck at them as they stood naked and without their armour, which they had pulled off to work with greater activity. If the besiegers fled, they instantly demolished the embankment, and set fire to the timbers and the wattles. Vespasian, perceiving that the intervals between the different breastworks, under which the separate parties were labouring, gave advantage to the assailants, ordered one to be carried all round, and, uniting all the working parties, effectually prevented these destructive attacks.

The garrison at length beheld this vast embankment completed; it almost reached to the height of their battlements; it stood towering right opposite to them, as if another city had arisen beside their own, and from the equal heights of their respective walls they were to join in deadly conflict for the mastery. Josephus hastily summoned his workmen, and gave orders that the city wall should be raised to a much greater height. The workmen represented that it was impossible, as long as the wall was thus commanded by the enemy, to carry on their labour. Josephus was not baffled; he ordered tall stakes to be driven on the top of the wall, upon which he suspended hides of oxen newly killed. On this yielding curtain the stones fell dead; the other missiles glided off without damage; and even the fire-darts were quenched by the moisture. Under this covering his men worked night and day, till they had raised the wall twenty cubits, thirty-five feet. He likewise built a great number of towers on the wall, and surrounded the whole with a strong battlement. The Romans, who thought themselves already masters of the city, were not a little discouraged, and were astonished at the skill and enterprise of the defenders; but Vespasian was only the more enraged at the obstinacy of the garrison, and the subtlety of the commander. For the defenders, become confident in the strength of their bulwarks, began to renew their former sallies: they fought in small bands, with the courage of regular troops and all the tricks and cunning of robbers. Sometimes they crept out and carried off whatever they could lay their hands on; sometimes, unperceived, set fire tc

the works. At length, Vespasian determined to turn
the siege into a blockade; and, as he could not take the
city by assault, to reduce it by famine. For, in a short
time, the garrison would either desire to capitulate, or
if they were still obstinate in their resistance, would
perish from want. At all events, if it was necessary to
renew the attack, their men would be enfeebled by privation and suffering. Accordingly, he kept his troops
in their quarters, and contented himself with strictly
blockading every avenue to the city.

The besieged were very well supplied with grain, and
every other necessary, excepting salt; but there was
great want of water. There was no spring in the city;
the inhabitants were obliged to be content with rain
water. But during the summer it rarely, if ever, rains
in that region; and, as the summer was the time of the
siege, they began to be dreadfully dispirited, and to look
forward in horrible apprehension to the period when
their supply would entirely fail. Josephus commanded
the water which remained to be rigidly measured out.
This scanty doling forth of that necessary refreshment to
men parched with fatigue, and many of them feverish
with wounds, seemed worse even than absolute privation;
the sense of want seemed to aggravate their thirst; and
many began to faint, as if already at the worst extremity
of drought. The Romans saw what was going on within
the walls; and, as the inhabitants crept along with
their pitchers to a particular spot to receive their daily
allotment of water, they pointed their engines at them,
and struck them down as they passed.

But the fertile mind of Josephus had not exhausted
its store of schemes: he ordered a great number of his
men to steep their clothes in water and hang them up
from the battlements till the wall ran down with the

dripping moisture.   The Romans were confounded ; for
men who could waste so much water out of mere wantonness, could not possibly be in the wretched state of
privation they had hoped.   Vespasian, weary of thus
blockading a city so amply supplied, returned to the
assault, the mode of attack to which the Jews wished to
drive him.   For in their state it was better to perish at
once by the sword, than by thirst and famine.

Josephus had another stratagem by which he kept up
intelligence with those without the city.   There was one
narrow and rugged path, down the dry bed of a torrent,
which led into the valley to the south.   It was so dangerous and seemingly impracticable, that the Romans
neglected to guard it.   By this way the messengers of
Josephus stole out of the city, bearing letters to and
from the commander, and every thing of small bulk of
which the garrison stood in need.   These men, in
general, crept out on all fours, covered with the skins of
beasts, that they might look like dogs.   This went on
for a long time, till at length the way was detected, and
closed up by the enemy.

At this perilous juncture Josephus honestly confesses
that he began to think of his own personal safety ; and
entered into deliberation with some of the chief leaders
of the garrison, as to the means of making their escape.
Their counsel transpired, and they were environed by
all the people of the city, earnestly entreating them not
to abandon the wretched town to the fury of the enraged
enemy ; for, so long as he and the garrison remained,
there was some hope of resistance.   Directly they were
gone, the city must inevitably fall ; and merciless extermination was the only fate which they could expect.
The crafty general endeavoured to persuade them, that
his only object in leaving the town would be to provide

more effectually for their safety; that he would raise
all Galilee, and so harass the Romans as to force them
to break up the siege: that his presence was of no real
service, but only made Vespasian the more obstinate in
his determination to capture the town. This language
but the more inflamed the multitude; the women with
their infants in their arms began to wail; boys and old
men fell at his feet, and embracing them, besought him
to remain and share their fate. "Not," Josephus adds,
"from any jealousy lest I should save my life, while
theirs were in danger, but because they entertained
some hope of saving their own through my means. As
long as I remained, they were safe." [1]

Partly moved by compassion, partly feeling that if he
did not consent to their entreaties, he might be detained
by force, Josephus determined to stand firm at his post,
and seized the moment of excitement, to lead his force
to a desperate attack. "If then," he exclaimed, "there
is no hope of safety, let us die nobly, and leave a glorious
example to posterity." The bravest crowded round him,
and some rushed suddenly forth, drove in the Roman
guard, and carried their inroads even into the camp;
they tore up the hides with which the works had been
defended, and set fire to the lines in many places. A
second and third day they continued these furious
attacks; and for many nights and days kept up, without
being wearied, a perpetual alarm.

Vespasian found the heavy armed legionaries ill-suited
to this desultory warfare; from the unwieldy weight of
their armour they could not, from their pride they would
not, retreat: and, when they turned again in any force,
the light-armed Jews in an instant disappeared within

---

[1] B. J. iii. 7. 16.

their walls.   Besides, the valour of the Jews was mere
desperation; like a fierce fire, if unresisted it would
burn out.   He ordered therefore the regular troops to
decline these attacks, and to repel the sallies of the besieged with the Arabian archers and Syrian slingers.
The engines in the mean time never ceased discharging
their showers of bolts and stones : these sorely distressed
the Jews, but sometimes getting under the range of
the engines, they fiercely attacked the Romans, never
sparing their own lives, and new troops continually filling up the places of those who were fatigued or slain.

The Roman general found that he was, as it were,
besieged in his turn; and as the embankment had now
reached close to the wall, he ordered the battering ram
to be advanced.   This was the most formidable of all
the besieging artillery used in ancient warfare.   It was
an immense beam, headed with iron, in the shape of a
ram's head, from which it took its name; it was suspended by cables from another beam, which was supported by strong tall posts; it was drawn back by a
great number of men, and then driven forward with so
tremendous a recoil, that tower or wall could scarcely
ever resist the shock.   The Romans were accustomed to see the bulwarks of the strongest cities
crumble as it were to dust, the instant they could bring
that irresistible machine to work.   As the heavy ram
slowly advanced towards the walls, covered with a pent-
house of wattles and hides, both for the protection of
the engine and of the men who were to work it, the
catapults and other engines, with the archers and
slingers, were commanded to play with increasing activity, to sweep the walls, and distract the besieged.
The battlements were entirely cleared of the defenders,
who lay crouching below, not knowing what was about

to happen. At the first blow of the ram the wall shook as with an earthquake, and a wild cry rose from the besieged, as if the city were already taken.

The engine went on battering at the same place shock after shock: the wall already began to totter and crumble, when Josephus thought of a new expedient. He ordered a number of sacks to be filled with straw, and let down by ropes from the walls, to catch the hard blows of the ram, wherever it might strike. The Romans were perplexed, for their blows fell dead on this soft and yielding substance; and in their turn they fastened the blades of scythes on long poles and cut asunder the ropes which held the sacks. Then the engine again began, without interruption, its work, when behold the Jews suddenly broke forth in three parties. They bore in their hands all the lighted combustibles they could find; they swept every thing before them, and set fire to the engines, the wattles and the palisadoes of the besiegers. The Romans, confounded with this unexpected daring, and blinded by the fire and smoke driving in their faces, made less courageous defence than usual. The timbers of the embankment were all dry: a great quantity of bitumen, pitch, and even sulphur had been used as cement. The conflagration spread with the greatest rapidity, and thus one hour destroyed the labour of many days.

The daring exploit of one man among the Jews met with universal admiration: he was a Galilean of Saab, named Eleazar, the son of Samaes. With an immense stone from the wall, he took such a steady aim, that he struck off the iron head of the battering ram; he then leaped down from the wall, secured his prize, and was bearing it back to the city. He was unarmed, and all the darts and arrows of the enemy were discharged at him. He was transfixed by five arrows; still, however, he pressed on, regained the walls, stood boldly up, displaying his trophy, in the sight of all—and then, still clinging to it with convulsive hands, fell down and expired. Two other Galileans, Netiras and Philip of Ruma, greatly distinguished themselves, breaking through the ranks of the tenth legion, and driving in all who opposed them.

Josephus and the rest followed this heroic example, and all the engines and the breast-work of the fifth and of the tenth legions which were driven in, were entirely consumed. Others followed the first rank of the assailants, and heaped the earth over what was destroyed as fast as they could.

Still, towards the evening, the Romans again set up the ram, and began to batter the wall at the same place. But while Vespasian himself was directing the assault, he was wounded in the heel by a javelin from the wall, slightly indeed, for the javelin was spent; but the greatest alarm spread through the army. Many gave up the attack to crowd around the general, who was bleeding. Titus showed the most affectionate solicitude. But Vespasian, suppressing the pain of his wound, speedily relieved their fears: and, to revenge the hurt of their commander, the whole army rushed on with a loud shout to the walls: all that night the awful conflict lasted. The Jews fell in great numbers; for though the missiles poured around them like hail, they would not abandon the walls, but continued heaving down great stones, and flinging fiery combustibles on the wattles which protected those that worked the ram. They fought at disadvantage, for the light of their own fires made the walls as light as day, and the enemy were thus enabled to take steady aim, while the black engines lay in shadow in the distance, and they could not distinguish when the bolts were about to be discharged. The scorpions and catapults raged more and more fiercely, and swept the walls; the stones from the other engines shattered the pinnacles and the corners of the turrets, which kept falling with a fearful crash. The stones penetrated right through dense masses of men, making as it were a furrow as they passed, and reaching to the rearmost man. Strange stories are reported of the force of these engines—one man was struck on the head, and his skull hurled, as by a sling, to the distance of three stadia, about three furlongs: a pregnant woman was hit in the lower part, and the child cast to the distance of half a stadium. It was a night of unexampled confusion. The clattering of the bolts, the shouts of the army, the heavy fall of the huge stones, the thundering shocks of the battering ram, were mingled with the frantic shrieks of women, and the screams of children—the whole space about the walls was like a pool of blood; and men could mount the wall upon the bodies of their slaughtered friends. All this deafening din was echoed back and multiplied by the surrounding mountains. Many fell, many more were wounded, but till the morning watch the wall stood firm: it then yielded: still, however, those who were well provided with defensive armour, laboured with all their might to form new buttresses and bulwarks, wherever a breach was threatened, before the machines, by which the enemy were to mount the breach, could be advanced.

Towards the morning Vespasian allowed his troops a short time for refreshment. In order to repel the besieged from the breach, he made the bravest of his horsemen dismount, and divided them into three parties.

They were completely cased in armour, and had long
pikes in their hands, to be ready to charge, instantly
that the machines for mounting the breach were fixed.
Behind these he stationed the flower of the infantry.
The rest of the horse were extended all over the
mountains, which encircled the town, that none might
make their escape; behind the foot were the archers,
the slingers, and engineers; and others with scaling
ladders, which were to be applied to such parts of the
walls as were yet uninjured, to call off the attention
of the defenders from the breach.   When Josephus
discovered this, he selected the old, the infirm, the
fatigued, and the wounded to defend those parts of
the wall. The bravest he chose to man the breach;
six, of whom himself was one, formed the first line.   He
addressed them in a few words, enjoining them not to
be alarmed at the shout of the legionaries; to kneel
down and cover their heads with their bucklers, and
retreat a little, till the bowmen had exhausted their
quivers; when the Romans had fixed the mounting
machines to leap down upon them and fight, remember-
ing that they could now scarcely be thought to fight for
safety, for of that they had no hope, but for a brave
revenge: finally, to set before their eyes their fathers
and children massacred, their wives defiled, and anticipate a just vengeance for these, now inevitable, calamities.

While this was going on, the idle multitude, with the
women and children, saw the city still surrounded by
triple lines, for the Romans did not withdraw any part
of their guards for the approaching conflict—the appalling force standing with their drawn swords before
the breach—the whole mountain gleaming with the
lances of the cavalry, and the Arabian archers with

their bows already levelled — they were seized with
universal consternation; one shrill and agonizing shriek
ran through the whole city, as if the horrors of the capture were not only dreaded, but actually begun.   Josephus, lest they should dispirit his men, ordered all the
women to be locked up in the houses, and threatened
all others with exemplary punishment if they raised any
disturbance.   He then took his post in the breach.   At
once the trumpets of the legions sounded, and the whole
Roman host raised one terrific shout.   At that instant
the sun was darkened with the clouds of arrows.   The
Jews closed their ears to the noise, and, shrouded under
their bucklers, avoided the arrows.   The moment that
the mounting engines were fixed, the Jews were upon
them before the assault, fighting hand to hand with the
most resolute courage; till at length the Romans, who
could continually pour new troops upon them, while the
besieged had none to supply their place when weary,
formed a solid phalanx, and moving on as one man,
drove back the Galileans, and were already within the
walls.   Still Josephus had a last expedient.   He had
prepared an immense quantity of boiling oil, and, at a
signal, this was poured, vessels and all, which burst
with the heat, upon the ascending phalanx.   The
ranks were broken, and the men rolled down, wild
with agony; for the boiling oil, which kindles easily
and cools slowly, trickled within their armour.   They
had not time to tear off their breastplates and bucklers
before it had penetrated to the skin; but they leaped
about and writhed with anguish, or plunged headlong
from the bridges; or, if they attempted to fly, were
pierced through their backs, the only part which was
without defensive armour.   Yet the steady courage of
the Romans was not thus to be repelled.   However those

behind might pity their suffering companions, they still
pressed forward, and sternly rebuked them for standing
in their way, and for impeding braver men in the performance of their duty. But the Jews had still another
stratagem. They poured boiled fenugreek, a kind of
herb, upon the planks on which the enemy were
mounting the breach, and made them so slippery, that
no one could gain a firm footing, either to ascend or
retreat. Some fell on their faces, and were trampled
down by those who followed; others rolled back upon
the embankment. The Jews struck at them as they
lay and grovelled; or, the close combat being thus interrupted, discharged their javelins, and heaped darts
and stones upon them. At length, about the evening,
the general recalled his worsted men, with considerable loss in killed and wounded. Those of Jotapata
had six killed, and three hundred wounded.[k]

Vespasian found his troops rather exasperated than
disheartened by this obstinate resistance; but yet it
was necessary to proceed by more slow and cautious
approaches. He gave orders that the embankment
should be raised considerably; and that fifty towers
should be built upon it, strongly girded with iron, both
that the weight might make them more firm, and to
secure them against fire. In these he placed his javelin-
men, his slingers, and archers, and the lighter engines
for the discharge of missiles. These, being concealed by
the height and the breast-works of their towers, might
take deliberate aim at all who appeared upon the walls.
This was a fatal measure to the Jews. The darts and

---

[k] εἶδος ὀσπρίου, ἥτις ἐφθὴ ἐπιχε-
σμένη ὄλισθον ἐμποιεῖ τοῖς ποσὶ
τῶν ἀνθρώπων ἐπισφαλῆ, ὅπερ Ἰώση-
πος πρὸς τὴν πολιορκίαν ἐμηχανή-
σατο. Suidas in voce. Confer Plin. xvii.
16; Col. ii. 10. 10. "Mihi quidem (ait
Lipsius, Polior. v. 3) hoc novum et alibi
non lectum." Cardwell, note on B. J.

arrows came pouring from above, so that they could not
shift and avoid them.   They could have no revenge
against these invisible foes; for their own arrows could
not reach to the height of the towers, and the towers,
being solid and compact with iron, could not be set on
fire.   All they could do was to abandon their walls,
and, when any party approached, make a rapid and
desperate sally to beat them off.   Thus their own loss
was considerable—that of the Romans very slight.   Still,
however, they kept up a manful resistance, and constantly repelled the enemy from the walls.

But now the fall of a neighbouring fortress was a
dreadful omen, and a warning of their own approaching
fate to the defenders of Jotapata.   A city called Japha,[1]
at no great distance, emboldened by the vigorous defence of Jotapata, closed its gates against the Romans.
Vespasian detached Trajan, the father of the Emperor,
with 2000 foot and 1000 horse, to reduce the place.[m]
The city was strongly situated, and surrounded by a
double wall.   The men of Japha came boldly forth to
meet the enemy; but this hardihood was their ruin.
They were repulsed and chased to the walls.   The pursuers and pursued entered pell-mell within the outer
gates.   Those who defended the inner wall instantly
closed their gates, and shut out the flower of their own
garrison as well as the enemy.   The fugitives, hotly
pursued, were cooped up between the two walls, and
mowed down with horrible carnage.   They rushed to
the gates, called upon their fellow citizens by name,

---

[1] Japha (see above, p. 232), the most
populous κώμη in Galilee. B. J. iii. 7.
31. Jafa is thought to be the Japha of
Josephus: it was visited by Mr. Wol-
cot. Bibliotheca Sacra, 1843. Ritter,
Erdkunde, p. 701.

[m] Plin. Panegyr. c. 89. Spanheim,
de Usu Numm., Diss. xi. p. 328.
Rasche, Lexicon, ii. i. 378.

and entreated them to open and let them in—but in
vain; to admit them, was to admit the conquering
enemy. Totally disheartened, not only by the terror of
the foe, but by the apparent treachery of their friends,
they had no courage to resist; but either stood still to
be tamely butchered, reproaching, as it were, those who
looked down from the walls with their miserable end—
or, in desperate frenzy, rushed on each other's swords,
or fell upon their own: and so they died, execrating
their fellow citizens rather than the enemy. In the
flight and in the suburb 12,000 perished; and those
who had thus, either out of panic or miscalculating
prudence, betrayed their fellow citizens, obtained only a
brief respite; for Trajan, rightly concluding that the
garrison must be greatly enfeebled by this loss, formed
the blockade of the city—and with courtier-like reserve,
as if he already anticipated the imperial destiny of the
Flavian family, sent despatches to Vespasian to request
that his son Titus might be detached to complete the
victory. Titus speedily arrived with 1000 foot and
500 horse. He took the command, and, placing Trajan
at the head of the left wing, and himself leading the
right, gave orders for a general assault. No sooner had
the soldiers fixed the scaling-ladders than the Galileans,
after a feeble resistance, abandoned the walls. Titus
and his soldiers leaped down into the city, and, the
Galileans rallying, a furious conflict ensued; for the
citizens blocked up the narrow streets and lanes, and
fought desperately, while the women, from the roofs of
the houses, hurled down everything on which they
could lay their hands. The battle lasted for six hours,
when all who could bear arms were slain; and the rest,
old and young—part in the public streets, part in the
houses—were indiscriminately put to the sword. The

women alone and infants were reserved as slaves : 15,000 were killed, 2130 taken.

It is remarkable that the Samaritans, who are generally accused by the Jews as disclaiming their kindred in every period of danger, made common cause in this insurrection. Roman oppression must indeed have weighed heavily, if the indignation it excited could overpower the rooted animosity of Samaritan and Jew, and set them in arms together against the same enemy. The Samaritans had not openly joined the revolt, but stood prepared with a great force on the sacred mountain of Gerizim—for most of their strong cities were garrisoned by the Romans. Vespasian determined to anticipate and suppress the insurrectionary spirit which was manifestly brooding in the whole region. Cerealis[n] was sent with 600 horse, and 3000 infantry, who suddenly surrounded the foot of the mountain. It was the height of summer, and the Samaritans, who had laid in no provision, suffered grievously from the want of water : some actually died of thirst ; others deserted to the Romans. As soon as Cerealis supposed that they were sufficiently enfeebled, he gradually drew his forces up the side of the mountain, enclosing the enemy in a narrower compass, as in the toils of a skilful hunter. He then sent to them to throw down their arms, and promised a general amnesty. On their refusal, he charged them with irresistible fury, and slew the whole, to the number of 11,600.

And now the end of Jotapata drew near. For forty-seven days its gallant inhabitants had resisted the discipline and courage of the whole Roman army, under their most skilful general; they had confronted bravery

---

[n] Petilius Cerealis, who commanded the ninth legion. Tac. Ann. xiv. 32; Hist. iv. 71; Vit. Agric. 8. 17; Dion, lxv. 18; lxvi. 30, with Reimar's note.

with bravery, and stratagem with stratagem. They were now worn out with watching and fatigue, with wounds and thirst. Their ranks were dreadfully thinned, and the overwearied survivors had to fight all day and watch all night. A deserter found his way to the camp of Vespasian, and gave intelligence of the enfeebled state of the garrison, urging him to make an assault at the early dawn of morning, when the sentinels were apt to be found sleeping on their posts. Vespasian suspected the traitor, for nothing had been more striking during the siege than the fidelity of the Jews to their cause. One man who had been taken had endured the most horrible torments, and though burnt in many parts of his body, steadily refused to betray the state of the town, till at length he was crucified. Still the story bore marks of probability; and Vespasian, thinking that no stratagem could inflict great injury on his powerful army, prepared for the assault.

A thick morning mist enveloped the whole city, as at the appointed hour the Romans, with silent step, approached the walls. Titus was the first to mount, with Domitius Sabinus, a tribune, and a few soldiers or the fifteenth legion. They killed the sentinels, and stole quietly down into the city. Sextus Cerealis, and Placidus, followed with their troops. The citadel was surprised: it was broad day, yet the besieged, in the heavy sleep of fatigue, had not discovered that the enemy were within the walls; and even now, those who awoke saw nothing through the dim and blinding mist. But by this time the whole army was within the gates, and the Jews were awakened to a horrible sense of their situation by the commencement of the slaughter. The Romans remembered what they had suffered during the siege, and it was not a time when mercy and compassion, foreign to their usual character, could arrest the arm of vengeance. They charged furiously down from the citadel, hewing their way through the multitude, who, unable to defend themselves, stumbled, and were crushed in the uneven ways; or were suffocated in the narrow lanes, or rolled headlong down the precipices. Nothing was to be seen but slaughter; nothing heard but the shrieks of the dying and the shouts of the conquerors. A few of the most hardy had gathered round Josephus, and mutually exhorted each other to self-destruction; as they could not slay the enemy, they would not be tamely slain by them. A great number fell by each other's hands. A few of the guard who had been at first surprised, fled to a tower on the northern part of the wall, and made some resistance. At length they were surrounded, and gave themselves up to be quietly butchered. The Romans might have boasted that they had taken the city without the loss of a man, had not a centurion, named Antonius, been slain by a stratagem. There were a great number of deep caverns under the city, in which many took refuge; one of these, being hotly pursued, entreated Antonius to reach his hand to him, as a pledge of accepting his surrender, as well as to help him to clamber out. The incautious Roman stretched out his hand, the Jew instantly pierced him in the groin with a lance, and killed him.

That day all were put to the sword who appeared in the streets or houses; the next, the conquerors set themselves to search the caverns and underground passages, still slaughtering all the men, and sparing none but infants and women. 1200 captives were taken. During the siege and capture 40,000 men fell. Vespasian gave orders that the city should be razed to the

ground, and all the defences burnt. Thus fell Jotapata, on the 1st day of Panemus (July).

But among all the dead, the Romans sought in vain
for the body of their obstinate and subtle enemy, Josephus.° Vespasian himself expressed great anxiety for
his capture; but all their search was baffled, and they
began to fear that the wily chieftain had, after all, withdrawn himself from their vengeance. During the confusion of the massacre, Josephus had leaped down the
shaft of a dry well, from the bottom of which, a long
cavern led off, entirely concealed from the sight of
those above. There he, unexpectedly, found himself
among forty of the most distinguished citizens of Jotapata, who had made this their hiding place, and furnished it with provisions for several days. He lay hid
all the day, while the enemy were prowling about, and
at night crept out, and endeavoured to find some way
of escape from the city; but the Roman guards were
too vigilant, and he was obliged to return to his lair.
Two days he remained without detection; on the third,
a woman who had been with those within the cavern,
being captured, betrayed the secret. Vespasian immediately despatched two tribunes, Paulinus ᵖ and Galli-
canus, to induce Josephus, by a promise of his life, to
surrender. Josephus, while he lay quiet in his cavern,
was suddenly startled by hearing himself called on by
name. It was the voice of the tribune with the message
of Vespasian. But Josephus had no great confidence
in Roman mercy, and refused to come forth, till Vespasian sent another tribune, Nicanor, with whom he
had been well acquainted. Nicanor stood at the mouth

° B. J. iii. 8. 1.
ᵖ Probably Valerius Paulinus, not the famous Suetonius Paulinus.

of the well, and enlarged on the natural generosity of
the Romans, and their admiration of so gallant an
enemy; he assured the suspicious Josephus that Vespasian had no intention against his life, but was anxious
to save a man who had displayed such noble self-devotion; and strongly urged that his delay would be of
little use, as they might easily take him by force. He
even added, that Vespasian would not have employed
the friend of Josephus on such a mission, if he had any
secret or treacherous design.

The Roman soldiers would have settled the affair in
a much more summary manner: they were with difficulty restrained by their commander from throwing
fire into the cavern, which would either have suffocated
those within, or forced them to make their way out. At
this moment Josephus remembered his dream, which
had so precisely foretold all the calamities of the Jews,
and all which was to happen to the future emperor of
Rome.   Now, Josephus was an adept in the interpretation of dreams: as a priest he had deeply studied the
prophecies of the Holy Books.   He was suddenly and,
doubtless, most opportunely seized with divine inspira-
tion, which inwardly assured him that it was the will of
Heaven that his country should fall, and Rome triumph,
and he himself save his life.   So, if he passed over to
the Roman party, he would do so, not as a renegade,
but as an obedient servant of God.

Saying this within himself, he consented to the terms
of Nicanor.   But, unhappily, a new difficulty occurred.
However satisfactory to his own conscience this determination of humbly submitting to the will of God, the
companions of Josephus were not religious enough to enter
into his motives.   They reproached him with the vulgar
desire of saving his life, and with cowardly defection

from the laws of his country. They reminded him of
his own eloquent exhortations to despise death in such
a noble cause ; exhortations with which so many had
generously complied. They intimated somewhat plainly,
that they would assist his failing patriotism, and enable
him to obtain all the honours of martyrdom ; in short,
that their hands and swords were ready to enable him
to die, not as a renegade, but as the chieftain of the
Jews. At the same time they showed their zealous
interest in his character by surrounding him with
drawn swords, and threatening to put him to death if
he stirred. Josephus was in great embarrassment, for
he felt that it would be impious resistance to the will of
God if he should thus submit to die. He began (in his
own words) to *philosophize* to them. It is not very
probable that at this perilous instant Josephus should
have the self-command to make, or his fierce assailants
the patience to listen to, a long set speech ; but his
oration, as it stands in the History, is so curious, that we
must insert the chief topics on which he dwelt. " Why,
my friends," he began, " should we be so eager for self-
murder? why should we separate associates so dear to
each other as the soul and body? It is noble to die in
war, true ! but according to the legitimate usage of war,
by the sword of the enemy. If I had supplicated for
mercy, I should have deserved to die ; but if the Romans
freely offer to spare us, why should we not spare ourselves? For what have we been fighting all this time?
—to save our lives ; and now we are to be such fools as
to throw our lives away. It is noble, indeed, to die for
our liberty, yes, in battle :—that man is equally a
coward who fears to die when death is necessary, and
he who chooses to die when there is no necessity. Why
do we refuse to surrender? In fear lest the Romans

should kill us ; and therefore we would kill ourselves.
In fear lest we be made slaves? at present, indeed, we
enjoy great liberty !"　He then entered at large into
the common-place arguments against self-murder ; the
disgrace of abandoning the helm when the bark is in
danger ; the natural fondness of all animals for life, and
their aversion to death ; above all, the sin of throwing
away the most precious gift of God.　" Our bodies are
mortal, and made of perishable matter; but the soul is
immortal ; as a part of the Divinity it dwells within our
bodies.　He is base and treacherous who betrays that
with which he is entrusted by man; how much more he
who basely gives up the precious trust which God has
confided to him !　We punish slaves even if they desert
the service of a cruel master, yet we have no scruple to
desert the service of a good and merciful Deity.　Know
ye not, that those who depart this life according to the
law of nature, and pay the debt when it is demanded
by God, obtain everlasting glory? their houses and
families prosper ; their souls remain pure and obedient,
and pass away to the holiest mansions in heaven : from
whence, in the revolution of ages, they again take up
their dwelling in pure bodies.　But for those who have
madly lifted their hands against their own lives, the
darkest pit of hell receives their souls, and God avenges
their crime upon their children's children.　Hence God
and our wise lawgiver have enacted a severe punishment against the suicide : his body is cast forth at sunset without burial ; the guilty hand, which dared to
separate the soul from the body, is cut off."　(Here
Josephus seems to have calculated on the ignorance of
his audience, and boldly engrafted a Grecian supersti
tion on the Mosaic law.)　He concluded with protesting
that he had no thought of deserting to the ranks of the

Romans, but that he rather looked forward to their putting him to death, in which case he should die gladly, having affixed the stain of the basest treachery on the enemy. But, unfortunately, these subtle arguments, these sublime doctrines, and magnanimous sentiments were lost on the dull ears of the obstinate Galileans; they only became more enraged; they ran at him with their swords, they reproached him with his cowardice, and every one of them was ready to plunge his sword to the heart of the craven. Josephus stood like a wild beast at bay, constantly turning to the man that was rushing at him; one he called familiarly by his name; at another he looked sternly, as if he were still his commander; here he clasped a hand, there he entreated; at all events determined to save his life, if possible. At length his distress so wrought upon them, that some out of respect, some out of attachment, perhaps some out of contempt, dropped their swords; those of not a few, he says, fell out of their hands, others were quietly returned into their sheaths. The wily leader marked his time, and had a stratagem ready on the instant. " If we must die, then, let us not die by our own, but by each other's hands. Let us cast lots, and thus fall one after another; for if the rest perish, it would be the deepest disgrace for me to survive." They all readily agreed, thinking that Josephus would inevitably share their fate. How the lots were cast, we are not informed, or whether, among his other soldierlike and noble qualities, the worthy commander had some skill in sleight-of-hand. But it so happened (by good fortune or the will of Providence) that they all, one after another, as the lots came up, offered their breasts to the sword. Josephus found himself left, with one other, to the last. Not in the least inclined that the lot should fall on himself, and with a nice and scrupulous reluctance to imbrue his hands in the blood of a fellow creature, Josephus persuaded this man to accept of the offered terms; and so they both came out together, leaving their dead friends in the cavern. Nicanor immediately led him to Vespasian. The Romans crowded from all parts to see this redoubted chieftain. A great rush and uproar ensued. Some were rejoicing at his capture, others threatening him with vengeance; all pressing forward to get a sight of him: those who were at a distance cried out that he should be put to death; those near him were seized with admiration, and remembrance of his noble actions. Not one of the officers, who had been most furious against him, but inclined to mercy directly they saw him, particularly Titus, who was struck with his dignified fortitude, and vigour of manhood. He was thirty years old at the beginning of the war. The influence of Titus was of great weight with Vespasian to dispose him to lenity; the prisoner was ordered to be closely guarded, with the design that he might be sent to Nero at Rome.

Josephus instantly demanded to be admitted to a private conference with Vespasian. All, excepting Titus and two friends, retired. Josephus assumed at once the air and language of a prophet: he solemnly protested that nothing would have tempted him to avoid the death which became a noble Jew, but the conviction that he was a messenger of God, to announce to Vespasian that he and his son would speedily assume the imperial dignity :[q] "Send me not to Nero: bind me, and keep me in

---

[q] Tacitus observes with his bitter shrewdness, "Occultâ lege fati, et ostentis, ac responsis, destinatum Vespasianum liberisque ejus imperium, *post fortunam* credidimus." Hist. i 10 ; compare Suet. Vesp. c. iv.

chains, as thy own prisoner; for soon wilt thou be the
sovereign lord of earth and sea, and of the whole human
race." Vespasian naturally mistrusted the adroit flatterer; but, before long, permitted himself to be fully
persuaded of his prophetic character. Josephus appealed
to the inhabitants of Jotapata, whether he had not predicted the taking of the city, and their own capture at
the end of forty-seven days. The captives, who could
only have been women, as all the men were put to the
sword, readily avouched his story; and the prophet,
though still kept in chains, was treated with great distinction, and received presents of raiment and other
valuable donatives.

This is a strange adventure. It is impossible not to
admire the dexterity with which the historian extricates
himself from all the difficulties of his situation, which,
however highly coloured, must have been one of the
greatest peril. What secrets that dark cavern may
have concealed, can never be known; but we should
certainly have read with deep interest the account of
these transactions, and indeed of the whole Galilean administration of Josephus, in the work of his rival, Justus
of Tiberias, unhappily lost. But, after every deduction
for his love of the marvellous, and the natural inclination to paint highly where he was the hero of his own
story, the valour and skill displayed in the defence of
Jotapata, and the singular address with which he insinuated himself into the favour of Vespasian and his
son, give a very high impression of the abilities of Josephus. As to the sincerity of his belief in his own inspi-
ration, it would more easily have obtained credit, if he
had shown himself, on other occasions, either more
scrupulous or less addicted to stratagem. The prediction itself was far from requiring any great degree of

political sagacity. It was impossible to suppose that the bloody Nero would be allowed to burthen the throne much longer. The imperial family was all but extinct. The empire would, in all probability, fall to the lot of the boldest and most ambitious of the great military leaders, among whom Vespasian stood, if not confessedly the first, yet certainly, with few competitors, in the first rank. It was therefore no very bold hazard to designate him as the future sovereign : at all events, and perhaps Josephus looked no further, the prediction served his immediate turn ; and, if it had not eventually proved true, yet the life of the prophet was secure, and his history, if ever written, might have preserved a prudent silence with regard to a prediction which the event had not justified.[r]

The progress of this year's campaign was not according to the usual career of the Roman arms: a powerful army had marched to subdue a rebellious and insignificant province ; two months had nearly elapsed, and they were little beyond the frontier. Now, however, they proceeded with greater rapidity. Vespasian returned to Ptolemais, from whence he marched along the coast to Cæsarea. The Greek inhabitants of that city

---

[r] The interest which attaches to the siege of Jotapata, the extraordinary minuteness of the description in Josephus, the character of Josephus himself, with its strange power and still stranger inconsistency, the perplexing problem as to his veracity as well as his patriotism, with the extraordinary fact that with no instruction or experience in military affairs he should have acted here with the skill of a consummate general, there with the obstinate courage, fertility of resources, craft and readiness of the guerrilla partisan—all this tempted me perhaps to draw out this siege and this personal history to a disproportionate length. Having done so, I am not inclined to shorten it, so significant does it still appear to me of the state of the Jewish mind, and the nature of the conflict of the Jews with the Roman supremacy, against which, in the wide circle of the Empire, they were the last desperate combatants for freedom.

had now, by the massacre of their Jewish competitors,
the whole region at their command.   They threw open
their gates, went forth to receive the Romans with the
loudest and most sincere demonstrations of joy; for
their vengeance was not yet satiated with Jewish blood
They sent a petition for the execution of Josephus; but
Vespasian did not condescend to reply.[a]   He took possession of Cæsarea, as pleasant winter-quarters for two
of his legions; for though very hot in summer, the
climate of Cæsarea was genial in winter: he fixed on
Scythopolis for the station of the other legion, the
fifteenth.

Cestius Gallus, during his flight, had abandoned
Joppa.   A strong body of insurgents had collected from
all quarters, and taken possession of the town, where
they had built a great number of barks, with which they
made piratical excursions, and plundered all the rich
merchant vessels which traded between Syria, Phœnicia,
and Egypt. Vespasian sent a considerable force against
this city.   The troops reached Joppa by night; and the
walls being unguarded, entered at once.   The inhabitants made no resistance, but fled to their ships, and
moored for the night out of the reach of the enemy's
darts and arrows.   Joppa is a bad harbour: the shore is
steep and rugged, making a kind of semicircular bay,
the extreme headlands of which approach each other.
These headlands are formed by precipitous rocks and
breakers, which extend far into the sea: when the north
wind blows, there is a tremendous surge, which makes
the port more dangerous than the open sea.   In the
morning this wind, called by the sailors of Joppa the
black north wind, began to blow furiously; it dashed

---

[a] B. J. iii. 9. 8.

the ships against each other, or against the rocks.
Some endeavoured to push to sea against the swell; for
they dreaded alike the lee-shore breakers and the
enemy: but all these, unable to stem the rolling of the
swell, foundered.   The rest the wind drove towards the
city, which the Romans would not let them enter.   The
shrieks of the men, the crashing of the vessels, made an
awful din; many were drowned; many were seen
swimming on broken pieces of wreck; many, to escape
drowning, fell on their own swords.   The whole shore
was strewn with mutilated bodies; those who struggled
to the beach were slain by the Romans: 4200 lives
were lost.   The Romans razed the city, but garrisoned
the citadel, lest it should again become a nest of pirates.

At first, vague rumours of the fall of Jotapata reached
Jerusalem: not a man had escaped to bear the fatal intelligence.   But bad tidings are apt to travel fast; and,
as is usual, when the truth became known, it was accompanied with many circumstances of falsehood. Josephus
was said to have fallen; and all Jerusalem united in
lamenting his loss: his death was a public calamity.
There was scarcely a family which had not to deplore
some private affliction; they bewailed those who had
been their guests, (probably at the great festivals,) or
relations, or friends, or brothers: but all deplored Josephus.   For thirty days, wailings were heard in the city;
and musicians were hired to perform funeral chants.
When, however, the news arrived that Josephus was not
merely alive, but treated with distinction by Vespasian,
sorrow gave place to the fiercest indignation.   By some
he was called a dastard, by others a traitor; his name
was execrated; and to their motives for fierce and obstinate resistance to the Romans was added an eager
desire to revenge themselves on the apostate.   But they

were yet left for some time to exhale their fury in words, and display their bravery, not against the enemy, but against each other.

Vespasian—whether his army had been too severely handled at Jotapata, or whether, as is possible, he wished, in case any effort should be made at Rome to rid the world of the tyrant, to find himself at the head of a powerful and unbroken force—turned aside from the direct road of victory, and declined to advance upon the rebellious capital. He accepted the invitation of Agrippa, who earnestly solicited his presence, in order that the king might make a splendid display of his devotion to the Roman cause, and, by the terror of the Roman arms, quell the spirit of revolt in his own dominions. From Cæsarea by the sea, Vespasian passed to Cæsarea Philippi, where the army reposed for twenty days. Tarichea and Tiberias, though on the western coast of the Lake of Gennesaret, belonged to the dominions of Agrippa. Evident symptoms of insurrection appeared in both these cities. Titus was ordered to concentrate all the forces on Scythopolis, which is at no great distance from Tiberias: there Vespasian met him; and they advanced to a place on an eminence, within half a mile of Tiberias, named Sennabris. From thence he sent forward a decurion, named Valerian, with fifty horse, to exhort the inhabitants to surrender; for the people were peaceably disposed, but forced into war by a small turbulent party. Valerian, when he came near the city, dismounted, that his troop might not appear like a body of skirmishers; but before he could utter a word, the insurgents, headed by Jesus, the son of Saphat, charged him with great fury. Valerian, though he might easily have dispersed them, had no orders to fight; and, astonished at the boldness of the Jews, fled

on foot, with five of his companions. The captured
horses were led in triumph into the city. The senate of
Tiberias took the alarm, and fled to the Roman camp:
they entreated Vespasian not to act precipitately against
a city almost entirely disposed to the Roman interest,
and not to visit the crime of a few desperate insurgents
on the unoffending people. Vespasian had given orders
for the plunder of the city; but partly in compliance
with their supplication, partly from respect for Agrippa,
who trembled for the fate of one of the fairest towns in
his dominions, he accepted their submission. The insurgents, under Jesus, fled to Tarichea. The people opened
their gates, and received the Romans with acclamations. As the entrance to the city was too narrow for
the army to march in, except in very slender files, Vespasian commanded part of the wall to be thrown down;
but he strictly prohibited all plunder or outrage against
the inhabitants; and, at the intervention of Agrippa,
left the rest of the wall standing.

Not only the insurgents from Tiberias, but from all
the adjacent country, assembled in Tarichea, which
likewise stood, south of Tiberias, on the shore of Gennesaret. This beautiful lake has been compared by travellers with that of Geneva. In those days the shores
were crowded with opulent towns, which lay embowered
in the most luxuriant orchards, for which the whole
district was celebrated. Such was the temperature of
the climate, that every kind of fruit-tree flourished in
the highest perfection—nuts, which usually grow in a
colder climate, with the palm of the sultry desert, and
the fig and olive, which require a milder air. "Nature,"
says Josephus, "is, as it were, ambitious of bringing
together the fruits of different climates, and there is a
strife among the seasons of the year, each claiming this

favoured country as its own: for not only do fruits of
every species flourish, but continue to ripen; the grapes
and figs for ten months, and other kinds throughout the
year. The water of the lake is remarkably salubrious,
milder than that of fountains, and as cool as snow. It
abounds in fish of several kinds, peculiar to its waters."
This lake had been the chief scene of the miracles and
preaching of Jesus Christ. Its blue and quiet waters
were now to be broken by other barks than those of the
humble fishermen who spread their nets upon its surface; and to reflect, instead of the multitudes who listened to the peaceful Teacher, the armour of embattled
squadrons and the glittering pride of the Roman eagles.
Tarichea had been carefully fortified by Josephus;
not indeed so strongly as the more important town of
Tiberias, but still every part that was not washed by the
lake had been surrounded with a substantial wall. The
inhabitants had a great number of vessels in their port,
in which they might escape to the opposite shore, or, if
necessary, fight for the naval command of the lake.
The Romans pitched their camp under the walls; but
while they were commencing their works, Jesus, at the
head of the Tiberians, made a vigorous sally, dispersed the
workmen, and when the legionaries advanced in steady
array, fled back without loss. The Romans drove a
large party to their barks; the fugitives pushed out into
the lake, but still remained within the range of missiles,
cast anchor, and drawing up their barks, like a phalanx,
began a regular battle with the enemy on the land.

Vespasian heard that the Galileans were in great
force on the plain before the city. He sent Titus with
600 picked horse to disperse them. The numbers were
so immense that Titus sent to demand further succours;
but before they arrived, he determined to charge the

enemy. He addressed his men, exhorting them not to
be dismayed by numbers, but to secure the victory
before their fellow-soldiers could come up to share their
glory. He then put himself at their head, and his men
were rather indignant than joyful at beholding Trajan, '
at the head of 400 horse, make his appearance in the
field. Vespasian had likewise sent Antonius Silas with
2000 archers to occupy the side of a hill opposite to the
city, in order to divert those who were on the walls.
Titus led the attack; the Jews made some resistance,
but overpowered by the long spears and the weight of
the charging cavalry, gave way, and fled in disorder
towards Tarichea. The cavalry pursued, making
dreadful havock, and endeavoured to cut them off from
the city. The fugitives made their way through by the
mere weight of numbers. When they entered the city,
a tremendous dissension arose. The inhabitants, anxious
to preserve their property, and dismayed by their defeat,
urged capitulation. The strangers steadily and fiercely
refused compliance. The noise of the dissension reached
the assailants, and Titus immediately cried out, "Now
is the time for a resolute attack, while they are distracted by civil discord." He leaped upon his horse,
dashed into the lake, and, followed by his men, entered
the city. Consternation seized the besieged ; they
stood still, not attempting resistance. Jesus and his
insurgents, at the alarm, fled with others towards the
lake, and came right upon the Romans. They were
killed endeavouring to reach the shore; the inhabitants without resistance, the strangers fighting gallantly,
for the former still cherished a hope that their well-
known peaceful disposition might obtain them mercy.
At length Titus having punished the ringleaders, gave
orders that the carnage should cease. Those who had

before fled to the lake, when they saw the city taken, pushed out to sea as far as possible. Titus sent information to his father of this signal victory, and gave orders that vessels might instantly be prepared to pursue the fugitives. When these were ready, Vespasian embarked some of his troops, and rowed into the centre of the lake. The poor Galileans in their light fishing-boats could not withstand the heavy barks of the Romans, but they rowed round them, and attacked them with stones —feeble warfare, which only irritated the pursuers! for if thrown from a distance they did no damage, only splashing the water over the soldiers or falling harmless from their iron cuirasses; if those who threw them approached nearer, they could be hit in their turn by the Roman arrows. All the shores were occupied by hostile soldiers, and they were pursued into every inlet and creek; some were transfixed with spears from the high banks of the vessels, some were boarded and put to the sword, the boats of others were crushed or swamped, and the people drowned. If their heads rose as they were swimming, they were hit with an arrow, or by the prow of the bark; if they clung to the side of the enemy's vessel, their hands and heads were hewn off. The few survivors were driven to the shore, where they met with no more mercy. Either before they landed, or in the act of landing, they were cut down or pierced through. The blue waters of the whole lake were tinged with blood, and its clear surface exhaled for several days a foetid steam. The shores were strewn with wrecks of boats and swollen bodies that lay rotting in the sun, and infected the air, till the conquerors themselves shrank from the effects of their own barbarities. Here we must add to our bloody catalogue the loss of 6000 lives.

These, however, were the acts of an exasperated soldiery against enemies with arms in their hands. But Vespasian tarnished his fame for ever, by a deed at once of the most loathsome cruelty and deliberate treachery. After the battle, his tribunal was erected in Tarichea, and he sat in solemn judgement on those of the strangers who had been taken captives, and had been separated from the inhabitants of the city. According to his apologist Josephus, his friends encircled the seat of justice, and urged the necessity of putting an end to these desperate vagabonds, who, having no home, would only retreat to other cities, forcing them to take up arms. Vespasian, having made up his sanguinary resolution, was unwilling to terrify the inhabitants of Tarichea by commanding the massacre in their streets; he feared that it might excite insurrection: nor did he wish the whole city to be witness of his open violation of that faith which had been pledged when they surrendered. But his friends urged that every act was lawful against the Jews, and that right must give way to expediency. The insurgents received an ambiguous assurance of amnesty, but were ordered to retreat from the city only by the road to Tiberias. The poor wretches had implicit reliance on Roman faith. The soldiers immediately seized and blockaded the road to Tiberias; not one was allowed to leave the suburbs. Vespasian, in person, pursued them into the stadium; he ordered 1200 of the aged and helpless to be instantly slain, and drafted off 6000 of the most ablebodied to be sent to Nero, who was employed in a mad scheme of digging through the Isthmus of Corinth : 30,400 were sold as slaves, besides those whom he bestowed on Agrippa, who sold his portion also. The greater part of these, if we may believe Josephus, were desperate and ferocious ruffians, from Trachonitis, Gaulonitis, Gadara,

and Hippos, men who sough; to stir up war, that they
might escape the punishment of the crimes they had
committed during peace.   Had they been devils, it
could not excuse the base treachery of Vespasian.

This terrible example appalled the whole of Galilee,
and most of the towns capitulated at once to avoid the
same barbarities; three cities alone still defied the conqueror, Gamala, Gischala, and Itabyrium, the city which
Josephus had fortified on Mount Tabor.   Though the inhabitants of Gamala, situated on the side of the Lake of
Gennesaret, opposite to Tarichea, at no great distance
from the shore, might have inhaled the tainted gales,
which brought across the waters the noisome and pestilential odours of the late massacre; though probably
some single fugitive may have escaped, and hastening
to the only city of refuge, have related the dreadful
particulars of those still more revolting deeds which had
been perpetrated in the stadium of Tarichea; yet Gamala, proud in the impregnable strength of its situation,
peremptorily refused submission.   Gamala was the
chief city of Lower Gaulonitis, and belonged to the
government of Agrippa.   It was even more inaccessible
than Jotapata.   It stood on a long and rugged ledge of
mountains, which sloped downward at each end, and
rose in the middle into a sudden ridge, like the hump
of a camel, from which the town had its name Gamala.   The face and both sides of the rock ended in
deep and precipitous chasms or ravines; it was only
accessible from behind, where it joined the mountain
ridge.   On this side a deep ditch had been dug right
across, so as to cut off all approach.   The houses rose
one above another on the steep declivity of the hill, and
were crowded very thick and close.   The whole city
seemed as if hanging on a sharp precipice, and threaten-

ing constantly to fall and crush itself. It inclined to
the south, but on the southern crag, of immense
height, was the citadel, and above this was a precipice without a wall, which broke off sheer and abrupt,
and sank into a ravine of incalculable depth. There
was a copious fountain within the walls. This impregnable city, Josephus had still further strengthened by
trenches and water-courses. The garrison was neither
so numerous nor so brave as that of Jotapata, but still
confident in the unassailable position of their city. It
was crowded with fugitives from all parts, and had
already for seven months defied a besieging force which
Agrippa had sent against it. Vespasian marched to
Emmaus, celebrated for its warm baths, and then appeared before Gamala. It was impossible to blockade
the whole circuit of a town so situated. But he took
possession of all the neighbouring heights, particularly
of the mountain which commanded the city. He then
took up a position behind and to the east, where
there was a lofty tower. There the fifteenth legion
had their quarters, the fifth threw up works opposite
to the centre of the city, the tenth was employed
in filling up the ditches and ravines. Agrippa ventured
to approach the walls to persuade the inhabitants to
capitulation. He was struck by a stone from a sling on
the right elbow, and carried off with all speed by the
followers. This insult to the native king exasperated
the Roman soldiery. The embankments were raised
with great expedition by the skilful and practised
soldiers. Directly they were ready, the engines were
advanced. Chares and Joseph commanded in the city;
they had some misgivings of the event, for they were
but scantily supplied with provisions and water. Still,
however, they manned the wall boldly, and for some

time vigorously resisted the engineers who were fixing
the machines; but, at length, beat off by the catapults
and other engines for throwing stones, they drew back
into the city. The Romans immediately advanced the
battering-rams in three places, and beat down the wall.
They rushed in through the breaches, and broke into the
city amid the clang of their trumpets, the clashing of
their arms, and the shouting of their men.

The Jews thronged the narrow streets, and bravely
resisted the advance of the assailants. At length, overpowered by numbers, who attacked them on all sides,
they were forced up to the steep part of the city. There
they turned, and charging the enemy with great fury,
drove them down the declivities, and made great havock
among them, as they endeavoured to make their way
up the narrow streets, and along the rugged and craggy
paths. The Romans, who could not repel their enemy,
thus hanging as it were over their heads, nor yet break
through the throngs of their own men, who forced them
on from beneath, took refuge in the houses of the
citizens, which were very low. The crowded houses
could not bear the weight, and came crashing down.
One, as it fell, beat down another, and so all the way
down the hill. The situation of the Romans was tremendous. As they felt the houses sinking, they leaped
on the roofs, and fell with the tumbling buildings.
Many were totally buried in the ruins; many caught
by some part of their bodies, as in a trap; many were
suffocated with the dust and rubbish. The Gamalites
beheld the hand of God in this unexpected calamity ot
the foe. They rushed on, regardless of their own lives,
struck at the enemy on the roofs, or as they were slipping about in the narrow ways, and, aiming steadily
from above, slew every one who fell. The ruins fur

nished them with stones, and the slain of the enemy
with weapons. They drew the swords of the dead to
plunge into the hearts of the dying. Many of the Romans who had fallen from the houses killed themselves.
Flight was impossible, from their ignorance of the ways
and the blinding dust: many slew each other by mis-
take, and fell among their own men. Those who could
find the road retreated from the city. Vespasian himself, who had shared in the labours of his men, was
deeply afflicted to see the city rolling down in ruins
upon the heads of his soldiers. Neglectful of his own
safety, he had ascended by degrees, without perceiving
it, to the upper part of the city. He found himself in
the thick of the danger, with but few followers, for Titus
was absent on a mission to the prefect of Syria. It was
neither safe nor honourable to fly. With the readiness
of an old and experienced soldier, he called to those
who were with him to lock their shields over their heads
in the form of a testudo. The storm of darts and of the
falling ruins crashed about them without doing them
any injury. They persevered. The Gamalites, according
to Josephus, who now loses no opportunity of flattering
his protector, thinking the Romans' presence of mind
little less than divine, relaxed the fury of their attack.
The troops retreated with their faces to the enemy, and
did not turn till they were safe beyond the walls. The
loss of the Romans was great. The brave centurion
Æbutius was particularly lamented. A decemvir named
Gallus, with ten men, in the tumult, crept into a
house and concealed himself there. The good citizens,
at supper, sat quietly conversing on the exploits of the
day; Gallus, who was a Syrian, understood every word
they said. At night he broke out, cut all their throats,
and came safe off to the Roman camp.

The soldiers were dispirited with their defeat, and with the shame of having left their general in so perilous a situation. Vespasian addressed them in language of approbation and encouragement: he attributed their recent repulse to accident, and to their own too impetuous ardour, which had led them to fight with the frantic fury of their antagonists, rather than with the steady and disciplined courage of Roman legionaries. The Gamalites, in the mean time, were full of exultation at their unexpected success. But before long, pride gave way to melancholy foreboding, for their provisions began to fail. Their spirits sank, for now they had no hope of being admitted to capitulation. Yet they did not entirely lose their courage and activity. They repaired the shattered walls, and strictly guarded the parts that were still unshaken. When at length the Romans had completed their works, and threatened a second assault, many fled through the sewers, and passages which led into the ravines, where no guard was stationed. The rest of the inhabitants wasted away with hunger in silence; for the scanty provisions that remained were kept for the use of the garrison alone.

In the mean time Itabyrium had fallen. This town had been strongly fortified by Josephus. The ascent to the hill of Tabor is on the north, but extremely difficult.[1] The level area on the top, three miles and a quarter in circuit, occupied by the troops, was surrounded in forty days by a strong wall. The lower part of the hill had copious fountains, but the town depended

---

[1] The height of this mountain, according to the numbers as they stand in Josephus, would be three miles and three-quarters. Maundrell ascended it in an hour. The circumference of the town three miles and a quarter. Yet Maundrell states the area on the top to be only two furlongs in length, and one broad. Three miles and a quarter of wall and trench, built in forty days, seems rather beyond credibility.

on the cisterns of rain water. Against this city Placidus was sent with 600 horse. The hill seemed absolutely inaccessible. But the garrison, endeavouring to out-general the Roman commander, were themselves caught by their own stratagem. Each party pretended a desire to come to terms. Placidus used mild language; and the Itabyrians descended the hill as if to treat, but with a secret design of assailing the Romans unawares. At this unexpected assault Placidus feigned flight, to lure them into the plain. They pursued boldly, when he suddenly wheeled round, routed them with dreadful slaughter, and cut off their retreat to the mountain. Those who escaped fled to Jerusalem. The inhabitants of Itabyrium, distressed for want of water, surrendered.

In the mean time, the garrison of Gamala still made a vigorous resistance, while the people pined away with hunger. At length, two soldiers of the fifteenth legion contrived by night to creep under one of the highest towers, where they began to undermine the foundations. By the morning watch they had got, unperceived, quite under it. They then struck away five of the largest stones, and ran for their lives. The tower came down, guards and all, with a tremendous crash. The rest of the sentinels on the wall fled on all sides. Some were killed as they ran out of the city, among them Joseph, one of the valiant defenders. The whole city was in confusion, men running up and down, with no one to take the command; for the other leader, Chares, lay in the last paroxysm of a fever, and, in the agitation of the alarm, expired.

But all that day, the Romans, rendered cautious by their former repulse, made no attempt. Titus had now returned to the camp, and eager to revenge the insult on the Roman arms, with 200 horse and a

number of foot entered quietly into the city. As soon
as the Galilean guards perceived him, they rushed to
arms. Some catching up their children, and dragging
their wives along, ran to the citadel, shrieking and
crying; others, who encountered Titus, were slain without mercy. Those who could not make their escape to
the citadel rushed blindly on the Roman guard. The
steep streets ran with torrents of blood. Vespasian led
his men immediately against the citadel. The rock
on which it stood was rugged and impracticable, of
enormous height, and surrounded on all sides by abrupt
precipices. The Jews stood upon this crag, the top of
which the Roman darts could not reach, striking down all
their assailants, and rolling stones and throwing darts
upon their heads. But a tremendous tempest completed
their ruin. They could not stand on the points of the
rock, nor see the enemy as they scaled the crag. The Romans reached the top, and surrounded the whole party.
The memory of their former defeat rankled in their
hearts. They slew as well those who surrendered as
those who resisted. Numbers threw themselves headlong, with their wives and children, down the precipices.
Their despair was more fatal than the Roman sword.
4000 were killed by the enemy; 5000 bodies were found
of those who had cast themselves from the rock. Two
women alone escaped, the sisters of Philip, Agrippa's
general, and they only by concealing themselves, for the
Romans spared neither age nor sex; they seized infants
and flung them down from the rock. Thus fell Gamala
on the 23rd of September.[u]

Gischala[v] alone remained in arms. The inhabitants

---

[u] B. J. iv. 1. 10.
[v] Reland and Ritter place Gischala
at El Jisch, a short distance north-west
of Safed. Ritter, p. 771 and 783.

of this town were an agricultural people, and little inclined to war.   But the subtle and ambitious John, the
son of Levi, the rival of Josephus, commanded a strong
faction in the city, headed by his own desperate bandits.
The town, therefore, notwithstanding the desire of the
people to capitulate, assumed a warlike attitude.   Vespasian sent Titus against it with 1000 horse.   The
tenth legion moved to Scythopolis, he himself with the
other two went into winter quarters at Cæsarea.   When
he arrived before Gischala, Titus perceived that he
might easily take the city by assault.   But desirous
of avoiding unnecessary bloodshed, and probably well
acquainted with the disposition of the people, he sent
to offer terms of capitulation.   The walls were manned
by the faction of John; not one of the people was
allowed to approach them while the summons of Titus
was proclaimed.   John answered with the greatest
temper and moderation, that the garrison accepted with
the utmost readiness the generous terms that had been
offered; but that the day being the Sabbath, nothing
could be concluded without a direct infringement of
the law.   Titus not merely conceded this delay, but
withdrew his troops to the neighbouring town of
Cydoessa.

At midnight, John, perceiving that no Roman guard
was mounted, stole quietly with all his armed men out
of the city, followed by many others, with their families,
who had determined on flying to Jerusalem.[x]   To the
distance of twenty stadia, about two miles and a half,
the women and children bore on steadily: their strength
then began to fail.   They dropped off by degrees, while the

---

[x] In his implacable enmity to John   desperate but skilful retreat of John
of Gischala, Josephus represents this   to Jerusalem as a cowardly flight.

men pressed rapidly on, without regarding them. They
sat down wailing by the way side; and the more faint and
distant seemed the footsteps of their departing friends,
the more near and audible they thought the hurried
trampling of the enemy. Some ran against each other,
each supposing the other the foe; some lost their way;
many were trampled down by other fugitives. Those
who kept up longest, as they began to fail, stood calling
on the names of their friends and relations, but in vain.
The unfeeling John urged his men to save themselves,
and make their escape to some place where they might
have their revenge on the Romans. When Titus appeared the next day before the gates, the people threw
them open, and with their wives and children received
him as their deliverer. He sent a troop of horse in
pursuit of John. They slew 6000 of the fugitives, and
brought back 3000 women and children to the city.
Titus entered Gischala amidst the acclamations of the
people; and conducted himself with great lenity, only
threatening the city in case of future disturbance,
throwing down part of the wall, and leaving a garrison
to preserve the peace. Gischala was the last city
in Galilee which offered any resistance; and the campaign ended soon after, when Vespasian, having made
a rapid march against Jamnia and Azotus, both which
surrendered, and admitted Roman garrisons, returned to
Cæsarea, followed by a vast multitude from all quarters,
who preferred instant submission to the Romans to the
perils of war.[y]

But while the cities of Galilee thus arrested the
course of the Roman eagles—while Jotapata and
Gamala set the example of daring and obstinate resist-

---

[y] B. J. iv. 3. 2.

ance—the leaders of the nation in Jerusalem, instead of sending out armies to the relief of the besieged cities, or making an effort in their favour, were engaged in the most dreadful civil conflicts, and were enfeebling the national strength by the most furious collision of factions. It must be allowed that the raw and ill-armed militia of Judæa, if it had been animated by the best and most united spirit, could scarcely have hoped to make head in the open field against the experience and discipline of the Roman legions. Their want of cavalry, perhaps, prevented their undertaking any distant expedition, so that it may be doubted whether it was not their wisest policy to fight only behind their walls, in hopes that siege after siege might weary the patience, and exhaust the strength, of the invading army. But Jerusalem was ill-preparing herself to assume the part which became the metropolis of the nation, in this slow contest; and better had it been for her, if John of Gischala had perished in the trenches of his native town, or been cut off in his flight by the pursuing cavalry. His fame had gone before him to Jerusalem, perhaps not a little enhanced by the defection of his rival Josephus.[a] The multitude poured out to meet him, as well to do him honour, as to receive authentic tidings of the disasters in Galilee. The heat and the broken breathing of his men showed that they had ridden fast and long; yet they assumed a lofty demeanour, declared that they had not fled, but retreated to maintain a better position for defence—that for Gischala, and such insignificant villages, it was not worth risking the blood of brave men—they had reserved all theirs to be shed in the defence of the capital. Yet to many their retreat was

---

[a] B. J. iv. 3. 1.

too manifestly a flight, and from the dreadful details of
massacre and captivity, they foreboded the fate which
awaited themselves.   John, however, represented the
Roman force as greatly enfeebled, and their engines
worn out before Jotapata and Gamala; and urged, that
if they were so long in subduing the towns of Galilee,
they would inevitably be repulsed with shame from
Jerusalem.   John was a man of the most insinuating
address, and the most plausible and fluent eloquence.
The young men listened with eager interest and vehement acclamation: the old sat silent, brooding over
their future calamities.   The metropolis now began to
be divided into two hostile factions; but the whole province had before set them the fatal example of discord.
Every city was torn to pieces by civil animosities;
wherever the insurgents had time to breathe from the
assaults of the Romans, they turned their swords against
each other.   The war and the peace factions not only
distracted the public councils, but in every family,
among the dearest and most intimate friends, this vital
question created stern and bloody divisions.   Every one
assembled a band of adherents, or joined himself to
some organized party.   As in the metropolis, the youth
were everywhere unanimous in their ardour for war;
the older in vain endeavoured to allay the frenzy by
calmer and more prudent reasoning.   First individuals,
afterwards bands of desperate men, began to spread
over the whole country, spoiling either by open robbery,
or under pretence of chastising those who were traitors
to the cause of their country.   The unoffending and
peaceful, who saw their houses burning, and their
families plundered, thought they could have nothing
worse to apprehend from the conquest of the Romans
than from the lawless violence of their own country-

men. The Roman garrisons in the neighbouring towns, either not considering it their business to interfere, or rejoicing, in their hatred to the whole race, to behold their self-inflicted calamities, afforded little or no protection to the sufferers. At length, an immense number of these daring ruffians, satiated with plunder, by degrees, and in secret, stole into Jerusalem, where they formed a great and formidable troop. The city had never been accustomed to exclude strangers from its walls—it was the national metropolis ; and all of Jewish blood had a right to take up their temporary or permanent residence in the Holy City. They thought too that all who entered their gates would strengthen their power of resistance, and that it would be impolitic to reject any who came to offer their lives for the defence of the capital. But even had they not brought sedition and discord in their train, this influx of strangers would rather have weakened than strengthened the defence of Jerusalem ; for the provisions which ought to have been reserved for the soldiers, were consumed by an inactive and useless multitude, and famine was almost immediately added to the other evils which enfeebled and distracted the city.

These men, of fierce and reckless dispositions, and already inured to marauding habits, though gathering from all quarters, soon learned to understand each other, and grew into a daring and organized faction. They began to exercise their old calling; robberies, and burglaries, and assassinations, perpetually took place, not secretly, or by night, or of the meaner people, but openly in the face of day, of the most distinguished characters in Jerusalem. The first victim was Antipas, a man of royal blood, and a citizen of such high character as to be entrusted with the charge of the public

treasury. They seized and dragged him to prison.
The next were Levias, and Saphias the son of Raguel,
both of the Herodian family, with many others of the
same class. The people looked on in dismay, but, so
long as their own houses and persons were safe, they
abstained from interference.

Having gone so far in their daring course, the robbers
did not think it safe to proceed farther. They dreaded
the families of those whom they had imprisoned, for
they were both numerous and powerful; they even
apprehended a general insurrection of the people.
They sent a ruffian named John, the son of Dorcas, a
man ready for the worst atrocities, with ten others like
him, and under their warrant a general massacre of the
prisoners took place. The ostensible pretext of this
barbarity was the detection of a conspiracy to betray
the city to the Romans. They gloried in this act,
and assumed the titles of Saviours and Deliverers
of their country, for having thus executed condign vengeance on those who were traitors to the common
liberty.[a]

The people still cowered beneath the sway of these
Zealot robbers. Their next step was even more daring.
They took upon themselves the appointment to the
Chief Priesthood—that is, probably, to nominate the
members of the Sanhedrin. They annulled at once all
claim from family descent, and appointed men unknown, and of ignoble rank, who would support them
in their violence. Those whom they had raised by

---

[a] The acts of these Septembrisers of
Jerusalem are related, it must be remembered, by an enemy. This fatal
schism between the more timid and
prudent who would have submitted
to Rome, and the braver and more desperate determined to fight to the last
for their liberties, was inevitable: only
we should wish to have heard the other
side.

their breath, their breath could degrade. Thus all the leaders of the people were the slaves and puppets of their will. They undermined the authority of some who were before at the head of affairs by propagating false rumours, and by ascribing to them fictitious speeches—so that by their dissensions among each other, they might increase the power of the Zealots, thus united for evil. At length, satiated with their crimes against men, they began to invade the sanc tuary of God with their unhallowed violence.

After some time, the populace were at last goaded to resistance. Ananus, the oldest of the chief priests,[b] had been long the recognized head of the more peaceful party. He was a man of great wisdom, and in the opinion of Josephus, had he not been cut off by untimely death, might have saved the city. At his incitement, murmurs and threats of resistance spread among the people, and the robber Zealots immediately took refuge in the Temple of God, which they made their garrison and head quarters. They pretended to proceed according to a mockery of law, which was more galling to the popular feeling than their licentious violence. They declared that the High Priest ought to be appointed by lot, not according to family descent. They asserted that this was an ancient usage; but, in fact, it was a total abro gation of the customary law, and solely intended to wrest the supreme power into their own hands. Matthias, the son of Theophilus, was the rightful High Priest; but the Zealots assembled, for this purpose, one family of

---

[b] These ἀρχιερεῖς, whom we now meet with in the plural number, instead of the one ἀρχιερεύς, were probably the chiefs of the 24 sacerdotal classes. Those too who had held the High-priesthood retained the title. Compare Selden de Success. in Pontif. i. 12; Casaubon in Baron. xiii. 5· Krebs and Wetstein in Matt. ii. 4.

the priestly race, that of Eliachim,[c] and from this chose
a High Priest by lot. It happened that the choice fell
on one Phanias, the son of Samuel, a man not merely
unworthy of that high function, but a coarse clown, who
had lived in the country, and was totally ignorant even
of the common details of his office. They sent for
him, however, decked him in the priestly robes, and
brought him forth as if upon the stage. His awkward
ness caused them the greatest merriment and laughter;
while the more religious priests stood aloof, weeping in
bitter but vain indignation at this profanation of the
holy office.

The people could endure every thing but this. They
rose as one man, to revenge the injured dignity of the
sacred ceremonies. Joseph, the son of Gorion, and
Simon, the son of Gamaliel, went about, both in private
and public, haranguing the multitude, and exhorting
them to throw off the yoke of these desperate ruffians,
and to cleanse the Holy Place from the contamination of
their presence. The most eminent of the priestly order,
Jesus, son of Gamala, and Ananus, remonstrated with
the people for their quiet submission to the Zealots,
which had now become a name of opprobrium and detestation.

A general assembly was summoned. All were indignant at the robberies, the murders, and sacrileges of
the Zealots, but still they apprehended their numbers
and the strength of their position. Ananus came forward and addressed them; and as he spoke, he continually turned his eyes, full of tears, towards the
violated Temple. He reproached them with their tame
endurance of a tyranny more cruel and disgraceful than

---

* This is Reland's reading for Eniachim, as in 1 Chron. xxiv. 12.

that of the Romans. Would they, who could not endure
the yoke of the masters of the world, bear the tyranny of
their countrymen? [d] He reproached them for their abandonment of the Temple of their God to profane and
lawless men. It was a cause for bitter tears to see
the offerings of the heathen in the Holy Place: how
much worse to see the arms of murderers, the murderers
of the flower of the city, whom the Romans even if conquerors would have spared! The Romans remained
reverently without, in the court of the Gentiles: those
who were bound to the Law—who called themselves Jews,
trod the very Holy of Holies, their hands reeking
with the blood of their brethren. His long and animated
harangue was heard with the deepest interest, and the
people demanded with loud outcries to be immediately
led to battle. The Zealots had their partisans in the
assembly, and speedily received intelligence of what
was going on. While Ananus was organizing his force,
they began the attack. But Ananus was not less active;
and though the people were inferior in discipline, unused
to act together in bodies, and inexperienced in the
management of their arms, yet they had vast superiority
in numbers. Thus a fierce civil war broke out in a city
against whose gates a mighty enemy was preparing to
lead his forces. Both parties fought with furious valour;
many were slain; the bodies of the people were carried
off into their houses; those of the Zealots into the
Temple, dropping blood, as they were hurried along,
upon the sacred pavement. The robbers had always
the better in a regular conflict, but the people at length
increasing in numbers, those that pressed behind prevented those in front from retreating, and urged for-

---

[d] τοὺς τῆς οἰκουμένης δεσπότας μὴ φέροντες, τῶν ὁμοφύλων τυράν-
νων ἀνεξόμεθα;

ward in a dense and irresistible mass, till the Zealots
were forced back into the Temple, into which Ananus
and his men broke with them. The first quadrangle,
that of the Gentiles, being thus taken, the Zealots fled
into the next, and closed the gates. The religious
scruples of Ananus prevented him from pressing his advantage; he trembled to commit violence against the
sacred gates, or to introduce the people, unclean, and
not yet purified from slaughter, into the inner court of
the Temple. He stationed 6000 chosen and well-armed
men in the cloisters, and made arrangements that this
guard should be regularly relieved.[e]

In this state of affairs, the subtle and ambitious John
of Gischala, who had not long arrived in Jerusalem,
pursued his own dark course.[f] Outwardly, he joined the
party of Ananus; no one could be more active in the
consultations of the leaders, or in the nightly inspection
of the guards. But he kept up a secret correspondence
with the Zealots, and betrayed to them all the movements of the assailants. To conceal this secret he re-
doubled his assiduities, and became so extravagant in
his protestations of fidelity to Ananus and his party,
that he completely overacted his part, and incurred suspicion. The people could not but observe that their
closest consultations were betrayed to the enemy, and
they began gradually to look with a jealous eye on
their too obsequious servant. Yet it was no easy task

---

[e] B. J. iv. 3. 12.

The more wealthy, however, betrayed their want of spirit. They
hired substitutes among the poor to
keep guard for them. πολλοὶ δὲ τῶν
ἐν ἀξιώμασιν, ἀφεθέντες ἀπὸ τῶν
ἄρχειν δοκούντων, μισθούμενοι πε-
νιχροτέρους ἀνθ᾽ ἑαυτῶν ἐπὶ τὴν

φρουρὰν ἔπεμπον. Such a party was
not likely to succeed against such antagonists. Ibid.

[f] It must be remembered that this
description of the acts of John comes
from his deadly foe. Salvador is inclined to make a hero of John, but
somewhat cautiously and irresolutely

to remove him; he was much too subtle to be detected,
and had a formidable band of adherents, by no means
of the lowest order, in the council itself. The people
acted in the most unwise manner possible. They betrayed their suspicions of John by exacting from him
an oath of fidelity. John swore readily to all they demanded, that he would remain obedient to the people,
never betray their counsels, and entirely devote both his
courage and abilities to the destruction of their enemies.
Ananus and his party laid aside their mistrust, admitted
him to their most secret councils, and even deputed
him to treat with the Zealots. John undertook the mission, and proceeded into the court of the Temple. There
he suddenly threw off his character, and began to address the Zealots as if he had been their ambassador,
rather than that of the people. He represented the
dangers he had incurred in rendering them secret service, informed them that negotiations were going on for
the surrender of the city to the Romans, that their ruin
was resolved, for Ananus had determined either to enter
the Temple by fair means, under the pretext of worship,
and with that view had purified the people, or by main
force; they must either submit, or obtain succours from
some external quarter; and he solemnly warned them
against the danger of trusting to the mercy of the people.
John, with his characteristic caution, only intimated the
quarter from which this succour was to be sought. The
chieftains of the Zealots were Eleazar, the son of Simon,
the old crafty antagonist of Ananus, and Zacharias, the
son of Phalec. They knew that they were designated
for vengeance by the adherents of Ananus; their only
hope was in driving their own partisans to desperation.
The mention of negotiations, according to Josephus the
malicious invention of John, inflamed the whole party

of the Zealots to madness. A despatch was instantly
sent to call the Idumeans to their assistance, by messengers who were noted for their swiftness of foot and
promptitude of action.

These Idumeans, who, since the conquest of Hyrcanus,[g] had been incorporated with the Jews as a people,
were a fierce and intractable tribe; some of the old
Arab blood seemed to flow in their veins; they loved
adventure, and thronged to war as to a festivity. No
sooner was the welcome invitation of the Zealots made
known through the country, than they flew to arms,
and even before the appointed day had assembled an
immense force, proclaiming as they went, that they
were marching to the relief of the metropolis. They
were 20,000 in number, under John and James, the
sons of Susa, Simon, son of Cathla, and Phineas, son of
Clusoth. The messengers of the Zealots had escaped
the vigilance of Ananus; and the vast army came
suddenly, though not quite unexpectedly, before the
walls. The gates were closed, and Ananus determined
to attempt expostulation and remonstrance with these
formidable invaders. Jesus, the next in age of the chief
priests to Ananus, addressed them from a lofty tower on
the wall. He endeavoured to persuade them to follow
one of three lines of conduct—either to unite with them
in the chastisement of these notorious robbers and assassins; or to enter the city unarmed, and arbitrate between
the conflicting parties; or, finally, to depart, and leave
the capital to settle its own affairs.[h] Simon, the son of
Cathla, sternly answered, that they came to take the
part of the true patriots and defenders of their country
against men who were in a base conspiracy to sell the

---

[g] Compare Joseph. Ant. xiii. 9. 1; B. J. ii. 3. 1.   [h] B. J. iv. 4. 3

liberties of the land to the Romans. This charge the party of Ananus had always steadily disclaimed; with what sincerity it is impossible to decide.

At the words of the son of Cathla, the Idumeans joined in the loudest acclamations, and Jesus returned in sadness to his dispirited party, who now, instead of being the assailants, found themselves, as it were, besieged between two hostile armies. The Idumeans were not altogether at their ease. Though enraged at their exclusion from the city, they were disappointed at receiving no intelligence from the Zealots, who were closely cooped up in the Temple, and some began to repent of their hasty march. So they encamped, uncertain how to act, before the walls. The night came on, and with the night a tempest of unexampled violence, wind and pouring rain, frequent lightnings, and long rolling thunders. The very earth seemed to quake. All parties, in this dreadful state of suspense, sat trembling with the deepest awe, and construed the discord of the elements, either as a sign of future calamity, or as a manifestation of the instant wrath of the Almighty. The Idumeans saw the arm of God revealed to punish them for their assault on the Holy City, and thought that Heaven had openly espoused the cause of Ananus. Mistaken interpreters of these ominous signs! which rather foreboded their own triumph, and the discomfiture of the Jewish people. Yet they locked their shields over their heads, and kept off the torrents of rain as well as they could. But the Zealots, anxious about their fate, looked eagerly abroad to discover some opportunity of rendering assistance to their new friends. The more daring proposed, while the fury of the storm had thrown the enemy off their guard, to fight their way through the bands stationed in the cloisters of the

outer court, and to throw open the gates to the Idumeans. The more prudent thought it in vain to resort
to violence, because the sentinels in the cloisters had
been doubled, and the walls of the city would be
strongly manned for fear of the invading army, and they
expected Ananus every hour to go the round of the
guards. That night alone, trusting perhaps to the
number and strength of his doubled party, Ananus neglected all precaution. The darkness of the night was
increased by the horrors of the tempest; some of the
guard stole off to rest. The watchful Zealots perceived
this, and taking the sacred saws, began to cut asunder
the bars of the gates. In the wild din of the raging
wind and pealing thunder, the noise of the saws was not
heard. A few stole out of the gate, and along the
streets to the wall. There applying their saws to the
gate which fronted the Idumean camp, they threw it
open. The Idumeans, at first, drew back in terror, for
they suspected some stratagem of Ananus; they grasped
their swords, and stood awaiting the enemy, whom they
expected every instant to break forth. But when they
recognized their friends, they entered boldly; and so
much were they exasperated, that if they had turned
towards the city, they might have massacred the whole
people. But their guides earnestly besought them first
to deliver their beleaguered companions. Not only did
gratitude, but prudence likewise, advise this course : for
if the armed guard in the porticoes were surprised, the
city would speedily fall; if it remained entire, the
citizens would rally round that centre, speedily collect
an irresistible force, and cut off their ascent to the
Temple. They marched rapidly through the city, and
mounted the hill of Moriah. The Zealots were on the
watch for their arrival, and as they attacked the guard

in front, fell upon them from behind. Some were slain
in their sleep: others, awaking at the din, rushed
together, and endeavoured to make head against the
Zealots. But when they found that they were attacked
likewise from without, they perceived, at once, that the
Idumeans were within the city. Their spirits sank, they
threw down their arms, and uttered wild shrieks of distress. A few bolder youths confronted the Idumeans,
and covered the escape of some of the older men, who
ran shrieking down the streets, announcing the dreadful
calamity. They were answered by screams and cries
from the houses, and the shrill wailing of the women.
On their side, the Zealots and Idumeans shouted, and
the wind howled over all, and the black and flashing
sky pealed its awful thunders. The Idumeans spared
not a soul of the guard whom they surprised, being
naturally men of bloody character, and exasperated by
having been left without the gates exposed to the furious
pelting of the storm; those who supplicated, and those
who fought, suffered the same fate: it was in vain to
appeal to the sanctity of the Temple; even within its
precincts they were hewn down. Some were driven to
the very ledge of the rock on which the Temple stood,
and in their desperation precipitated themselves headlong into the city. The whole court was deluged with
human blood, and when day dawned, 8500 bodies were
counted. But the carnage ended not with the night.
The Idumeans broke into the city, and pillaged on all
sides. The High Priests, Ananus, and Jesus, the son of
Gamala, were seized, put to death, and,—an unprecedented barbarity among a people so superstitious about
the rites of sepulture, that even public malefactors were
buried before sunset !—the bodies of these aged and respected men, who had so lately appeared in the splendid

sacred vestments of the priests, were cast forth naked to the dogs and carrion birds.[1]

With the death of Ananus, all hopes of peace were extinguished, and from that night Josephus dates the ruin of Jerusalem. The historian gives him a high character. He was a man of rigid justice who always preferred the public good to his own interest, and a strenuous lover of liberty, of popular address, and of great influence over all the lower orders. Though vigilant and active in placing the city in the best posture of defence, yet he always looked forward, in eager hope, to a peaceable termination of the contest. In this respect, perhaps, he followed the wisest policy, considering the state of his country, and the strength of the enemy ;[k] yet we cannot wonder that a man with such views, at such a crisis, should be vehemently suspected of traitorous intentions by the more rash and zealous of his countrymen, who preferred death and ruin rather than submission to the tyrannous yoke of Rome. Jesus, the son of Gamala, was likewise a man of weight and character.

The vengeance of the Zealots and their new allies was not glutted by the blood of their principal enemies. They continued to massacre the people, in the words of Josephus, like a herd of unclean animals. The lower orders they cut down wherever they met them ; those of higher rank, particularly the youth, were dragged to prison, that they might force them, by the fear of death,

---

[1] κἄιτο, τοσαύτην Ἰουδαίων περὶ τὰς ταφὰς πρόνοιαν ποιουμένων, ὥστε καὶ τοὺς ἐκ καταδικης ἀνασταυρουμένους πρὸ δὺντος ἡλίου καθελεῖν τε καὶ θάπτειν. I cite this passage as illustrating the crucifixion of our Lord, and because it shows how the Jewish mind had now become familiar with this Roman mode of execution.

[k] ἄμαχα γὰρ ἤδει τὰ Ῥωμαίων is the expression of Josephus, with a sympathy of opinions prudent or base (as different minds might judge). B J. iv. 5. 2.

to embrace their party. No one complied; all preferred death to an alliance with such wicked conspirators. They were scourged and tortured, but still resolutely endured, and at length were relieved from their trials by the more merciful sword of the murderer. They were seized by day, and all the night these horrors went on; at length their bodies were cast out into the streets, to make room for more victims in the crowded prisons. Such was the terror of the people, that they neither dared to lament nor bury their miserable kindred; but retired into the farthest part of their houses to weep, for fear the enemy should detect their sorrow; for to deplore the dead was to deserve death. By night they scraped up a little dust with their hands, and strewed it over the bodies; none but the most courageous would venture to do this by day. Thus perished 12,000 of the noblest blood in Jerusalem.[1]

Ashamed, at length, or weary of this promiscuous massacre, the Zealots began to affect the forms of law, and set up tribunals of justice. There was a distinguished man, named Zacharias, the son of Baruch,[m] whose influence they dreaded, and whose wealth they yearned to pillage, for he was upright, patriotic, and rich. They assembled, by proclamation, seventy of the principal men of the populace, and formed a Sanhedrin. Before that court they charged Zacharias with intelligence with the Romans. They had neither proof nor

---

[1] B. J. iv. 5. 3.

[m] The singular coincidence between this man and the Zacharias, son of Barachias, mentioned by Christ (St. Matt. xxiii. 35), is explained in very different ways. Some go so far as to interpret it as a prophecy of this event, and cite instances of an aorist used in a future sense. This is to me very improbable. I should be inclined to suppose "the son of Barachias" a gloss crept into the text of the Gospel, or an error of a copyist.

witness, but insisted on their own conviction of his guilt.
Zacharias, despairing of his life, conducted himself with
unexampled boldness; he stood up, ridiculed their
charges, and, in a few words, clearly established his own
innocence.   He then turned to the accusers, inveighed
with the most solemn fervour against their iniquities,
and lamented the wretched state of public affairs.   The
Zealots murmured, and some were ready to use their
swords; but they were desirous of seeing whether the
judges were sufficiently subservient to their will.   The
seventy unanimously acquitted the prisoner, and preferred to die with Zacharias rather than be guilty of
his condemnation.   The furious Zealots raised a cry of
indignation; two of them rushed forward, and struck
him dead, where he stood, in the Temple court, shouting
aloud, "This is our verdict—This is our more summary
acquittal!"   Then dragging the body along the pavement, they threw it into the valley below.   The judges
they beat with the flat blades of their swords, and drove
them, in disgrace, back into the city.

At length the Idumeans began to repent of this
bloody work; they openly declared that they had
advanced to Jerusalem to suppress the treason of the
leaders, and to defend the city against the Romans;
that they had been deceived into becoming accomplices
in horrible murders; no treason was really apprehended, and the Roman army still suspended their
attack.   They determined to depart; first, however, they
opened the prisons, and released 2000 of the people, who
instantly fled to Simon the son of Gioras, of whom we
shall hereafter hear too much.   Their departure was
unexpected by both parties.   The populace, relieved
from their presence, began to gain confidence; but the
Zealots, as if released from control, rather than deprived

of assistance, continued their lawless iniquities. Every day new victims fell by rapid and summary proceedings; it seemed as if they thought their safety depended on the total extermination of the higher orders. Among the rest perished Gorion, a man of the highest birth and rank, and the greatest zeal for liberty : incautious language caused his ruin. Even Niger of Peræa, their most distinguished soldier, who had escaped from the rout at Ascalon, was dragged along the streets, showing in vain the scars which he had received for his ungrateful country. He died with fearful imprecations, summoning the Romans to avenge his death, and denouncing famine and pestilence, and civil massacre, as well as war, against this accursed city. Niger was the last whose power they dreaded. After that deed they carried on their sanguinary work without scruple : none could escape. He who paid them no court, was stigmatized as haughty; he who spoke boldly, as one who despised them ; he who merely flattered them, as a traitor; they had but one punishment for great or small offences—death; none but the very meanest in rank and fortune escaped their hands.[n]

In this state of the city, many of the Roman leaders strongly urged Vespasian to march immediately on Jerusalem, and put an end to the rebellion. The more politic general replied, that nothing would extinguish these feuds which were wasting the strength of the rebels, or unite their forces, but an attack from the Romans; he determined to allow them, like wild beasts, to tear each other to pieces in their dens. Every day deserters came in ; not but that the roads were closely

***

[n] B. J. iv. 6. 1. Thus writes Josephus—perhaps here as elsewhere, rather with the vehemence of an orator, than with the cautious accuracy of a historian.

guarded, yet those who had the power to bribe largely, and those alone, were sure to find their way; yet some, such was the attachment to the very soil of Jerusalem, after they had got off, returned of their own accord, only in hopes that they might find burial in the Holy City. Hopes too often baffled; for, so hardened were all hearts become, that even the reverence for that sacred rite was extinct. Both within the city, and in the villages, lay heaps of bodies rotting in the sun. To bury a relative, was death; thus compassion itself was proscribed and eradicated from the heart. Such was the state of the people, that the survivors envied the dead as released from suffering; those who were tormented in prisons even thought them happy whose bodies were lying unburied in the streets. Religion seemed utterly abolished: the law was scorned, the oracles of the prophets were treated with ridicule, as the tricks of impostors. "Yet by these men," says Josephus, "the ancient prediction seemed rapidly drawing to its fulfilment; that when civil war should break out in the city, and the Temple be profaned by the hands of native Jews, the city would be taken, and the Temple burned with fire."

During all this horror and confusion, John of Gischala steadily pursued his path of ambition. From the most desperate of these desperate men, he attached a considerable party to his own person; and, though suspected by all as aiming at kingly power, and watched with jealous vigilance, yet such was his craft and promptitude, that he imperceptibly centred all real authority and influence in his single person. In the public councils, he contradicted every one, and delivered his own sentiments with a sort of irresistible imperiousness. Some were cajoled by his subtlety, others awed by his

decision, till at length his adherents almost threw off
the mask, and formed, as it were, a body-guard around
their leader.   Thus the Zealots were divided.   In one
part John ruled like a king; in the other a kind of
democratical equality prevailed.   Yet the factions only
watched each other, and contending but in occasional
skirmishes, combined readily for the persecution of the
people, and vied with each other in the quantity of
plunder they could extort.

Thus the miserable city was afflicted by the three
great evils, war, tyranny, and sedition: a fourth was
soon added to complete their ruin.   The Sicarii or
Assassins, it may be remembered, had seized the strong
fortress of Masada, near the Dead Sea.   They had
hitherto been content to subsist on the adjacent country.   Encouraged by the success of the daring robbers
who had thus become masters of Jerusalem, they surprised Engeddi during the night of the Passover, dispersed all who resisted, and slew about 700, chiefly
women and children.   They brought away great quantities of corn, and followed up the blow by wasting the
whole region.   Other bands collected in other parts,
and the province became a scene of plunder and confusion.

It was now the spring—the commencement of a new
campaign.   The refugees in the camp of Vespasian
earnestly besought him to march at once upon the
capital; but the wary Roman chose rather to reduce the
rest of the country.   The first place against which he
moved was Gadara, the chief city of Peræa.   The more
wealthy inhabitants sent a deputation to Vespasian.
The opposite party, surprised by the rapid advance of
the Romans, after revenging themselves on some of
those who had treated for surrender, withdrew, and

Gadara received the conqueror with open gates, and with joyful acclamations. Vespasian granted the inhabitants a garrison for their protection, for they had destroyed their walls of their own accord.

Vespasian having despatched Placidus, with 500 horse and 3000 foot, to pursue the fugitives from Gadara, returned to Cæsarea. They had taken possession of a large village named Bethanabris, which they armed in their defence. Placidus attacked them, and employing his usual stratagem, a feigned retreat, to allure them from their walls, then faced round, and cut off the greater part. Some forced their way back, and Placidus had well nigh entered the village with them. Before night it was taken and laid waste with the usual carnage. Those who escaped, raised the country as they passed, and grown again to a considerable body, fled towards Jericho, the populous and strongly fortified city on the other side of the river. Placidus pursued them to the Jordan; the river was swollen and impassable. They were obliged to turn and fight. It must have been near the place where the waters, of old, receded at the word of Joshua, but now the deep and rapid flood rolled down in unchecked impetuosity. The Romans charged with their accustomed vigour. Multitudes fell, multitudes were driven into the stream, others plunged in of their own accord. Not only the river, but the Dead Sea also, was almost choked with bodies, which lay floating upon its dark and heavy waters. 15,000 were killed, 2500 taken prisoners, with an immense booty from all that pastoral region, asses, sheep, camels, and oxen. Placidus followed up his victory, reduced the whole country of Peræa, and the coast of the Dead Sea as far as Machærus.

In the mean time the state of the Roman empire

began to command the attention of Vespasian.   Vindex
had revolted in Gaul, and Vespasian was anxious to put
an end to the war in Palestine, in order that his army
might be at liberty for any further service.   He advanced from Cæsarea, took successively Antipatris,
Lydda, and Jamnia, and blockaded Emmaus, which
made resistance.   He then moved southward through
the toparchy of Bethleptepha, to the frontier of Idumæa, wasting as he went with fire and sword, and
leaving garrisons in all the defensible castles.   In Idumæa he took two large villages, Betharis and Cephar-
toba, put to the sword above 10,000 men, and brought
away 1000 captives.   Leaving there a strong force to
waste the country, he returned to Emmaus, passed by
Samaria and Neapolis, encamped in Corea, and at
length appeared before Jericho, where the troops which
had subdued Peræa met him.   The insurgents of
Jericho fled to the wilderness of Judæa, which lay to
the south along the shores of the Dead Sea.   The
city was deserted, and the Roman soldiery reposed
among the delicious gardens and palm groves in the
neighbourhood, before they encountered the dreary and
mountainous wilderness which lay between them and
Jerusalem.

Vespasian sent to reduce all the neighbouring country.   Lucius Annius was detached against Gerasa, where
1000 of the youth were put to the sword, the rest made
captives, and the city pillaged by the soldiery.   And
now Jerusalem already beheld the Roman at her gates ;
every approach to the city was cut off, and every hour
they expected to see the plain to the north glitter with
the arms and eagles of the fated enemy.   Suddenly
intelligence came from Rome which checked the march
of Vespasian, and Jerusalem had yet a long period

either to repent and submit, or to prepare for a more orderly and vigorous resistance. The first event was the death of Nero: and during the whole of the year 68–9, in which Galba, Otho, and Vitellius, successively attained and lost the imperial crown, Vespasian held his troops together, without weakening, by unnecessary exertions against the enemy, that force by which he might eventually win the sovereignty of the world.

But Jerusalem would not profit by the mercy of the Almighty in thus suspending for nearly two years the march of the avenger. An enemy more fatal than the Roman immediately rose up to complete the sum of her misery, and to add a third party to those which already distracted her peace. Simon, son of Gioras, a native of Gerasa, was a man as fierce and cruel, though not equal in subtlety to John of Gischala. He had greatly distinguished himself in the rout of Cestius. Since that time, it has been seen that he pillaged Acrabatene, and being expelled from that region by Ananus, entered Masada, where by degrees he became master of the town. His forces increased; he had wasted all the country towards Idumæa, and at length began to entertain designs upon Jerusalem. The Zealots marched out in considerable force against him, but were discomfited and driven back to the city. Simon, instead of attacking Jerusalem, turned back and entered Idumæa at the head of 20,000 men. The Idumeans suddenly raised 25,000, and after a long and doubtful battle Simon retreated to a village called Nain, the Idumeans to their own country. Simon a second time raised a great force and entered their border. He encamped before Tekoa, and sent one of his adherents named Eleazar to persuade the garrison of Herodium, at no

great distance, to surrender. The indignant garrison
drew their swords upon him; he leaped from the wall
and was killed. On the other hand the Idumeans,
betrayed by one of their leaders, were struck with a
panic and dispersed. Simon entered the country, took
Hebron, and wasted the whole region. His army consisted of 40,000 men, besides his heavy-armed troops.
They passed over the whole district like a swarm of
locusts, burning, destroying, and leaving no sign of life
or vegetation behind them.

The Zealots in the mean time surprised the wife of
Simon, and carried her off in triumph to Jerusalem.
They hoped that by this means they should force Simon
to terms. Simon came raging like a wild beast before
the walls of Jerusalem. The old and unarmed people
who ventured out of the gates were seized and tortured.
He is said scarcely to have refrained from mangling
their bodies with his teeth. Some he sent back with
both hands cut off, vowing that unless his wife were
returned, he would force the city, and treat every man
within the walls in the same manner. The people, and
even the Zealots themselves, took the alarm; they
restored his wife, and he withdrew.

It was now the spring of the second year, 69, and
Vespasian once more set his troops in motion. He
reduced the toparchies of Gophnitis and Acrabatene.
His cavalry appeared at the gates of Jerusalem.
Cerealis in the mean time had entered Idumæa, and
taken Caphethra, Capharabis, and Hebron: nothing
remained to conquer but Herodium, Masada, Machærus,
and Jerusalem itself.

Still no attempt was made on Jerusalem; it was left
to its domestic enemies. Simon had remained in
Masada, while Cerealis wasted Idumæa. He then broke

forth again, entered Idumæa, drove a vast number of that people to Jerusalem, and again encamped before the walls, putting to the sword all the unfortunate stragglers who quitted the protection of the city.

Simon thus warred on the unhappy city from without, and John of Gischala within. The pillage and licence of the opulent capital had totally corrupted his hardy Galileans, who had been allowed to commit every excess. Pillage was their occupation, murder and rape their pastime. They had become luxurious and effeminate; they had all the cruelty of men with the wantonness of the most abandoned women. Glutted with plunder and blood, and the violation of women, they decked their hair, put on female apparel, painted their eyes, and in this emasculate garb wandered about the city, indulging in the most horrible impurities, yet, on an instant, reassuming their character of dauntless ruffians, drawing their swords, which were concealed under their splendid clothes, and fighting fiercely or stabbing all they met without mercy. Thus was the city besieged within and without. Those who stayed were tyrannized over by John; those who fled, massacred by Simon.

At length the party of John divided. The Idumeans, who were still in considerable numbers in Jerusalem, grew jealous of his power; they rose and drove the Zealots into a palace built by Grapte, a relation of King Izates. This they entered with them, and thence forced them into the Temple. This palace was the great treasure-house of John's plunder, and was now in turn pillaged by the Idumeans. But the Zealots assembled in overwhelming force in the Temple, and threatened to pour down upon the Idumeans and the people. The Idumeans did not dread their bravery so

much as their desperation, lest they should sally and set
the whole city on fire over their heads.   They called an
assembly of the chief priests, and that counsel was
adopted which added the final consummation to the
miseries of the city.   " God," says Josephus, "overruled
their wills to that most fatal measure."   They agreed
to admit Simon within the gates.   The High Priest,
Matthias, a weak but, from his rank, an influential
man, supported this new proposition: he was sent in
person to invite Simon within the walls, and amid the
joyful greetings of the misguided populace, the son of
Gioras marched through the streets, and took possession
of all the upper city.

Simon immediately proceeded to attack the Zealots
in the Temple, but the commanding situation of the
building enabled them to defend themselves with success.   They fought with missiles from the porticoes and
pinnacles, and many of Simon's men fell.   To obtain
still further advantage from the height of their ground,
they reared four strong towers, one on the north-east
corner, one above the Xystus, one at another corner
opposite the lower city, and one above the Pasto-
phoria, where the priests were accustomed to sound
the silver trumpet to announce the commencement
and termination of the Sabbath.   On these towers
they placed their military engines, their bowmen and
slingers, which swept the enemy down at a great distance; till at length Simon in some degree relaxed his
assaults.

Vespasian had now assumed the purple; the East
declared in his favour; Josephus received the honour
and reward of a prophet, and was delivered from his
bonds.   After the defeat and death of Vitellius, the
new Cæsar was acknowledged at Rome, and the whole

empire hailed in joyful triumph the accession of the
Flavian dynasty. At the commencement of the ensuing
year the Emperor had time to think of the reduction of
the rebellious city which had long resisted his own
arms. His son Titus was sent to complete the subjugation of Palestine by the conquest of the capital.

BOOK XVI.

SIEGE OF JERUSALEM.

State of the City — Advance of the Roman Army — Danger of
Titus — Capture of the first Wall — Of the second — Famine —
Murders within the City — Crucifixions without — The City
encircled with a Trench and Wall — Antonia taken — Capture
— Conflagration of the Temple — Capture and Demolition of the
City — Fate of John and Simon — Numbers slain and taken
Prisoners — Triumph of Vespasian and Titus.

A.C. 69, 70.

THE last winter of Jerusalem passed away in the same
ferocious civil contests; her streets ran with the blood
of her own children; and instead of organizing a regular
defence against the approaching enemy, each faction
was strengthening its own position against the uninter-
mitting assaults of its antagonists. The city was now
divided into three distinct garrisons, at fierce and implacable hostility with each other.[a] Eleazar, the son of
Simon, the man who was the first cause of the war, by
persuading the people to reject the offerings of the
Roman Emperors, and who afterwards had set himself
at the head of the Zealots, and seized the Temple, saw,
with deep and rankling jealousy, the superiority assumed
by John of Gischala. He pretended righteous indignation at John's sanguinary proceedings, and at length,

---

[a] Joseph. B. J. v.
" Nam pervicacissimus quisque illuc
perfugerat, eoque seditiosius agebant.
Tres Duces, totidem exercitus." Tac.
Hist. v. 12.

with several other men of influence, Judas, the son of
Hilkiah, Simon, the son of Ezron, and Hezekiah, the
son of Chobar, he openly seceded from the great band
of Zealots who remained true to John, and seized the
inner court of the Temple. And now the arms of savage
men, reeking with the blood of their fellow citizens,
were seen to rest upon the gates and walls of the Holy
of Holies. The sacred songs of the Levites gave place
to the ribald jests of a debauched soldiery. Instead of
the holy instruments of music, were heard the savage
shouts of fighting warriors; and among the appointed
victims, men, mortally wounded by the arrows of their
own brethren without, lay gasping on the steps of the
altar. The band of Eleazar was amply supplied with
provisions; for the stores of the Temple were full, and the
Zealots were not troubled with religious scruples. But
they were few, and could only defend themselves within,
without venturing to sally forth against the enemy.
The height of their position gave them an advantage
over John, whose numbers were greatly superior: yet,
though he suffered considerable loss, John would not
intermit his attacks; clouds of missiles were continually
discharged into the inner court of the Temple, and the
whole sacred pavement was strewn with dead bodies.

Simon, the son of Gioras, who occupied the upper
city, attacked John the more fiercely, because the
strength of John was divided, and he was likewise
threatened by Eleazar from above. But John had
the same advantage over Simon, which Eleazar had
over John. It was a perilous enterprise to scale the
ascent to the Temple, and on such ground the Zealots
had no great difficulty in repelling the incessant assaults
of Simon's faction. Against Eleazar's party they turned
their engines, the scorpions, catapults, and balistas, with

which they slew not a few of their enemies in the upper
court, and some who came to sacrifice. For it was a
strange feature in this fearful contest, that the religious
ceremonies still went on upon the altar, which was often
encircled with the dead. Beside the human victims
which fell around, the customary sacrifices were regularly offered. Not only the pious inhabitants of Jerusalem constantly entreated and obtained permission to
offer up their gifts and prayers before the altar of
Jehovah; but even strangers from distant parts would
still arrive, and, passing over the pavement slippery
with human blood, make their way to the Temple of
their fathers, where they fondly thought the God of
Abraham, Isaac, and Jacob still retained his peculiar
dwelling within the Holy of Holies.—Free ingress and
egress were granted; the native Jews were strictly
searched, the strangers were admitted with less difficulty: but often in the very act of prayer, or sacrifice,
the arrows would come whizzing in, or the heavy stone
fall thundering on their heads; and they would pay
with their lives the price of kneeling and worshipping
in the sacred place.

The contest raged more and more fiercely—for the
abundant stores within the Temple so unsparingly supplied the few adherents of Eleazar, that, in their
drunkenness, they would occasionally sally out against
John. When these attacks took place, John stood on
the defensive; from the outer porticoes repelled Simon,
and with his engines within harassed Eleazar. When
the drunken or overwearied troops of Eleazar gave him
repose, he would sally forth against Simon, and waste
the city. Simon, in his turn, would drive him back;
and thus the space around the Temple became a mass of
ruin and desolation; and in these desultory conflicts,

the granaries, which, if carefully protected and prudently
husbanded, might have maintained the city in plenty
for years, were either wantonly thrown to waste or set
on fire by Simon, lest they should be seized by John.

The people in the mean time, particularly the old
men and the women, groaned in secret; some uttered
their prayers, but not aloud, for the speedy arrival of
the Romans, to release them from the worse tyranny of
these fierce strangers. In one point the three parties
concurred, the persecution of the citizens, and in the
condign punishment of every one whom they suspected
of wishing well to the Roman army as their common
enemy. It was dreadful to witness the deep and silent
misery of the people; they dared not utter their griefs;
their very groans were watched, and stifled in their
hearts. But it was even more dreadful to see the
callous hard-heartedness which had seized all ranks.
All were alike become reckless from desperation; there
was no feeling for the nearest kindred, their very burial
was neglected. All the desires, the hopes, the interests
of life were extinguished; death was so near, it was
scarcely worth while to avoid it. Men went trampling
over dead bodies as over the common pavement; and
this familiarity with murder, as it deadened the hearts
of the citizens, so it increased the ferocity of the
soldiers. Yet, even in the midst of all this, the old
religious prejudices were the last to yield. Among the
atrocities of John, the promiscuous spoliations and
murders, one act made still a deep impression upon the
public mind—his seizing some sacred timbers of great
size and beauty which Agrippa had brought from
Lebanon for the purpose of raising the Temple twenty
feet, and his converting them to the profane use of
raising military towers to annoy the faction of Eleazar

in the inner Temple. He erected these towers on the west side, where alone there was an open space, the others being occupied by flights of steps.[b] The force of the three factions was as follows: Simon had 10,000 Jews, and 5000 Idumeans; John 6000; Eleazar 2400.[c]

At length, after this awful interval of suspense, the war approached the gates of Jerusalem. Titus, having travelled from Egypt, arrived at Cæsarea, and began to organize his forces. In addition to the three legions which Vespasian had commanded, the twelfth returned to Syria, burning with revenge for its former disgraceful defeat under Cestius Gallus. The Syrian kings sent large contingents. The legions were full, the men who had been drafted off by Vespasian having been replaced by 2000 picked troops from Alexandria, and 3000 of those stationed on the Euphrates. Tiberius Alexander, who was distinguished not only by his wisdom and integrity, but by the intimate friendship of Titus, was appointed to a high command. He had been the first, in the recent political changes, to espouse the party of Vespasian; and his experience in arms, and his know-ledge of the country which he had once governed, added weight to his counsels. The army advanced in its customary order of march: first the allies; then the pioneers; the baggage of the principal officers, strongly guarded; then Titus himself, with a select guard of spearmen; then the horse attached to the legions; the military engines next, also strongly guarded; the eagles and the trumpeters followed; then the legionaries in

---

[b] B. J. v. 6. 1.

[c] The general suspicion which attaches to the enormous numbers of killed and prisoners, given by Josephus, is increased by observing the compara tively small force of fighting men at this period, which rests on the same authority.

their phalanx, six deep; the slaves with their baggage; last of all, the mercenaries with the rear-guard to keep order. The host moved slowly through Samaria into Gophna, and encamped in the valley of Thorns, near a village called Gaboth Saul, the Hill of Saul, about 3¾ miles from Jerusalem. Titus himself, with 600 horse, went forward to reconnoitre. As they wound down the last declivities which sloped towards the walls, the factious and turbulent city seemed reposing in perfect peace. The gates were closed; not a man appeared. The squadron of Titus turned to the right, filed off and skirted the wall towards the tower of Psephina.

On a sudden the gate behind him, near the tower of the Women, towards the monument of Helena, burst open; and countless multitudes threw themselves, some across the road on which Titus was advancing, some right through his line, separating those who had diverged from the rest of the party.[d] Titus was cut off with only a few followers. To advance was impossible; the ground was covered with orchards and gardens, divided by stone walls and intersected by deep trenches and water-courses, which reached to the city walls. To retreat was almost as difficult, for the enemy lay in thousands across his road. Titus saw that not a moment was to be lost: he wheeled his horse round, called to his men to follow him, and charged fiercely through. Darts and javelins fell in showers around him; he had ridden forth to reconnoitre, not to battle, and had on neither helmet nor breastplate. Providentially not an arrow touched him. Clearing his way with his sword on both sides, and trampling down the enemy with his fiery steed, he continued to cleave his passage through

---

[d] B. J. v. 2. 2.

the dense masses. The Jews shouted with astonishment at the bravery of Cæsar, but exhorted each other to secure the inestimable prize. Yet still they shrank and made way before him. His followers formed around him as well as they could, and at length they reached their camp in safety. One man had been surrounded and pierced with a thousand javelins. Another, having dismounted, was slain, and his horse was led away into the city. The triumph of the Jews was unbounded. Cæsar himself had been seen to fly. It was the promise and presage of more glorious and important victories.

The legion from Emmaus now joined the camp, and advanced to Scopos, within a mile of the city, from which all its extent could be surveyed. A level plain lay between the army and the northern wall; the Romans encamped, two legions in front, the fifteenth three stadia behind. The tenth legion now likewise arrived from Jericho, and occupied a station at the foot of the Mount of Olives.

Each from his separate watch-tower, Eleazar from the summit of the Temple, John from the porticoes of the outer courts, and Simon from the heights of Sion, beheld three camps forming immediately under the walls of the city. For the first time they felt the imperious necessity of concord. They entered into negotiations, and agreed on a simultaneous attack. Their mutual animosity turned to valiant emulation; they seized their arms, and rushing along the Valley of Jehoshaphat, fell with unexpected and irresistible impetuosity upon the tenth legion at the foot of the Mount of Olives. The legionaries were at work on their entrenchments, and many of them unarmed. They fell back, overpowered by the suddenness of the onset; many were

VOL. II.   Y

killed before they could get to their arms. Still more
and more came swarming out of the city; and the consternation of the Romans yet further multiplied their
numbers. Accustomed to fight in array, the legionaries
were astonished at this wild and desultory warfare; they
occasionally turned, and cut off some of the Jews, who
exposed themselves in their blind fury; but, overborne
by numbers, they were on the verge of total and irre-
parable defeat, when Titus, who had received intelligence of the assault, with some picked men, fell as
unexpectedly on the flank of the Jews, and drove them
up the valley with great loss. Still the battle raged
the whole day. Titus, having planted the troops who
came with him in front across the valley, sent the rest
to seize and fortify the upper part of the hill. The
Jews mistook this movement for flight, their watchmen
on the walls shook their garments violently as a signal;
it seemed as if the whole city poured forth, roaring and
raging like wild beasts. The ranks of the Romans were
shattered by the charge, as if by military engines; they
fled to the mountain. Titus was again left with but
a few followers, on the declivity. With the advantage
of the ground he defended himself resolutely, and at
first drove his adversaries down; but like waves broken
by a promontory, they went rushing up on both sides,
pursuing the other fugitives, or turning and raking his
party on both flanks. Those on the mount, as they saw
the enemy swarming up the hill, were again seized with
a panic, and dispersed on all sides, until a few, horror-
struck at the critical situation of their commander, by a
loud outcry raised an alarm among the whole legion,
and bitterly reproaching each other for their base desertion of their Cæsar, with the resolute courage of men
ashamed of their flight, rallied their scattered forces.

made head, and drove the Jews down the hill into the valley. The Jews contested every foot of ground, till at length they were completely repulsed; and Titus again having established a strong line of outposts, dismissed his wearied men to their works.

It was now the Passover, the period during which, in the earlier days of the Mosaic polity, or during the splendour of the Hebrew monarchy, the whole people used to come up with light and rejoicing hearts to the hospitable city, where all were welcome; where every house was freely opened and without reward; and the united voices of all the sons of Abraham blessed the Almighty for their deliverance from Egypt. Even in these disastrous days the Festival retained its reverential hold upon the hearts of the people. Not merely multitudes of Jews from the adjacent districts, but even from remote quarters, were assembled to celebrate the last public Passover of the Jewish nation. Dion Cassius states that many Jews came from beyond the Euphrates to join in the defence of the city; probably he meant those strangers who had come to the Festival.[e] These numbers only added to the miseries of the inhabitants, by consuming the stores and hastening the general distress and famine. Yet, even the day of sacrifice was chosen by John of Gischala for an act of treachery and bloodshed. When Eleazar opened the gates of the court to admit the worshippers, some of John's most desperate adherents, without having performed their ablutions, (Josephus adds this as a great aggravation of the crime,) stole in among the rest with their swords under their cloaks. No sooner were they within, than

---

[e] δι Ιουδαῖοι, πολλοὶ μὲν αὐτόθεν, πολλοὶ δὲ καὶ παρὰ τῶν ὁμοήθων, ὁυχ ὅτι ἐκ τῆς αὐτῆς τῶν Ῥωμαίων ἀρχῆς, αλλὰ καὶ ἐκ τῶν πέραὶ Ἐυφράτου προσβεβηκότες. lxvi. 4.

they threw away their cloaks, and the peaceful multitude beheld the swords of these dauntless ruffians flashing over their heads. The worshippers apprehended a general massacre. Eleazar's Zealots knew well on whom the attack was made. They leaped down and took refuge in the subterranean chambers of the Temple. The multitude cowered round the altar; some were slain out of wantonness, or from private animosity—others trampled to death. At length, having glutted their vengeance upon those with whom they had no feud, the partisans of John came to terms with their real enemies. They were permitted to come up out of their hiding places, even to resume their arms, and Eleazar was still left in command; but one faction became thus absorbed in another, and two parties instead of three divided the city.

In the mean time Titus was cautiously advancing his approaches. The whole plain from Scopos to the outward wall was levelled. The blooming gardens with their bubbling fountains, and cool water-courses, in which the inhabitants of Jerusalem had enjoyed sweet hours of delight and recreation, were ruthlessly swept away. The trees, now in their spring flower, fell before the axe, the landmarks were thrown down, the water-courses destroyed: even the deep and shady glens were levelled and filled up with the masses of rugged and picturesque rocks which used to overshadow them. A broad and level road led from Scopos to the tomb of Herod, near the pool of Serpents.

While this work was proceeding, one day, a considerable body of the Jews was seen to come, driven out, as it appeared, from the gate near the Tower of the Women. They stood cowering under the walls as if dreading the attack of the Romans. It seemed as though the peace party had expelled the fiercer insurgents, for many were

seen upon the walls, holding out their right hands
in token of surrender, and making signs that they
would open the gates.   At the same time they began to
throw down stones on those without; the latter appeared
at one moment to endeavour to force their way back,
and to supplicate the mercy of those on the walls; at
another to advance towards the Romans, and then
retreat as if in terror.   The unsuspecting soldiers were
about to charge in a body, but the more wary Titus
ordered them to remain in their position.   A few, however, who were in front of the workmen, seized their
arms and advanced towards the gates.   The Jews fled, till
their pursuers were so close to the gates as to be within
the flanking towers.   They then turned, others sallied forth
and surrounded the Romans, while those on the walls
hurled down stones and every kind of missile on their
heads.   After suffering great loss in killed and wounded,
some of the Romans effected their retreat, and were
pursued by the Jews to the monument of Helena.   The
Jews, not content with their victory, stood and laughed
at the Romans for having been deceived by so simple a
stratagem, clashed their shields, and assailed them with
every ludicrous and opprobrious epithet.   Nor was this
the worst; they were received with stern reproof by
their tribunes, and Cæsar himself addressed them in the
language of the strongest rebuke: "The Jews," he said,
"who have no leader but despair, do every thing with
the utmost coolness and precaution, lay ambushes,
and plot stratagems; while the Romans, who used to
enslave fortune by their steady discipline, are become so
rash and disorderly as to venture into battle without
command."   He then threatened, and was actually
about to put into execution, the military law, which
punished such a breach of order with death—had not

the other troops surrounded him, entreating mercy fo.
their fellow soldiers, and pledging themselves to redeem
the disaster by their future regularity and discipline.
Cæsar was with difficulty appeased.

The approach to the city was now complete, and the
army took up a position along the northern and western
wall. They were drawn up, the foot in front, seven deep,
the horse behind, three deep, with the archers between
them. The Jews were thus effectually blockaded; and
the beasts of burthen, which carried the baggage, came
up to the camp in perfect security. Titus himself encamped about a quarter of a mile from the wall, near
the tower Psephina; another part of the army near the
tower called Hippicus, at the same distance; the tenth
legion kept its station near the Mount of Olives.

Jerusalem at this period was fortified by three walls,
in all those parts where it was not surrounded by abrupt
and impassable ravines; there it had but one. Not
that these walls stood one within the other, each in a
narrower circle running round the whole city; but each
of the inner walls defended one of the several quarters
into which the city was divided—or it might be almost
said, one of the separate cities. Since the days in
which David had built his capital on the rugged heights
of Sion, great alterations had taken place in Jerusalem.
That eminence was still occupied by the upper city;
but in addition, first the hill of Moriah had been taken
in, on which the Temple stood; then Acra, which was
originally, although a part of the same ridge, separated
by a deep chasm from Moriah. This chasm was almost
entirely filled up and the top of Acra levelled by the
Asmonean princes, so that Acra and Moriah were united,
though on the side of Acra the Temple presented a formidable front, connected by several bridges or cause-

ways with the lower city. To the south the height of
Sion, the upper city, was separated from the lower
by a ravine, which ran right through Jerusalem, called
the Tyropœon, or the valley of the Cheesemongers: at
the edge of this ravine, on both sides, the streets suddenly broke off, though the walls in some places must
have crossed it, and it was bridged in more than one
part. To the north extended a considerable suburb
called Bezetha, or the new city.[f]

The first or outer wall encompassed Bezetha. Agrippa
the First had intended, as it has been mentioned, to
make this of extraordinary strength. He had desisted
from the work on the interference of the Romans; who
appear to have foreseen that this refractory city would
hereafter force them to take arms against it. Had this
wall been built according to the plan of Agrippa, the
city, in the opinion of Josephus, would have been impregnable. This wall began at the tower Hippicus,
which stood, it seems, on a point at the extreme corner
of Mount Sion: it must have crossed the western mouth

---

[f] This topography and description of
the walls is almost entirely from Josephus, whose authority on this subject
is unquestionable. It may be compared with Mr. Fergusson's elaborate
article in Smith's Dictionary of the
Bible. Mr. Fergusson agrees with me
in full reliance on the accuracy of
Josephus: the difficulty is in adapting
the description to the present state of
the ground, and the traditionary sites
of some of the towers and other landmarks. With Mr. Fergusson's view of
the site of the Holy Sepulchre this History has no concern. My difficulty
is in supposing a place of sepulture,
with the Jews' deep feeling of the uncleanness of the dead, being permitted
on the hill of the Temple. Still it
may have been the site of Constantine's church; but I venture to doubt
whether Constantine knew more of the
actual site than we do. The only indication—the Temple of Venus, said to
have been built by Hadrian, in contempt of the Christians—I am confident
is utterly unhistoric, out of character
with Hadrian and his times, and perhaps the fiction which has perplexed
the question for ever. That temple,
if really built, was much more likely
raised in scorn of the rebellious and
hardly conquered Jews, in front of
what had been their glorious Temple.

of the valley of Tyropœon, and run directly north to the
tower of Psephina, proved clearly by D'Anville to have
been what was called during the Crusades Castel Pisano.
It then bore towards the monument of Helena, ran by
the royal caverns to the Fuller's monument, and was
carried into the valley of Kedron or Jehoshaphat, where
it joined the old or inner wall under the Temple. The
wall, however it fell short of Agrippa's design, was
of considerable strength. The stones were 35 feet.
long, so solid as not easily to be shaken by battering
engines, or undermined. It was 17½ feet broad; it had
only been carried to the same height by Agrippa, but
it had been hastily run up by the Jews to 35 feet; on
its top stood battlements 3½ feet, and pinnacles 5¾; so
the whole was nearly 45 feet high.

The second wall began at a gate in the old or inner
one, called Gennath, the gate of the gardens; it intersected the lower city, and having struck northward for
some distance, turned to the east and joined the north-
west corner of the citadel of Antonia. The Antonia
stood at the north-west corner of the Temple, and was
separated from Bezetha by a deep ditch, which probably protected the whole northern front of the Temple
as well as of the Antonia.

The old or inner wall was that of Sion. Starting from
the south-western porticoes of the Temple, to which it
was united, it ran along the ridge of the Tyropœon,
passed first the Xystus, then the Council house, and
abutted on the tower Hippicus, from whence the northern wall sprang. The old wall then ran southward
through Bethso to the gate of the Essenes, all along the
ridge of the valley of Hinnom, then eastward again to
the pool of Solomon, so on through Ophla, probably a
deep glen: it there joined the eastern portico of the

Temple. Thus there were, it might seem, four distinct
towns, each requiring a separate siege. The capture of
the first wall only opened Bezetha; the fortifications of
the northern part of the Temple, the Antonia, and the
second wall still defended the other quarters. The
second wall forced, only a part of the lower city was
won; the strong rock-built citadel of Antonia and the
Temple on one hand, and Sion on the other, were not in
the least weakened.

The whole circuit of these walls was guarded with
towers, built of the same solid masonry with the rest of
the walls. They were 35 feet broad, and 35 high; but
above this height were lofty chambers, and above those
again upper rooms, and large tanks to receive the rain-
water. Broad flights of steps led up to them. Ninety
of these towers stood in the first wall, fourteen in the
second, and sixty in the third. The intervals between
the towers were about 350 feet. The whole circuit of
the city according to Josephus was 33 stadia—rather
more than 4 miles. The most magnificent of all these
towers was that of Psephina, opposite to which Titus encamped. It was $122\frac{1}{2}$ feet high, and commanded a
noble view of the whole territory of Judæa, to the
border of Arabia, and to the sea: it was an octagon.
Answering to this was the tower Hippicus, and, following
the old wall, stood those of Mariamne and Phasaelis,
built by Herod, and named after his brother and friend
and his wife. These were stupendous even as works of
Herod. Hippicus was square; $43\frac{3}{4}$ feet each way. The
whole height of the tower was 140 feet—the tower
itself $52\frac{1}{2}$, a deep tank or reservoir 35, two stories of
chambers $43\frac{3}{4}$, battlements and pinnacles $8\frac{3}{4}$. Phasaelis
was a solid square of 70 feet. It was surrounded by a
portico $17\frac{1}{2}$ feet high, defended by breastworks and bul-

warks; and above the portico was another tower, divided
into lofty chambers and baths.   It was more richly or-
namented than the rest with battlements and pinnacles,
so that its whole height was above 167 feet.   It looked
from a distance like the tall Pharos of Alexandria. This
stately palace was the dwelling of Simon.   Mariamne,
though not equal in elevation, was more luxuriously
fitted up; it was built of solid wall 35 feet high, and
the same width: on the whole, with the upper chambers,
it was about 76¾ feet high.   These lofty towers appeared
still higher from their situation.   They stood upon the
old wall, which ran along the steep brow of Sion.   The
masonry was perfect: they were built of white marble,
cut in blocks 35 feet long, 17½ wide, 8¼ high, so fitted
that the towers seemed hewn out of the solid quarry.

Such was the strength of the city which Titus surveyed from the surrounding heights, if with something
like awe at its impregnable strength, with still greater
wonder and admiration at its unexampled magnificence:
for within these towers stood the palace of the Kings,
of the most extraordinary size and splendour.   It was
surrounded by a wall 35 feet high, which was adorned
by towers at equal distances, and by spacious barrack
rooms with 100 beds in each.   It was paved with every
variety of rare marble; timbers of unequalled length
and workmanship supported the roofs.   The chambers
were countless, adorned with all kinds of figures, the
richest furniture, and vessels of gold and silver.   There
were numerous cloisters, of columns of different orders,
the squares within of beautiful verdure; around were
groves and avenues, with fountains and tanks, and bronze
statues pouring out the water.   There were likewise
large houses for tame doves.   Much of this magnificence, however, had already run to waste and ruin.

during the conflict within the city.   The beautiful gardens were desolate, the chambers plundered.   A fire, that originated in the Antonia, had crossed over to the palace and injured a considerable part, even the roofs of the three towers.[g]

The fortress Antonia stood alone, on a precipitous rock near 90 feet high, at the north-west corner of the Temple.   It was likewise a work of Herod.   The whole face of the rock was fronted with smooth stone for ornament, and to make the ascent so slippery as to be impracticable; round the top of the rock there was first a low wall, rather more than 5 feet high.   The fortress was 70 feet in height.   It had every luxury and convenience of a sumptuous palace, or even of a city; spacious halls, courts, and baths.   It appeared like a vast square tower, with four other towers at each corner; three of them between 80 and 90 feet high : that at the corner next to the Temple above 120.   From this the whole Temple might be seen, and broad flights of steps led down into the northern and western cloisters or porticoes of the Temple, in which, during the Roman government, their guard was stationed.

High above the whole city rose the Temple, uniting the commanding strength of a citadel with the splendour of a sacred edifice.   According to Josephus the esplanade on which it stood had been considerably enlarged by the accumulation of fresh soil, since the days of Solomon, particularly on the north side.   It now covered a square of a furlong each side.[h]   Solomon had

---

[g] καὶ ἀπὸ τῆς ᾿Αντωνίας ἤρξατο τὸ πῦρ, μετέβη δ᾽ ἐπὶ τὰ βασίλεια, καὶ τῶν τριῶν πύργων τὰς στέγας ἀπενεμήθη. B. J. v. 4. This is rather difficult to comprehend, unless the roofs were of very combustible material, set in flames by flying sparks and flakes of fire.

[h] D'Anville, from an estimate of the present area of the hill, is inclined to suppose that the whole ought to be nearly ten instead of six stadia.

faced the precipitous sides of the rock on the east, and perhaps the south, with huge blocks of stone; the other sides likewise had been built up with perpendicular walls to an equal height. These walls in no part were lower than 300 cubits, 525 feet; but their whole height was not seen, excepting on the eastern and perhaps the southern sides, as the earth was heaped up to the level of the streets of the city. Some of the stones employed in this work were of the size of 70 feet, probably in length.

On this gigantic foundation ran on each front a strong and lofty wall without; within, a spacious double portico or cloister $52\frac{1}{2}$ feet broad, supported by 162 columns, which supported a cedar ceiling of the most exquisite workmanship. The pillars were entire blocks hewn out of solid marble, of dazzling whiteness, $43\frac{3}{4}$ feet high. On the south side the portico or cloister was triple.

This quadrangle had but one gate to the east, one to the north, two to the south, four to the west; one of these led to the palace, one to the city, one at the corner to the Antonia, one down towards the gardens.

The open courts were paved with various inlaid marbles. Between this outer court of the Gentiles, and the second court of the Israelites, ran rails of stone, but of beautiful workmanship, rather more than 5 feet high. Along these, at regular intervals, stood pillars with inscriptions in Hebrew, Greek, and Latin—warning all strangers, and Jews who were unclean, from entering into the Holy Court beyond. An ascent of 14 steps led to a terrace $17\frac{1}{2}$ feet wide, beyond which arose the wall of the Inner Court. This wall appeared on the outside 70 feet, on the inside $43\frac{3}{4}$; for besides the ascent of 14 steps to the terrace, there were 5 more up to the gates. The Inner Court had no gate or opening to the west, but four on the north and four on the south, two to the east, one of which was for the women, for whom a portion of the Inner Court was set apart—and beyond which they might not advance; to this they had access likewise by one of the northern, and one of the southern gates, which were set apart for their use. Around this court ran another splendid range of porticoes or cloisters: the columns were quite equal in beauty and workmanship, though not in size, to those of the outer portico. Nine of these gates, or rather gateway towers, were richly adorned with gold and silver on the doors, the door-posts, and the lintels. The doors of each of the nine gates were 52½ feet high, and half that breadth. Within, the gateways were 52½ feet wide and deep, with rooms on each side, so that the whole looked like lofty towers: the height from the base to the summit was 70 feet. Each gateway had two lofty pillars 21 feet in circumference. But that which excited the greatest admiration was the tenth, usually called the Beautiful Gate of the Temple. It was of Corinthian brass of the finest workmanship. The height of the Beautiful Gate was 87½, its doors 70 feet. The father of Tiberius Alexander had sheeted these gates with gold and silver; his apostate son was to witness their ruin by the plundering hands and fiery torches of his Roman friends. Within this quadrangle there was a further separation; a low wall which divided the priests from the Israelites: near this stood the great brazen altar. Beyond, the Temple itself reared its glittering front. The great porch or Propyleon, according to the design of the last, or Herod's Temple, extended to a much greater width than the body of the Temple; in addition to the former width of 105 feet, it had two wings of 35

each, making in the whole 175.   The great gate of this
last quadrangle, to which there was an ascent of twelve
steps, was called that of Nicanor.   The gateway tower
was 132½ feet high, 43½ wide : it had no doors, but the
frontispiece was covered with gold, and through its spacious arch was seen the golden gate of the Temple
glittering with the same precious metal, with large plates
of which it was sheeted all over.   Above this gate hung
the celebrated golden vine.   This extraordinary piece of
workmanship had bunches, according to Josephus, as
large as a man.   The Rabbins add that, "like a true
natural vine, it grew greater and greater ; men would
be offering, some, gold, to make a leaf, some a grape,
some a bunch : and these were hung up upon it, and so
it was increasing continually."

The Temple itself, excepting in the extension of the
wings of the Propyleon, was probably the same in its
dimensions and distribution with that of Solomon.   It
contained the same holy treasures, if not of equal magnificence, yet by the zeal of successive ages the frequent plunder to which it had been exposed was constantly replaced ; and within, the golden candlestick
spread out its flowering branches ; the golden table supported the show bread, and the altar of incense flamed
with its costly perfume.   The roof of the Temple had
been set all over on the outside with sharp golden
spikes, to prevent the birds from settling, and defiling
the roof ; and the gates were still sheeted with plates
of the same splendid metal.   At a distance, the whole
Temple looked literally like " a mount of snow, fretted
with golden pinnacles."

Looking down upon its marble courts, and on the
Temple itself, when the sun arose above the Mount of
Olives, which it directly faced, it was impossible, even

for a Roman, not to be struck with wonder, or even for a Stoic, like Titus, not to betray his emotion. Yet this was the city which in a few months was to lie a heap of undistinguished ruins; and the solid Temple itself, which seemed built for eternity, not " to have one stone left upon another."

Surveying all this, Titus, escorted by a strong guard of horse, rode slowly round the city. But if thoughts of mercy occasionally entered into a heart, the natural humanity of which seems to have been steeled during the whole course of the siege, the Jews were sure to expel them again by some new indication of their obstinate ferocity. As he passed along, Nicanor, an intimate friend of the Emperor, was so imprudent as to venture near the walls with Josephus, to parley with the besieged; he was answered by an arrow through the right shoulder. Titus immediately ordered the suburbs to be set on fire, and all the trees to be cut down to make his embankments. He determined to direct his attack against the part of the outer wall which was the lowest, on account of the buildings of Bezetha not reaching up to it, near the tomb of John the high priest. As the approaches were made, and the day of assault was visibly drawing near, the people began to have some cessation of their miseries, as their worst enemies, those within the gates, were employed against the Romans; and they looked forward to a still further release when the Romans should force the city.

Simon, it has been before stated, had 10,000 of his own men, and 5000 Idumeans; John 6000; 2400 remained under the command of Eleazar. The cautious John would not venture forth himself from his lair in the Temple, not from want of valour or animosity against the enemy, but from a suspicion of Simon;

but his men went forth to fight in the common cause.
The more open and indefatigable Simon was never at
rest: he mounted all the military engines taken from
Cestius, on the walls; but they did little damage, as his
men wanted skill and practice to work them. But they
harassed the Roman workmen by stones and missiles
from the walls, and by perpetual sallies. Under their
penthouses of wicker work, the Romans laboured diligently; the tenth legion distinguished itself, and having
more powerful engines, both for the discharge of arrows
and of stones, than the others, not merely repelled those
who sallied, but threw stones, the weight of a talent, a
distance of two furlongs, upon the walls. The Jews set
men to watch the huge rocks, which came thundering
down upon their heads. They were easily visible, from
their extreme whiteness, (this, it seems, must have been
by night;) the watchmen shouted aloud in their native
tongue, *The bolt is coming!* on which they all bowed
their heads, and avoided the blow. The Romans found
out this, and blackened the stones, which, now taking
the Jews unawares, struck down and crushed, not merely
single men, but whole ranks. Night and day the
Romans toiled; night and day, by stratagem and force,
the Jews impeded their progress. When the works
were finished, the engineers measured the space to the
walls with lead and line, thrown from the engines, for
they dared not approach nearer. Having first advanced
the engines, which discharged stones and arrows, nearer
the wall, so as to cover the engineers, Titus ordered the
rams to play. At three different places they began
their thundering work; the besieged answered with
shouts, but shouts of terror. It became evident that
nothing less than an united effort could now repel the
foe. Simon proclaimed an amnesty to all John's fol-

lowers who would descend to man the wall. John, though still suspicious, did not oppose their going; and the two parties fought side by side from the walls with emulous valour, striving to set the engines on fire by discharging combustibles from above; others sallied forth in troops, tore the defences from the engines, and killed the engineers. Titus, on his side, was indefatigable; he posted horsemen and bowmen in the intervals between the machines, to repel the assailants. So the formidable machines, called Helepoleis, the takers of cities, pursued undisturbed their furious battering. At length a corner tower came down, but the walls stood firm, and offered no practicable breach.

Whether awed by this circumstance, or weary with fighting, the Jews seemed on a sudden to desist from their ferocious sallies. The Romans were dispersed about the works and entrenchments. Suddenly, through an unperceived gate, near the tower of Hippicus, the whole united force of the besieged came pouring forth with flaming brands to set the machines on fire. They spread on to the edge of the entrenchments. The Romans gathered hastily, but Jewish valour prevailed over Roman discipline. The besiegers were put to flight, and then a terrible conflict took place about the engines, which had all been set on fire, but for the manful resistance of some Alexandrians, who gave Cæsar time to come up with his horse. Titus killed twelve men with his own hand, and the rest at length suddenly retreated; one Jew was taken prisoner, and crucified—the first instance of that unjustifiable barbarity—before the walls. John, the captain of the Idumeans, was shot by an Arab, during a parley with a Roman soldier; he was a man of courage and prudence, and his death was greatly lamented. Exhausted with the conflict of the day, the

Roman army retired to repose. There was a total
silence throughout the vast camp, broken only by the
pacing of the sentinel; when suddenly a tremendous
crash seemed to shake the earth, and the crumbling
noise of falling stones continued for a few moments.
The legionaries started to arms, and, half naked, looked
through the dim night, expecting every instant to see
the gleaming swords and furious faces of their enemies
glaring upon them. All was still and motionless. They
stood gazing upon each other, and hastily passed the
word; and as their own men began to move about, they
mistook them for the enemy, and were well nigh seized
with a panic flight. The presence of Titus reassured
them, and the cause of the alarm soon became known.
They had built three towers upon their embankment,
nearly ninety feet high; one of them had fallen with its
own weight, and given rise to the confusion.

These towers did the most fatal damage to the Jews.
Beyond the range of arrows from their height, from
their weight they were not to be overthrown, and,
being plated with iron, would not take fire. From the
tops of these the men showered continually every kind of
missile, till at length the defenders retired from the
walls, and left the battering engines to perform their
work undisturbed. There was one of these Helepoleis,
or battering engines, called by the Jews themselves
Nico, the Victorious, for it beat down every thing before
it. Nico did not cease to thunder day and night, till at
length the wall began to totter. The Jews, exhausted
by fatigue, and harassed with passing the night far from
their own houses within the city, began to grow careless
and indifferent about the suburb; and at once, abandoning their posts, retreated to the second wall. The
Romans entered Bezetha, and threw down a great part

of the wall. Titus took up a position, near what was
called the Camp of the Assyrians, stretching as far as
the brook Kedron, and he immediately gave orders for
the attack of the second wall. Here the conflict became
more terrible than ever; the party of John defended
the Antonia and the northern cloister of the Temple;
that of Simon, the rest of the wall to a gate through
which an aqueduct passed to the tower Hippicus.
The Jews made perpetual sallies, and fought with the
most dauntless courage. Without the wall the Roman
discipline in general prevailed, and they were driven
back; from the walls, on the other hand, they had
manifest advantage. Both parties passed the night in
arms—the Jews, in fear of leaving their walls defenceless—the Romans, in constant dread of a surprise. At
dawn the battle began again; on the one hand, Simon
acted the part of a most gallant commander, and his
influence and example excited his men to the most
daring exploits; on the other, the desire of speedily
putting an end to the war; the confidence in their own
superior discipline; the assurance that the Roman arms
were irresistible; the pride of their first success; above
all, the presence of Titus, kept up the stubborn courage
of the assailants. Longinus, a Roman knight, greatly
distinguished himself by charging singly into a whole
squadron of the Jews; he killed two men, and came
safely off. But the Jews were entirely reckless of their
own lives, and sacrificed them readily if they could but
kill one of their enemies. Before long the great Helepoleis began to thunder against the central tower of the
wall. The defenders fled in terror, except a man named
Castor, and ten others. At first these men lay quiet;
but as the tower began to totter above their heads, they
rose, and stretched out their hands in an attitude of

supplication. Castor called on Titus by name, and entreated mercy. Titus ordered the shocks of the engine
and the discharge of arrows to cease, and gave Castor
permission to speak. Castor expressed his earnest
desire to surrender, to which Titus replied, that he
would the whole city were of the same mind, and inclined honourably to capitulate. Five of Castor's men
appeared to take his part; the other five, with savage
cries, to reproach them for their dastardly baseness. A fierce quarrel seemed to ensue. The attack
was entirely suspended, and Castor sent secret notice
to Simon, that he would amuse the Emperor some
time longer. In the mean while, he appeared to
be earnestly expostulating with the opposite party,
who stood upon the breast-works, brandishing their
swords; and at length striking their own bosoms,
seemingly fell dead. The Romans, who did not see
very distinctly from below, were amazed at what they
supposed the desperate resolution of the men, and even
pitied their fate. During this, Castor was wounded
in the nose by an arrow, which he drew out, and
showed it indignantly to Cæsar, as if he had been un-
generously treated. Titus sternly rebuked the man
who had shot it, and desired Josephus to go forward and
parley with Castor. But Josephus knew his countrymen too well, and declined the service. Upon this, one
Æneas, a deserter, offered his services. Castor called
him to come near to catch some money, which he
wished to throw down. Æneas opened the folds of his
robe to receive it, and Castor immediately levelled a
huge stone at his head; it missed Æneas, but wounded
a soldier near him. Cæsar, furious at having been thus
tricked, ordered the engines to be worked more vigorously than ever. Castor and his men set the tower on

fire, and when it was blazing, appeared to leap boldly into the flames; in fact, they had thrown themselves into a subterraneous passage, which led into the city.

The fifth day the Jews retreated from the second wall, and Titus entered that part of the lower city which was within it, with 1000 picked men. The streets of the wool-sellers, the braziers, and the clothiers, led obliquely to the wall.

Instead of throwing down the walls and burning as he went on, Titus, with a view of gaining the people, issued orders that no houses should be set on fire, and no massacre committed. He gave out, that he was desirous of separating the cause of the people from that of the garrison; that to the former he would readily restore all their property. The fierce insurgents hailed this as a sign of weakness, threatened all the people with instant death if they stirred, slew without mercy every one who uttered a word about peace, and then fell furiously on the Romans. Some fought on the houses, some from the walls; some along the narrow streets; others, sallying from the upper gates, fell on the camp behind. The guards who were upon the walls leaped down, and totally abandoned their companions within the newly conquered part of the city. All was confusion; those who reached the wall were surrounded, and looked in vain for succour from their associates without, who had enough to do to defend their own camp. The Jews increased every instant in numbers; they knew every lane and alley of the city, they appeared on every side, and started up where they were the least expected. The Romans could not retreat, for the narrowness of the breach would only allow them to retire very slowly. Titus, at last, came to their assistance, and by placing archers at the ends of the lanes and streets, kept the assailants back, and at last brought off most of his men, but they had totally lost the fruits of their victory.

This success raised the spirits of the besieged to the highest pitch of elevation ; they thought that whenever the Romans should venture again into the streets, if indeed they would be rash enough to do so, they would be repelled with the same loss and disgrace. But they thought not of the secret malady which was now beginning to sap their own strength—the want of provisions.[1] As yet, indeed, though many were absolutely perishing with hunger, as these were only the disaffected populace, they rather rejoiced at being rid of the burthen than deplored the loss. As for the breach, they manned it boldly, and made a wall of their own bodies, fighting for three days without intermission. On the fourth they were forced to retire, and Titus, entering the wall a second time, threw down the whole northern part of it, and strongly garrisoned the towers towards the south.

Two walls had fallen, but still the precipitous heights of Sion, the impregnable Antonia, and the stately Temple, lowered defiance on the invaders. Titus determined to suspend the siege for a few days, in order to allow time for the terror of his conquests to operate on the minds of the besieged, and for the slow famine to undermine their strength and courage. He employed the time in making a magnificent review of all his troops, who were to receive their pay in view of the whole city. The troops defiled slowly in their best attire with their arms taken out of their cases and their breast-plates on ; the cavalry leading their horses,

---

[1] B. J. v. 9. 1.

accoutred in their most splendid trappings. The whole suburbs gleamed with gold and silver. The Romans beheld the spectacle with pride, the Jews with consternation. The whole length of the old wall, the northern cloisters of the Temple, every window, every roof, was crowded with heads, looking down, some with stern and scowling expressions of hate and defiance; others in undisguised terror, some emaciated with famine, others heated with intemperance. The sight might have appalled the boldest; but the insurgents knew that they had offended too deeply to trust to Roman mercy, and that nothing remained but still to contend with the stubborn obstinacy of desperation. For four days this procession continued defiling beneath the walls; on the fifth, as no overtures for capitulation were made, Titus gave orders to recommence the siege. One part of the army was employed to raise embankments against the Antonia, where John and his followers fought: the rest against the monument of John the high priest, on part of the wall defended by Simon. The Jews had now learned, by long practice, the use of their military engines, and plied them from their heights with tremendous effect. They had 300 scorpions, for the discharge of darts; and 40 balistas, which threw enormous stones. Titus used every means to induce them to surrender, and sent Josephus to address them in their native language. Josephus with some difficulty found a place from whence he might be heard, and, at the same time, be out of arrow-shot. Whether his prudence marred the effect of his oratory or not, by his own statement he addressed to them a long harangue. He urged their own interest in the preservation of the city and Temple, the unconquerable power of the Romans, their mercy in offering terms of capitulation, and he dwelt on the famine which had begun to waste their strength. Neither the orator himself, nor his topics, were very acceptable to the fierce Zealots. They scoffed at him, reviled him, and hurled their darts against his head. Josephus then reverted to the ancient history of the nation; he urged that the Jewish people had never yet relied on such defenders, but ever on their God. "Such was the trust of Abraham, who did not resist when Necho, the Pharaoh of Egypt, took away his wife Sarah!" The orator seems here to have reckoned on the ignorance of his audience. He then recounted first the great deliverances, then the great calamities of the nation, and proceeded in a strain of vehement invective, little calculated to excite anything but furious indignation in the minds of the Zealots.[k] They, as might be expected, were only more irritated. The people, by his account, were touched by his expostulations; probably their miseries and the famine argued more powerfully to their hearts; they began to desert in numbers. Some sold their property at the lowest price, others swallowed their more valuable articles, gold and jewels, and when they fled to the Romans, unloaded themselves of their precious burthens. Titus allowed them to pass unmolested. The news of their escape excited many others to follow their example, though John and Simon watched every outlet of the city, and executed without mercy all whom they suspected of a design to fly. This too was a convenient charge, on which they could put to death as many of the more wealthy as they chose.

---

[k] Josephus even appealed to miracles wrought in favour of the Romans: he asserted that the fountain of Siloam, and other water springs, which had failed entirely while they were in the power of the Jews, no sooner came into the possession of the Romans than they began to flow abundantly.

In the mean time the famine increased, and with the famine the desperation of the insurgents.[1] No grain was exposed for public sale: they forced open and searched the houses; if they found any, they punished the owners for their refusal; if none was discovered, they tortured them with greater cruelty for concealing it with such care. The looks of the wretched beings were the marks by which they judged whether they had any secret store or not. Those who were hale and strong were condemned as guilty of concealment: the plunderers passed by only the pale and emaciated. The wealthy secretly sold their whole property for a measure of wheat, the poorer for one of barley, and shrouding themselves in the darkest recesses of their houses, devoured it underground: others made bread, snatched it half-baked from the embers, and tore it with their teeth. The misery of the weaker was aggravated by seeing the plenty of the stronger. Every kind feel-

---

[1] While the famine was thus grievous, the supply of water seems never to have failed. In this they had great advantage over the besiegers. Josephus indeed (see above) intimates a sort of miracle, that Siloam, and other sources of water which had dried up, when in possession of the Jews, began to flow again for the Romans. Τίτῳ μὲν γὰρ πηγαὶ πλουσιώτεραι ῥέουσιν, ἃι ξηρανθεῖσαι πρότερον ὑμῖν· πρὸ γοῦν τῆς αὐτοῦ παρουσίας τήν τε Σιλωὰμ ἐπιλιποῦσαν ἴστε, καὶ τὰς ἔξω τοῦ ἄστεος ἁπάσας, ὥστε πρὸς ἀμφορεῖς ὠνεῖσθαι τὸ ὕδωρ· τὸ δὲ ῥῦν οὕτω πληθύνουσι τοῖς πολεμίοις ὑμῶν, ὡς μὴ μόνον αὐτοῖς καὶ κτήνεσιν, ἀλλὰ καὶ κήποις διαρκεῖν. Josephus would persuade us that he uttered this in the hearing of the besiegers, thus appealing to themselves for its truth. It is evidently a flower of later rhetoric. Strabo had before described Jerusalem as ἐντὸς μὲν ἔυυδρον, ἐκτὸς δὲ παντελῶς διψηρὸν. xvi. p. 763. So Tacitus: " Fons perennis, cavati sub terrâ montes; et piscinæ cisternæque servandis imbribus." Hist. v. 12. Dion Cassius is even more explicit: τὸ δὲ δὴ πλεῖστον δι Ρωμαῖοι τῇ ἀνυδρίᾳ ἐκακοπάθουν, καὶ φαῦλον καὶ πόῤῥωθεν ὕδωρ ἐπαγόμενοι· δι δὲ Ιουδαῖοι διὰ τῶν ὑπονόμων ἴσχυον. Not only had they plenty of water, but at times they issued out through the subterraneous aqueducts, attacked the Romans when seeking water, and cut off stragglers. Vesp. lxvi. 3.

ing — love — respect — natural affection — were extinct through the all absorbing want. Wives would snatch the last morsel from husbands, children from parents, mothers from children; they would intercept even their own milk from the lips of their pining babes. The most scanty supply of food was consumed in terror and peril. The marauders were always prowling about. If a house was closed, they supposed that eating was going on; they burst in, and squeezed the crumbs from the mouths and the throats of those who had swallowed them. Old men were scourged till they surrendered the food, to which their hands clung desperately, and even were dragged about by the hair, till they gave up what they had. Children were seized as they hung upon the miserable morsels they had got, whirled around and dashed upon the pavement. Those who anticipated the plunderers by swallowing every atom, were treated still more cruelly, as if they had wronged those who came to rob them. Tortures, which cannot be related with decency, were employed against those who had a loaf, or a handful of barley. Nor did their own necessities excuse these cruelties; sometimes it was done by those who had abundance of food, with a deliberate design of husbanding their own resources. If any wretches crept out near the Roman posts to pick up some miserable herbs or vegetables, they were plundered on their return; and if they entreated, in the awful name of God, that some portion at least might be left them of what they had obtained at the hazard of their lives, they might think themselves well off if they escaped being killed as well as pillaged.[m]

---

[m] Of all high wrought descriptions of human suffering, what can surpass this paragraph in the history of the war? v. 10. 3. Josephus would console himself with the bold assertion that the men who perpetrated these enormities

Such were the cruelties exercised on the lower orders by the satellites of the tyrants; the richer and more distinguished were carried before the tyrants themselves. Some were accused of treasonable correspondence with the Romans; others with an intention to desert. He that was plundered by Simon was sent to John; he that had been stripped by John was made over to Simon; so, by turns, they, as it were, shared the bodies and drained the blood of the citizens. Their ambition made them enemies; their common crimes united them in friendship. They were jealous if either deprived the other of his share in some flagrant cruelty; and complained of being wronged if excluded from some atrocious iniquity.

The blood runs cold, and the heart sickens, at these unexampled horrors; and we take refuge in a kind of desperate hope that they have been exaggerated by the historian: those which follow, perpetrated under his own eyes by his Roman friends, and justified under the all-extenuating plea of necessity, admit of no such reservation—they must be believed in their naked and unmitigated barbarity. Many poor wretches, some few of them insurgents, but mostly the poorest of the people, would steal down the ravines by night, to pick up whatever might serve for food. They would, most of them, willingly have deserted, but hesitated to leave their wives and children to be murdered. For these Titus laid men in ambush; when attacked, they defended themselves; as a punishment, they were scourged, tortured, and crucified; and in the morning, some-

---

were not Jews of legitimate descent, but δοῦλοι καὶ σύγκλυδες, καὶ νόθα τοῦ ἔθνους φθάρματα. And yet these very men for freedom (dare we say for faith?) did deeds of valour and daring equal to the famous Maccabees.

times 500, sometimes more, of these miserable beings were seen writhing on crosses before the walls. This was done because it was thought unsafe to let them escape, and to terrify the rest.[a] The soldiers added ridicule to their cruelty; they would place the bodies in all sorts of ludicrous postures; and this went on till room was wanting for the crosses, and crosses for the bodies.

These executions produced a contrary effect to that which was contemplated. The Zealots dragged the relatives of the deserters, and all they suspected as inclined towards peace, up to the walls, and bade them behold those examples of Roman mercy. This checked the desertion, excepting in those who thought it better to be killed at once than to die slowly of hunger. Titus sent others back to Simon and John, with their hands cut off, exhorting them to capitulate, and not to force him to destroy the city and the Temple. It cannot be wondered, that as Titus went round the works, he was saluted from all parts, in contempt of the imperial dignity, with the loudest and bitterest execrations against his own name and that of his father.

At this time a son of the king of Commagene, called Antiochus Epiphanes, a name of ominous sound to Jerusalem, joined the Roman camp with a chosen band of youths, dressed and armed in the Macedonian fashion.

---

[a] Josephus is now become the stedfast flatterer of Titus. Not only does he colour most highly the personal prowess of the son of Cæsar; in this he has the concurrence of Tacitus: "Ipse, ut super fortunam crederetur, decorum se, promptumque in armis ostendebat, comitate et adloqui's officia provocans; ac plerumque in opere, in agmine, gregario militi mixtus, incorrupto ducis honore." Hist. v. 1.

Josephus would also attribute to Titus merciful compunction at these executions. I cannot but think that Bishop Heber's "stoic tyrant's philosophic pride" is more true to the character of Titus.

He expressed his wonder at the delay of the Romans in assaulting the wall. Titus gave him free leave to make the attempt, which he did with great valour, but with little success, notwithstanding his vaunting; for though he escaped, all his men were severely mutilated and wounded by the besieged.

After seventeen days' labour, on the 27th or 29th of May, the embankments were raised in four separate places. That of the fifth legion began near the pool of the Sparrows; that of the twelfth about thirty-five feet farther off; that of the tenth on the north, near the pool of the Almond Trees; and that of the fifteenth on the east, near the Monument of John. All was prepared; the engines mounted, and the troops stood awaiting the assault, when suddenly the whole ground between the embankments and the wall was seen to heave and roll like a sea. Presently thick masses of smoke came curling heavily up, followed by dim and lurid flames; the whole then sank, the engines and the embankments rolled down together into the fiery abyss, and were either buried or consumed. John had undermined the whole, piled below an immense quantity of pitch, sulphur, and other combustibles, set fire to the wooden supports, and thus destroyed the labours of seventeen days.

The Jewish captains were rivals in valour as in guilt. Two days after, Simon, on his side, made a desperate attack on the engines, which had already begun to shake the walls. Tepthaus, a Galilean, Megassar, formerly an attendant on Mariamne, and a man of Adiabene, the son of Nebat, called Chagiras, (the lame,) rushed fiercely out, with torches in their hands. These men were the bravest as well as the most cruel of the Zealots. They were not repelled till they had set fire

to the Helepoleis. The Romans crowded to extinguish
the fire; the Jews from the walls covered their men,
who, though the iron of the engines was red hot, would
not relax their hold. The fire spread to the other
works, and the Romans, encompassed on all sides by the
flames, retreated to their camp. The Jews followed up
their success, and, all fury and triumph, rushed upon
the trenches, and assailed the guards. By the Roman
discipline it was death to desert such a post. The guards
stubbornly resisted, and were killed in numbers. The
scorpions and balistas of the Romans rained a shower of
mortal missiles, but the Jews, utterly regardless of de-
fending themselves, still pushed fiercely on, swarm after
swarm pouring out of the city; so that Titus, who had
been absent reconnoitring the Antonia, in order to find
a new spot to fix his engines, found the whole army besieged, and even wavering. He charged with his men
resolutely against the Jews, who turned round and faced
his attack. Such was the dust and the noise, that no one
could see, hear, or distinguish friend from foe. The
event of the contest left the Romans dispirited by the
loss of their battering train, and with little hope of
taking the city with the ordinary engines that remained.
Titus summoned a council of war. Three plans were
discussed; to storm the city immediately, to repair the
works and rebuild the engines, or to blockade and
starve the garrison to surrender. The last was preferred;
and the whole army set to work upon the trench, each
legion and each rank vying with the rest in activity.
The trench ran from the "camp of the Assyrians,"
where Titus was encamped, to the lower part of Bezetha,
along the valley of Cedron, and the ridge of the Mount
of Olives, to a rock called Peristereon, at the mouth of
the valley of Siloam, and a hill which hangs over

Siloe, thence to the west to the valley of the Fountain, thence ascending to the sepulchre of the high
priest Ananias, round the mountain where Pompey's
camp was formerly pitched, by a village called that of
Erebinth, or Pulse, then turned eastward again and
joined the camp: the whole work was within a furlong
of five miles; it was surmounted by thirteen garrison
towers, and was entirely finished in three days.

It can scarcely be doubted that there must have
been, within the walls of Jerusalem, many so closely
connected with the Christians as to be well acquainted
with the prophetic warning which had induced that
people to leave the fated city. With what awful force
must the truth of the disbelieved or disregarded words
have returned to their remembrance, when their enemies had thus literally "cast a trench about them,
and compassed them round, and kept them in on every
side!" But the poor and the lowly would have little
time to meditate even on such solemn considerations;
for the instant effect of this measure was to increase
the horrors of the famine so far that whole families
lay perishing with hunger. The houses were full of
dying women and children, the streets with old men,
gasping out their last breath. The bodies remained unburied, for either the emaciated relatives had not strength
for the melancholy duty, or, in the uncertainty of their
own lives, neglected every office of kindness or charity.
Some, indeed, died in the act of burying their friends;
others crept into the cemeteries, lay down on a bier, and
expired. There was no sorrow, no wailing; they had not
strength to moan; they sat with dry eyes, and mouths
drawn up into a kind of bitter smile. Those who were
more hardy looked with envy on those who had already
breathed their last. Many died, says the historian, with

their eyes still steadily fixed on the Temple. There was a deep and heavy silence over the whole city, broken only by the robbers, as they forced open houses to plunder the dead, and in licentious sport dragged away the last decent covering from their limbs; they would even try the edge of their swords on the dead. The soldiers, dreading the stench of the corpses, at first ordered them to be buried at the expense of the public treasury; as they grew more numerous, they were thrown over the walls into the ravines below.

Titus, as he went his rounds, saw these bodies rotting, and the ground reeking with gore wherever he trod; he groaned, lifted up his hands to heaven, and called God to witness that this was not his work.° The Roman camp, in the mean time, was abundantly supplied; and Titus commanded timber to be brought from a distance, and recommenced his works in four places against the Antonia.

One crime remained of which the robbers had not yet been guilty, and that, Simon now hastened to perpetrate. The high priest, Matthias, a man of feeble character, had passively submitted to all the usurpations of the robber leaders. He it was who admitted Simon to counterpoise the party of John. Matthias was accused, whether justly or not, of intelligence with the Romans; he was led out and executed in the sight of the Romans, with his three sons: the fourth had made his escape. The inoffensive old man only entreated that he might be put to death first; this was denied him, and his sons were massacred before his face by Ananus, the son of Bamad, the remorseless executioner of Simon's cruelties. Ananias, the son of Masambal,

---

° B. J. v. 12. 4.

Aristeus, the secretary of the Sanhedrin, and fifteen of its members, were put to death at the same time. The father of Josephus was thrown into prison, and all access to him strictly forbidden. Josephus himself had a narrow escape; he was struck on the head by a stone, and fell insensible. The Jews by a vigorous sally endeavoured to make themselves masters of his body, but Titus sent troops to his rescue, and he was brought off, though with difficulty. The rumour of his death spread through the city, and reached his mother in her prison; his speedy appearance under the walls reassured his friends, and was quickly imparted to his afflicted parents.

The murder of the High Priest, and of the Sanhedrin, at last excited an attempt to shake off the yoke of the tyrants. A certain Judas, the son of Judas, conspired with ten others to betray one of the towers to the Romans. They offered to surrender it, but the Romans, naturally suspicious, hesitated. In the mean time Simon, as vigilant as he was cruel, had discovered the plot; the conspirators were put to death in the sight of the Romans, and their bodies tumbled from the walls. Still desertion became more frequent; some threw themselves from the walls, and fled for their lives; others, under pretence of issuing forth to skirmish, got within the Roman posts. Many of these famished wretches came to a miserable end. When they obtained food they ate with such avidity as was fatal to their enfeebled frames; few had self-control enough to accustom their stomachs by degrees to the unusual food. Others perished from another cause. A man was seen searching his excrements for some gold which he had swallowed and voided. A report spread through the camp that all the deserters had brought off their treasures in the same manner. Some of the fierce Syrian

and Arabian allies set on them and cut open their living
bodies in search of gold; two thousand are said to have
been killed in this way during one night. Titus was indignant at the horrid barbarity; he threatened to surround the perpetrators and to cut down their whole
squadrons. The number of offenders alone restrained
him from inflicting summary justice. He denounced
instant death against any one detected in such a crime:
but still the love of gold was, in many instances,
stronger than the dread of punishment, and that which
was before done openly, was still perpetrated secretly.

John, the Zealot, at this time committed an offence,
in the opinion of the devout Jews, even more heinous
than his most horrible cruelties, that of sacrilege; he
seized and melted the treasures of the Temple, and even
the dishes and vessels used in the service. Probably
with revengeful satisfaction he began with the offerings
of the Roman Emperors. He openly declared that the
holy treasures ought to assist in supporting a holy war.
He distributed, also, to the famished people, the sacred
wine and oil, which were used and drunk with the
greatest avidity. For this offence the historian, Josephus, has reserved his strongest terms of horror and ex-
ecration; "for such abominations, even if the Romans
had stood aloof, the city would have been swallowed
by an earthquake, or swept away by a deluge, or would
have perished, like Sodom, in a tempest of fire and
brimstone."

But by his own account, such calamities would have
been as tender mercies to the present sufferings of the
Jews. A deserter, who at one time had been appointed
to pay for the interment of the dead at a particular
gate, stated, that from the 14th of April, when the siege
began, to the 1st of July, 115,880 bodies had been

buried at the public charge, or thrown from the walls, not including those interred by their friends. Others said, that 600,000 of the poorer people had perished; that when they could no longer bury them, they shut them up in some of the larger houses, and left them there. A measure of wheat was selling for a talent, and the people were raking the very dungheaps for sustenance. Yet still, though dead bodies actually impeded the way of the defenders to the walls, and though the city, like one vast sepulchre, seemed to exhale a pestilential stench, with unbroken resolution which might have become better men, the soldiers both of John and Simon went sternly trampling over those dead bodies as over the senseless pavement, and manned the walls with that wild desperation which familiarity with death is apt to engender.[p]

The Romans, in the mean time, laboured hard at their military engines. There was great scarcity of timber; they were obliged to bring it from a considerable distance, so that not a tree was left standing within above ten miles of the city. All the delicious gardens, the fruitful orchards, the shady avenues, where, in their days of peace and happiness, the inhabitants of the devoted city had enjoyed the luxury of their delicious climate, the temperate days of spring, and the cool summer nights, were utterly destroyed. It was a lamentable sight to behold the whole gay and luxuriant suburban region turned to a frightful solitude.

At length, the tall and fearful engines stood again menacing the walls. Both the Jews and Romans looked at them with apprehension: the Jews from experience of their tremendous powers; the Romans in the con

---

[p] B. J. vi. 1. 1.

2 A 2

viction that if these were burned, from the total want of timber it would be impossible to supply their places. Josephus confesses that at this period the Roman army was exhausted and dispirited; while their desperate enemies, notwithstanding the seditions, famine, and war, were still as obstinately determined as ever, and went resolutely and even cheerfully forth to battle. Before the engines could be advanced against the walls, the party of John made an attempt to burn them, but without success; their measures were ill combined, their attack feeble and desultory. For once, the old Jewish courage seemed to fail; so that, advancing without their customary fury, and finding the Romans drawn up in disciplined array, the engines themselves striking down their most forward men, they were speedily repelled, and the Helepoleis advanced to the wall, amid showers of stones and fire and every kind of missile. The engines began to thunder; and the assailants, though sometimes crushed by the stones that were hurled upon them from above, locked their shields over their heads, and worked at the foundation with their hands and with crow-bars, till at length they got out four large stones. Night put an end to the conflict.

During the night, the wall suddenly fell in with a terrific noise; for it happened to stand over that part which John had formerly undermined, in order to destroy the enemy's engines. But when the Romans rushed, in the morning, to the breach, they found a second wall, which John, with true military foresight had built within, in case of such an emergency. Still this wall was newly made, and comparatively weak. Titus assembled the officers of the army, and made them an energetic address; in which, among other topics, he urged the manifest interference of Divine Providence in their favour, in the unexpected falling of the wall. They listened in silence, till at length a common soldier, a Syrian named Sabinus, a man of great courage but slender make and very dark complexion, volunteered to lead a forlorn hope. He threw his shield over his head, grasped his sword, and advanced deliberately to the wall. Only eleven men had courage to follow him. Javelins, weapons of all kinds, and huge stones, came whizzing and thundering around him. Some of his companions were beaten down, but, though covered with darts, he still persisted in mounting, till the Jews, panic stricken at his boldness, and supposing that he was followed by many more, took to flight. He had actually reached the top of the wall, when his foot slipped, and he fell. The Jews turned and surrounded him. He rose on his knees, still made a gallant defence, wounding many of the enemy; and at length expired, buried under a thousand spears. Of the eleven, three reached the top of the wall, and were killed by stones; eight were carried back, wounded, to the camp. This was on the 3rd of July. Two days after, at the dead of night, twenty soldiers of the guard, with a standard bearer of the fifth legion, two horsemen, and a trumpeter, crept silently up the breach, surprised and slew the watch, and gave orders to the trumpeter to blow with all his might. The rest of the sentinels, without waiting to see the number of the assailants, fled in terror. Titus, directly he heard the sound of the trumpet, armed his men and scaled the Antonia. The Jews fled on all sides; some fell into the mines which John had dug under the Roman embankments; but Simon and John, uniting all their forces, made a resolute effort to defend the entrance to the Temple. A fierce battle ensued, with spears and javelins; the troops of both parties were so mingled and confused, that no man knew where he was. The narrow passages were crowded with the dead, so that those engaged were obliged to scramble over heaps of bodies and of armour to get at each other. At length, after ten hours' hard fighting, Titus, contented with the possession of the Antonia, recalled his men. But a Bithynian centurion, named Julian, of uncommon strength and skill in the use of his weapons, sprang forward from the side of Titus, where he was standing, and singly charged the Jews with such extraordinary resolution, that they fled on all sides; and Julian forced his way, committing dreadful slaughter as he went on, up to a corner of the inner court of the Temple. Unfortunately his shoes were full of nails, and slipping upon the smooth pavement, he fell with his armour clattering around him. The fugitives turned upon him. A loud shout of terror arose from the Romans in the Antonia, answered by a fierce and exulting cry from the Jews. They surrounded the gallant Julian, and though he covered himself with his shield, and repeatedly struggled to rise, he was overpowered by numbers. Still, however, his breastplate and helmet protected the vital parts, till at length his limbs having been hewn off, he received a mortal wound, and fell dead. The Jews, to the great grief of Cæsar, dragged the body into the Temple, and again drove back the Romans into the Antonia.

It was now the 5th of July.[q] Titus commanded that the fortress of Antonia should be razed to the ground. He had heard that the daily sacrifice was now intermitted, from want of persons to make the offering; and

---

[q] There is here a difficulty about the day. This event is commemorated by the Jews on the 17th of July, the day indicated by Josephus, but it cannot easily be reconciled with the history.

understanding the deep impression made on all the
Jews by the suspension of that rite, he determined to
try another attempt on their religious feelings. Josephus was sent to offer free egress to John if he would
come forth to fight, that the Temple might escape defilement. Josephus placed himself so as to be heard by all
the Jews; and communicated, in the Hebrew language,
the offers of Titus. John replied in words of the fiercest
bitterness, imprecating curses on the head of the renegade Josephus; and concluded, that "he feared not the
taking of the city, for it was the city of God." Josephus broke out into a vehement invective, but neither
his words, nor the tears or sobs by which he was interrupted, had the slightest effect on John or his soldiers;
they rushed out and endeavoured to seize him. Some
few, however, were moved.

There were certain men of distinction, who, from
time to time, had seized an opportunity of desertion.
Among these were Joseph and four chief priests; three
sons of Ismael, the high priest; four of Mathias; one
of the other Matthias, whom Simon put to death with
three of his sons. Titus had received the fugitives with
kindness, promised them his protection, and dismissed
them to Gophni. These men were sent for, and with
Josephus, attempted to persuade the people, if not to
capitulate, at least to spare the Temple from inevitable
defilement and ruin. But all in vain! The sacred
gates were blocked up with balistas and catapults;
the peaceful Temple, with its marble courts and gilded
pinnacles, assumed the appearance of a warlike citadel.
Its courts were strewn with the dead—men with swords
reeking with the blood of the enemy, or of their own
countrymen, rushed to and fro along the Holy Place, or
even the Holy of Holies. Even the Roman soldiers, it

is said, shuddered at the profanation. Titus tried a last
remonstrance. " You have put up a barrier," he said,
" to prevent strangers from polluting your Temple: this
the Romans have always respected;—we have allowed
you to put to death all who violated its precincts. Yet
ye defile it yourselves with blood and carnage. I call
on your Gods—I call on my whole army—I call on the
Jews who are with me—I call on yourselves—to witness,
that I do not force you to this crime. Come forth, and
fight in any other place: and no Roman shall violate
your sacred edifice." But John and his Zealots suspected (it may be with justice) the magnanimity of
Titus, and would not surrender a place the strength of
which was their only trust. Perhaps they had still a
fanatic confidence, that, reeking as they were with
blood, steeped to the lips in crime, they were still the
chosen people of Jehovah ; and that yet, even yet, the
Power which smote Pharaoh, and Sennacherib, and the
enemies of the Maccabees, would reveal himself in irresistible terror.

  Titus, finding all his efforts of mercy rejected, determined on a night attack: as the whole army could not
make the assault, on account of the narrowness of the
approaches, thirty men were picked from each century,
tribunes appointed over each 1000, and Cerealis chosen
to command the whole. Titus himself announced that
he would mount a watch-tower which belonged to the
Antonia, in order that he might witness and reward
every act of individual bravery. They advanced when
night was three parts over, but found the enemy on the
watch. The battle began to the advantage of the Romans, who held together in compact bodies, while the
Jews attacked in small troops or singly. In the blind
confusion of the night, among the bewildering shouts on

all sides, many fell upon each other, and those who
were repelled were mistaken for the assailants, and
killed by their own men; so that the Jews lost more by
their own swords than by the foe.   When day dawned,
the combat continued on more even terms; after eight
hours' contest, though the Romans were thus fighting
as in a theatre, in view of the Emperor, they had not
gained a foot of ground; and the battle ceased, as it
were, by common consent.

In the mean time, the Romans had levelled part of
the Antonia, and made a broad way, by which they
could bring their engines to bear upon the Temple.
They erected their embankments, though with great
difficulty from the scarcity of timber, against four
places of the outer court; one opposite the north-east
corner of the inner court; one against a building between the two northern gates, one against the western,
and another against the northern cloisters.   Still the
indefatigable Jews gave them no rest; if the cavalry
went out to forage, and let their horses loose to feed,
the Jews would sally out in squadrons and surprise
them.   They made one desperate assault on the outposts, near the Mount of Olives, in open day; and,
but for a charge of cavalry on their flank, had almost
succeeded in forcing the wall.   In this contest, a horse-
man, named Pedanius, stooped down, caught up a Jew,
with all his armour, carried him by main strength, and
threw him down before the feet of Titus.   Titus admired the strength of Pedanius, and ordered the captive
to be put to death.

Overborne, exhausted, famine-stricken, still the Jews
fought, inch by inch; and, according to the historian,
sternly sacrificed, as it were, their own limbs, cutting
off every foot that the enemy had taken, as if to pre-

vent the progress of the disease.[r]   They set on fire the
portico which led from the Antonia to the Temple, and
made a breach of between twenty and thirty feet.   Two
days after, the Romans, in their turn, set fire to the
cloister, and burned above twenty feet more.   The
Jews looked on calmly, and allowed the flame to spread,
till the whole space between the Antonia and the
Temple was cleared.

But if the holy precincts were thus to perish by fire,
they determined that they should not fall unavenged.
Along the whole western cloisters they filled the space
between the beams and the roof with dry wood, sulphur,
and bitumen; they then retreated from the defence, as
if quite exhausted.   The more prudent of the assailants
suspected some stratagem, but many immediately applied the scaling ladders, and mounted boldly to the
roof.   At that instant the Jews below set fire to the
train; the flames rushed roaring and blazing up among
the astonished assailants.   Some flung themselves down
headlong into the city, others among the enemy; there
they lay bruised to death, or with broken limbs: many
were burnt alive, others fell on their own swords.   In
vain they looked to their companions below, in vain
they beheld the sorrow of Cæsar himself, who, though
they had acted without orders, commiserated their fate.
Escape or succour was alike impossible; a few on a
broader part of the roof fought valiantly, and died to a
man with their arms in their hands.   The fate of a
youth, named Longus, created general interest.   The
Jews offered to spare his life if he would go down and
surrender; on the other hand, his brother Cornelius,
from below, entreated him not to disgrace the Roman

---

character. The youth stabbed himself to the heart.
One Artorius escaped by a singular stratagem : he
called to one of his comrades, and offered to leave him
his whole property if he would catch him as he fell.
The man came below, Artorius jumped down, crushed
his friend to death in his fall, and escaped unhurt.
Thus a great part of the western cloister was burnt, the
Romans set fire to that of the north, and laid it in ashes
as far as the north-east corner, near Cedron.

In the mean time the famine continued its fearful
ravages. Men would fight, even the dearest friends,
for the most miserable morsel. The very dead were
searched, as though they might conceal some scrap
of food. Even the robbers began to suffer severely;
they went prowling about like mad dogs, or reeling,
like drunken men, from weakness; and entered and
searched the same houses twice or thrice in the same
hour. The most loathsome and disgusting food was
sold at an enormous price. They gnawed their belts,
shoes, and even the leathern coats of their shields—
chopped hay and shoots of trees sold at high prices.
Yet what were all these horrors to that which followed?
There was a woman of Perea, from the village of Bethe-
zob, Mary, the daughter of Eleazar. She possessed
considerable wealth when she took refuge in the city.
Day after day she had been plundered by the robbers,
whom she had provoked by her bitter imprecations. No
one, however, would mercifully put an end to her
misery; and her mind maddened with wrong, her body
preyed upon by famine, she wildly resolved on an expedient which might gratify at once her vengeance and
her hunger. She had an infant that was vainly endeavouring to obtain some moisture from her dry bosom
—she seized it, cooked it, ate one half, and set the

other aside. The smoke and the smell of food quickly reached the robbers—they forced her door, and with horrible threats commanded her to give up what she had been feasting on. She replied with appalling indifference, that she had carefully reserved for her good friends a part of her meal—she uncovered the remains of her child. The savage men stood speechless, at which she cried out with a shrill voice, "Eat, for I have eaten—be ye not more delicate than a woman, more tender-hearted than a mother—or if ye are too religious to touch such food, I have eaten half already, leave me the rest." They retired pale and trembling with horror. The story spread rapidly through the city, and reached the Roman camp; where it was first heard with incredulity, afterwards with the deepest commiseration.[*] How dreadfully must the words of Moses have flashed and wrought upon the minds of all those Jews who were not entirely unread in their holy writings!—*" The tender and delicate woman among you, which would not adventure to set the sole of her foot upon the ground for delicateness and tenderness, her eye shall be evil toward the husband of her bosom, and toward her son, and toward her daughter; and toward her young one that cometh out from between her feet, and toward her children which she shall bear: for she shall eat them for want of all things, secretly in the siege and straitness wherewith thine enemy shall distress thee in thy gates."*

The destruction of the outer cloisters had left the Romans masters of the great court of the Gentiles; on the 8th of August the engines began to batter the western gate of the inner court. For six previous days the largest

---

[*] Josephus mars this piteous history by false rhetoric: he makes the mother utter a speech to the child, which he thinks pathetic.

and most powerful of the battering rams had played upon
the wall; the enormous size and compactness of the stones
had resisted all its efforts.   Other troops at the same
time endeavoured to undermine the northern gate, but
with no better success; nothing therefore remained but to
fix the scaling ladders, and storm the cloisters.   The Jews
made no resistance to the Romans' mounting the walls;
but as soon as they reached the top hurled them down
headlong, or slew them before they could cover themselves with their shields.   In some places they thrust
down the ladders, loaded with armed men, who fell
back, and were dashed to pieces on the pavement.
Some of the standard-bearers had led the way; they
also were repelled, and the Jews remained masters of
the eagles.   On the side of the Romans fell many distinguished soldiers; on that of the Jews, Eleazar, the
nephew of Simon.   Repulsed on all hands from the top
of the wall, Titus commanded fire to be set to the gates.

In the mean time Ananus of Emmaus, the bloody
executioner of Simon, and Archelaus, son of Magadat,
deserted to the Romans.   Titus at first intended to put
them to death, but afterwards relented.

No sooner had the blazing torches been applied to
the gates than the silver plates heated, the wood
kindled, the whole flamed up and spread rapidly to the
cloisters.   Like wild beasts environed in a burning
forest, the Jews saw the awful circle of fire hem them
in on every side; their courage sank, they stood
gasping, motionless and helpless; not a hand endeavoured to quench the flames, or stop the silent progress
of the conflagration.   Yet still fierce thoughts of desperate vengeance were brooding in their hearts.
Through the whole night and the next day, the fire
went on consuming the whole range of cloisters.   Titus

at length gave orders that it should be extinguished,
and the way through the gates levelled for the advance
of the legionaries. A council of war was summoned, in
which the expediency of destroying the magnificent
building was solemnly discussed. It consisted of six
of the chief officers of the army, among the rest,
of Tiberius Alexander, whose offerings had formerly
enriched the splendid edifice. Three of the council
insisted on the necessity of destroying for ever
this citadel of a mutinous people: it was no longer a
temple, but a fortress, and to be treated like a military
strong-hold. Titus inclined to milder counsels; the
magnificence of the building had made a strong impression upon his mind, and he was reluctant to destroy
what might be considered one of the wonders of the
Roman empire. Alexander, Fronto, and Cerealis concurred in this opinion, and the soldiers were ordered to
do all they could to quench the flames.[t] But higher

---

[t] "Fertur Titus, adhibito consilio,
prius deliberasse an templum tanti
operis everteret. Etenim nonnullis
videbatur, ædem sacratam ultra omnia
mortalia illustrem non debere deleri,
quæ servata modestiæ Romanæ testi-
monium, diruta perennem crudelitatis
notam præberet. At contra alii et
Titus ipse evertendum templum impri-
mis censebant, quo plenius Judæorum
et Christianorum religio tolleretur.
Quippe has religiones, licet contrarias
sibi, iisdem tamen auctoribus profectas;
Christianos ex Judæis extitisse; radice
sublatâ stirpem facile perituram. Ita
Dei nutu, accensis omnium animis templum dirutum abhinc annos trecentos
triginta et unum." This passage from
Sulpicius Severus (Chronicon, xxx. 11

6) might appear of itself to be of slight
authority, directly contradicting, as it
does, the statement of Josephus. But
M. Jacob Bernays in a remarkable
dissertation (über die Chronik des
Sulpicius Severus, Berlin, 1861) has
shown, to my judgement conclusively,
that these are, with but slight modifi-
cations, the words of Tacitus, from the
lost portion of his History. M. Bernays
has clearly proved that Tacitus was one
of the chief authorities used by Sulpicius. There are several passages in which
he adopts the express words of Tacitus,
still extant, almost without alteration.
The style of this passage, with the exception of a few words, is very Tacitus, a passage which none but Tacitus
could write. For the "nonnulli" Taci-

counsels had otherwise decreed, and the Temple of Jerusalem was to be for ever obliterated from the face of
the earth. The whole of the first day after the fire
began, the Jews from exhaustion and consternation
remained entirely inactive. The next, they made a
furious sally from the eastern gate against the guards
who were posted in the outer court. The legionaries
locked their shields together and stood the brunt of the
onset: but the Jews still came pouring forth in such
overbearing multitudes, that Titus himself was forced to
charge at the head of some cavalry, and with difficulty
drove them back into the Temple.

It was the 10th of August, the day already darkened
in the Jewish calendar by the destruction of the former
Temple by the king of Babylon: that day was almost
passed. Titus withdrew again into the Antonia, intending the next morning to make a general assault. The
quiet summer evening came on; the setting sun shone
for the last time on the snow-white walls and glistening
pinnacles of the Temple roof. Titus had retired to rest;
when suddenly a wild and terrible cry was heard, and a
man came rushing in, announcing that the Temple was
on fire. Some of the besieged, notwithstanding their
repulse in the morning, had sallied out to attack the
men who were busily employed in extinguishing the
fires about the cloisters. The Romans not merely drove
them back, but, entering the sacred space with them,

---

tus wrote the names of the counsellors
who were for mercy; for "ultra omnia
mortalia illustrem," "inter omnes mor-
tales nobilem," or "illustrem." He wrote,
too, "superstitio," rather than "religio." The half knowledge and half
ignorance of the relations between the
Jews and Christians, the bitter prejudice
against both, are quite in character
with Tacitus. If then this be a fair
conclusion, as I doubt not it is, of M.
Bernays, it is a curious illustration
of the adulatory tone towards his Roman patrons with which Josephus composed his History.

forced their way to the door of the Temple.   A soldier,
without orders, mounting on the shoulders of one of his
comrades, threw a blazing brand into a small gilded
door on the north side of the chambers, in the outer
building or porch.[a]   The flames sprang up at once.   The
Jews uttered one simultaneous shriek, and grasped their
swords with a furious determination of revenging and
perishing in the ruins of the Temple.   Titus rushed
down with the utmost speed : he shouted, he made
signs to his soldiers to quench the fire : his voice was
drowned, and his signs unnoticed, in the blind confusion.   The legionaries either could not or would not
hear : they rushed on, trampling each other down in
their furious haste, or, stumbling over the crumbling
ruins, perished with the enemy.   Each exhorted the
other, and each hurled his blazing brand into the inner
part of the edifice, and then hurried to his work of
carnage.   The unarmed and defenceless people were
slain in thousands ; they lay heaped like sacrifices, round
the altar; the steps of the Temple ran with streams
of blood, which washed down the bodies that lay about.

Titus found it impossible to check the rage of the
soldiery; he entered with his officers, and surveyed the
interior of the sacred edifice.   The splendour filled
them with wonder; and as the flames had not yet
penetrated to the Holy Place, he made a last effort to
save it, and springing forth, again exhorted the soldiers
to stay the progress of the conflagration.   The centurion Liberalis endeavoured to force obedience with his
staff of office ; but even respect for the Emperor gave
way to the furious animosity against the Jews, to the
fierce excitement of battle, and to the insatiable hope of

---

[a] θυρίδι.   It may have been, and is usually described as a window.

plunder. The soldiers saw every thing around them radiant with gold, which shone dazzlingly in the wild light of the flames; they supposed that incalculable treasures were laid up in the sanctuary. A soldier, unperceived, thrust a lighted torch between the hinges of the door: the whole building was in flames in an instant. The blinding smoke and fire forced the officers to retreat, and the noble edifice was left to its fate.[x]

It was an appalling spectacle to the Roman—what was it to the Jew? The whole summit of the hill which commanded the city blazed like a volcano. One after another the buildings fell in, with a tremendous crash, and were swallowed up in the fiery abyss. The roofs of cedar were like sheets of flame: the gilded pinnacles shone like spikes of red light: the gate towers sent up tall columns of flame and smoke. The neighbouring hills were lighted up; and dark groups of people were seen watching in horrible anxiety the progress of the destruction: the walls and heights of the upper city were crowded with faces, some pale with the agony of despair, others scowling unavailing vengeance. The shouts of the Roman soldiery as they ran to and fro, and the howlings of the insurgents who were perishing in the flames, mingled with the roaring of the conflagration and the thundering sound of falling timbers. The echoes of the mountains replied or brought back the shrieks of the people on the heights:

---

[x] The curious reader may find in Eisenmenger, Entdecktes Judenthum, i. 19, 20, some strange Rabbinical stories of the bitter sorrow of God at the destruction of his Temple. "When God departed from his Temple, he went back, embraced and kissed the walls and the pillars, wept, and said, ' Alas for the peace of my House, of my Holy of Holies!' The angels in vain endeavoured to console the Almighty!!"

all along the walls resounded screams and wailings:
men who were expiring with famine, rallied their
remaining strength to utter a cry of anguish and
desolation.

The slaughter within was even more dreadful than
the spectacle from without. Men and women, old and
young, insurgents and priests, those who fought and
those who entreated mercy, were hewn down in indis-
criminate carnage. The number of the slain exceeded
that of the slayers. The legionaries had to clamber
over heaps of dead to carry on the work of extermination. John, at the head of some of his troops, cut his
way through, first into the outer court of the Temple,
afterwards into the upper city. Some of the priests
upon the roof wrenched off the gilded spikes, with their
sockets of lead, and used them as missiles against the
Romans below. Afterwards they fled to a part of the
wall, about fourteen feet wide; they were summoned
to surrender; but two of them, Mair, son of Belga,
and Joseph, son of Dalai, plunged headlong into the
flames.

No part escaped the fury of the Romans. The trea-
suries with all their wealth of money, jewels, and costly
robes—the plunder which the Zealots had laid up—
were totally destroyed. Nothing remained but a small
part of the outer cloister, in which about 6000 unarmed
and defenceless people, with women and children, had
taken refuge. These poor wretches, like multitudes of
others, had been led up to the Temple by a false prophet, who had proclaimed that God commanded all the
Jews to go up to the Temple, where he would display
his Almighty power to save his people. The soldiers
set fire to the building: every soul perished.

For during all this time false prophets, suborned by

the Zealots, had kept the people in a state of feverish excitement, as though the appointed Deliverer would still appear. They could not, indeed, but remember the awful, the visible signs which had preceded the siege —the fiery sword, the armies fighting in the air; the opening of the great gate, the fearful voice within the sanctuary, "Let us depart;" the wild cry of Jesus, son of Ananus—*Woe, woe to the city!* which he had continued from the government of Albinus to the time of the siege, when he suddenly stopped, shrieked out—*Woe to myself!* and was struck dead by a stone. Yet the undying hopes of fierce fanaticism were kept alive by the still renewed prediction of that Great one, who would at this time arise out of Judæa, and assume the dominion of the world. This prophecy the flattering Josephus declared to be accomplished in the Roman, Vespasian; but more patriotic interpreters still, to the last, expected to see it fulfilled in the person of the conquering Messiah, who would reveal himself in the darkest hour, wither the Roman legions with one word, and then transfer the seat of empire from the Capitol to Sion.[y]

The whole Roman army entered the sacred precincts, and pitched their standards among the smoking ruins; they offered sacrifice for the victory, and with loud acclamations saluted Titus as Emperor. Their joy was not a little enhanced by the value of the plunder they had obtained, which was so great that gold fell in Syria to half its former value. The few priests were still on the top of the walls to which they had escaped.

---

[y] τὸ δὲ ἐπᾶραν αὐτοὺς μάλιστὰ πρὸς τὸν πόλεμον, ἦν χρησμὸς ἀμφίβολος, ὁμοίως ἐν τοῖς ἱεροῖς εὑρημένος γράμμασιν, ὡς κατὰ τὸν καιρὸν ἐκεῖνον ἀπὸ τῆς χώρας τις αὐτῶν ἄρξει τῆς οἰκουμένης. B. J. vi. 5. 4. Compare Tacitus, Hist. v. 13; and Suetonius, Vesp. 4.

A boy emaciated with hunger came down on a promise that his life should be spared. He immediately ran to drink, filled his vessel, and hurried away to his comrades with such speed that the soldiers could not catch him. Five days afterwards the priests were starved into surrender; they entreated for their lives, but Titus answered, that the hour of mercy was past; they were led to execution.

Still the upper city held out; but Simon and John, disheartened by the capture of the Temple, demanded a conference. It was granted, and Titus, stationing himself at the western verge of the hill, addressed them through an interpreter.[a] He offered to spare their lives on the condition of instant surrender. John and Simon demanded free egress with their wives and children, promising to evacuate the city, and depart into the wilderness. The terms were rejected, and Titus vowed the unsparing extermination of the whole people; his troops had immediate licence to plunder and burn Acra.[a] The archives, the council house, the whole of Acra and Ophla, were instantly set on fire. The insurgents took possession of the palace, where, from its strength, the people had laid up much of their wealth; they drove the Romans back, and put to death 8400 of the people who had taken refuge there, and plundered all the treasures.[b] They took two Roman soldiers

---

[a] This is the worst, most rhetorical, and most unsuited to the occasion, of all those speeches which Josephus, fondly supposing no doubt that he is following and rivalling Thucydides, ascribes to the Emperor; and all this, as he says, to be interpreted to the fierce warriors.

[a] The sons and brothers of King Izates, who, whether of their free will or from compulsion, had remained in the city (a singular fact), with several of the heads of the people, now surrendered: their lives were spared; they were sent prisoners to Rome, Titus no doubt anticipating the pride of his triumph.

[b] This, of all the extravagant and incredible numbers in Josephus, seems the most extravagant and incredible.

alive; one they put to death, and dragged his body through the city; the other, pretending to have something to communicate to Simon, was led before him, but as he had nothing to say, he was made over to one Ardala, to be put to death. He was led forth with his hands bound, and his eyes bandaged, to be killed in sight of the Romans, but while the Jew was drawing his sword, the prisoner contrived to make his escape. Titus, unwilling to punish him with death after he had thus escaped, but wishing to show that it was unworthy of a Roman soldier to be taken alive, had him stripped of his armour, and dismissed him with disgrace. The next day the Romans entirely cleared the lower city, and set the whole on fire. The insurgents, cooped up in the upper city, lay in ambush near the outlets, and slew every one who attempted to desert. Their great trust was in the subterranean passages, in which they hoped to lie hid.

On the 20th of August, Cæsar at length raised his mounds against the steep cliffs of the upper city; he had the greatest difficulty in obtaining timber. But at last his works were ready in two places, one opposite the palace, the other near the Xystus. The Idumean chieftains now endeavoured secretly to make their terms. Titus reluctantly consented; but the vigilant Simon detected the plot, threw the leaders into prison, and entrusted the defence of the walls to more trusty soldiers. Still the guards could not prevent desertion; though many were killed, yet many escaped. The Romans, weary of the work of slaughter, spared the people, but sold all the rest as slaves; though they bore but a low price, the market being glutted, and few purchasers found—40,000 were thus spared, the number sold as slaves was incalculable. About the same time a priest named Jesus, son of Thebuth, obtained his life on condition of surrendering some of the treasures of the Temple which he had secured, two candlesticks, tables, goblets and vessels of pure gold, as well as the curtains and the robes of the High Priests. Another, who had been one of the treasurers, showed a place where the vests and girdles of the priests were concealed, with a great quantity of purple and scarlet thread, and an immense store of cinnamon, cassia, and other spices.

Eighteen days elapsed before the works were completed; on the 7th of September the engines were advanced to batter down the last bulwark of the besieged. Some did not await the conflict, but crept down into the lower city; others shrank into the subterranean passages; others, more manfully, endeavoured to beat down the engineers. The Romans advanced in the pride of victory; the Jews were weary, famine-stricken, disheartened. A breach was speedily made, some of the towers fell, the leaders did not display their customary valour and conduct; they fled on all sides. Some who were accustomed to vaunt the most loudly, now stood pale, trembling, inactive; others endeavoured to break through the Roman works and make their escape. Vague rumours were spread abroad that the whole western wall had fallen, that the Romans were in the city; the men looked around for their wonted leaders; they neither saw their active figures hurrying about in the thickest of the fray, nor heard their voices exciting them to desperate resistance. Many threw themselves on the ground and bitterly lamented their fate. Even John and Simon, instead of remaining in their three impregnable towers, where nothing but famine could have reduced them, descended into the streets, and fled into the valley of Siloam. They then made an attempt to force their way through the wall; but their daring and strength seemed alike broken, they were repulsed by the guard, dispersed, and at length crept down into the subterranean vaults. The Romans ascended the wall with shouts of triumph at a victory so much beyond all hope, easy and bloodless; they spread through the streets, slaying and burning as they went. In many houses where they expected rich plunder, they found nothing but heaps of putrid bodies, whole families who had died of hunger; they retreated from the loathsome sight and insufferable stench. But they were not moved to mercy towards the living; in some places the flames were actually retarded or quenched with streams of blood; night alone put an end to the carnage. When Titus entered the city he gazed with astonishment at the massy towers, and recognized the hand of God in a victory which had thus made him master of such fortresses without a struggle. The multitudes of prisoners who pined in the dungeons, where they had been thrown by the insurgents, were released. The city was ordered to be razed, excepting the three towers, which were left as standing monuments of the victory.

The soldiers themselves were weary of the work of slaughter, and orders were issued to kill only those who resisted. Yet the old and infirm, as unsaleable, were generally put to death. The rest were driven into a space of the Temple, called the Court of the Women. There a selection was made; the noted insurgents were put to death, excepting some of the tallest and most handsome, who were reserved to grace the triumph of Titus. Of the rest, all above seventeen years old were sent to Egypt to work in the mines, or distributed among the provinces to be exhibited as gladiators in the public theatres, and in combats against wild beasts. Twelve thousand died of hunger—part from want or neglect of supplies, part obstinately refusing food. During the whole siege the number killed was 1,100,000, that of prisoners 97,000. In fact, the population not of Jerusalem alone, but that of the adjacent districts— many who had taken refuge in the city, more who had assembled for the feast of unleavened bread—had been shut up by the sudden formation of the siege.

Yet the chief objects of their vengeance, the dauntless Simon, son of Gioras, and John the Gischalite, still seemed to baffle all pursuit. The Roman soldiers penetrated into the subterranean caverns: wherever they went, they found incalculable treasures and heaps of dead—some who had perished from hunger, others from their wounds, many by their own hands. The close air of the vaults reeked with the pestilential effluvia; most recoiled from these pits of death; the more rapacious went on, breathing death for the sake of plunder. At length, reduced by famine, John and his brethren came forth upon terms of surrender; his life was spared—a singular instance of lenity, if indeed his conduct had been so atrocious as it is described by his rival Josephus. He was condemned to perpetual imprisonment, and finally sent to Italy.[c]

Many days after, towards the end of October, when Titus had left the city, as some of the Roman soldiers were reposing amid the ruins of the Temple, they were surprised by the sudden apparition of a man in white raiment, and with a robe of purple,[d] who seemed to rise

---

[c] B. J. vii. 2. 2.

[d] κατ᾽ αὐτὸν ἐκεῖνον τὸν τόπον, ἐν ᾧ τὸ ἱερὸν ἦν πρόσθεν, ἐκ γῆς ἀνεφάνη. This may seem to imply that there was a subterranean connexion between the upper city and the substructures of the Temple.

from the earth in silent and imposing dignity. At first they stood awestruck and motionless: at length they ventured to approach him; they encircled him, and demanded his name. He answered, "Simon, the son of Gioras; call hither your general." Terentius Rufus was speedily summoned, and to him the brave, though cruel, defender of Jerusalem surrendered himself. On the loss of the city, Simon had leaped down into one of the vaults, with a party of miners, hewers of stone, and iron workers. For some distance they had followed the natural windings of the cavern, and then attempted to dig their way out beyond the walls; but their provisions, however carefully husbanded, soon failed, and Simon determined on the bold measure of attempting to overawe the Romans by his sudden and spectral appearance. News of his capture was sent to Titus; he was ordered to be set apart for the imperial triumph.

Thus fell, and for ever, the metropolis of the Jewish state. Other cities have risen on the ruins of Jerusalem, and succeeded, as it were, to the inalienable inheritance of perpetual siege, oppression, and ruin. Jerusalem might almost seem to be a place under a peculiar curse: it has probably witnessed a far greater portion of human misery than any other spot upon the earth.

Terentius Rufus, or Turnus Rufus, (as his name appears in the Rabbinical traditions, ever coupled with the most rancorous expressions of hatred, and confounded with the no less obnoxious T. Annius Rufus, the governor of Judæa in the time of Hadrian,) executed the work of desolation, of which he was left in charge, with unrelenting severity. Of all the stately city—the populous streets, the palaces of the Jewish kings, the

fortresses of her warriors, the Temple of her God—not a
ruin remained, except the tall towers of Phasaelis, Mariamne, and Hippicus, and part of the western wall, which
was left as a defence for the Roman camp. Titus
having distributed praises and rewards to his army, and
offered sacrifice to his gods, had departed. Wherever
he went, miserable gangs of captives were dragged
along, to glut the eyes and ears of the conquerors by
their sufferings in those horrible spectacles which are
the eternal disgrace of the Roman character. At
Cæsarea Philippi, 2500 were slain in cold blood, either
in combats with wild beasts, or fighting as bands of
gladiators. This was in honour of the birth-day of his
brother Domitian—an appropriate celebration for such
an event. Vespasian's birth-day was also commemorated at Berytus with the same horrible festivities.
One act of mercy alone, towards the Jewish race,
marked the journey of Titus. The inhabitants of Antioch, incited by a Jewish apostate, Antiochus, the son of
the first man among the Jews in the city, had cruelly
persecuted his brethren. This apostate had accused his
kindred of a design of setting fire to the whole city.
For this many were burnt alive, and the whole community threatened with destruction. An accidental
fire happened afterwards to take place, which was
again laid to the charge of the Jews. In short, the
whole Grecian population was so exasperated against
the Jews, that they petitioned Titus for their expulsion
from the city, or at least to cancel their privileges.[d]
Titus at first gave no answer, but afterwards, on his
return from the Euphrates, he refused their demands in
these affecting words: "The country of the Jews is

---

[d] B. J. vii. 5. 2.

destroyed—thither they cannot return: it would be hard to allow them no home to which they can retreat —leave them in peace." As he passed from Antioch to Alexandria, he surveyed the ruins of Jerusalem, and is said to have been touched with pity at the total desolation of that splendid city. For this work of havock, for the destruction of near a million and a half of human lives, and the reduction of above 100,000 to the most cruel servitude, Titus was considered as entitled to a splendid triumph. If the numbers in Josephus may be depended on, the fearful catalogue of those who lost their lives or their liberty in this exterminating war, and its previous massacres, stands as follows :°

---

* I have ventured to doubt the vast numbers (in this respect the discrepancies in the sacred books are the most striking and most irreconcileable) in the earlier Jewish history. Josephus, as if it were a strange habit in the people, instead of confirming, in my judgement, by his boundless extravagance, only strengthens the doubtfulness of the whole. In one passage he gravely asserts that the smallest villages in Galilee had 15,000 inhabitants (B. J. iii. 3. 2), besides a great number of cities, πόλεις πυκναὶ, of course with far larger populations.

The only approach to statistics is the calculation from the number of lambs sacrificed at the Passover, from which he would conclude that three millions of persons attended at Jerusalem during these festivals. (See ii. p. 218.) Though it cannot be asserted that these persons were not all together in the capital, that some were coming and going (f r all, to keep the law there, must have been present at least at the Great Day), yet we may fairly suppose that many found accommodation in the adjacent villages (as our Lord seems to have passed the nights at Bethany and on the Mount of Olives); and whoever has seen even a modern pilgrimage in the South will make fair allowance for the multitudes which, in such climates, sleep in the open air. Still, taking the circuit of Jerusalem, I cannot conceive the possibility of crowding such numbers, even with the deductions suggested, within the walls.

It is right, however, to add a passage from Strabo confirmatory of the great populousness of part of Galilee. Jamnia and the adjacent villages furnished a levy of 40,000 armed men. καὶ δὴ καὶ εὐάνδρησεν οὗτος ὁ τόπος, ὥστ' εκ τῆς πλησίον κώμης Ἰαμνείας, καὶ τῶν κατοικιῶν τῶν κυκλῷ τέτταρας μυριάδας ὁπλίζεσθαι. Lib. xvi. p. 759.

Before the War under Vespasian.

At Jerusalem, killed by Florus	3,600
At Cæsarea	20,000
At Scythopolis	13,000
At Ascalon	2,500
At Ptolemais	2,000
At Alexandria	50,000
At Damascus	10,000
At Joppa	8,400
Upon the mountain Asamon	2,000
The battle near Ascalon	10,000
The Ambuscades	8,000
	129,500

During the War in Galilee and Judæa.

At Japha	15,000
On Gerizim	11,600
At Jotapata	40,000
At Joppa	4,200
At Tarichea	6,500
At Gamala	9,000
At Gischala	6,000
In Idumæa	10,000
At Gerasa	1,000
Near the Jordan	15,000
	118,300
At Jerusalem	**1,100,000**

After the Fall of Jerusalem.

At Machærus	1,700
At Jardes	3,000
At Masada	960
In Cyrene	3,000
	8,660
TOTAL KILLED	**1,356,460**

Prisoners.

In Gischala	2,200
Near the Jordan	2,500
At Jerusalem	97,000
TOTAL PRISONERS	**101,700**

The loss in many skirmishes and battles,—that of Itabyrium, for instance,—is omitted, as we have not the numbers; besides the immense waste of life from massacre, famine, and disease, inseparable from such a war, in almost every district. The number of prisoners is only given from two places besides Jerusalem.

Nothing could equal the splendour of the triumph which Vespasian shared with his son Titus for their common victories. Besides the usual display of treasures, gold, silver, jewels, purple vests, the rarest wild beasts from all quarters of the globe, there were extraordinary pageants, three or four stories high, representing, to the admiration and delight of those civilized savages, all the horrors and miseries of war; beautiful countries laid waste, armies slain, routed, led captive; cities breached by military engines, stormed, destroyed with fire and sword; women wailing; houses overthrown; temples burning; and rivers of fire flowing through regions no longer cultivated or peopled, but blazing far away into the long and dreary distance. Among the spoils, the golden table, the seven-branched candlestick, and the book of the Law, from the Temple of Jerusalem, were conspicuous.[f]

The triumph passed on to the Capitol, and there paused to hear that the glory of Rome was completed by the insulting and cruel execution of the bravest general of the enemy. This distinction fell to the lot of Simon, the son of Gioras. He was dragged along to a place near the Forum, with a halter round his neck, scourged as he went, and there put to death.[g]

---

[f] Was Pliny's remarkable expression that Jerusalem was the most famous city in the East ("in qua fuere Hierosolymæ, longe clarissima urbium Orientis non Judææ modo," l. v. c. viii.) the common sentiment of the times, or a skilful adulation of its conquerors, Vespasian and Titus, his special patrons?

[g] B. J. vii. 5. 6

The antiquary still endeavours to trace, among the defaced and mouldering reliefs of the arch raised to Titus, "the Delight of human-kind," and which still stands in the Forum of Rome, the representation of the spoils taken from the Temple of Jerusalem—the golden table and candlestick, the censers, the silver trumpets, and even the procession of captive Jews.[h]

---

[h] On the subsequent fate of these spoils compare a dissertation of Reland, de Spoliis Templi; Gibbon, c. xli.; Le Beau, Bas Empire, viii. p. 260.

BOOK XVII.

TERMINATION OF THE WAR.

Fall of Herodion — Machærus — Masada — Fate of Josephus —
Agrippa — Berenice.

IT might have been expected that all hopes of resistance,
even among the most stubborn of the Jews, would have
been buried under the ruins of the capital; that after
the fall of Jerusalem, with such dreadful misery and
carnage, every town would at once have opened its
gates, and laid itself at the mercy of the irresistible
conqueror. Yet, when Lucilius Bassus came to take
the command of the Roman army, he found three
strong fortresses still in arms—Herodion, Masada, and
Machærus. Herodion immediately capitulated; but
Machærus, beyond the Jordan, relying on its impregnable position, defied all the power of the enemy.
Machærus stood on the summit of a lofty crag, surrounded on all sides by ravines of enormous depth,
which could not easily be crossed, and could not possibly
be filled up. One of these ravines, on the western side,
ran down, a distance of nearly eight miles, to the Dead
Sea. Those to the north and the south were less deep,
but not less impassable; on the east the hollow was 175
feet to the bottom, beyond which arose a mountain
which faced Machærus. The town had been built and
strongly fortified by Alexander Jannæus, as a check
upon the Arabian freebooters. It was a place of great

beauty, as well as strength, adorned with noble palaces, and amply supplied with reservoirs of water. Bassus determined to form the siege on the eastern side; the garrison took possession of the citadel, and forced the strangers, who had taken refuge there from all quarters, to defend the lower town. Many fierce conflicts took place under the walls; the garrison sometimes surprising the enemy by the rapidity of their sallies; sometimes, when the Romans were prepared for them, being repulsed with great loss. There happened to be a young man, named Eleazar, of remarkable activity and valour, who greatly distinguished himself in these attacks, being always the first to charge and the last to retreat, often by his single arm arresting the progress of the enemy, and allowing his routed compatriots time to make good their retreat. One day, after the battle was over, proudly confident in his prowess, and in the terror of his arms, he remained alone without the gates, carelessly conversing with those on the wall. Rufus, an Egyptian, serving in the Roman army, a man of singular bodily strength, watched the opportunity, rushed on him, and bore him off, armour and all, to the Roman camp. Bassus ordered the captive to be stripped and scourged in the sight of the besieged. At the sufferings of their brave champion the whole city set up a wild wailing. Bassus, when he saw the effect of his barbarous measure, ordered a cross to be erected, as if for the execution of the gallant youth. The lamentations in the city became more loud and general. Eleazar's family was powerful and numerous. Through their influence it was agreed to surrender the citadel, on condition that Eleazar's life should be spared. The strangers in the lower town attempted to cut their way through the posts of the besiegers; a few of the bravest succeeded; of those who remained, 1700 perished. The treaty with the garrison was honourably observed.

Bassus proceeded to surround the forest of Jardes, where a vast number of fugitives had taken refuge: they attempted to break through, but were repulsed, and 3000 put to the sword. During the course of these successes Bassus died, and Flavius Silva assumed the command in Palestine. Silva immediately marched against Masada, the only place which still held out.[1] Masada was situated on the south-western side of the Dead Sea. Like the other hill fortresses of Palestine, it stood on a high rock, girt with precipitous chasms, the sides of which a goat could scarcely clamber. It was accessible only by two narrow and very difficult paths, from the east and from the west. On the east, the path, or rather a rocky stair, led up from the shore of the Dead Sea, called the Serpent, from its winding and circuitous course. It ran along the verge of frightful precipices, which made the head giddy to look down; it was necessary to climb step by step; if the foot slipped, instant death was inevitable. After winding in this manner nearly four miles, this path opened on a level space, on which Masada stood, in the midst of a small and highly cultivated plain of extraordinary beauty and fertility. The city was girt with a wall, nearly a mile in circuit; it was twenty-two feet high, fourteen broad, and had thirty-seven lofty towers. Besides this wall, Masada had a strong and magnificent palace, with sixty towers, built by Herod, on the western cliff, and connected, by an underground way, with the citadel. The western ascent was com-

---

[1] There is an engraving in Traill's Josephus from a drawing of Masada, which gives a striking impression of its sombre grandeur and strength.

manded, in its narrowest part, by an impregnable tower.

The city was amply supplied with excellent water, and with provisions of all kinds, wine, oil, vegetables, and dates. According to the strange account of Josephus, the air of Masada was of such a temperature, that, although some of these fruits had been laid up for a hundred years, since the time of Herod, they were still sound and fresh. There were likewise armories sufficient to supply 10,000 men, with great stores of unwrought iron, brass, and lead. In fact, Masada had been the fortress which Herod the Great had always looked to, as a place of security, either in case of foreign invasion, or the revolt of his own subjects. The town was now as strongly manned as fortified. Eleazar, the commander, was a descendant of Judas the Galilean, and inherited the principles of his ancestor in their sternest and most stubborn fanaticism. To yield to a foreign dominion, was to him and his zealous associates the height of impiety ; death was far preferable to a treacherous dereliction of the sovereignty of God. They acted, to the end, up to their lofty tenets.

Silva having blockaded the town, so that none could make their escape, seized a point of rock, called the White Promontory, to the westward. There he erected his works, a mound, 350 feet high, and above that a second bank of enormous stones ; and at length he brought a battering ram to bear upon the walls. After long resistance, a breach was made ; but the besieged had run up another wall within, of great timbers laid parallel with each other, in two separate rows, the intervening space being filled with earth : this sort of double artificial wall was held together by transverse beams, and the more violently it was battered, the more solid and compact it became, by the yielding of the earth.. Silva ordered his men to throw lighted brands upon it : the timbers speedily kindled, and the whole became a vast wall of fire. The north wind blew the flames into the faces of the besiegers, and the Romans trembled for their own works and engines. On a sudden the wind shifted to the south, the flames burned inwards, and the whole fell down, a heap of smouldering ashes. The Romans withdrew to their camp, to prepare for the attack on the next morning, and stationed strong and vigilant outposts to · prevent the flight of the garrison. But Eleazar was not a man either himself to attempt flight or to permit others to follow so dastardly a course. He assembled his followers in the palace, and reminded them that the time was now come when they must vindicate to the utmost their lofty principles. God had evidently abandoned his people ; the fall of Jerusalem, the ruin of the Temple, too sadly proved this. The sudden change of the wind, on the day before, distinctly announced that they, too, were deserted by his protecting providence. Still it was better to fall into the hands of God than of the Roman ; and he proposed that they should set the city on fire, and perish together, with their wives unviolated, their children yet free from captivity, on that noble funeral pile.

His men gazed on each other in wonder. Some were kindled at once with his enthusiasm ; others thought of their wives and children, and tears were seen stealing slowly down their hardy cheeks. Eleazar saw that they were wavering, and broke out in a higher and more splendid strain. He spoke of the immortality, the divinity of the soul; its joyful escape from its imprisonment in its mortal tenement. He appealed to the example of the Indians, who bear life as a burthen, and

2 c 2

cheerfully throw it off.[k]   Perhaps with still greater effect he dwelt on the treatment of the conquered by the Romans, the abuse of women, the slavery of children, the murderous scenes in the amphitheatres.   "Let us die," he ended, "unenslaved; let us depart from life in freedom with our wives and children.   This our law demands, this our wives and children entreat; God himself has driven us to this stern necessity; this the Romans dread above all things, lest we should disappoint them of their victory.   Let us deny them the joy and triumph of seeing us subdued, and rather strike them with awe at our death, and with enforced admiration of our indomitable valour."

He was interrupted by the unanimous voice of the multitude, vying with each other in eagerness to begin on the instant the work of self-devotion.   On their intoxicated spirits no softer feelings had now the slightest effect.   They embraced their wives, they kissed their children even with tears, and, at the moment, as though

---

[k] Μέγα μὲν οὖν δύναται ψυχὴ καὶ σώματι συνδεδεμένη· ποιεῖ γὰρ αὐτῆς ὄργανον αἰσθανόμενον ἀοράτως αὐτὸ κινοῦσα, καὶ θνητῆς φύσεως περαιτέρω προάγουσα ταῖς πράξεσιν. 'Ου μὴν ἀλλ' ἐπειδὰν ἀπολυθεῖσα τοῦ καθέλκοντος αὐτὴν βάρους ἐπὶ γῆν καὶ προσκρεμαμένου, χῶρον ἀπολάβῃ τὸν οἰκεῖον, τότε δὴ μακαρίας ἰσχύος καὶ πανταχόθεν ἀκωλύτου μετέχει δυνάμεως, ἀόρατος μένουσα τοῖς ἀνθρωπίνοις ὄμμασιν, ὥσπερ αὐτὸς ὁ θεός.   This is a fine passage, though one may doubt whether it was uttered by the fierce Sicarians : if it was, they were nobler fellows than Josephus represents them.[*]   But the speech is sadly marred by its length.   The long analogy with the Indians is very curious, but very tame.   And who reported the speech ?[†] for according to the History all were killed and burned, except two old women and five children who were in the caverns below.

[†] The reference of Eleazar to the Indians, even as ascribed as it must be to Josephus, is remarkable.   One might almost suppose that he had read the Bhagavat Gita. See Wilkins's translation.   "How can the man who believeth that this thing is incorruptible, eternal, inexhaustible, and without birth, think that he can either kill it or cause it to be killed?" Compare the whole passage in Wilkins's translation, p. 37 or the original in Schlegel's Bhagavat Gita, Lectio ii. p. xi.

[*] B. J. vii. 8.

they had been the passive instruments of another's will, they stabbed them to the heart. Not a man declined the murderous office. But they thought that they should wrong the dead if they survived them many minutes. They hastily drew together their most valuable effects, and, heaping them up, set fire to these sumptuous funeral piles. Then, ten men having been chosen by lot as the general executioners, the rest, one after another, still clasping the lifeless bodies of their wives and children, held up their necks to the blow. The ten then cast lots; nine fell by each other's hands; the last man, after he had carefully searched whether there was any more work for him to do, seized a lighted brand, set fire to the palace, and so, with resolute and unflinching hand, drove the sword to his own heart.

One old woman, another female who was a relative of Eleazar and distinguished for her learning, and five children, who had crept into an underground cavern, were all that escaped; 960 perished. The next morning the Romans advanced to the wall in close array and with the greatest caution. They fixed the scaling-ladders, mounted the wall, and rushed in. Not a human being appeared; all was solitude and silence, and the vestiges of fire all around filled them with astonishment. They gave a shout as they were wont when they drove the battering ram, as if to startle the people from their hiding-places. The two women and the five children came creeping forth. The Romans would not believe their story, till, having partially extinguished the fire, they made their way into the palace, and, not without admiration, beheld this unexampled spectacle of self-devotion.

Thus terminated the final subjugation of Judæa. An edict of the Emperor to set up all the lands to sale had been received by Bassus. Vespasian did not pursue the usual policy of the Romans, in sharing the conquered territory among military colonists. He reserved to the imperial treasury the whole profits of the sale. Only 800 veterans were settled in Emmaus, about seven miles and a half from Jerusalem. At the same time another edict was issued for the transfer of the annual capitation tax of two drachms, paid by the Jews in every quarter of the world, for the support of the Temple worship, to the fund for rebuilding the Temple of Jupiter Capitolinus, which, as Gibbon observes, " by a remarkable coincidence, had been consumed by the flames of war about the same time with the Temple of Jerusalem." Thus the Holy Land was condemned to be portioned out to strangers, and the contributions for the worship of the God of Abraham levied for the maintenance of a heathen edifice.

Yet, though entirely extinguished in Judæa, the embers of the war still burned in more distant countries. Some of the Assassins (the Sicarii) fled to Egypt, and began to display their usual turbulence, putting to death many of the more influential Jewish residents, who opposed their seditious designs, and exciting the rest to revolt. The Jews assembled in council, and determined to put down these dangerous enemies to their peace, by seizing and delivering them up to the Romans. Six hundred were immediately apprehended; a few, who fled to the Thebais, were pursued and captured. But the spirits of these men were still unsubdued; the most protracted and excruciating torments could not induce one of them, not even the tenderest boy, to renounce his Creed, or to own Cæsar as his Lord. On the news of this commotion, Vespasian sent orders that the temple of Onias in Heliopolis should be closed. Lupus, the Prefect, obeyed the order, took away part of the treasures, and shut up the temple. The edict was executed with still greater rigour by Paulinus, the successor of Lupus, who entirely stripped the treasury, and made the way to the temple impassable.

The last of these fanatics, having previously endangered the peace of Cyrene, had almost involved in his own fate the few distinguished Jews who had escaped the ruin of their country. A certain turbulent weaver of Cyrene, named Jonathan, pretended to supernatural signs and visions, and led a multitude of the lower orders into the Desert. The chief Jews denounced him to Catullus, the governor of the Pentapolis. Troops of horse were sent out, the deluded multitude brought back, and the impostor, after having long baffled their search, was apprehended. Before the tribunal of the governor this man accused many of the chief Jews as accomplices in his plot. Catullus listened with greedy ear to his charges, and even suggested the names of those whom he was anxious to convict. On the evidence of Jonathan and a few of his comrades, a man named Alexander, and Berenice his wife, who had been on bad terms with Catullus, were seized and put to death. Three thousand more shared their fate; their property was confiscated to the imperial treasury. Jonathan went still farther; he denounced, as the secret instigators of his revolt, some of the Jews of the highest rank who resided in Rome—among the rest, Josephus the historian.[1]

Catullus came to Rome with his witnesses. Vespasian ordered a strict investigation, the event of which was the exculpation of the accused, and the condemnation of Jonathan, who was first scourged and then burnt alive.

---

[1] Joseph. B. J., vii. cap. ult.

Catullus escaped animadversion; but Josephus, who spares no opportunity of recounting the judgements of Providence on his own personal enemies, gives a frightful picture of his end. He was seized with a dreadful malady of body and mind. Racked with remorse of conscience, he would rave, and scream out that he was environed by the ghosts of those whom he had murdered. He would then leap out of bed, and writhe and roll on the ground, as though on the rack, or burning alive in the flames. At length his entrails fell out, and death put an end to his agonies.

There were several persons who escaped from the general wreck of their country, whose fate may excite some interest. Josephus, the historian, after his surrender, married a captive in Cæsarea; but in obedience, it may be supposed, to the law which prohibited such marriages to a man of priestly line, he discarded her, and married again in Alexandria. We have seen that he was present during the whole siege, endeavouring to persuade his countrymen to capitulate. Whether he seriously considered resistance impossible, or, as he pretends, recognizing the hand of God, and the accomplishment of the prophecies, in the ruin of his country, esteemed it impious as well as vain; whether he was actuated by the baser motive of self-interest, or the more generous desire of being of service to his miserable countrymen, he was by no means held in the same estimation by the Roman army as by Titus. They thought a traitor to his country might be a traitor to them; and they were apt to lay all their losses to his charge, as if he kept up secret intelligence with the besieged. On the capture of the city, Titus offered him any boon he would request. He chose the sacred books, and the lives of his brother and fifty friends. He was afterwards permitted to

select 190 of his friends and relatives, from the multitudes who were shut up in the Temple to be sold for
slaves. A little after, near Tekoa, he saw a number of
persons writhing in the agonies of crucifixion, among
the rest three of his intimate associates. He rode off
with all speed to entreat their pardon. It was granted;
but two of them expired as they were being taken down
from the cross, the third survived. The estate of Josephus lying within the Roman encampment, Titus assigned him other lands in lieu of it. Vespasian also
conferred on him a considerable property in land. Josephus lived afterwards in Rome, in high favour with
Vespasian, Titus, and Domitian. The latter punished
certain Jews, and an eunuch, the tutor of his son, who
had falsely accused him; exempted his estate from tribute, and advanced him to high honour. He was a great
favourite with the Empress Domitia. He took the
name of Flavius, as a dependant on the Imperial family.

By his Alexandrian wife Josephus had three sons:
one only, Hyrcanus, lived to maturity. Dissatisfied with
his wife's conduct, he divorced her likewise, and married
a Cretan woman, from a Jewish family, of the first rank
and opulence in the island, and of admirable virtue.

At Rome, Josephus first wrote the History of the
Jewish War, in the Syro-Chaldaic language, for the use
of his own countrymen in the East, particularly those
beyond the Euphrates.[m] He afterwards translated the
work into Greek, for the benefit of the Western Jews
and of the Romans. Both king Agrippa and Titus
bore testimony to its accuracy. The latter ordered it
to be placed in the public library, and signed it with
his own hand, as an authentic memorial of the times.

---

[m] Whiston assigns the Jewish War to about A.C. 75; the Antiquities to 93.

Many years afterwards, about A.C. 93, he published his great work on the Antiquities of the Jews, of which the main object was to raise his nation in the estimation of the Roman world, and to confute certain calumnious accounts of their early history, which increased the hatred and contempt in which they were held. With the same view he wrote an answer to Apion, a celebrated grammarian of Alexandria, who had given currency to many of the ancient fictions of Egyptian tradition concerning the Jews. He likewise published his own Life, in answer to the statements of his old antagonist, Justus of Tiberias, who had sent forth a history of the war, written in Greek with considerable elegance. When he died is uncertain: history loses sight of him in his 56th or 57th year.[n]

The last of the royal house of Herod, who ruled in Palestine, king Agrippa, among the luxuries of the Roman capital, where he generally resided, forgot the calamities of his country, and the ruin of his people. He died, as he had lived, the humble and contented vassal of Rome. He had received the honours of the prætorship, and an accession of territory, from Vespasian. In him the line of the Idumean sovereigns was extinct.

His sister, Berenice, had nearly attained a loftier

---

[n] The view taken by later Jewish writers of the character of Josephus and of his History is thus expressed by Jost :—

"Die Kriegsgeschichte, höchst merkwürdig in ihrer Art, erzählt der eitele, eigennützige und verrätherische Joseph, oft die Thatsachen entstellend, mit schauderhafter Kälte : nach ihm sind die freiheitsliebenden Genossen nur Verbrecher und Räuber, derer Ueberwindung und graussige Behandlung er in behaglicher Genuss seines Sündenlohnes mit sichtlichen Beifall schildert. Er hat mit seinen übrigens unschätzbaren Geschichtswerken sich selbst ein ewiges Brandmahl aufgedrückt." Judenthum, i. p. 445.

I cannot quite assent to the coldness, though Josephus too often writes like a rhetorician—certainly not to his taking delight in the sufferings of his countrymen.

destiny. She was received with the highest honours at the imperial court, where her beauty and attractions, notwithstanding that she had been twice married, and had no great character for virtue,[o] so inflamed the heir of the empire and the conqueror of Judæa, Titus, that Rome trembled lest a Jewish mistress should sit on the imperial throne.[p] The public dissatisfaction was so loud and unambiguous, that Titus was constrained to dismiss her. She returned afterwards to Rome, but never regained her former favour. The time of her death, as well as that of her brother, is uncertain.

---

[o] The Roman satirist, Juvenal, has given currency to a report of a scandalous connexion with her brother.

"Deinde adamas notissimus, et Berenices
In digito factus pretiosior: hunc dedit olim
Barbarus incestæ, dedit hunc Agrippa sorori."—Satir. vi. 156.

[p] " Propterque insignem reginæ Berenices amorem cui etiam nuptias pollicitus ferebatur. Berenicem statim ab urbe dimisit invitus invitam."—Suet. in Tit. vii. Compare Dion Cassius. Aurelius Victor in his Epitome adds further scandal.

BOOK XVIII.

BARCOCHAB.

Character of the ensuing History — Re-establishment of Jewish Communities — Origin and Growth of Rabbinism — History to the Time of Trajan — Insurrections in Egypt, Cyrene, Cyprus, Mesopotamia, Palestine — Rabbi Akiba — Barcochab — Fall of Bither.

THE political existence of the Jewish nation was annihilated; it was never again recognised as one of the states or kingdoms of the world. Judæa was sentenced to be portioned out to strangers—the capital was destroyed—the Temple demolished—the royal house almost extinct—the High-priesthood buried under the ruins of the Temple. Our history has lost, as it were, its centre of unity; we have to trace a despised and obscure race in almost every region of the world; and connect, as we can, the loose and scattered details of their story. We are called back, indeed, for a short time to Palestine, to relate new scenes of revolt, ruin, and persecution. We behold the formation of two separate spiritual states, under the authority of which the whole nation seems to range itself in willing obedience. But in later periods we must wander over the whole face of the habitable globe to gather the scanty traditions which mark the existence of the Jewish people among the different

states of Asia, Africa, and Europe—where, refusing
to mingle their blood with any other race of mankind, they dwell in their distinct families and communities, and still maintain, though sometimes long and
utterly unconnected with each other, the principle of
national unity. Jews in the indelible features of the
countenance, in mental character, in customs, usages,
and laws, in language and literature, above all, in
religion; in the recollections of the past, and in the
hopes of the future; with ready pliancy they accommo-
date themselves to every soil, every climate, every gra-
dation of manners and civilization, every form of government; with inflexible pertinacity they practise their
ancient usages, circumcision, abstinence from unclean
meats, eating no animal food which has not been killed
by a Jew; rarely intermarry, except among each other;
observe the fasts and festivals of their church; and
assemble, wherever they are numerous enough, or dare
to do so, in their synagogues for public worship. Denizens every where, rarely citizens; even in the countries
in which they have been the longest and most firmly
established, they appear, to a certain degree, strangers
or sojourners; they dwell apart, though mingling with
their neighbours in many of the affairs of life. For
common purposes they adopt the language of the country they inhabit; but the Hebrew remains the national
tongue, in which their holy books are read, and their
religious services conducted—it is their literary and
sacred language, as Latin was that of the Christian
church in the dark ages.

The history of the modern Jews may be comprehended under three heads: 1st, Their literature, which,
in fact, is nearly the same with that of their law and
their religion, the great mass of their writings being

entirely devoted to those subjects:[a] 2. Their persecutions: 3. Their industry and their wealth, in general the fatal causes of those persecutions. With regard to the first point, it would not be consistent with the popular character of our work to enter into it, further than as it has influenced the character and circumstances of the nation. The second will be too often forced upon our notice: at one period the history of the Jews is written, as it were, in their blood; they show no signs of life but in their cries of agony; they only appear in the annals of the world to be oppressed, robbed, tortured, massacred. Yet still, patient and indefatigable, they pursue, under every disadvantage, the steady course of industry. Wherever they have been allowed to dwell unmolested, or still more, in honour and respect, they have added largely to the stock of national wealth, cultivation, and comfort. Where, as has been more usually the case, they have been barely tolerated, where they have been considered, in public estimation, the basest of the base, the very outcasts and refuse of mankind, they have gone on accumulating those treasures which they dared not betray or enjoy. In the most barbarous periods they kept up the only traffic and communication which subsisted between distant countries; like hardy and adventurous miners, they were always at work under the surface of society, slowly winning their way to opulence. Perpetually plundered, yet always wealthy; massacred by thou-

---

[a] I have rather expanded the view of the Jewish literature; still, however, avoiding a barren catalogue of the names of writers unknown beyond the sphere of Judaism, and dwelling almost entirely on those who have exercised an influence beyond that circle. The list of Jewish writers must be sought in the Buxtorfs, in Bartolocci, in De Rossi, and other writers, among whom I would name especially the Essays of M. Munk (Paris, 1859) as the latest and among the most learned.

sands, yet springing up again from their undying stock; the Jews appear at all times, and in all regions. Their perpetuity, their national immortality, is at once the most curious problem to the political inquirer; to the religious man a subject of profound and awful admiration.

It was not long after the dissolution of the Jewish state that it revived again in appearance, under the form of two separate communities, mostly independent upon each other: one under a sovereignty purely spiritual; the other partly temporal and partly spiritual —but each comprehending all the Jewish families in the two great divisions of the world. At the head of the Jews on this side of the Euphrates appeared the Patriarch of the West; the chief of the Mesopotamian community assumed the striking but more temporal title of Resch-Glutha, or Prince of the Captivity. The origin of both these dignities, especially of the Western patriarchate, is involved in much obscurity. It might have been expected that, from the character of the great war with Rome, the people, as well as the state of the Jews, would have fallen into utter dissolution, or, at least, verged rapidly towards total extermination. Besides the loss of nearly a million and a half of lives during the war, the markets of the Roman empire were glutted with Jewish slaves. The amphitheatres were crowded with these miserable people, who were forced to slay each other, not singly, but in troops; or fell in rapid succession, glad to escape the tyranny of their masters by the more expeditious cruelty of the wild beast. And in the unwholesome mines hundreds were doomed to toil for that wealth which was not to be their own. Yet still this inexhaustible race revived before long to offer new candidates for its inalienable inheritance of detestation and misery. Of the state of Palestine, indeed, immediately after the war, we have little accurate information. It is uncertain how far the enormous loss of life, and the numbers carried into captivity, drained the country of the Jewish population; or how far the rescript of Vespasian, which offered the whole landed property of the province for sale, introduced a foreign race into the possession of the soil. The immense numbers engaged in the rebellion during the reign of Hadrian imply, either that the country was not nearly exhausted, or that the reproduction in this still fertile region was extremely rapid. In fact, it must be remembered, that whatever havock was made by the sword of the conqueror, by distress, by famine; whatever the consumption of human life in the amphitheatre and the slave market, yet the ravage of the war was, after all, by no means universal in the province. Galilee, Judæa, and great part of Idumæa, were wasted, and, probably, much depopulated; but, excepting a few towns which made resistance, the populous regions and wealthy cities beyond the Jordan escaped the devastation. The dominions of king Agrippa were, for the most part, respected. Samaria submitted without resistance, as did most of the cities on the sea-coast. Many of the rich and influential persons fell off from their more obstinate countrymen at the beginning or during the course of the war, were favourably received, and dismissed in safety by Titus.[b]

---

[b] " Noch bestanden überall im Reiche, und selbst in Palästina Gemeinden, welche am Kampfe sich nicht betheiligt hatten, römisch-gesinnte, welche keinen Grund zur Verfolgung darboten, oder solche, deren kriegeslüstige Männer ihre Kühnheit gebüsst hatten; noch blieben im Schutz der Römer gemässigte Männer, welche frühzeitig übergetreten waren, und denen Erhaltung ihre Besitzen zugesagt worden; noch waren stille Bewohner übrig,

According to Jewish tradition, the Sanhedrin escaped the general wreck. Before the formation of the siege, it had followed Gamaliel, its Nasi, or Prince, to Jabne (Jamnia).[c] Simeon, the son and successor of Gamaliel, had gone up to the Passover; he was put to death. Rabban Jochanan ben Zaccai, after having laboured in vain to persuade the people to peace, made his escape to the camp of Titus, and afterwards became Nasi at Jamnia. It was Rabban Jochanan who, on the awful night when the great eastern gate of the Temple flew open of its own accord, quoted the ominous words of the prophet Zechariah—"*Open thy doors, O Lebanon, that the fire may devour thy cedars.*" He escaped the fury of the Zealots by being laid out on a bier as dead, and carried forth by his scholars, R. Joshua, and R. Eliezar. Jochanan is famous in Jewish tradition: he is the first of the elder Tanaim. Of the various anecdotes and sayings attributed to him, this appears to me the most striking:—His son died; he was inconsolable. His five famous scholars met to comfort him; four of them urged the examples of Adam, of Job, of Aaron, of David, who had suffered the same affliction. "How can the sufferings of others alleviate my sorrow?"

---

welche nach Erstickung des Aufstandes keinen Argwohn einflössten. Der Römer war viel zu stolz, um seine Rache weiter auszudehnen, und die Klugheit fcrderte Schonung derer, welche durch Bestellung des Bodens und andere friedliche Beschäftigungen dem Reiche noch Abgaben eintragen könnten. Von den ohnehin dem Kriege abgeneigten Gelehrten war eher eine Beschwichtigung der Gemüther zu erwarten. Die Religion lebte wieder auf." Jost, Judenthum, ii. 4. (Published since the first editions of this work.)

[e] I am inclined to think that the permission granted, according to the Rabbins, by Titus, to the Sanhedrin, to depart to Jamnia, Jabne, or Jafne, is another version of the account in Josephus, of the eminent persons who were courteously received by Titus, sent to *Gophni*, and afterwards recalled, for a short time, to try their influence, with Josephus, in persuading the besieged to surrender.

The fifth said—"A man had a precious jewel entrusted
to his care. He was troubled by the thought, 'How
can I render up this treasure uninjured?' Thou art in
the same case—thou hast had the happiness to restore
thy well-trained son uncorrupt to the Giver."—"My
son," he said, "thou hast truly comforted me." Jochanan's dying words were—"Fear God even as ye fear
men." His disciples seemed astonished. He added—
"He who would commit a sin, first looks round to discover whether any man sees him; so take ye heed that
God's all-seeing eye see not the sinful thought in your
heart." There is another account of his last words.
His disciples addressed him—"Why weepest thou, thou
Light of Israel?" — "If they were about to lead me
before a king of flesh and blood, who to-day is and to-
morrow is in the grave; if he were wroth with me,
his wrath were not eternal; if he should put me in
chains, his chains were not eternal; if he should put me
to death, that death would not be eternal; I might
appease him with words or bribe him with gifts. But
now they are about to lead me before the King of kings,
the Lord Blessed for ever, who lives and remains in
sæcula et sæcula sæculorum. If he is wroth with me, his
wrath is eternal; if he casts me into chains, his chains
are eternal; if he puts me to death, it is eternal death;
him no words can appease, no gifts soften. And further, there are two ways—one to hell, one to Paradise;
and I know not which way they will lead me. Is there
not cause for tears?"[d] Gamaliel, the son of Simeon,
likewise escaped the fate of his father, slain during the

---

[d] Lightfoot, in the spirit of his time
and opinions, says insultingly, "Oh the
wretched and failing faith of a Pharisee
in the hour of death!" Lightfoot, Academiæ Jafnensis Historiæ Fragm.
Works. 8vo. Edit. Pitman, - 44a

siege. With the permission of Titus, he followed Jochanan to Jamnia, and afterwards succeeded him in the presidency.[a]

---

[a] The Sanhedrin, the Rabbins say, had ten flittings.[1] From Gazith (the chamber in the Temple) to Khanoth (the Tabernæ, or shops, in the outer court)—from Khanoth to Jerusalem—from Jerusalem to Jabneth—from Jabneth to Osha—from Osha to Shepharaam—from Shepharaam to Bethshaaraim—from Bethshaaraim to Sepphoris—from Sepphoris to Tiberias. Its Nasi, or Presidents, on the same authority, were as follows :[2]—

Ezra.

Simon the Just.

Antigonus of Socho (the master of Sadoc).

Joseph ben Joezer, President. Joseph ben Jochanan, Vice-President.[3]

Joshua ben Perachiah—persecuted by Alexander Janneus; fled to Alexandria.[4]

Judah ben Tabbai, P. Simon ben Shetach, V.P.—according to Lightfoot, many *eminent* actions were performed by them ;—*they hanged eighty witches in one day.*[5]

Shemaiah, P. Abtalion, V. P.—descended from Sennacherib !—their mothers of Jewish blood. Probably the Sameas and Pollio of Josephus.

Hillel, P. Shammai, V. P.—Hillel was a second Moses : at forty years old he came up to Jerusalem; forty years he studied the law; forty years he was president.[6]

Simeon, son of Hillel—supposed by some the Simeon who took our Saviour in his arms; but there is considerable chronological difficulty.

Gamaliel, son of Simeon, (the teacher of St. Paul,)—with him the honour of the law failed, purity and Pharisaism died.[7]

Simeon, his son—slain at Jerusalem.[8]

Jochanan

---

[1] Jost, Judenthum, ii. 16, et seqq.

[2] Jost writes thus: "Wenn daher berichtet wird, dass das Synedrion nach verschiedenen Orten gewandert sei, so hat man nicht einen fortwährend gesetzgebenden Körper zu denken, der bloss dem Ort gewechselt habe, sondern einen nach Unterbrechungen wieder neu zusammen-getretenen." ii. 87.

[3] Lightfoot, Fall of Jerusalem, Section iv.

[4] On Joshua ben Perachiah—Jost, Israeliter, iii. p. 79, &c. On Simon ben Shetach, p. 89.

[5] Compare Jost, Geschichte, iii. 91, for the whole story, and the "Anhang" to the passage. It is worth observing that though Jost has complained that the printing in Lightfoot's works, especially of the Chaldaic, is very incorrect, yet he fully appreciates the profound erudition of our great Talmudist. "Der gelehrte Engländer in seine Sammlung die in Hinsicht der Gelehrsamkeit die Bewunderung der Nachwelt verdient." Anhang, iii. p. 167.

[6] The school of Hillel and the school of Shammai, established a permanent and distinctive influence over the Jewish mind. The great distinction was, that Hillel always adhered to the milder and more merciful, Schammai to the more strict and severe interpretation of the Law.

[7] Jost seems to give this saying as relating to the young Gamaliel of Jamnia.

On Jochanan ben Zacchai—Jost, Judenthum, ii. p. 16 et seqq.

[8] Rabban Simeon, the President of the Council, was caught in Jerusalem as in a trap, and lost his life. Lightfoot, Fall of Jerusalem, Section iii.

That this school of Gamaliel[f] had any legitimate title to the dignity of the Sanhedrin, may be reasonably doubted; but it seems clear, that the great school of Jamnia obtained considerable authority, and whether from the rank and character of its head, or from the assemblage of many of the members of the ancient Sanhedrin, who formed a sort of community in that place, it was looked up to with great respect and veneration by the Jews who remained in Palestine. The Romans would regard with contemptuous indifference the establishment of this kind of authority. Like Pilate, or Gallio in the Acts, they would leave to the conquered people to settle among themselves "*questions relating to their law.*" But these points were of vital interest to the Jew: they far surpassed in importance all sublunary considerations; on these depended the favour of their God, their only refuge in their degradation and misery; and with unexampled, though surely not reprehensible pertinacity, the more they were depressed, the more ardently they were attached to their own institutes. They were their only pride—their only treasure—their only patrimony, now that their Temple was in ashes, and their land had been confiscated. The enemy could not wrest them away; they were the continual remembrancers of the glories of the past, the only consolation and pledge of blessing for the future.[g]

Jochanan ben Zaccai.
Gamaliel of Jabneh, son of Simeon.
Simeon, son of Gamaliel, first Patriarch of Tiberias.
Judah, son of Simeon.
Gamaliel, son of Judah.

[f] Jost, true to his own system, makes Gamaliel the *founder* of a new Sanhedrin. To Gamaliel is attributed a table which showed the phases of the moon. p. 25, note.

[g] From the Capita Patrum in the Mischna, Part iv., may be seen the profound reverence, attachment, almost adoration of the Law. "He who learneth in the Law, in the name of the Law, he is worthy of many things, not only of many things, of the whole

It is indeed a strange transition in Jewish history from the wild contests of the fanatic Zealots, to the disputations of learned expounders of the Law—from the bloody tribunals of Simon Bar Gioras, John of Gischala, and Eleazar the Zealot, to the peaceful scholars at the feet of Gamaliel—from the din of arms, the confusion of besieged cities, the miseries of famine, massacre, and conflagration, to discussions about unclean meats, new moons, and the observance of the Sabbath.[h] But of all things it is most strange, that a people apparently occupied in these scholastic triflings, should, in sixty years, spring up again in a revolt scarcely less formidable to the ruling powers, or less calamitous to themselves, than the great Jewish war under Titus.

Gamaliel,[i] the last of the Gamaliels, the son of

---

world. . . . He loves God, he loves men; he makes God to rejoice, he makes men to rejoice. The Law clothes him with humility and fear. It makes him fit to become just, pious, upright, faithful. It removes him far off from sin, approaches him to innocence. Men derive from the Law all that is useful, counsel, wisdom, prudence, fortitude, as it is written, 'With me is counsel, with me is understanding and power;' and the Law gives to him the kingdom, and the dominion, and the searching out of judgement, and the secrets of the Law are revealed to him, and he is made as a perennial fountain, and as a river which waxes more and more strong. And he becomes modest and patient, and pardons him who affects him with ignominy. Such a man the Law magnifies, and sets him above all work." Mischna, iv. p. 48. This almost deification of the Law should be studied to understand St. Paul's argument when contrasting it with the Gospel.

[h] Lightfoot, Fall of Jerusalem, sect. iv. Compare Jost, Geschichte, iii. 283, and Judenthum, ii. 25 et seqq.

[i] It was a saying, it should seem, of this Gamaliel, son of Judah the Prince:—" He who multiplies flesh multiplies woes; he who multiplies riches multiplies cares; he who multiplies woes multiplies witches; he who multiplies women-servants multiplies wickedness; he who multiplies men-servants multiplies robbery; he who multiplies the land multiplies life; he who multiplies schools multiplies wisdom; he who multiplies counsel multiplies the Law; he who multiplies justice (or almsgiving) multiplies peace; he who gains to himself a good name gains himself; he who gains the Law gains eternal life." Mischna, Capita Patrum. iv. p. 416.

Judah, the president of the school in Jamnia, or, as the Jews assert, the Nasi of the Sanhedrin, was deeply learned, but proud and overbearing. He studiously depressed his rivals in learning, R. Eliezer, son of Hyrcan, and R. Joshua, son of Hananiah. It was a question, whether a first-born animal, wounded on the lip, was a lawful offering. Joshua decided in the affirmative. Gamaliel not merely annulled his sentence, but inflicted a humiliating penance on Joshua, making him stand up while himself was lecturing. A scholar asked Joshua, whether evening prayer was a duty or a free-will offering. Joshua decided for the latter. Another contradiction and another penance ensued, till at length the indignant scholars determined to throw off the yoke, and Gamaliel was formally deposed. Much difficulty arose about his successor. R. Joshua, his great rival, was passed by, and the choice lay between R. Akiba, a man whose fiery and impetuous character afterwards plunged himself and the nation in the darkest calamities, and R. Eliezer, a young man of noble family, said to be descended from Ezra. The choice fell on Eliezer. He hesitated to accept the dignified office. "Why?" he was asked. "Because I have not a grey beard;" and immediately his beard began to sprout, and grew, on the instant, to the most orthodox length and venerable whiteness.[k]   Other

---

[k] For Eliezer Akiba had the highest respect. R. Eliezer dying, at Cæsarea, desired to be buried at Lydda, whom R. Akiba bewailed as well with blood as with tears. "For when he met his hearse between Cæsarea and Lydda, he beat himself in that manner that blood flowed down upon the earth. Lamenting, thus he spake, 'O my father, my father! the chariot and horsemen of Israel! I have much money, but I want a moneyer to change it.'" The gloss is this, "I have very many questions, but now there is no man to whom I may propound them." Lightfoot, Chor. Cent. x. p. 38.

schools were gradually established. Eliezer, son of Hyrcan, taught in Lydda ; Joshua, son of Hananiah, in Pekun ; Akiba, in Baar-brak. Of all these Rabbins, or Masters of the Law, stories are told, sometimes puerile, sometimes full of good sense and profound moral wisdom, sometimes most absurdly extravagant; and characteristic incidents, which bear the stamp of truth, occur in the midst of the most monstrous legends.[1] But all these show the authority of Rabbinism —for so that system of teaching may be called—over the public mind ;—of Rabbinism, which, supplanting the original religion of the Jews, became, after the ruin of the Temple and the extinction of the public worship, a new bond of national union, the great distinctive feature in the character of modern Judaism. Indeed it is absolutely necessary, for the distinct comprehension of the later Jewish history, to enter into some farther consideration of the origin, growth, and nature of that singular spiritual supremacy assumed by the Rabbinical oligarchy, which, itself held together by a strong corporate spirit, by community of interest, by identity of principle, has contributed, more than any other external cause, to knit together in one body the widely dispersed members of the Jewish family, and to keep them the distinct and separate people which they appear in all ages of the world. It is clear that, after the return from the Babylonian Captivity, the Mosaic constitution

---

[1] Some of the Rabbins refused to eat flesh, or drink wine, after the destruction of the Temple. "Shall we eat meat when meat offerings are forbidden, or drink wine when wine offerings are no more made in the Temple?" "By that rule," answered the shrewd R. Joshua, "you must abstain from bread, for the shew-bread is no more set out —from fruits, for the first fruits are no longer offered—from water, for there is now no water by the altar. Go: exact no duties from the people which the many cannot discharge.' Jost, Geschichte; also Judenthum, ii. 72.

could be but partially re-established. The whole building was too much shattered and its fragments too
widely dispersed, to reunite in their ancient and regular
form. Palestine was a dependent province of the great
Persian empire; and neither the twelve confederate
republics of older times, nor the monarchies of the later
period, could be permitted to renew their existence.
But in no respect was the original Mosaic constitution
so soon or so entirely departed from, as in the distinctions and endowments of the great learned aristocracy,
the tribe of Levi; in no point was it more impossible to
reinstate the polity on its primitive model. To ascend
no higher, the tribe of Levi seem to have lost all their
possessions in the provinces of Israel on the separation
of the kingdoms. On the return from the Captivity,
the Levites are mentioned as distinct from the priests,
and are present, as it were, giving authority at the
public reading of the Law.[m] But they were by no
means numerous, perhaps scarcely more than sufficient
to furnish the different courses to minister in the
Temple. At all events they were no independent or
opulent tribe; their cities were gone; and though they
still retained the tithe, it was so far from supporting
them in great affluence, that when the higher class
encroached upon the rights of the lower order, the
latter were in danger of absolute starvation. In fact,
they were the officiating priesthood, and no more;
bound to be acquainted with the forms and usages of
the sacrificial ritual; but the instruction of the people,
and the interpretation of the Law, by no means fell
necessarily within their province. On the other hand,
the Jews who returned from the Captivity brought with

---

[m] Ezra and Nehemiah passim, especially Nehemiah, iv. v. vii.

them a reverential, or rather a passionate attachment
to the Mosaic Law. This it seems to have been the
prudent policy of their leaders, Ezra and Nehemiah, to
encourage by all possible means, as the great bond of
social union, and the unfailing principle of separation
from the rest of mankind.   The consecration of the
second Temple, and the re-establishment of the state,
was accompanied by the ready and solemn recognition
of the Law. By degrees attachment to the Law sank
deeper and deeper into the national character; it was
not merely at once their Bible and their Statute Book,
it entered into the most minute detail of common life.
But no written law can provide for all possible exi-
gencies; whether general and comprehensive, or minute
and multifarious, it equally requires the expositor to
adapt it to the immediate case which may occur, either
before the public tribunal, or that of the private conscience.   Hence the Law became a deep and intricate
study. Certain men rose to acknowledged eminence for
their ingenuity in explaining, their readiness in applying,
their facility in quoting, and their clearness in offering
solutions of the difficult passages of the written statutes.[a] Learning in the Law became the great distinction to which all alike paid reverential homage. Public
and private affairs depended on the sanction of this self-
formed spiritual aristocracy.   In an imperfect calendar
the accurate settling of the proper days for the different
fasts and festivals was of the first importance. It would
have been considered as inevitably tending to some
great national calamity, if it had been discovered that
the new moon, or any other moveable festival, above

---

[a] See at the end of Jost, Judenthum, i., the 613 Laws, 248 Commandments,
365 Prohibitions.

all if the Passover, had been celebrated on a miscalculated day. The national sacrifice, or that of the individual, might be vitiated by an inadvertent want of conformity to the strict letter of the ritual. Every duty of life, of social intercourse between man and man, to omit its weightier authority as the national code of criminal and civil jurisprudence, was regulated by an appeal to the Book of the Law. Even at every meal, the scrupulous conscience shuddered at the possibility, lest by some neglect, or misinterpretation of the statute, it might fall into serious offence. In every case the learned in the Law could alone decide to the satisfaction of the inquirer.

Moreover, by degrees, another worship, independent of the Temple, grew up—that of the Synagogue. The nation still met in the great Temple, for the purpose of national expiation or thanksgiving. The individual went there to make his legal offerings, or to utter his prayers in the more immediate presence of the God of Abraham. But besides this he had his synagogue— where, in a smaller community, he assembled, with a few of his neighbours, for Divine worship, for prayer, and for instruction in the Law. The latter more immediately, and gradually the former, fell entirely under the regulation of the learned interpreter of the Law, who, we may say, united the professions of the clergy and the law—the clergy, considered as public instructors; for the law-school and the synagogue were always closely connected, if they did not form parts of the same building.[o] Thus there arose in the state the curious phenomenon of a spiritual supremacy, distinct

---

[o] On the manner in which the Sanhedrins or Courts were ultimately connected with the Academies or Schools, compare Vitringa.

from the priesthood; for though many of these teachers were actually priests and Levites, they were not necessarily so—a supremacy which exercised the most unlimited dominion, not formally recognised by the constitution, but not the less real and substantial; for it was grounded in the general belief, ruled by the willing obedience of its subjects, and was rooted in the very minds and hearts of the people, till at length the maxim was openly promulgated, "the voice of the Rabbi, the voice of God." Thus, though the high priest was still the formal and acknowledged head of the state, the real influence passed away to these recognised interpreters of the Divine word.[p]

The circumstances of the Jewish history concurred in depressing the spiritual authority of the priesthood; and, as in such a community spiritual authority must have existed somewhere, its transfer to the Rabbins, though slow and imperceptible, was no less certain. During the reign of the Asmoneans the high priesthood became a mere appendage of the temporal sovereignty; but the Pharisaic, or learned party, were constantly struggling for superiority with the throne, which nominally united both the religious and worldly supremacy. Herod ruled as a military despot; but it was not the priesthood, the chief dignity of which he filled with his own dependants, but this body of men, learned in the law of the Fathers, which alone resisted the introduction of Grecian manners and customs, and kept alive the

---

[p] The learned treatise of Vitringa De Synagogâ Vetere not only gives his own views on all the questions relating to the growth and constitution of the Synagogue, but also those of most of the learned scholars before or during his time, especially Selden and Altingius. Vitringa is in agreement on the whole, though not throughout and in every particular, with Jost, Herzfeld, and the modern writers.

waning embers of Judaism. We have seen that, in the
zenith of his power, he dared not exact an oath of
allegiance, from his dread of a most influential class
zealously attached to the Law. The Sanhedrin was, in
general, the organ by which they acted, as the seats of
that half-senatorial, half-judicial body, were usually
filled by the most learned and influential of the Rabbins, or teachers. It is probable that general opinion
would point them out as the fittest persons to fill the
places of the twenty-three judges, appointed, according
to Josephus, in every considerable town. Still their
power was more deeply rooted than in the respect paid
to any court or office: it consisted rather in the education and daily instruction of the people, who looked up
to them with implicit confidence in their infallibility.[q]

The ideal Sopher or Scribe (the reader of the Gospel
knows these Scribes only on their darker side) may be
read in the Book of Ecclesiasticus. The great bulk
of the Jews were employed in commerce or in handi-
craft. They could not read, still less study the Law;
the Scribe was therefore absolutely necessary for the
instruction and edification of the people. " *The wisdom
of a learned man cometh by opportunity of leisure: and he
that hath little business shall become wise. The husband-*

---

[q] On the Sopherim, the Scribes, the
chief instructors of the people, during
the centuries which followed Ezra, till
their teaching assumed a definite form,
compare Jost, i. 93. Their power and
influence from the time of Ezra down-
wards were gradually developed. They
read, translated, and expounded the
Law in the Synagogues. "Natürlich
wurde nunmehr mancher stehende
Gebrauch durch die Schrift begründet
und wohl auch mancher verwerfliche
Gebrauch oder Begriff berichtigt.
Daraus entwickelte sich denn der spä-
terhin allgemein anerkannte Grund-
satz." *Die Aussprüche der Sopherim
seien wichtiger als die der Thora.*
Thus in almost all cases the interpretation overrode the written Law. All
these comments were afterwards (see
below) embodied in the Mischna.

man, the carpenter, the smith, the potter, all these trust to their hands, and every one is wise in his work. Without these cannot a city be inhabited. But they cannot sit in the council, nor on the judges' seat, they shall not be found where parables are spoken. . . . . . But he that giveth his mind to the Law of the Most High, and is occupied in the meditation thereof, will seek out the wisdom of the ancients, and be occupied in prophecies. He will keep the sayings of the renowned men: and where subtle parables are, he will be there also. . . . . He shall serve among great men, and appear before princes: he will travel through strange countries; for he hath tried the good and evil among men. . . . . When the great Lord will, he shall be filled with the spirit of understanding. . . . . He shall show forth that which he hath learned, and shall glory in the Law of the Covenant of the Lord. . . . . Many shall commend his understanding; and so long as the world endureth, it shall not be blotted out; his memorial shall not depart away, and his name shall live from generation to generation. Nations shall show forth his wisdom, and the congregation shall declare his praise. If he die, he shall leave a greater name than a thousand: and if he live, he shall increase it. Yet have I more to say, which I have thought upon; for I am filled as the moon at the full." [r]

But besides the interpretation of the written statutes, according to the rules of plain common sense or more subtle reason, the expounders of the Law assumed another ground of authority over the public mind, as the depositaries and conservators of the unwritten or traditionary law. This was not universally acknowledged

---

[r] This striking climax shows the estimate in which the *Learned* were held. Eccles. xxxviii. xxxix.

—and, from the earliest period, the great schism, in
Jewish opinion, was, on this important point, the authority of tradition. But the traditionists were far
superior in weight and numbers—and, by the mass of
the people, the Masora, or unwritten tradition, received, as the Rabbins asserted, by Moses on Mount
Sinai, and handed down, in regular and unbroken
descent, through all the great names of their early
history, the heads of the Sanhedrin its successive conservators, till it finally vested in themselves, was listened to with equal awe, and received with equal
veneration with the statutes inscribed by the hand of the
Almighty on the tables of stone. This was generally
called Masora, or *Tradition*, or Cabala [a]—the *received*
doctrine of the schools—thus uniting, as it were, the
sanctity of tradition in the Church of Rome, with the
validity of precedent in our law courts.

Hence the demolition of the Temple, the final cessation of the services, and the extinction of the priesthood,
who did not survive their occupation—events which, it
might have been expected, would have been fatal to the
national existence of the Jews as destroying the great
bond of union, produced scarcely any remarkable effect.
The Levitical class had already been superseded as the

---

[a] The term Cabala is usually applied to that wild system of Oriental
philosophy which was introduced, it is
uncertain at what period, into the
Jewish schools; in a wider sense, it
comprehended all the decisions of the
Rabbinical courts or schools, whether on
religious or civil points—whatever, in
short, was considered to have been ruled
by competent judges; but in its more
exclusive sense it meant that knowledge which was traditionally derived
from the hidden mysteries contained in
the letters of the Law, in the number
of times they occurred, and in their relative position. Even Maimonides uses
Kabala as synonymous with oral tradition. The figurative meaning of all
the anthropomorphic expressions for
God may be taught to the simplest.
"Easque per Kabbalam et oralem tra-
ditionem tradere parvulis et mulieribus,
indoctis et imperitis, est necessarium."
More Nevochim, i. c. xxxv.

judges and teachers of the people, the Synagogue, with
its law school, and its grave and learned Rabbi, had
already begun to usurp the authority, and was prepared
to supply the place of the Temple with its solemn rites,
regular sacrifices, and hereditary priesthood.   Hence
the remnant of the people, amid the general wreck of
their institutions, the extinction of the race, at least the
abrogation of the office of High-priest, and even the
defection of the representative of their late sovereign
Agrippa, naturally looked round with eagerness to see
if any of their learned Rabbins had escaped the ruin;
and directly they found them established in comparative
security, willingly laid whatever sovereignty they could
dare to offer at their feet.   Their Roman masters had
no tribunal which they could approach; the administration of their own law was indispensable; hence,
whether it assumed the form of an oligarchy, or a
monarchy, they submitted themselves with the most
implicit confidence, and in the most undoubting spirit,
to the Rabbinical dominion.

The Jews, though looked upon with contempt as well
as detestation, were yet regarded, during the reign of
Vespasian and his immediate successors, with jealous
watchfulness. A garrison of 800 men occupied the ruins
of Jerusalem, to prevent the reconstruction of the city
by the fond and religious zeal of its former inhabitants.
The Christian Hegesippus relates that Vespasian commanded strict search to be made for all who claimed
descent from the house of David—in order to cut off, if
possible, all hopes of the restoration of the royal house,
or of the Messiah, the confidence in whose speedy coming
still burned with feverish excitement in the hearts of all
faithful Israelites.   This barbarous inquisition was continued in the reign of Domitian ; nor did the rest of the

nation escape the cruelties which desolated the empire under the government of that sanguinary tyrant. The tax of two drachms, levied according to the rescript of Vespasian, for the rebuilding the temple of Jupiter Capitolinus, was exacted with unrelenting rigour; [t] and, if any denied their Judaism, the most indecent means were employed against persons of age and character, to ascertain the fact. Suetonius, the historian, had seen a public examination of this nature before the tribunal of the procurator. [u] Still it may be doubted whether these persecutions, which, perhaps, were chiefly directed at the Judaizing Christians, oppressed the Jewish people very heavily in their native land. It is impossible, unless communities were suffered to be formed, and the whole race enjoyed comparative security, that the nation could have appeared in the formidable attitude of resistance which it assumed in the time of Hadrian.

The reign of Nerva gave a brief interval of peace to the Jews with the rest of the world. The Jews, if not released from the payment to the Capitoline Temple, were not so ignominiously treated as in the reign of Domitian. No man who did not openly acknowledge himself to be a Jew was subject to the fiscal regulation. [x] In the reign of Trajan either the oppressions of their

---

[t] Καὶ ἀπ' ἐκείνου δίδραχμον ἐτάχθη, τοὺς τὰ πάτρια ἔθη περιστέλλοντας, τῷ Καπιτωλίῳ Διὶ κατ' ἔτος ἀποφέρειν. Dion Cassius, lxvi. 7. Φόρον δὲ τοῖς ὅπου δήποτ' οὖσιν 'Ιουδαίοις ἐπέβαλε, δύο δραχμὰς ἕκαστον κέλευσας ἀνὰ πᾶν ἔτος εἰς τὸ Καπιτώλιον φέρειν, ὥσπερ πρότερον εἰς τὸν ἐν 'Ιεροσολύμοις νεὼν συνετέλουν. Joseph. B. J., vii. 6. 6. Though the mode of levying the tax was mitigated

by Nerva, it continued to later times. Καὶ νῦν 'Ιουδαίων τὸ δίδραχμον αὐτοῖς ('Ρωμαίοις) τελούντων. Origen. ad. Afric.

[u] In Domitian. c. xii.

[x] Eckhel agrees with Spanheim that the famous coin of Nerva, with the epigraph

"Fisci Judaici calumnia sublata,"

does not mean the abolition of the tax, but the prohibition of the delations

enemies, or their own mutinous and fanatic disposition, drove them into revolt, as frantic and disastrous as that which had laid their city and Temple in ashes. In every quarter of the world, in each of their great settlements, in Babylonia, Egypt and Cyrene, and in Judæa, during the sovereignty of Trajan and his successor, the Jews broke out into bold and open rebellion—not without considerable successes—and were finally subdued, only after an obstinate struggle and enormous loss of life.[y]

The wise and upright Trajan was not superior to the intolerant religious policy of his predecessors. From the memorable letter of Pliny, it is manifest that the existing laws, though not clearly defined, were rigid against all who practised foreign superstitions. It is by no means improbable that its descent from Judaism, of which Christianity was long considered a modification, tended to increase the hostility against the unoffending Christians, which their rapid progress had excited.[z] If, even under a man of the temper and moderation of

and insulting usage of ascertaining the liability to it. "Non ipsam fiscam Judaicam, quod censuere varii, a Nerva abolitam dici, sed tantum ejus *calumniam* sublatam esse, hoc est ab eodem fiscali debito solvendo immunes in postremum mansisse, quicunque se haud erant Judæos professi, nec inde pro Judæis in fiscales tabulas relati." Eckhel, iv. p. 148.

The whole question of Jewish taxation is worked out with great labour and general accuracy, in the article Juden Geschichte, in Ersch and Gruber, Encyclopædia, l. xxvii.

[y] Gibbon attributes all these insurrections to the unprovoked turbulence and fanaticism of the Jews. But his mind, notwithstanding its boasted liberality, was by no means exempt from the old vulgar prejudices against the Jews; heightened, perhaps, by his unfriendly feeling, not more philosophical, to the religion from which Christianity took its rise.

[z] Salvador, though of course as a Jew from an opposite point of view, concurs with me in connecting, as I have done in other works, the hostility of the Roman Government towards the Christians, shown in the persecutions during the reign of Trajan, with the commotions of the Jews in the East. "Jews and Christians were still, to a certain extent, confounded in the popular mind; and fear, political jealousy, and hatred do not sharpen the powers of just discrimination." Salvador, ii. 514.

Pliny, and by the express rescript of the Emperor, all the Christians obtained, was not to be "hunted out with the implacable zeal of an inquisitor;" if scenes like those, so strikingly described in the acts of the martyrdom of Ignatius, were by no means unfrequent: we may fairly conclude that the odious Jews, under worse governors, or where the popular feeling was not repressed by the strong hand of authority, would be liable to perpetual insult, oppression, and persecution. The Rabbinical traditions [a] are full of the sufferings of the people during this melancholy period, but they are so moulded up with fable,[b] that it is difficult to decide whether they rest on any groundwork of truth. This, however, is certain, that during the war of Trajan with Parthia, when the Roman legions were probably with-

---

[a] Many of these traditions may be read in Eisenmenger, Das Entdecktes Judenthum. This curious book was written in avowed and bitter hostility to the Jews, but the quotations are copious and full, and there is no reason to suspect their accuracy. See below.

[b] It is related that, unfortunately, the birthday of a prince fell on the anniversary of the fatal 9th of August; and while the whole Roman empire was rejoicing, the Jews alone were bewailing, in ill-timed lamentations, the fate of their Temple. Again, while the imperial family were in the deepest mourning for the loss of a daughter, the unlucky Jews were celebrating with noisy mirth their Feast of Lamps. The indignant Empress exclaimed, "Before you march against the barbarians, sweep this insolent people from the face of the earth." Trajan, in Syria, surrounded a vast number of Jews with his legions, and ordered

them to be hewn down. He afterwards offered to their wives, either to share the fate of their husbands, or to submit to the embraces of his soldiery. "What thou hast done to those beneath the earth, do to those who are upon it:" such was the answer of the women. Their blood was mingled with that of their husbands; and the sea that broke upon the shores of Cyprus was tinged with the red hue of carnage. If there be any truth in this legend, that sea recoiled before long from those shores in a tide, which showed still more visible signs of unrelenting vengeance. But, independent of the improbability of the whole story, and its inconsistency with the character of the Emperor, the family of Trajan make a great figure in this, as in other Jewish legends; yet it is almost certain that he had no children.—Hierosolym. Talmud. Socra, quoted by Jost, Geschichte der Israeliten, iii. p. 218.

drawn from the African provinces, and a few feeble
garrisons alone remained to maintain the peace, intelligence was received that the Jews of Egypt and Cyrene
had taken up arms, and were perpetrating the most
dreadful atrocities against the Greek inhabitants of those
districts. The cause of this insurrection is unknown;
but when we remember the implacable animosities of
the two races, which had been handed down as an inheritance for centuries, it is by no means surprising,
that, directly the coercive authority of the Roman troops
was withdrawn, a violent collision should take place.[c]
Nor is it improbable that the Greeks, who had been
suffering grievous exactions from a rapacious Roman
governor, might take up their old quarrel, and, in the
absence of the Romans, endeavour to indemnify themselves by the plunder of their more industrious, perhaps
more wealthy, neighbours. On which side hostilities
began, we know not; but the Jews, even if they only
apprehended an attack, had horrible reminiscences of
recent disasters, or traditions, not very remote, of the
days of Caligula; and might, not unnaturally, think
that there was wisdom in endeavouring to be the first in
the field; that it was better to perish with arms in
their hands, than stand still, as in former times, to be
tamely pillaged and butchered. All Egypt, both
Alexandria and the Thebais, with Cyrene, arose at
once.[d] In Egypt the Jews had at first some success;
but the Greeks fell back on Alexandria, mastered the
Jews within the city, and murdered the whole race.

---

[c] Compare Der Judische Krieg unter
den Kaisern Trajan und Hadrian, von
D. Friedrich Munter, Altona, 1821. This
valuable tract has been translated in
an American journal, under the direction of Dr. Robinson, the traveller.

[d] Look back to the outbreak in the
Cyrenaica under Jonathan, at the
close of the war under Vespasian.—
Euseb. H. E., iv. 3.

Maddened by this intelligence, as well as by the memory
of former cruelties, the Jews of Cyrene, headed by
Lucuas and Andrew, by some supposed, though improbably, two names of the same man, swept all over
Lower Egypt, where they were joined by a host of their
countrymen, and penetrated into the Thebais, or even
farther, and exacted the most dreadful retribution for
the present and the past. Horrid tales were told of the
atrocities they committed. Some of their rulers they
sawed asunder from head to foot; they flayed their
bodies, and clothed themselves with the skins, twisted
the entrails and wore them as girdles, and anointed
themselves with blood.* We are even told that this
people, so scrupulous in the refusal of all unclean food,
nevertheless feasted on the bodies of their enemies.
With barbarity for which they could quote better precedent, they are said to have thrown their enemies to
wild beasts, and forced them to fight on the theatres as
gladiators: 220,000 fell before their remorseless vengeance.[f] Whether these cannibal atrocities were true
or not, that they should be propagated and credited,
shows the detestation in which the race was held.
Lupus, the Roman governor, meanwhile, without troops,
sat an inactive spectator of this devastation; while

---

* In the Book Zemach David, quoted
by Eisenmenger, Das Entdecktes Judenthum, i. 654-5, it is written that
at this time they killed a multitude of
people countless as the sands of the
sea. In the Book Meor Enaim, on the
authority of Rabbi Asariah, they killed
above 200,000 in Egypt; in Cyprus
they did not leave one of the Gentiles
(Gojim) alive. It adds that the Emperor Trajan sent his general, Hadrian,
against them, who destroyed them, so
many as were never heard of or seen
in the days of Nebuzaradan or of
Titus.

[f] Munter supposes that they may
have turned the usual atrocities of the
Romans against themselves, have seized
the amphitheatres, and forced their
prisoners to fight with wild beasts or
gladiators (p. 15). This is hardly
possible.

Lucuas, the Jewish leader, is reported to have assumed the style and title of king.

The flame spread to Cyprus, where the Jews were numerous and wealthy.[s]   One Artemio placed himself at their head; they rose and massacred 240,000 of their fellow-citizens; the whole populous city of Salamis became a desert.   The revolt in Cyprus was first suppressed; Hadrian, afterwards emperor, landed on the island, and marched to the assistance of the few inhabitants who had been able to act on the defensive. He defeated the Jews, expelled them from the island, to whose beautiful coasts no Jew was ever after permitted to approach.   If one were accidentally wrecked on the inhospitable shore, he was instantly put to death.[h] Martius Turbo was sent by sea for the purpose of expedition, with a considerable force of horse and foot to the coast of Cyrene.   As far as the campaign can be traced, it seems that he marched against Andrew, and, after much hard fighting, suppressed the insurrection in that province, and then turned upon Egypt, where Lucuas still made head.   Lucuas, according to a tradition preserved by Abulfharagi, attempted to force his way by the Isthmus of Suez; and some, at least, of his followers found their way to Palestine.[i]   The loss of the Jews, as might be expected, was immense; their own traditions report, that as many fell in this disastrous war, as ori-

---

[s] Herod the First farmed the copper-mines in Cyprus. Joseph. Ant. xvi. 2.

[h] Euseb. H. E. iv. 6. Dion Cassius, loc. cit.

[i] This seems confirmed by a passage in Appian, B. C. ii. 90, who incidentally mentions the destruction of a Heathen temple near Mount Casius during the exterminatory war (ἐξολλύντα τὸ ἐν Αἰγύπτῳ 'Ιουδαίων γένος) waged by Trajan *at this time* against the Jews.

Orosius describes the Jewish insurrection in his vague way. They had so utterly desolated Libya, that the Emperor Hadrian was obliged to send colonists to people the desert which they had left. lib. vii.

ginally escaped from Egypt under Moses—600,000
men.[k]

Cyprus was scarcely subdued, and the war was still
raging in Egypt, when tidings arrived that the Jews of
Mesopotamia were in arms.[1] Probably the Eastern Jews
had found that, by the conquests of Trajan, they had
changed masters for the worse. Under the Parthian
kings they had lived in peace, unmolested in their religion, sometimes making proselytes of the highest rank
—in the case of Izates, even of kings; and they were
oppressed by no exclusive taxation. The Jews of Africa
and Syria might have looked with repining envy on
their more prosperous brethren in Babylonia. The
scene of the great Captivity was now become the only
dwelling of Jewish peace and Jewish independence;
while the land of milk and honey flowed with the bitter
streams of servitude and persecution. Even if the
Babylonian Jews did not, as gratitude and policy would
equally have urged, during the war between Rome and
her Eastern rival, manfully take arms in favour of their
protectors against the enemies and oppressors of their
race—if they left the armies of Parthia to fight their
own battles, and quietly waited to be transferred to the
conqueror; yet, when they were included, by the victories of Trajan, within the pale of Roman oppression—
visited in their turn by that fierce soldiery which had
trampled on the ruins of Jerusalem—made liable, perhaps, to a capitation tax for the maintenance of a
heathen temple,—it was by no means surprising if they
endeavoured to shake off the galling and unwonted

---

[k] So much destruction was caused
by this war in Alexandria, that in the
Chronicon Eusebianum (Mediol. 1818)
it is said, "Hadrianus Alexandriam a

Judæis labefactatam reparavit." See
on the Coins Munter, p. 21.
[1] Euseb. H. E. loc. cit.

yoke. Their insurrection was soon suppressed by the vigour of Lusius Quietus, a man of Moorish race, and considered the ablest soldier in the Roman army. The commission of Quietus was not only to subdue, but to expel the Jews from the whole district. The Jews defended themselves with obstinate courage, and, though overpowered, still remained in Mesopotamia.[m] The immediate appointment of L. Quietus to the government of Judæa, seems to intimate some apprehension of commotions in that province, which might be kept down by the terrors of his name.

In the next year (A.C. 117) Trajan died, and Hadrian ascended the throne. For the Mesopotamian Jews alone this was a fortunate occurrence; for as the prudent Hadrian abandoned all the conquests of his predecessor in the East, and re-established the Euphrates as the boundary of the Roman empire, they fell again under the milder dominion of their Parthian sovereigns. The new emperor was not likely to entertain very favourable sentiments towards his Jewish subjects. He had been an eye-witness of the horrible scenes which had desolated the lovely island of Cyprus; he had seen the voluptuous Idalian groves reeking with blood, or unwholesome with the recent carnage of their inhabitants; the gay and splendid cities reduced to the silence of desolation. It is not improbable that the same mischiefs might seem to be brooding in Palestine. Hadrian himself visited Judæa and Egypt. Extant coins establish this fact. The famous letter to Servianus, in which he casts his mockery impartially on Jews, Samaritans, and

---

[m] Euseb. H. E. iv. 2 : ὃς καὶ παρα-
ταξάμενος, πάμπολυ πλῆθος τῶν
αὐτόθι φονεύει. Eusebius quotes as
his authority the great writers of the
time.

Christians, was written in Alexandria;[n] but sterner measures followed, how far from suspicions, not without ground, of meditated revolt and insurrection, does not appear. An edict was issued tantamount to the total suppression of Judaism: it interdicted circumcision,[o] the reading of the Law, and the observance of the Sabbath. It was followed by a blow, if possible, more fatal: the intention of the Emperor was announced to annihilate at once all hopes of the restoration of the Holy City by the establishment of a Roman colony in Jerusalem, and the foundation of a fane, dedicated to Jupiter, on the site of their fallen Temple. A town had probably risen by degrees out of the ruins of Jerusalem, where the three great towers and a part of the western wall had been left as a protection to the Roman garrison:[p] but the formal establishment of a colony implied the perpetual alienation of the soil, and its legal appropriation to the *stranger*.[q] The Jews looked on with dismay, with

---

[n] " Nemo illic archesynagogus Judæorum, nemo Samarites, nemo Christianorum presbyter non mathematicus, non aruspex, non aliptes." I understand Hadrian's implied meaning to be, that they were alike what we call quacks and charlatans. Vopisci Saturninus, H. A. S., p. 966. Compare Juvenal, vi. 543.

[o] Spartian speaks of this with true Roman contemptuousness: "Moverunt eâ tempestate et Judæi bellum, quod vetabantur mutilare genitalia." Hadr. c. 14.

[p] The devotion of a city to perpetual desolation, so as never to be again inhabited by man, was marked by a peculiar ceremony in the Roman religion, the drawing a ploughshare over its whole site: " Nam ideo ad diruendas vel exaugurandas urbes aratrum adhi-

bitum, ut eodem ritu, quo conditæ, subvertantur." Serv. ad Æneid. iv. p. 527. " Cur perirent funditus, imprimeretque muris hostile aratrum." Hor. Od. 1, 16. That it was also an Eastern custom, compare Jer. xxvi. 8. It was probably by application of this prophecy that some of the Jews asserted this to have been done by Titus. But the sentence of Josephus seems conclusive against this as an historical fact; and this devotion of the site of the city to perpetual desolation does not seem to have been consummated as to Jerusalem after the capture by Titus.

[q] ἐς δὲ τὰ Ἱεροσόλυμα πόλιν αὐτοῖ ἀντὶ τῆς κατασκαφείσης οἰκισάντος, ἣν καὶ Αἰλίαν Καπιτολίναν ὠνόμασε, καὶ ἐς τὸν τοῦ ναοῦ τοῦ Θεοῦ τόπον, ναὸν τῷ Διὶ ἕτερον ἀντεγείραντος,

anguish, with secret thoughts of revenge, at length with hopes of immediate and splendid deliverance. It was an opinion deeply rooted in the hearts of all faithful Israelites, that in the darkest hour of the race of Abraham, when his children were at the extreme point of degradation and wretchedness, even then the arm of the Lord would be revealed, and the expected Messiah would make his sudden and glorious appearance. They were now sounding the lowest depths of misery. They were forbidden, under penalties sternly enacted and rigidly enforced, to initiate their children into the chosen family of God. Their race was in danger of becoming extinct; for even the blood of Abraham would little avail the uncircumcised. Their city was not merely a mass of ruins, inhabited by the stranger, but the Pagans were about to make their permanent residence upon the site of Sion, and a temple to a Gentile idol was to usurp the place of the Holy of Holies.

At this momentous period it was announced that the Messiah had appeared. He had come in power and in glory: his name fulfilled the great prophecy of Balaam. Bar-cochab, the Son of the Star, was that star which was to "arise out of Jacob." Wonders attended upon his person: he breathed flames from his mouth, which, no doubt, would burn up the strength of the proud oppressor, and wither the armies of the tyrannical Hadrian.

πόλεμος οὔτε μικρὸς οὔτ' ὀλιγοχρόνιος ἐκινήθη, lxix. 12. I follow Dion's distinct statement, in preference to the loose one of Eusebius, that Ælia was founded *after* the siege. Nothing could be more according to the policy of Rome than to fix a colony, as a garrison, in a place of such importance as Jerusalem, the strength of which had so severely tried the Roman arms, especially after the rebellions in the time of Trajan. The designed Temple to Jupiter is in character with, and perhaps a first beginning of, that system, so widely carried out by the Antonines, of rebuilding and *Romanising* the vast ancient temples in the East, as at Baalbec, Petra, and in Egypt.

Above all, the greatest of the Rabbins, the living oracle
of divine truth, whose profound learning was looked up
to by the whole race of Israel, acknowledged the claims
of the new Messiah, and openly attached himself to his
fortunes; he was called the standard-bearer of the Son
of the Star. Rabbi Akiba was said not to be of the
pure blood of Israel, but descended (such is the Rabbinical genealogy) from Sisera, the general of Jabin, king
of Tyre, by a Jewish mother. For forty years he had
lived a simple shepherd, tending the flocks of a rich
citizen of Jerusalem, named Calba Sheva. Love made
him the wisest of his age. He became enamoured of
his master's daughter: the wealthy Jew rejected the
indigent shepherd, who was an alien from the race of
Israel. But the lovers were secretly married, and
Akiba left his bride immediately, and spent twelve years
in study, under the tuition of R. Eliezer and R. Joshua.
He returned, it is said, with 12,000 disciples. But the
unrelenting father had disinherited his daughter. They
lived in the greatest penury; and she bore her first
child on a bed of straw. Akiba went back for twelve
years more to the seat of learning. He returned again,
followed by 24,000 disciples; and the father, at length
appeased or overawed by the fame of his son-in-law,
broke his vow of implacable resentment, and bestowed
on Akiba and his wife sufficient property to enable them
to live in splendour. A thousand volumes would not
contain the wonderful things which Akiba did and
said.[r] He could give a reason for the use of the most

---

[r] Pirke Aboth, quoted by Jost (Geschichte, p. 206). See in the same book
the further account of Akiba's life,
with the Talmudic authorities. Jost,
in his later work (Judenthum, ii. c. vi.
p. 59), is much more copious: "The
characteristics of Akiba were, matchless
acuteness in penetrating the obscure
passages of the traditions; he was
rigorous on all actors of injury, severe

insignificant letter of the Law; and it is boldly averred, that God revealed more to him than he did to Moses. He first committed the traditions to writing, and thus laid the groundwork for the celebrated Mischna, or Comment on the Law. A striking story is told of Akiba. His great maxim was "that every thing is ordained of heaven for the best." With this axiom on his lips, he was riding with some of his followers near the ruins of Jerusalem. They burst into tears at the melancholy sight; for, to heighten their grief, they beheld a jackal prowling upon the Hill of the Temple. Akiba only observed, that the very successes of the idolatrous Romans, as they fulfilled the words of the prophets, were grounds of loftier hopes for the people of God.[s] The end of these lofty hopes must have severely

---

on moral questions; his learning was a 'well-ordered treasury.'"

Geiger quotes the following :—"If Shaphan had not arisen at his time (that of Hezekiah), if Ezra had not arisen at his time, and Akiba at his, the Law of Israel had been forgotten; the Word, which was spoken at the right time, outweighs all words." p. 156.

A saying of Akiba would show that he was superior to some of the prejudices of his race: "R. Akiba dicebat, Quicunque sepelitur in reliquis terris perinde est ac si sepeliretur in Babyloniâ. Quicunque sepelitur in Babyloniâ perinde est ac si sepeliretur in terrâ Israel. Quicunque sepelitur in terrâ Israel perinde est ac si sepeliretur sub altari, quia tota terra Israel conveniret ut esset locus altaris. Quicunque autem sepelitur sub altari perinde est ac si sepeliretur sub

throno gloriæ, quia dicitur, Jer. xvii. 2, 'Thronus gloriæ altitudo a primo, locus sanctuarii nostri.'" Quoted in Menschen Talmudien, p. 226.

Other sayings of Akiba, in Eisenmenger, i. 10, and 25.

[s] Jost (Judenthum, p. 66) has another striking story. "Akiba had a firm conviction that Jerusalem and the Temple would be speedily restored. He visited Rome with three of his disciples. These were so overpowered by the splendour and strength of the Capitol, that they burst into tears. To their astonishment, Akiba smiled. He asked, 'Why do ye weep?' 'Ought we not to be in pain when we behold the Idolaters living in magnificence and peace, while the footstool of our God is a prey to the flames, and a haunt of wild beasts?' 'Good,' Akiba replied, 'and therefore did I smile. If it fares so well with God's enemies, must

tried the resignation of Akiba. He was yet in the zenith of his fame, though now nearly 120 years old, the period of life to which his great prototype, Moses, attained (his biographers have no doubt conformed his life to that model); he is said, also, by some, to have been the head of the Sanhedrin, when Barcochab, or Coziba, announced his pretensions as the Messiah. Akiba had but newly returned from a visit, or from a flight, to his Mesopotamian brethren, and whether the state of affairs at Nahardea and Nisibis had awakened his hopes and inflamed a noble jealousy, which induced him to risk any hazard to obtain equal independence for his brethren in Judæa; or whether there was any general and connected plan for the reassertion of Jewish liberty, he threw himself at once into the party of the heaven-inspired insurgent. "Behold," said the hoary enthusiast, in an assembly of the listening people, " the Star that is come out of Jacob; the days of the redemption are at hand." "Akiba," said the more cautious R. Jochanan, "the grass will spring from thy jawbone, and yet the Son of David will not have come." The period of the first appearance of the pretended Messiah is by no means certain, even his real name is unknown;[t] he is designated only by his title, Bar-cochab, the Son of a Star, which his disappointed countrymen, afterwards, in their bitterness, changed to Bar-cosba, the Son of a Lie. He is said to

---

not his obedient children expect a far better doom?' "

[t] Jost is inclined to connect the travels of Akiba with the general insurrection: "Und in verschiedenen Zeiten der Bewegung, welche eine Reihe von Jahren dauerte, und trotz grosser Niederlagen der Anführer sich wiederholte, bis Bethar gänzlich zerstört wurde, finden wir ihn in den Gegenden, wo der Aufstand zunächst ausbrach." p. 67. He was in Cilicia, Cappadocia, perhaps Galatia, in Arabia and Africa. See also p. 76.

have been a robber; [u] he had learned a trick of keeping
lighted tow, or straw, in his mouth, which was the
secret of his breathing flames, to the terror of his
enemies, and the unbounded confidence of his partisans.[x]
He seems to have been a man of no common vigour and
ability; but, unhappily, this second Jewish war had no
Josephus, and the whole history of the campaigns,
where the Jews manifestly gained great advantages, and
in which the most able general of Rome, Severus, found
it expedient to act on the defensive, and reduce the
province rather by blockade and famine than by open
war, can only be made out from three short chapters of
Dion Cassius,[y] occasional brief notices in other authors,
and the Legends of the Talmud. Lusius Quietus, the
able conqueror of Mesopotamia, suspected of ambitious
designs on the empire, had been deprived, first of his
kindred Moorish troops, then of his province, and finally
of his life. By a curious coincidence, the Roman commander, to whom the final demolition of Jerusalem had
been committed by Titus, bore the name of Terentius
Rufus; the prefect in Palestine, at the commencement
of the revolt under Bar-cochab was T. Annius, or Tyn-
nius, called, by the Rabbins, Tyrannus, or Turnus
Rufus, the Wicked.[z] Thus, the two men who were the

---

[u] Basnage, p. 342; but he cites no
authority. Jost asserts that his early
life was quite unknown. p. 244.

[x] So the slave Eunus, in the servile
war in Sicily:—"Idque ut divinitus
fieri probaret in ore abdita nuce, quam
sulphure et igne stipaverat, leniter
inspirans, flammam inter verba fun-
uebat." Florus, iii. 19. "Atque ut
ille Barchochebas auctor seditionis Ju-
daicæ stipulam in ore suo accensam
anhelitu ventilabat ut flammas evo-

mere videretur." We can hardly understand how such things could be thought
miraculous. Heronym. Apol. ii. ad Ru-
finum. Maimonides, on the other hand,
asserts (Münter, note p. 48) "Sapientes
nullum ab eo signum vel miraculum
petierunt." See the traditions about
Bar-cochab, Eisenmenger, ii. 654.

[y] Or rather Xiphilin. There is a
passage about the war in Moses of
Chorene, the Armenian historian, c. 57.

[z] Jost, Anhang, p. 180.

objects of the deepest detestation to the Jews, are perpetually confounded. Rufus is said, by the command
of Hadrian, to have driven the plough over the ruins of
Jerusalem.[a] At the first threatening of the revolt, probably after the visit of Hadrian to the East, in the year
130 (A. C.), Rufus poured all the troops at his command
into Judæa; he seized and imprisoned Akiba: but
either his forces or his abilities were unequal to the
crisis. The Romans could not believe that, with the
memory of the former war still on the lips of the fathers
of the present generation, the Jews would provoke the
danger of a second exterminating conflict. But for
some time the insurgents had been busily employed in
laying up stores of arms. By degrees, they got possession of all the strong heights, raised walls and fortifications, dug or enlarged subterranean passages and caverns
both for retreat and communication, and contrived, by
holes from above, to let light and air into those secret
citadels, where they deposited their arms, held their
councils, and concealed themselves from the vigilance
of the enemy. Multitudes crowded openly, or stole in
secret, to range themselves under the banner of the
Messiah. Native Jews and strangers swelled his ranks.
It is probable that many of the fugitives from the insurgents in Egypt and Cyrene had found their way to
Palestine, and lay hid in caves and fastnesses. Even
many who were not Jews, for the sake of plunder and
the licence of war, united themselves with the rebels.
No doubt, some from the Mesopotamian provinces came
to the aid of their brethren. The whole Jewish race
throughout the world was in commotion; those who
dared not betray their interest in the common cause

---

[a] See note ante, p. 424.

openly, did so in secret, and perhaps some of the wealthy Jews in the remote provinces privately contributed from their treasures. Bar-cochab, if we may believe the Rabbins, found himself at the head of 200,000 men, a statement somewhat invalidated by the addition, that there was not a soldier who could not, putting his horse at full speed, tear up a cedar of Lebanon by the roots. Those who had denied or disguised their circumcision, hastened to renew that distinguishing mark of their Israelitish descent, and to entitle themselves to a share in the great redemption. The Christians, alone, stood aloof, and would lend no ear, nor pay respect to the claims of another Messiah, a man of robbery and bloodshed, of earthly pretensions, and the aspirant founder of a temporal kingdom. Bar-cochab is reported to have revenged himself by the most cruel persecutions on those most dangerous opponents to his claim as the Messiah.[b]

The first expedition of Bar-cochab was to make himself master of the ruins of Jerusalem. As we have before observed, probably some sort of rude town had grown up amid the wreck of the city, even if no preparations had been made for the foundation of Ælia. Pious pilgrims, no doubt, stole in secret to pay their adorations on the sacred hill; and some would think it worth while to venture all hazards, if their last remains might repose within the circuit of the Holy City. With what triumph must they have crowded to the same spot, when the conquering banner of the Messiah was unfolded, for

---

Eusebius, quoting Justin Martyr: καὶ γὰρ ἐν τῷ νῦν γενομένῳ Ἰουδαϊκῷ πολέμῳ, Βαρχωχέβας ὁ τῆς Ἰουδαίων ἀποστασέως ἀρχηγέτης, Χριστιανοὺς μόνους εἰς τιμωρίας δεινάς, εἰ μὴ ἀρνοῖντο Ἰησοῦν τὸν Χριστόν, καὶ βλασφημοῖεν, ἐκέλευεν ἄγεσθαι. H. E. iv. 8. Justin Martyr was nearly contemporary with these events, and, as born in Palestine, of good authority. Compare his Apolog., c. 31.

here Bar-cochab openly assumed the name of king, and
is said to have issued coins with his superscription, and
with the year of the freedom of Jerusalem as the date.[c]
Still the Jews avoided a battle in the open field. Turnus
Rufus revenged himself with the most unrelenting
cruelties on the defenceless. According to Eusebius,
he put to death thousands of men, women, and children.
But the obstinate courage and activity of the Jews were
unbroken ; they pursued their deliberate system of
defence, so that, on the arrival of the famous Julius
Severus to take the command, they were in possession
of fifty of the strongest castles, and 985 villages. But
Severus had learned the art of war against desperate
savages in Britain. He turned their own policy against
the insurgents. He ventured on no general battle
with an enemy now perhaps grown to an overwhelming
force ; [d] but he attacked their strongholds in detail, cut
off their supplies, and reduced them to the greatest
distress by famine. Yet the Romans experienced, on
their side, considerable losses, for Hadrian, whether
with the army or in the neighbourhood, did not adopt
the customary form in his despatches to the senate, " I

---

[c] There is no historical account of
this event, though there seems little
doubt of the fact. It is, however, denied, I know not on what grounds, by
some modern Jewish writers. Jost,
Judenthum, ii. 79, note. Tychsen and
others have concluded, from extant
coins, that he was in possession of Jerusalem for three years ; if so, it was from
132 to 135. The coins, however, are
of very doubtful date and authority.

There is a long note of Heinichen,
on Eusebius, H. E. iv. p. 300, on the
whole subject of the war. Heinichen

is of the same opinion with me, that
the foundation of a new city by Hadrian
on the site of Jerusalem was the cause
of the war. " Quod vero ad conditum
Æliæ spectat, tantum abest ut condita
fuerit ab Hadriano post partam de
Judæis victoriam. Immo bellum Judaicum ex Æliæ conditu originem
cepit."

[d] ὃς ἄντικρος μὲν οὐδαμόθει
ἐτόλμησε τοῖς ἐναντίοις συμβαλεῖν,
τό τε πλῆθος καὶ τὴν ἀπογνώσιν
αὐτῶν ὁρῶν. Dion Cassius.

rejoice if all is well with you and your children; with myself and the army all is well."[e] In Jerusalem the insurgents were disheartened and confounded by the sudden falling in of some vast subterranean vaults, where, according to tradition, the remains of Solomon were buried. It was reported that this had been the treasure-house, as well as the sepulchre, of the Jewish kings, and stories were current that John Hyrcanus and Herod had successively violated the cemeteries, and enriched themselves with their spoils. Now their sudden fall not only made the defences insecure, but was considered as of awful omen.[f] The Romans, probably after a hard contest,[g] made themselves masters of Jerusalem, and razed every building that remained to the ground: it was then, perhaps, not before, that the plough was passed by Rufus over the devoted ground.[h]

---

[e] A fragment of Fronto addressed to M. Antoninus on the Parthian war shows how terrible were the reminiscences of the Jewish war, which is compared with that of the Parthians and of the Britons. "Nonne a Parthis consularis æque vir in Mesopotamiâ trucidatus? Quid avo vestro Hadriano imperium obtinente quantum militum a Judæis, quantum ab Britannis cæsum?" Epist. p. 107.

[f] This was called the μνημεῖον τοῦ Σολομῶντος—the very brief account in Dion Cassius does not indicate the situation of this tomb of Solomon, but the incident must have been of great importance, as being the only fact in the siege thought worthy of record. Cedrenus adds, σημεῖον δὲ γέγονε τῆς ἁλώσεως αὐτοῦ ὡς τὸ τοῦ Σολομῶντος σημεῖον (melius μνημεῖον) αὐτόματον διαλυθῆναι.—

Edit. Bonn. i. 438.

[g] The whole war appears to have lasted at least three years—132 B.C. to 135.

[h] Appian, B.C., speaks of the different destructions of Jerusalem, by Ptolemy king of Egypt, by Titus, and in his own time by Hadrian: καὶ Ἀδριανὸς αὖθις ἐπ᾽ ἐμοῦ. The war was related at length in the Samaritan Book of Joshua: "Obsidio urbis Hierosolymitanæ per Adrianum fusè pertexitur"—apud Fabric. Cod. Epig. V.T. p. 887. It does not appear at this length in the later edition of that book. Euseb. Dem. Evang. vi. 18: μετ᾽ οὐ πολὺν δὲ χρόνον κατὰ Ἀδριανὸν Αὐτοκράτορα κινήσεως αὖθις Ἰουδαϊκῆς γενομένης τὸ λοιπὸν τῆς πόλεως μέρος ἡμίσυ πολιορκηθὲν αὖθις ἐξελαύνεται, ὡς ἐξ ἐκείνου καὶ εἰς δεῦρο πάμπαν ἄβατον γενέσθαι τὸν

At length the discipline of the Roman troops, and the consummate conduct of Severus, brought the war nearly to a close. The strong city of Bither alone remained, the metropolis and citadel of the insurgents. The situation of this city is not certainly known; it is placed by Eusebius near Beth-horon, by others near the sea.[1] How long Bither stood out after the siege was actually formed, is equally uncertain. When affairs began to wear a gloomy aspect, (thus write the Rabbins,) Eliezer, the son of Hamadai, enjoined the besieged to seek their last resource, prayer to the God of their fathers. All day long the zealous Rabbi was on his knees. As long as he prayed, like Moses during the battle with the Amalekites in the Desert, so long the Jews assumed new courage, and fought with unconquerable fury.[k] A Samaritan undertook to silence by treachery the devout and prevailing Rabbi. He stole up to him where he was kneeling in prayer on a conspicuous eminence, and

---

τόπον. Chrysostom, Orat. iii. in Judæos, says that Hadrian, τὰ λείψανα ἀφανίσας πάντα, raised his own statue on the ruins. This may, however, be mere oratory. Jerome is the authority for the ploughshare driven over the Temple: "aratum Templum in ignominiam gentis oppressæ, a Tito Annio Rufo" (In Zechariam c. 8), but Jerome confounds the two Tituses. See other passages from the Byzantines (of no authority) in Münter, p. 70-1.

[1] Jost says that it was a mountain city, not belonging to Judæa, not far from the sea, between Cæsarea and Diospolis, but he cites no authorities (see, however, Itinerarium Antonini). Judenthum, ii. p. 79.

[k] Jost, Geschichte, iii. p. 251, with authorities.

The reader curious about these extravagancies may find them, with quotations at length from the Rabbinical writings, in the Pugio Fidei of Raimond Martin, p. 258, et seqq., Edit. du Voisin. Throughout there is utter confusion between this war and that under Vespasian and Titus. Rabbi Jochanan said that there were 80,000 pair of trumpeters, each of whom commanded many hosts. Bar-cochab had 200,000 men, who, to prove their boldness and courage, had cut off one of their fingers. "How," said the wise man, "will you try the prowess of these mutilated men? He who cannot ride full speed and pluck up, as he passes, a cedar of Lebanon by the roots, may be discharged."

whispered some indistinct words in his ear. The vigilant Bar-cochab demanded what was the object of his message. The Rabbi could not answer. The Samaritan, after long pretended reluctance, declared that it was an answer to a secret message confided to him by the Rabbi, about capitulation. Bar-cochab commanded the Rabbi to be executed on the spot. This barbarous measure alienated and dispirited his followers. Bither was at length stormed, Bar-cochab was killed, and his head carried in triumph to the Roman camp. It was again on the fatal 9th of Ab[l] (August), the anniversary of the double destruction of Jerusalem, that Bither fell, it was razed to the ground.[m]

Of the massacre the Rabbins tell frightful stories, but their horror is mitigated by their extravagance. More are said to have fallen at Bither than escaped with Moses from Egypt. The horses waded up to their bits in carnage. Blood flowed so copiously, that the stream carried stones weighing four pounds into the sea, according to their account, forty miles distant. The dead covered eighteen square miles, and the inhabitants of the adjacent region had no need to manure their ground for seven years. A more trustworthy authority, Dion Cassius,[n] states, that during the whole war the enormous number of 580,000 fell by the sword,

---

[l] The Jewish day of mourning has always been kept on the 9th, though it seems from Josephus that the 10th was the real day of the destruction.

[m] The absurd statements of the Rabbinical authorities as to the size and populousness of Bither are hardly worth notice except as illustrations of the extraordinary amplifying power of Jewish writers as to numbers. According to the Tract Gittin (Eisenmenger, ii. 656) there were 400 synagogues, each synagogue had 400 schoolmasters, each schoolmaster 400 scholars. According to Echa Rabbathi (ibid.) there were 500 schoolhouses, in the smallest not less than 300 scholars. See another monstrous story—Jost, Anhang iii. p. 185.

[n] Dion Cassius, in loc.

not including those who perished by famine, disease,
and fire. The whole of Judæa was a desert; wolves
and hyænas went howling along the streets of the desolate cities. Those who escaped the sword were scarcely
more fortunate ; they were reduced to slavery by thousands. There was a great fair held under a celebrated
Terebinth, which tradition had consecrated as the very
tree under which Abraham had pitched his tent.[o]
Thither his miserable children were brought in droves,
and sold as cheap as horses. Others were carried away
and sold at Gaza; others transported to Egypt. The
account of the fate of Rabbi Akiba is singularly characteristic.[p] He was summoned for examination before
the odious Turnus Rufus. In the middle of his in-
terrogations, Akiba remembered that it was the hour
of prayer. He fell on his knees, regardless of the
presence of the Roman, and of the pending trial for
life and death, and calmly went through his devotions. This is in another place related more at length :
"In the midst of his tortures Akiba remembered
the moment when the Schema ('Hear O Israel,' &c.)
ought to be repeated. He spoke it with devotion, and
a glad countenance. T. Annius Rufus . . . . . beheld
him and said, 'Akiba, thou art either become obtuse,
or by your stubbornness wouldest provoke still sharper
sufferings. Why dost thou smile?' Akiba answered,
'I have had the happy lot almost entirely to fulfil the
verse in our daily devotions, "Thou shalt love the Lord
thy God with all thy heart, and with all thy soul, and
with all thy strength," for I have yielded myself up
entirely to the love of God, and willingly made sacri-

---

* Hieronym. in Zechariam c. 8.
* Beraeoth. l. 59. Erubiu, s. 8, quoted by Jost, iii. 253.

fice of all my possessions. One thing alone was wanting, to show my love by the offering up of my life; I rejoice that this last trial is come, and I will endure it.'"[q] In the prison, while his lips were burning with thirst, he nevertheless applied his scanty pittance of water to his ablutions. The barbarous Roman ordered the old man to be flayed alive, and then put to death. The most furious persecution was commenced against all the Rabbins, who were considered the authors and ringleaders of the insurrection. Chanania, the son of Theradion, was detected reading and expounding the Law; he was burned with the book which he was reading. It was forbidden to fill up the number of the great Synagogue, or Sanhedrin, but Akiba, just before his death, had named five new members; and Judah, the son of Bavah, secretly nominated others in a mountain glen, where he had taken refuge. Soldiers were sent to surprise Judah; he calmly awaited their coming, and was transfixed by 300 spears.

Hadrian, to annihilate for ever all hopes of the restoration of the Jewish kingdom, accomplished his plan of establishing a new city on the site of Jerusalem, peopled by a colony of foreigners.[r] The city was called Ælia Capitolina; Ælia after the prænomen of the emperor, Capitolina as dedicated to the Jupiter of the Capitol.[s] An edict was issued, prohibiting any

---

[q] Jost might well call this martyrdom. Judenthum, i. p. 69. Chiarini, ii. 336, has another version.

[r] The Chronic. Alexandrinum, after a description of the sale of the Jewish captives under the terebinth, contains an account of buildings erected by Hadrian in Ælia, among them a theatre. Edit. Bonn. i. p. 474.

[s] This fact strengthens my utter disbelief in the erection of a Temple of Venus over the sepulchre of Christ. Hadrian had no special hostility to the Christians. I am glad to find myself in perfect agreement with Bishop Münter: "Er (Hadrianus) war übrigens kein Feind und Verfolger der Christen." p. 92. Münter suggests that the

Jew from entering the new city on pain of death, or
approaching its environs, so as to contemplate even at
a distance its sacred height.[t] More effectually to keep
them away, the image of a swine was placed over the
gate leading to Bethlehem. The more peaceful Christians were permitted to establish themselves within the
walls, and Ælia became the seat of a flourishing church
and bishopric.

Apologies of Quadratus and Aristides,
presented by them to Hadrian at
Athens, were intended to aid him in
discriminating between Christians and
Jews.   I cannot lay great stress on
Moses of Chorene, who not merely represents Hadrian as not unfriendly but
as settling the Christians in his new
city : "Atque ipse Hierosolymam a
Vespasiano, Tito, et ab se devastatam
instauravit, et ab nomine suo Æliam
nominavit; cum ipse Adrianus Sol esset
appellatus, atque ibi Ethnicos locavit et
Christianos, quorum · Episcopus erat
Marcus."   Mos. Chor. Hist. c. 57.

Jost dates from the war of Bar-cochab
the distinction drawn by the Romans
between the Jews and Christians :
"Die erste bedeutende Trennung beider
zeigte sich in dem letzten Kriege unter
Barcochba, der gegen die Christen
Gewalt brauchte." iv. p. 13.

[t] This prohibition is mentioned by
many writers. Justin Martyr, Apolog.;
Euseb. H. E. iv. 16; Dem. Ev. viii.
18; Tertullian, in Jud. xv.; Sulpic.
Sever. ii. 45, cited at full length, in
Heinichen's note on H. E. i. p. 298;
Talmud. Bab. Taan. p. 14; Mischna,
cited by Jost, 252.

BOOK XIX.

THE PATRIARCH OF THE WEST, AND THE PRINCE OF THE CAPTIVITY.

Re-establishment of the Community — Patriarch of Tiberias — His Power and Dominions — Jews in Egypt — Asia Minor — Greece — Italy— Spain — Gaul — Germany — Origin and Nature of the Rabbinical Authority — The Worship of the Synagogue — Early History of the Patriarchate — Civil Contests — Contests with the Babylonian Jews — Relation with Rome — The Prince of the Captivity — Jews in China.

FOR the fourth time the Jewish people seemed on the brink of extermination. Nebuchadnezzar, Antiochus, Titus, Hadrian, had successively exerted their utmost power to extinguish, not merely the political existence of the state, but even the separate being of the people. Hadrian's edict had interdicted circumcision, keeping the Sabbath, instruction in the Law — all the outward acts and usages of the race. These offences were to be punished at the will of the prefect with fine, even with death.[a] It might have appeared impossible that anything like a community should again revive within Palestine; still more so, that the multitudes of Jews scattered over the whole face of the world should maintain any correspondence or intelligence, continue a distinct and unmingled race, or resist the process of absorption into the general population, the usual fate of

---

[a] Jost quotes Die Hadrians Verfolgung, in Frankel's 'Monatschrift,' 1852, p. 80.

small bodies of strangers settled in remote and unconnected regions. In less than sixty years after the war
under Hadrian, before the close of the second century
after Christ, the Jews present the extraordinary spectacle of two regular and organized communities: one
under a sort of spiritual head, the Patriarch of Tiberias,
comprehending all of Israelitish descent who inhabited
the Roman empire; the other under the Prince of the
Captivity, to whom all the eastern Jews paid their
allegiance. Gibbon has briefly stated the growth of
the former of these principalities with his usual general
accuracy, as regards facts, though the relation is coloured by his sarcastic tone, in which the bitter anti-
pathy of his school to the Jewish race is strongly
marked. " Notwithstanding these repeated provoca-
tions, the resentment of the Roman princes expired
after the victory; nor were their apprehensions continued beyond the period of war and danger. By the
general indulgence of polytheism, and by the mild temper of Antoninus Pius, the Jews were restored to their
ancient privileges, and once more obtained the permission of circumcising their children, with the easy re-
straint that they should never confer on any foreign
proselyte that distinguishing mark of the Hebrew race.
The numerous remains of that people, though they were
still excluded from the precincts of Jerusalem, were
permitted to form and to maintain considerable esta-
blishments both in Italy and in the provinces, to acquire the freedom of Rome, to enjoy municipal
honours, and to obtain, at the same time, an exemption from the burthensome and expensive offices of
society. The moderation or the contempt of the Romans gave a legal sanction to the form of ecclesiastical
police which was instituted by the vanquished sect.

The patriarch, who had fixed his residence at Tiberias, was empowered to appoint his subordinate ministers and apostles, to exercise a domestic jurisdiction, and to receive from his despised brethren an annual contribution. Now synagogues were frequently erected in the principal cities of the empire; and the sabbaths, the fasts, and the festivals, which were either commanded by the Mosaic Law, or enjoined by the traditions of the Rabbins, were celebrated in the most solemn and public manner. Such gentle treatment insensibly assuaged the stern temper of the Jews. Awakened from their dream of prophecy and conquest, they assumed the behaviour of peaceable and industrious subjects. Their irreconcileable hatred of mankind, instead of flaming out in acts of blood and violence, evaporated in less dangerous gratifications. They embraced every opportunity of overreaching the idolaters in trade;[b] and they pronounced secret and ambiguous imprecations against the haughty kingdom of Edom."[c]

---

[b] Jost, Geschichte, iv. 7, traces, of course in a more friendly tone, the growth of this love of wealth, the natural result of the commercial spirit.

[c] According to the false Josephus, Tsepho, the grandson of Esau, conducted into Italy the army of Æneas, King of Carthage. Another colony of Idumeans, flying from the sword of David, took refuge in the dominions of Romulus. For these, or for other reasons of equal weight, the name of Edom was applied by the Jews to the Roman empire.—Gibbon's Note. The false Josephus is a romancer of very modern date, though some of these legends are possibly more ancient. It may be worth considering whether many of the stories in the Talmud are not history, in a figurative disguise, adopted from prudence. The Jews might dare to say many things of Rome, under the significant appellation of Edom, which they feared to utter publicly. Later and more ignorant ages took literally, and, perhaps, embellished, what was intelligible among the generation to which it was addressed. Rabbi Jehuda the Holy prophesied that the destroyers of the second Temple should be conquered by the Persians. He grounded this on Jer. xl. 20 : "Therefore hear the counsel of the Lord that he hath taken against Edom." Jost, iv. 129. See a curious passage (Eisenmenger, i. 237)

Unfortunately it is among the most difficult parts of Jewish history to trace the growth of the patriarchal authority established in Tiberias, and its recognition by the whole scattered body of the nation, who, with dis-interested zeal, and I do not scruple to add, a noble attachment to the race of Israel, became voluntary sub-jects and tributaries to their spiritual sovereign, and united with one mind and one heart to establish their community on a settled basis. It is a singular spectacle to behold a nation dispersed in every region of the world, without a murmur or repugnance, submitting to the regulations, and taxing themselves to support the greatness, of a supremacy which rested solely on public opinion, and had no temporal power whatever to en-force its decrees. It was not long before the Rabbins, who had been hunted down with unrelenting cruelty, began to creep forth from their places of concealment. The death of Hadrian, in a few years after the termina-tion of the war, and the accession of the mild Anto-ninus,[d] gave them courage, not merely to make their public appearance, but openly to re-establish their schools and synagogues. The school of Jamnia,[e] called

from Aben-Ezra on Isaiah lxiii. 1, also ii. 69, a passage predicting the de-struction of Rome by the Israelites, manifestly Post-Mohammedan: "In Talmud namque in locis innumeris quandoque Esau, quandoque Edom, quandoque Seir, quandoque etiam filii Esau vel Edom, vocati sunt Romani, et Roma mons Seir, atque mons Esau." R. Martin, Pugio Fidei, p. 319. See quotations. Basnage has much, too much, of this Idumean descent of the Romans, from Abarbanel and other late writers. lvii., cviii.

[d] Basnage has heaped together all the romances about the connexion of the elder Antoninus with the Jews, in-vented by later writers. He had been nursed on Jewish milk, circumcised himself, was a pupil of Rabbi Jehuda the Holy (lib. viii. 1). They were not worth refutation.

[e] Lightfoot, Academiæ Jafnensis Historiæ Fragmenta, and Jost, Ge-schichte, iv. 29. This school seems tc have removed to Ussa or Oscha, the site of which is unknown.

the Vineyard, because the scholars stood in regular rows, was reopened, and the Jewish youth crowded to the feet of their acknowledged teachers.[f] Of the Rabbins who were considered legitimate members of the great Sanhedrin, there escaped the storm, Simon the son of Gamaliel, who had an hereditary title to the presidency (he is said to have been the only young scholar who escaped the wreck of Bither): five who had been named by Judah the son of Bavah, Judah the son of Ilai, Simon the son of Jochai, R. Jose,[g] R. Elasar, R. Nehemiah, and lastly, R. Meir.[h] The first pious care of the Rabbins was to obtain permission to perform funeral rites for their brethren; this indulgence was long celebrated by a thanksgiving in their daily prayers; their next was to obtain an abrogation of the persecuting edicts.[i] For this purpose Simon Ben Jochai, and a youth of great promise, were sent to Rome. This journey is adorned with the customary fables. They obtained the favour of the Emperor by a miraculous cure of his sick daughter. It is certain, however, that Antoninus issued an edict which permitted the Jews to perform the rite of circumcision;[k]

---

[f] Jost, Geschichte, iv. 25, from Sanhedrin, 14.

[g] The Talmud describes these teachers as Jose B. Halepha, the deep thinker; Judah B. Ilai, the holy; Meir, the judicious; Simon ben Jochai, the Cabbalist; Simeon ben Gamaliel, the Nasi. Jost, Geschichte, iv. p. 32. In his later work, Judenthum, ii. 87, et seqq., Jost is not much more full on their specific characters and sayings, though he adduces other instances of their learning and wisdom.

[h] Of R. Meir it is reported in the Talmud that he was not of Jewish descent, but sprung from the Impostor who set himself up for Nero (after the death of that Emperor) in the East. He was a scholar of Akiba.

[i] Jost, Geschichte, iv. 44.

[k] Digest. xlviii. viii. 11: "Circumcidere Judæis filios suos tantum, rescripto Divi Antonini permittitur, in non ejusdem religionis qui hoc fecerit, castrantis pœna irrogatur." A law of this period was necessary to prohibit Jews from making and circumcising converts. "Cives Romani, qui se Ju-

but, as though he apprehended that the religion of this despised people might still make proselytes, they were forbidden to initiate strangers into the family of Israel.[l] Still it should seem that in Palestine they were watched with jealous vigilance.[m] A story is related of the fall of the school in Jamnia (Jabne), which shows as well the unruly spirit of the Jews, as the rigorous police of the Romans. Simon Ben Jochai, who appears to have been by no means a safe person to be entrusted with a mission to Rome, makes a prominent figure in the narrative.[n] During a public debate, at which R. Jehuda, R. Jose, and R. Simon Ben Jochai were present, the topic of discussion was the national character of their Roman masters. The cautious Jehuda turned the dangerous subject to their praise, on those points on which a Jew might conscientiously admire his oppressors. "How splendid," he exclaimed, "are the public works of this people! In every city they have built spacious market-places for the public use, for the commerce and for the amusement of the inhabitants. They throw noble bridges over rivers, and thus unite separate pro-

daico ritu vel servos suos circumcidi patiuntur, bonis ademptis in insulam perpetuo relegantur; *medici capite puniantur.*"

"Judæi si alienæ nationis comparatos servos circumciderint, aut deportantur aut capite puniuntur." Jul. Paulus, Rec. Sent. v. 22, De Seditiosis.

[l] Perhaps the confusion between the Jews and Christians, whose rapid progress excited great alarm, might be the real cause of this limitation; or it might be aimed at the Judaizing Christians, who insisted on circumcising their new converts; though, after all, it is by no means improbable that Judaism still made proselytes from the heathen.

[m] It is impossible to date the vague sentence in Capitolinus, who, among the victories of Antoninus Pius, writes, " Judæos rebellantes contudit per præsides et legatos." H. A, S. p. 133. Vit. Anton.

[n] Jost in his Judenthum places this embassy under the reign of M. Aurelius. But compare the Anhang (Israeliter), iv. 226. A Christian bishop is a rival for the cure, by dispossession, of the Princess Lucilla. According to Baronius, sub ann. 163, Lucilla was the daughter of M. Aurelius.

vinces, and facilitate the mutual intercourse of distant regions.   How beautiful are their baths, which contribute as much to the health as to the enjoyment of the people!"   Thus spoke R. Jehuda, the president. The fiery Simon Ben Jochai sprang up, and cried aloud, "Why this adulatory encomium on heathens? For what purpose are all these works erected, but to gratify their own rapacity and to facilitate their exactions?   Why do they build spacious market-places, but for the assembling together of harlots to gratify their licentiousness?   Their baths are erected only for their own sensual delights; their bridges, that their collectors of tribute may pass from land to land.   *We* occupy ourselves in Divine lore; *we* study eternal and disregard temporal advantages."°

The consequence of this imprudent speech was a formal accusation before the authorities.   Simon was adjudged to have forfeited his life.   R. Jose, because he had maintained a suspicious silence, was banished. R. Jehuda alone obtained a general licence to teach. Simon fled, but the school was suppressed.   Another proof of the perpetual apprehension of insurrection is

---

° This remarkable story from the Talmudic Treatise Schabbath, cited by Jost, is curious on account of the boldness of what the Jews said, and not less from their prudential silence. They cannot have been ignorant of the magnificent heathen temples which were erected or restored, if not in Palestine, all around it, during the reigns of the Antonines.   To this the costliness and splendour, as well as the noble, if debased, architecture, still bear witness. To that time belong, as well as many temples in Egypt, the temples of Baalbec, probably of Palmyra, of Petra, Gerasa, and those other cities beyond the Jordan visited by Mr. Cyril Graham.   On this remarkable subject the history of the Antonines (in truth almost a total blank) gives no information, and it has not been worked out with sufficient accuracy by architects, the masters in the history of their art, from the buildings themselves Capitolinus, after reciting the magnificent buildings of Antoninus at Rome, adds, " Multas etiam civitates adjuvit pecuniâ, ut opera vel nova facerent, vel vetera restituerent."   In Antonin.

thus related:—The trumpet blast, which was sounded at the commencement of the month Tisri, awakened the suspicion of a governor, ignorant of Hebrew customs : it was reported to be a signal for general revolt. The governor was appeased by a prudent arrangement of Simon, the son of Gamaliel,[p] who ordered that the trumpet should sound, not at the commencement, only in the middle of the prayers, thus clearly forming part of the service.

Nor was the reign of the philosophic M. Aurelius without danger to, perhaps not without well-grounded suspicion of, the Jews. The victories of Avidius Cassius over Vologeses, king of Parthia, and the capture of Ctesiphon, after a long siege, brought the Mesopotamian Jews once more under the dominion of Rome. Seleucia, in which there were many Jews, capitulated; but, in violation of the terms, four or five thousand were put to the sword. Cassius assumed the purple in Syria; the Jews are supposed to have joined his standard, for Marcus Aurelius, though he displayed his characteristic lenity towards the Roman insurgents, punished the intractable Jews with the repeal of the favourable laws of Antoninus Pius. Their conduct seems to have ruffled the temper of the philosophic emperor, who declared that they were more unruly than the wild Sauromatæ and Marcomanni, against whom he was engaged in war.[q]

Yet these severe laws were either speedily annulled,

---

[p] Jost, iv. 52.

[q] "Ille (M. Aurelius), cum Palæstinam transiret *fœtentium* Judæorum et tumultuantium tædio percitus dolenter dicitur exclamasse, O Marcomanni! O Quadi! O Sauromatæ! tandem alios vobis inquietiores inveni?" Ammian. Marcel. xxii. 5. Inquietiores must be the right reading, not inertiores. The "fœtentium" is rather of the time of Ammianus than of M. Aurelius.

or never carried into execution. The Rabbinical dominion gradually rose to greater power; the schools
flourished; perhaps in this interval the great Synagogue
or Sanhedrin had its other migrations, from Osha to
Shepharaam, from Shepharaam to Bethshaaraim, from
Bethshaaraim to Sepphoris, and finally to Tiberias, where
it fixed its pontifical throne, and maintained its supremacy for several centuries. Tiberias, it may be remembered, was a town built by Herod Antipas, over an
ancient cemetery, and therefore abominated by the more
scrupulous Jews, as a dwelling of uncleanness. But
the Rabbins soon obviated this objection. Simon Ben
Jochai,[r] by his cabalistic art, discovered the exact spot
where the burial-place had been; this was marked off,
and the rest of the city declared, on the same unerring
authority, to be clean. Here, then, in this noble city,
on the shore of the sea of Galilee, the Jewish pontiff
fixed his throne; the Sanhedrin, if it had not, as the
Jews pretend, existed during all the reverses of the
nation, was formally re-established. Simon, the son and
heir of Gamaliel, was acknowledged as the Patriarch of
the Jews, and Nasi or President of the Sanhedrin.
R. Nathan was the Ab-beth-din; and the celebrated
R. Meir, the Hachim, or Head of the Law. In every
region of the West, in every province of the Roman
empire, the Jews of all ranks and classes submitted,
with the utmost readiness, to the sway of their Spiritual
Potentate. His mandates were obeyed, his legates
received with honour, his supplies levied without difficulty, in Rome, in Spain, in Africa. At a somewhat
later period, probably about the reign of Alexander
Severus, the Christian writer, Origen, thus describes the

---

[r] Jost, iv. 69.

power of the Jewish Patriarch: "Even now, when the
Jews are under the dominion of Rome, and pay the
didrachm, how great, by the permission of Cæsar, is the
power of their Ethnarch! I myself have been a witness
that it is little less than that of a king. For they
secretly pass judgements according to their Law, and
some are capitally condemned, not with open and acknowledged authority, but with the connivance of the
emperor. This I have learned, and am fully acquainted
with, by long residence in their country."[*]

Here, then, it may be well to take a survey of these
dominions of the Western Patriarch, to ascertain, as far
as possible, the origin and condition of the different
settlements of Jews in Europe, Western Asia, and Africa,
the constitution of their societies, and the nature of the
authority exercised by the supreme pontiff.

It will have been seen, in many incidental notices,
that long before the dissolution of the Jewish state, and
before the promulgation of Christianity, this people were
widely dispersed over the whole face of the globe. The
following passage of Philo, in his letter of Agrippa,
which might be confirmed by other quotations from
Josephus, describes their state in his own days (the reign
of Caligula): "Jerusalem is the city of my ancestors,
the metropolis, not only of Judæa, but of many other
provinces, in consequence of the colonies which it has
at different times sent out into the neighbouring countries, Egypt, Phœnicia, Syria, and Cœlesyria; and into
more distant regions, Pamphylia, Cilicia, the greatest
part of Asia Minor, as far as Bithynia, and the remotest
shores of the Euxine; so also into Europe, into Thessaly,
Bœotia, Macedonia, Ætolia, Attica, Argos, Corinth, and

---

[*] Origenes ad Africanum Epist., cxiv.

into most, and those the best, parts of the Pelcponnesus: and not only are the Continents full of Jewish colonies, but the principal islands also, Euboea, Cyprus, and Crete. I say nothing of the countries beyond the Euphrates; for all of them, except a small portion, particularly Babylon and the Satrapies of the rich adjacent districts, have many Jewish inhabitants."[t] The events of Jewish History in Palestine tended to increase rather than to diminish the number of those who were either dragged away as captives, or sought peace and security from the devastation of their native land in the less troubled provinces of the empire. Even where they suffered most, through their own turbulent disposition or the enmity of their neighbours, they sprang again from their undying stock, however it might be hewn by the sword or seared by the fire. Massacre seemed to have no effect in thinning their ranks, and, like their forefathers in Egypt, they still multiplied under the most cruel oppression. In Egypt and Cyrene, indeed, they had experienced the greatest losses, but on the visit of Hadrian to Alexandria, he found the city and country still swarming with Jews. The origin and history of the Egyptian, as well as of the Syrian Jews, have been already traced. The Jews of Asia Minor owed their first establishment to Antiochus the Great, who settled vast numbers in the different cities in that region.

---

[t] Many passages in Josephus illustrate and confirm this statement of Philo. The following, quoted from Strabo, is of perhaps higher authority than the statement of any Jew: — καὶ τόπον οὐκ ἔστι ῥᾳδίως εὑρεῖν τῆς οἰκουμένης, ὃς οὐ παραδέδεκται τοῦτο τὸ φῦλον, μηδ' ἐπικρατεῖται ὑπ' αὐτοῦ. Strabo enlarges on their vast numbers in Egypt and Cyrene. Οὐ γὰρ ἔστιν ἐπὶ τῆς οἰκουμένης δῆμος, ὁ μὴ μοῖραν ὑμετέραν ἔχων—from the speech of Agrippa, B. J. ii. 16. 4. Compare B. J. vii. 3, as to the vast numbers in Syria, especially in Antioch. Proselytes were numerous in Antioch.

From Asia Minor they probably spread to Greece and to the Islands. The clearest notion of their numbers in all this part of the world, including Galatia, Bithynia, and Cappadocia, may be formed from the narrative of the Apostolic journeys. Whatever city Paul enters, he seems to find a synagogue and a number of his country-men, many of whom were powerful and opulent. I need only name the cities of Ephesus, Laodicea, Per-gamus, Thessalonica, Athens, and Corinth. It is pro-bable that in Asia Minor, and in Alexandria, the later Jews first generally adopted their commercial habits; but their condition was much more secure in the former country than among the fiery inhabitants of the factious Egyptian city. Many public decrees are extant,[a] not only of the Roman authorities, particularly Julius Cæsar, which secure important privileges to the Jewish residents in Asia Minor, but likewise local ordinances of the dif-ferent cities, Pergamus, Halicarnassus, Laodicea, Ephe-sus, and Miletus, highly favourable to these foreign denizens, and seeming to show that the two races lived together on terms of perfect amity. In some of the occurrences related in the Acts of the Apostles, the Jews, in those times, appear a considerable and influen-tial, by no means the proscribed and odious, race which they were held to be in other quarters. The public decrees usually gave them the title of Roman citizens, a privilege to which many of the Jews (the well-known instance of St. Paul will occur to every one) had un-doubtedly attained. It was their great object to obtain exemption from military service. In other times they do not seem to have objected to enrol themselves in the

---

[a] Read the elaborate dissertation of Krebs, Decreta Romanorum pro Judæis facta, Lipsiæ, 1768.

armies of their rulers. Some are said to have been in
Alexander's army; and an improbable story is told, by
a doubtful authority, Hecatæus, of their refusing, and
obtaining an exemption from being employed in building
an idolatrous temple in Babylon. The striking story of
Mosellama is more authentic.[x] But most likely, having
betaken themselves to the more lucrative occupations of
peace, at later periods they pleaded that it was contrary
to their religion to fight, or to work, or even to march
on the Sabbath, and that they could not partake of the
same meat with the other soldiers; their plea seems to
have been admitted. Of their wealth we have a curious
evidence. Their contributions to the Temple were so
ample as to excite the jealous rapacity of the Roman
governor. Cicero, in a memorable oration, vindicates
Flaccus for not having permitted the provinces to be
drained of their wealth for such a purpose, and holds up
his example to other governors, complaining that Italy
itself suffered by the exportation of so much wealth.[y]

The origin of the Jews in Italy, or rather in Rome, is
very obscure. It is usually ascribed to the vast number
of slaves brought to the capital by Pompey after his
conquest of Jerusalem. These slaves were publicly sold
in the markets; yet, if we are to believe Philo, they
were emancipated almost without exception by their
tolerant masters, who were unwilling to do violence to
their religious scruples. Is it not more probable that
there were some, if not many, opulent commercial

---

[x] While some Greek soldiers were
watching with superstitious anxiety
the flight of a bird, which was to be of
good or evil omen, they were horror-
struck to see it fall, transfixed by the
arrow of their Jewish comrade. The
Jew calmly answered, "How much
must yonder bird have known of the
secrets of futurity, which knew not
how to avoid the arrow of Mosellama
the Jew?"

[y] Cic. pro Flacco. Comp. ii. p. 50.

Jews already in Rome, who, with their usual national spirit, purchased, to the utmost of their means, their unhappy countrymen, and enabled them to settle in freedom in the great metropolis? The passage in Cicero alluded to above, is conclusive evidence to the wealth of the Jewish community in Italy. They were among the mourners, the most sincere mourners, at the obsequies of Julius Cæsar.[a] They wailed for many nights around his entombment. No doubt their detestation of Pompey, the first Roman violator of their sanctuary, would deepen their respect for his rival and conqueror. However they obtained their freedom, it is certain that a vast number of Jewish libertines or freed-slaves inhabited Rome. Tacitus states their number at 4000.[a] It appears from Josephus, as we have seen,

---

[a] " Præcipuè Judæi qui noctibus continuis bustum frequentârunt." Suet. Jul. c. 84.

[a] If credit is to be given to a reading in Valerius Maximus, as it is found in two Epitomators, Julius Paris and Januarius Nepotianus, the Jews were of much older date in Rome. The old reading was, " Idem (C. Cornelius Hispalla, prætor peregrinus) [Hispalla lived in the consulship of M. Popilius Lænas and Cn. Calpurnius, A.U. 615, B.C. 139] qui Sabazii Jovis cultu simulato mores Romanos inficere conati sunt, domos suas repetere coegit."

The Epitomators read :—

Paris.	*Nepotianus.*
" Idem *Judæos* qui Sabazi Jovis cultu Romanos inficere mores conati erant, repetere domos suas coegit."	" Judæos quoque qui Romanis tradere sacra sua conati erant, idem Hispalus urbe exterminavit, arasque privatas a publicis locis abjecit."

If this reading be genuine, we find the Jews not merely settled in Rome, but a dangerous and proselyting people, three-quarters of a century before the taking of Jerusalem by Pompey. But this fact requires, in my judgement, much better authority. The age of Julius Paris is altogether uncertain ; he has been placed as early as Hadrian (Kemf. Præf. p. 66). Nepotianus is not earlier than the fourth century. But both are post-Christian writers. The fact itself is sufficiently startling. And what have the Jews to do with Jupiter Sabazius—a Phrygian god? Some indeed have suggested Sabati ; others D. Sabaoth. The private altars of the Jews erected in public places is a manifest absurdity. I have no hesitation in rejecting the whole as a

that 8000 were present when Archelaus appeared before
Augustus, and a vast number poured out to welcome
the false Alexander. They formed the chief population
of the Transtiberine region.[b] They shared (that is, the
less wealthy) in the general largess of corn which was
distributed among the poorer inhabitants of the city:
by a special favour of Augustus,[c] if the distribution fell
on a Sabbath, their portion was reserved. They were
expelled by Tiberius, and a great number drafted off as
soldiers to the unwholesome island of Sardinia;[d] by
Caligula they were oppressed; by Claudius once more
expelled, or at least their synagogues closed on account
of the feuds between the Jews and Christians.[e] Yet
here, as elsewhere, oppression and persecution seemed

---

flagrant anachronism, introduced into
the text of Valerius, after the time
when the Jews, either of themselves or
as connected with the Christians, had
become much more familiar to the
general ear. See the new edition of
Valerius, by Kemf, Berlin, 1834. The
Epitomators were first published by
Cardinal Mai.

[b] "Hoc quod *Transtiberinus* ambulator,
　　Qui pallentia sulfurata fractis
　　Permutat vitreis."—MART. L. 42.

This was the case in the time of
Caligula: τὴν πέραν τοῦ Τιβέρεως
ποταμοῦ μεγάλην τῆς Ῥωμῆς ἀπο-
τομὴν, ἣν οὐκ ἠγνόει κατεχομένην
καὶ οἰκουμένην πρὸς Ἰουδαίων. Ῥωμαῖοι δὲ ἦσαν οἱ πλείους ἀπελευθερω-
θέντες· αἰχμάλωτοι γὰρ ἀχθέντες
εἰς Ἰταλίαν, ὑπὸ τῶν κτησαμένων
ἐλευθερώθησαν, οὐδὲν τῶν πατρίων
παραχαράξαι βιασθέντες. Philo, Leg.
ed Mangey. ii. p. 560.

It is amusing to see the malicious satisfaction with which Basnage
attempts to prove against his Roman

Catholic opponents that they were
possessors of the Vatican.

[e] It seems to have been the amusement of the idle youth of Rome to
visit the Jewish synagogue. The well-
known passage in the ninth satire of
Horace will occur to the classical
reader. Though I have some doubts
whether the Judaism of the poet's
friend, Fuscus Aristius, has not been
inferred on insufficient grounds.

[d] "Si ob gravitatem cœli interirent,
vile damnum," writes the contemptuous historian.

[e] "Judæos impulsore Chresto assi-
duè tumultuantes Româ expulit." Suet.
Claudius.

Dion gives a milder edict. They were
not expelled, on account of their numbers: τοὺς δὲ Ἰουδαίους, πλεονασάν-
τας αὖθις, ὥστε χαλεπῶς ἂν ἄνευ
ταραχῆς, ὑπὸ τοῦ ὄχλου σφῶν τῆς
πόλεως εἰρχθῆναι, οὐκ ἐξήλασε μὲν,
τῷ δὲ δὴ πατρίῳ νόμῳ καὶ βίῳ χρη-
σαμένους ἐκέλευσε μὴ συναθροίζε-
σθαι. I. lx. 6.

not to be the slightest check to their increase. They
had a sort of council, or house of judgement, which
decided all matters of dispute. To this, no doubt, either
in the synagogue or law court attached to it, St. Paul
expected to give an account of his conduct. The numbers of the Jews in Rome were doubtless much increased,
but their respectability as well as their popularity much
diminished, by the immense influx of the most destitute
as well as of the most unruly of the race, who were swept
into captivity by thousands after the fall of 'Jerusalem.
The change appears to be very marked. The language
of the incidental notices which occur about the Jews in
the Latin authors, after this period, seems more and
more contemptuous, and implies that many of them
were in the lowest state of penury, the outcasts of society. Juvenal[f] bitterly complains that the beautiful
and poetic grove of Egeria was let out to mendicant
hordes of Jews, who pitched their camps like gipsies, in
the open air, with a wallet and a bundle of hay for their
pillow, as their only furniture. Martial[g] alludes to
their filth, and, what is curious enough, describes them
as pedlers, venders of matches, which they trafficked
for broken glass.[h]

---

[f] "Nunc sacri fontis nemus et delubra
    locantur
  Judæis, quorum cophinus fœnumque
    supellex."—*S.* iii. 12.

See also the passage about the Jews,
riv. 96 et seqq.

[g] More fœtid

  ". . . . quam jejunia sabbatariorum."
                                —iv. 6, 7.
  "A matre doctus nec rogare Judæos,
  Nec sulfuratæ lippus institor mercis."
                                —xii. 57.
Compare vi. 94; vii. 30, 35, 82.

So too Statius :—

"Illic agmina confremunt Syrorum,
Hic plebs scenica, quisque comminutis
Permutant vitreis gregale sulphur."
                            Silvæ, i. iv. 72.

[h] Another curious illustration of
the numbers of Jews in Rome is to be
found in their catacombs. There can
be no doubt, as observed by a late
writer, Mr. Burgon, "that the motive
of burying in a catacomb was in
the first instance neither heathen nor
Christian, but Jewish." Burgon,
Letters from Rome, p. 130. The
Jews had a religious horror of burning

Of their establishment in the other provinces in the Roman Empire, we have no certain information.   In the Middle Ages the most extraordinary fables were invented concerning their first settlement in Germany, France, and Spain.   Those relating to the latter country may serve as a specimen.   There they claimed descent from maritime adventurers in the time of Solomon, or from a part of their race transported to that country when Nebuchadnezzar[1] conquered Spain![J]   Hebrew derivations were found for many of the Spanish cities,

---

the dead. The catacombs, whatever their origin, would bear a strong likeness to the caves in the rocks, in which, from Abraham to the burying place of Nicodemus, they had been wont to inter their ancestors. The chapter of Bosio (xxii.) is full on the Jewish catacomb near the Porta Portese, conveniently situated for the Transtiberine Jews. It is curious that another Jewish catacomb has been recently discovered at no great distance from their settlement, alluded to by Juvenal, near the fountain of Egeria. In this, all the inscriptions, I believe, as far as yet discovered, have been in Greek, except one or two Latin. Of the older Jewish inscriptions Mr. Burgon cites four in Greek. In Bosio may be seen the seven-branched candlestick from the catacomb near the Porta Portese. Nor is it only at Rome that Jewish catacombs have been discovered. At Venosa there have been found some very remarkable ones, with many inscriptions, twenty-four in Hebrew. They bear the seven-branched candlestick and a pigeon with an olive branch. "The Latin and Greek inscriptions are misspelt, but the Hebrew ones are more correct; they generally consist of a

prayer for the repose and blessing of the dead." Others are well known at Naples, also in other places (Lavello and Oria) in that kingdom. Murray's Handbook for Southern Italy, p. 382.

By the favour of Signore Visconti I am able to insert one or two of the inscriptions from the newly-discovered catacomb, and some of the rude emblems, perpetually found in the Jewish catacombs (see next page).

In the Études sur les Juifs d'Espagne (translated by J. G. Magnabal, from the Spanish of J. Amador de los Rios, Paris, 1861), these fables are related, and rejected as utterly unhistoric. The curious reader may find the letter said to have been written by the Head of the Synagogue at Toledo, reproving the High Priest Eleasar . . . Annas and Caiaphas with the unjustifiable death of our Saviour.

[J] These fables were probably invented for the purpose of exculpating themselves with the Christians, as, having long before been separated from the nation, they could not have borne any part in the guilt of the Crucifixion of Christ. When the Christians took Toledo, this plea was urged; perhaps it was invented at that time.

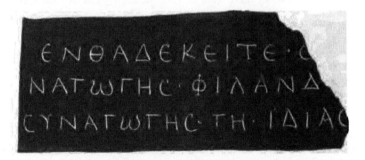

JEWISH INSCRIPTIONS IN THE CATACOMBS—ROME.

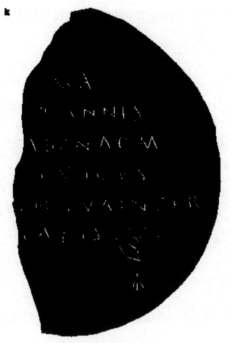

JEWISH INSCRIPTIONS FROM THE CATACOMBS.

ᵇ Later excavations have brought to light other curious circumstances concerning this Jewish catacomb. See *Cimitero degli Antiche Ebrei, per Raffaelli Garrucci, Romæ*, 1862. I. Before the entrance of the actual cemetery, there appears to have been a synagogue or proseucha (p. 5), closely resembling the mortuary chapels or places of worship of the early Christians. II. Of forty-three inscriptions, twelve only were in Latin (p. 63), thirty-one Greek, a singular illustration of the prevalence of Greek among the early Christians. But "the Latin proper names are double the number of the Greek; the Greek, again, twice as many as the Hebrew or Aramaic." Is not this easily accounted for? A large proportion of the Jews were freedmen, who, as usual, took the name of the master who had emancipated them. There is not a single Hebrew or Aramaic epitaph, but the words שלום and שלום על ישראל frequently occur (p. 26).

Moreover, if Signore Garrucci is right in his conclusions, there were seven synagogues of the Jews in different quarters of the city, each with its special name, the prototypes of the Christian tituli or parishes of Rome. Each had its archon or archontes, the archisynagogi, or presbyters—elders (p. 53), &c.

which proved, to the satisfaction even of later antiquaries,[1] the early settlement of the Jews in that region; forgetting entirely the close affinity of the Phœnician and Punic dialects with the Hebrew, and the successive occupation of (at least maritime) Spain by these kindred nations. In fact, the Jews spread with the dominion of the Roman arms, part as slaves, part as free men with commercial objects, or seeking only a safe and peaceful settlement. Some, no doubt, made their livelihood by reputable traffic or industry, and attained to opulence; others were adventurers, more unscrupulous as to the means by which they obtained their subsistence. The heathen could not but look with something of the interest excited by wonder on this strange, unsocial, and isolated people, who dwelt among them and yet were not of them. While the philosopher despised the fanaticism which he could not comprehend, the populace mingled something like awe with their dislike. The worse and more destitute of the race probably availed themselves of this feeling; many, half impostors and half enthusiasts, gained their livelihood by working on the superstitious terrors of the people, who were never more open to deception than in this age of comparative advancement. The empire swarmed with Jewish wonder-workers, mathematicians, astrologers, or whatever other name or office they assumed or received from their trembling hearers.[m]

Yet, in some points, all of Hebrew blood, rich and poor, high and low, concurred, in their faithful attachment to their synagogue, their strict subordination to their religious teachers, and through their synagogue and teachers to the great spiritual head of their commu-

---

[1] i. e. Escalone from Ascalon, Toledo from Toledoth, " the Generations," &c.

[m] "Qualiacunque voles Judæi somnia vendunt."—Juv. vi. 547.

nity, the Patriarch of Tiberias. While the Temple stood, these scattered settlements of the Jews were colonies of a nation; after its fall, they became independent communities, yet held together by their unchangeable usages, by the worship in the synagogues, by the Law and the interpreters of the Law (the Rabbins), by their schools of learning, by aversion, not without ground, for the idolatries and vices, as well as the hatred, of the heathen.[n]   Wherever Jews resided, a

---

[n] Among the tracts in the Mischna, one of the most historically curious and instructive is the Avoda Sara on foreign worship. It is directed exclusively against idolatry, and manifestly belongs to a period when Heathenism, not Christianity, was the enemy and antagonist of Judaism. It is the Law of a people dwelling among, and in constant intercourse with, idolaters. Three entire days before the great festivals of the heathen, and three after, it was prohibited to Israelites to have commerce, either of buying or selling, lending or borrowing with them, lest the Jew should contribute to the worship of false gods. The great festivals were the Calends, the Saturnalia, the commemoration of conquests, the days of the inauguration of the birth and of the death of the Emperor. All funeral pomp, of burning, or apotheosis, was idolatrous; where this did not take place it was not idolatrous. It was prohibited to have intercourse with the heathen on days of private worship, as when a man began to shave his beard to commemorate his escape from shipwreck or from prison. If a city celebrated a festival, the Jew might have intercourse with the heathen in the suburbs, and there only; if the suburbs, only in the city. Certain things might not be sold to idolaters—citrons, large white and some other kinds of figs, frankincense, white fowls (if these were sold, the sellers were to cut off a claw, as the heathen would not offer mutilated victims); neither bears nor lions, nor any hurtful things, arms, or military engines, chains, or fetters. They were not to aid in building basilicas or scaffolds for execution, neither circuses nor theatres; as to baths, not the niches or shrines which contained images; neither to work ornaments for idols, such as chains, earrings, rings. (But R. Elieser said these might be sold, if a fair price were paid!) They might not let houses or fields to the heathen in Judæa; in Syria or elsewhere they might. No Jewish woman might remain alone with an idolater. They might buy medicines of the heathen, but not allow idolaters to mix up medicines for them. These are but a few of the subtle provisions which went into the most minute questions of food, the use of the same vessels and furniture, even of personal contact. The Jew might drink milk if he saw it drawn by a pagan (he must see it, lest the animal should be

synagogue might be, and usually was, formed. Every synagogue was visited in turn by the Legate of the Patriarch. These legates were called apostles. The office probably existed before the fall of Jerusalem. The apostles collected the contributions for the Temple. They had authority to regulate all differences which might arise, and to receive the revenue of the Patriarch. Every year a proclamation was made by sound of trumpet in every synagogue, commanding the payment of the tribute: its final day of settlement was on the last of May. On the return of these legates they informed the Patriarch of the state of the synagogues, assisted him as counsellors, and held a distinguished rank among the people. The early Christians accuse the Jews of having sent messengers throughout the world, for the purpose of anathematizing them in their synagogues, and uttering a solemn curse upon the name of Jesus Christ. It is by no means unlikely that these ordinary legates received instructions to warn all the faithful Israelites against this detested innovation, and to counteract by every means in their power the progress

---

unclean). He might not sit under the shade of a tree worshipped by an idolater ; trees by the public wayside did not make unclean ; wood might not be used cut from a sacred tree unless the tree had been profaned. There were certain rules by which a pagan was considered to have rendered even an idol profane. If *he sold or purchased it, it became profane.* I conclude this brief summary of these singular provisions with this story:—The senators of Rome asked the Jews, " If God, the one true God as you assert, is not within those things which we worship as idols, why does he not utterly destroy them ? "

" No doubt," answered the Jews, " he would so destroy them, if they were things of which the world has no great need. But idolaters worship the sun, the moon, and the stars. Were it just that, on account of fools, God should make desolate the world ?" They rejoined, " But why does he not destroy those things of which we make idols, which the world needs not ? " The Jews answered, " The idolaters would only be confirmed in their superstition ; they would say there must be divinity in those things left for our worship, all other things being destroyed."

of the new religion. No doubt the rapid growth of
Christianity tended to strengthen the power of the synagogue, by constantly keeping alive the vigilance, and
inflaming the zeal, of the more stedfast and ardent
adherents to the Law. Indeed the point which miti-
gates, more than any other, our compassion for the
sufferings of the Jews, is the readiness with which they
joined the heathen in the persecution of the Christians.
Too often the Jews, though themselves eating the bitter
bread of slavery, and instructed in the best school for
the humaner feelings, adversity, were seen rejoicing by
the stake of the expiring Christian. In the beautiful
description of the death of Polycarp, there is a frightful
incident of the Jews shouting for the execution, and
busy in keeping the wood around the body of the holy
martyr.[o]

The worship of the synagogue, with its appendant
school or law court, where lectures were given, and
knotty points of the Law debated, became the great bond
of national union, and has continued, though the monarchical centre of unity in Tiberias disappeared in a few
centuries, to hold together the scattered nation in the
closest uniformity.[p] The worship of the synagogue is
extremely simple.[q] Wherever ten Jews were found,
there a synagogue ought to be formed. The Divine

---

[o] Polycarp. Martyr. c. xii. xiii. et
seqq. There is a curious passage in
the account of the martyrs of Palestine, by Eusebius, recently discovered
in Syriac, and translated by Dr.
Cureton. It describes the Jews of
Lydda (Diospolis), when witnessing
several martyrdoms of Christians, surprised to hear the Christians, being
Egyptians, called by Jewish names,

Elias, Jeremiah, Isaiah, Daniel. One
of the martyrs prayed for the Jews
and Samaritans who stood around.
Cureton, pp. 37, 38.

[p] This is chiefly compiled from
Lightfoot, Vitringa de Syn. Vet.,
Jost, and other authorities.

[q] On the Liturgies or forms of
prayer, read Jost, i. 173 et seqq.

Presence, the invisible Shechinah, descends not but where ten are met together; if fewer, the Divine Visitant was supposed to say, "Wherefore come I, and no one is here?" It was a custom, therefore, in some of the more numerous communities, to appoint ten "men of leisure," whose business it was to form a congregation.[r] The buildings were plain; in their days of freedom it was thought right that the house of prayer to God, from its situation or its form, should overtop the common dwellings of man; but in their days of humiliation, in strange countries, the lowly synagogue, the type of their condition, was content to lurk undisturbed in less conspicuous situations.[s] Even in Palestine the synagogues must have been small, for Jerusalem was said to contain 460 or 480; the foreign Jews, from the different quarters of the world, seem each to have had their separate building, where they communicated in prayer with their neighbours and kindred. Such were the synagogues of the Alexandrians, the Cyrenians, and others. Besides the regular synagogues, which were roofed, in some places they had chapels or oratories open to the air, chiefly perhaps where their worship was not so secure of protection from the authorities; these were usually in retired and picturesque situations, in groves, or on the seashore. In the distribution of the synagogue, some remote resemblance to the fallen Temple was kept up. The entrance was from the east: in the centre stood an elevated tribune or rostrum, in the place of the great altar, where prayer, the only permitted sacrifice, and if from an humble and contrite

---

[r] Such seems the simple solution of a question on which learned volumes have been written.

[s] We shall see hereafter that in their days of splendour in the Spanish peninsula, and perhaps in some other countries, they aspired to higher architectural grandeur.

heart, doubtless most acceptable to their Almighty Father, was constantly offered, and the Book of the Law was read. At the west end stood a chest, in which the Book was laid up, making the place, as it were, an humble Holy of Holies, though now no longer separated by a veil, nor protected by the Cherubim and Mercy Seat. Particular seats, usually galleries, were railed off for the women.

The chief religious functionary in the synagogue was called the angel, or bishop. He ascended the tribune, repeated or chanted the prayers, his head during the ceremony being covered with a veil. He called the reader from his place, opened the book before him, pointed out the passage, and overlooked him that he read correctly. The readers, who were three in number on the ordinary days, seven on the morning of the Sabbath, five on festivals, were selected from the body of the people. The Law of course was read, and the prayers likewise repeated, in the Hebrew language.[t] The days of public worship in the synagogue were the Sabbath,[u] the second and fifth days of the week, Monday and Thursday. There was an officer in the synagogues

---

[t] In the earlier times there can be no doubt that the version of the LXX. was read in the Greek or Hellenist synagogues (Basnage, viii. 1). But the gradual withdrawal of the Jews within themselves, the disputes with the Christians, who almost invariably cited the LXX. (read Justin Martyr against Trypho), first limited this usage, as the Gemara states, to the five Books of the Law, afterwards proscribed it ; and the old adage, "he who teaches his son Greek, is as he who eats swineflesh," became an orthodox maxim. The Hellenists from a respectable class of brethren became an odious sect. But the later Jews were too wise rigidly to confine their prayers, however they might keep their Scriptures in their inviolable sanctity, to a learned language.

[u] For the thirty-nine things forbidden on the Sabbath, see Jost, Judenthum, i. 178. They were chiefly works of husbandry, sowing, ploughing, reaping, &c. ; of handicrafts, spinning, weaving, &c. ; hunting, killing game, &c. ; writing two letters, or effacing them to write them again ; building ; putting out or lighting fires. To these

out of Palestine, and probably even within its borders, called an interpreter, who translated the Law into the vernacular tongue, usually Greek in the first case, or Syro-Chaldaic in the latter. Besides the bishop, there were three elders, or rulers, of the synagogue, who likewise formed a court or consistory for the judgement of all offences. They had the power of inflicting punishment by scourging;[v] from Origen's account, the Patriarch of Tiberias had assumed the power of life and death. But the great control over the public mind lay in the awful sentence of excommunication. The anathema of the synagogue cut off the offender from the Israel of God; he became an outcast of society. The first process, usually, was the censure; the name and the offence of the delinquent were read for four succeeding Sabbaths, during which he had time to make his peace with the congregation. At the end of that period the solemn Niddui, or interdict, was pronounced with the sound of trumpets,[w] which for thirty days separated the criminal from the hopes and privileges of Israel. For more heinous offences, and against contumacious delinquents, the more terrific Cherem, or the still more fatal Shammata, the excommunication, was proclaimed. The Cherem inflicted civil death, but, on due repentance and reparation for the crime, the same authority which

---

prohibitions the *wise* added many others: playing with nuts or almonds, climbing, riding, or whatever gave cause for forbidden work.

[v] The scourging with forty stripes save one was long in the power of the synagogue. "Has any Montanist," demands the orthodox writer against the Montanists (Euseb. v. 16), "ever been scourged or stoned in the synagogue of the Jews?" The adventurer Acosta, in the seventeenth century, describes his own scourging in Amsterdam. Bayle, Acostæ.

[w] Compare Vitringa on the blowing of trumpets at the time of excommunication, i. 204; on the general subject, p. 743 et seqq.; Eisenmenger, i. 119.

denounced, might repeal the Cherem—the absolved offender was restored to life. But no power could cancel the irrevocable Shammata. Some indeed have doubted whether the last sentence was ever pronounced, or even was known to the Law.[1] Prudence would certainly have advised the disuse of a practice which might drive the desperate offender to seek that consolation in another faith which was irrevocably denied him in his own: the Church would have opened its gates to receive him who was doomed to perpetual exile from the Synagogue. The sentence of excommunication was couched in the most fearful phrases. The delinquent was excommunicated, anathematized, accursed—by the Book of the Law, by the ninety-three precepts, by the malediction of Joshua against Jericho, by that of Elisha against the children who mocked him, and so on through all the terrific threatenings of the ancient law and history. He was accursed by the mysterious names of certain spirits of deadly power. He was accursed by heaven and earth, by the Seraphin, and by the heavenly orbs. "Let nothing good come out of him, let his end be sudden, let all creatures become his enemies, let the whirlwind crush him, the fever and every other malady and the edge of the sword smite him, let his death be unforeseen, and drive him into outer darkness." Excommunication, as we have said, inflicted a civil death; how far, at least in the milder form, it excluded from the synagogue, seems not quite clear. But no one, except his wife and children, might approach the moral leper—all others must avoid him the distance of a toise. If there were a dead body in his house, no one might inter it; if a child were born, the father must circumcise it. Public

---

[1] Vitringa questions the use of the Shammata.

detestation was not appeased by death. No one mourned him who died excommunicated; his coffin was stoned, and a heavy slab was placed over his remains by the hands of justice, either as a mark of infamy, or to prevent him from rising again at the last day. No doubt these spiritual terrors were often abused by the domineering Rabbi; but it is as little to be questioned that they exercised a high moral influence. The excommunication smote the adulterer, or the unnatural father, who, in their striking language, more cruel than the ravens, neglected the children whom God had given.

The influence of the Rabbins was not grounded on the public services of religion alone. The whole course of education was committed to their care, or at least to their superintendence.[y] In all those interesting epochs of domestic life in which the heart is most open to impressions of reverence and attachment, the Rabbi, even where the ancient Levite had no office, had made himself an indispensable part of the ceremony. When the house rejoiced in the birth of a man child, though circumcision was not necessarily performed in the syna-

---

[y] The following is considered the authorized course of Jewish education. As soon as the children can speak, they are taught certain religious axioms; from three or four to six or seven they learn their letters; at that age they go to school, and are taught to read the Pentateuch; at ten they commence the Mischna; at thirteen and one day they are considered responsible, and are bound to keep the 613 precepts of the Law; at fifteen they study the Gemara, i. e., the Talmud; at eighteen they marry; at twenty they enter into business.

"Filius quinque annorum ad Biblia. Filius decem annorum ad Mischna. Filius tredecim annorum ad præcepta. Filius quindecim annorum ad Talmud. Filius decem et octo annorum ad nuptias. Filius viginti annorum ad sectandum (divitias). Filius triginta annorum ad robur. Filius quadraginta annorum ad prudentiam. Filius quinquaginta annorum ad consilium. Filius sexaginta annorum ad senectutem. Filius septuaginta annorum ad canitiem. Filius nonaginta annorum ad foveam. Filius centum annorum (reputatus est) quasi mortuus sit, et transierit ex hoc mundo." Mischna, Capita Patrum, iv. p. 481

gogue, nor was the operator usually of that order, yet
ill-omened and unblest was the eighth-day feast which
was not graced by the presence of a Rabbi. In marriages the Rabbi joined the hands, pledged the cup, and
pronounced the seven prayers of benediction over the
wedded pair. The Rabbi attended the sick man, and consoled him with the assurance of the certain resurrection
of all faithful Israelites to their exclusive Paradise, and
he was present at the interment of the dead. Nor was
this all: by degrees the whole life of the Jew was vo-
luntarily enslaved to more than Brahminical or monkish
minuteness of observance. Every day, and every hour
of the day, and every act of every hour, had its appointed
regulations, grounded on distorted texts of Scripture, or
the sentences of the Wise Men, and artfully moulded up
with their national reminiscences of the past or their distinctive hopes of the future,—the divine origin of the
Law, the privileges of God's chosen people, the restoration
to the Holy City, the coming of the Messiah. The Jew
with his early prayer was to prevent the rising sun, but
more blessed he who encroached upon the night to
lament, before the dawn, the fate of Jerusalem.[a] His
rising from his bed, his manner of putting on the different articles of dress, the disposition of his fringed
tallith, his phylacteries on his head and arms, his ablutions, his meals, even the calls of nature were subjected
to scrupulous rules—both reminding him that he was of
a peculiar race, and perpetually reducing him to ask the
advice of the Wise Men, which alone could set at rest the

---

[a] It was ruled, and there is something deeply pathetic in the rule,
"that the Jew should rise early in
the morning; his first thoughts and
prayers should be on the desolation
and restoration of Jerusalem. God
hears the prayers of those who rise by
night to weep for Jerusalem." Bux-
torf, De Synagoga.

trembling and scrupulous conscience. Nor was it enough
that the all-seeing eye of God watched with jealous
vigilance the minutest acts of His Chosen.   Rabbinical
authority peopled the air with spirits of beneficent or
malign aspect: the former might be revolted by the
least uncleanness, the latter were ever ready to take advantage of every delinquency. The Wise Men alone were
well acquainted with the nature, the orders, the powers,
or the arts of these mysterious beings; and thus a new
and unbounded field was opened for their interference.
Such was the character of the Rabbinical dominion as it
was gradually, though perhaps not as yet perfectly,
developed.   The Rabbins slowly withdrew into a
spiritual order; they stood aloof from the worldlings
(the Amhaarez); they avoided all familiar intercourse
with them, they would not degrade themselves to inter-
marriage with them ; they expected to be treated with
reverence, would hardly return the common salutation.[a]
Such (for this dominion now assumed a monarchical form)
was the kingdom of the Patriarch of Tiberias, in its
boundaries as extensive as that of Rome, and founded
on the strongest basis, the blind and zealous attachment
of its subjects.[b]

Before long the Sanhedrin of that city began to
assume a loftier tone; their edicts were dated as from
Jerusalem, their school was called Sion.[c] But into
this spiritual court, as into that of more splendid and
worldly sovereigns, ambition and intrigue soon found
their way. The monarch could not brook any constitutional limitation to his state or authority ; the subordinate officers, the aristocracy of this singular republic, were

---

[a] Jost, iv. 133, gives several pages
of instances of their haughtiness, to
which R. Jehuda was not superior.

[b] Jost, iv. 75.

[c] Chiefly from Jost, Geschichte des
Israeliter, with his authorities.

eager to usurp the rights of the throne. The first collision
was on the all-important point of etiquette. No sooner
was Simon, son of Gamaliel, quietly seated in the Patriarchate, than he began to assert or enlarge his prero-
gative. His Ab-beth-din, R. Nathan, and his Hachim, R.
Meir, enjoyed a larger share of his state than he was
willing to concede. When any one of these heads of
the spiritual senate entered, the whole assembly was
accustomed to rise, and to remain standing till he was
seated. This equality of respect was galling to the
pride of Simon; he determined to vindicate the superior
dignity of his chair, and took an opportunity of moving,
in the absence of the parties concerned, that the whole
assembly should rise only on the entrance of the
Patriarch, on that of the Ab-beth-din two rows, on
that of the Hachim only one. The next time that R.
Nathan and R. Meir made their appearance, this order
was observed. The degrading innovation went to their
hearts. They dissembled their resentment, but entered
into a secret conspiracy to dethrone or to humiliate the
unconstitutional despot. "He," said R. Meir, "who
cannot answer every question which relates to the Word
of God, is not worthy to preside in the great Sanhedrin.
Let us expose his ignorance, and so compel him to
abdicate. Then you shall be Patriarch, and I your
Ab-beth-din." In secret council they framed the most
intricate and perplexing questions to confound the
despot. Happily for him, their conversation was overheard by a learned and friendly member of the Sanhedrin, who began to discuss in a loud tone, so as to be
heard by Simon in the neighbouring chamber, the points
on which it was agreed to attack and perplex the overbearing Patriarch. At the next sitting, the rebels,
Nathan and Meir, advanced to the charge with their

formidable host of difficulties.   To their confusion, Simon, forewarned, repulsed them on all points, and unravelled, with the utmost readiness, the most intricate questions.   Simon triumphed, the rebellious Ab-beth-din and Hachim were expelled from the Sanhedrin. But still they kept up the war, and daily assailed the Patriarch with a new train of difficulties, for which they required written answers.   At length the civil contest ended, through the intervention of the more moderate. The ex-Ab-beth-din and ex-Hachim were reinstated; but, on the momentous point whether the whole San-hedrin rose on their entrance, or only two rows, I deeply regret that I must leave the reader in the same lamentable ignorance with myself.

Not content, or rather flushed with this advance towards unlimited monarchy in his own dominions, the high-minded Simon began to meditate schemes of foreign conquest.[d]   The independence or equality of the head of the Babylonian community haunted him, as that of the Patriarch of Constantinople did the early Popes; and a cause of quarrel, curiously similar to that about the time on which Easter was to be kept, speedily arose.   The schools of Babylonia and Palestine fell into an open schism concerning the calculation of the day for the Paschal feast.   Simon determined to assert the superiority of the Patriarchate of Tiberias over his dis-obedient brethren.   The scene is in the highest degree characteristic.   It must, however, be premised, that it is by no means certain at what time the Princes of the Captivity commenced their dynasty.   In the following story, Ahia appears as the head of the community; but

---

[d] Jost, Geschichte der Israeliter, iv. 59 et seqq., with Talmudic authori-ties. Compare Judenthum, ii. p. 168 et seqq.

probably the Prince had not yet obtained the influence, or assumed the state, which, during the first fifty years of the third century, distinguished the Jewish sovereign of the East. Hananiah, who taught at Nahar-pakod, and Judah ben Bethuriah, were the most eminent of the learned teachers in the schools of Babylon; and to humble their pride and bring them into subordination to the seat of learning in Tiberias, was the great object of the mission which was despatched by the Patriarch. The two legates were furnished with three letters. They delivered the first to Hananiah, which bore the superscription, "To your Holiness." Delighted with their recognition of a title considered of high importance, Hananiah courteously inquired the reason of their coming,—"To learn your system of instruction." Still more flattered, Hananiah received the ambassadors with the utmost cordiality, and commended them to the people, as worthy of every honour, both as descendants of the high priest (for the Patriarch of Tiberias claimed his lineage from Aaron) and for their own personal merit. When the treacherous legates had secured their ground in the good opinion of the people, they began to controvert the judgements of Hananiah, to animadvert on his opinions, and to lessen him by every means in the public estimation. Hananiah, enraged at this abuse of his kindness, summoned a second assembly of the people, and denounced the legates as traitors and ignorant men. The people replied, "That which thou hast built, thou canst not so soon pull down; the hedge which thou hast planted, thou canst not pluck up without injury to thyself." Hananiah demanded their objections to his system of instruction. They answered, "Thou hast dared to fix intercalations and new moons, by which great inconformities have arisen between the brethren in Babylonia and Palestine." "So did Rabbi Akiba," said Hananiah, "when in Babylon." "Akiba," they rejoined, "left not his like in Palestine." "Neither," cried the desperate Rabbi, "have I left my equal in Palestine." The legates produced their second letter, which ran in these mysterious words : "That which thou leftest a kid, is grown up a strong-horned goat ;" it meant that the Sanhedrin, which he left without power, had regained all its authority. Hananiah was struck dumb. R. Isaac, one of the deputies, saw his time : he mounted the tribune, from which the Law was usually read. "These," he said, naming them, "are the holy days of God—these the holy days of Hananiah !" An indistinct murmur ran through the synagogue. R. Nathan, the second deputy, arose and read the verse of Isaiah, "Out of Sion goeth forth the Law, and the Word of God from Jerusalem." Then, with a bitter intonation, "Out of Babylon goeth forth the Law, the Word of God from Nahar-pakod !" The assembly was in an uproar. "Alter not the Word of God," was the universal cry. The legates followed up their advantage and produced their third letter, which threatened excommunication against the factious opponents of their authority. They added these emphatic words :—"The *learned* have sent us, and commanded us thus to say : 'If he will submit, well ; if not, utter at once the interdict. So likewise set the choice before our brethren in foreign parts. If they will stand by us, well ; if not, let them ascend their high places ; let Ahia build them an altar, and Hananiah [he was of Levitical descent] sing at the sacrifice ; and let them at once set themselves apart and say, We have no portion in the Israel of God.'" From all sides an instantaneous cry arose, "Heaven preserve us from heresy ! We have still a portion in the Israel of

God." The authority of the Sanhedrin in Tiberias was universally recognized. Judah ben Bethuriah, as well as Hananiah, was forced to bow to the yoke; and till the political separation of the Babylonian from the Western Jews, on the restoration of the Persian monarchy (for the province had now been again brought under the Roman dominion by the conquests of Verus), the Patriarch of Tiberias maintained his uncontested supremacy over the whole Jewish commonalty. In the preceding history, both in the object and the manner in which it was conducted, we are almost tempted to inquire whether it is not a scene borrowed from the annals of the Papal Church.

But before we describe the re-establishment of the Resch-Glutha, or Prince of the Captivity, in all the state and splendour of an Oriental sovereign, far outshining, at least in pomp, his rival sovereign in Tiberias, we return to the West to trace the history of the Palestinian Jews, as connected with that of their Roman masters.[*] During all the later conflicts with Rome, the Samaritans had escaped by quiet submission the miseries which had so perpetually fallen on their more unruly brethren; they had obtained the rights of Roman citizenship for their fidelity. During the first establishment of the Rabbinical dominion at Tiberias, its chiefs had displayed an unprecedented degree of liberality towards their once detested neighbours. Though they sarcastically denominated them "the proselytes of the lions," yet they would inhabit the same city, sleep in the same house, eat at the same table, and even partake of animals which they had killed This unusual mildness rested on the authority of R. Akiba, and seems to strengthen the suspicion that it

---

[*] Jost, iv. p. 79 et seqq.

was grounded on policy, and that the enterprising Rabbi had laid a deliberate scheme of uniting in one league all who claimed Jewish descent. But this amity between the two hostile sects was but transient. One Rabbi declared it was better to use water for an offering than Samaritan wine. Another, in their own city, openly accused them of worshipping idols on Gerizim; he hardly escaped with his life. Political circumstances increased the jealousies, which at last broke out into open hostilities; and opportunities occurred in which they might commit mutual acts of violence, without the interference of the ruling powers.

In one of the great contests for the empire, they espoused opposite parties. The Samaritans, unfortunately for themselves, were on the losing side. Pescennius Niger had assumed the purple in Syria. The Jews presented a petition for the reduction of their taxation. "Ye demand," said the stern Roman, "exemption from tribute for your soil—I will lay it on the air you breathe."[f] The Samaritans took up arms for Niger, the Jews threw themselves into the party of Severus. That able general soon triumphed over all opposition, and severely punished the partisans of his rival: the Samaritans forfeited their privilege of Roman citizenship. The presence of the Emperor overawed the conflicting factions, though Severus himself was in great danger from a daring robber of the country, named Claudius, who boldly rode into his camp, saluted and embraced him, and, before orders could be given for his seizure, had escaped.[g] Severus celebrated a Jewish triumph, probably on account of the general pacification of the province. His laws were favourable to the Jews.

---

[f] Spartian, Pescennius Niger, H. A. S., p. 377; Eusebii Chronicon, ccii.
[g] Spartiani d. Severus.

The edict of Antoninus was re-enacted, though still with its limitation against circumcising proselytes.[h] The Jews were permitted to undertake the tutelage of pagans, which shows that they had still the privileges of Roman citizenship, and they were exempt from burthens incompatible with their religion. Still they were interdicted from approaching the walls of the Holy City, and their general condition is thus described by Tertullian, who wrote during the reign of Severus: "Dispersed and vagabond, exiled from their native soil and air, they wander over the face of the earth, without a king, either human or divine; and even as strangers, they are not permitted to salute with their footsteps their native land."[i]

The Jews and Christians contest the honour of having furnished a nurse to the fratricide son of Severus, Caracalla.[j] If this tyrant indeed sucked the milk of Christian gentleness, his savage disposition turned it to gall.[k] According to the Rabbinical legends, he was so

---

[h] "Judæos fieri vetuit."

[i] Tertullian, Apologet. xxii. Tertullian, it must be remembered, writes as an orator, not as a historian.

[j] Jost, in his Geschichte der Israeliten seit der Zeit der Maccabäer, conceives that the strange stories in the Jewish writers, about the intercourse between one of the Antonines (most assert the first, the Pious) and the head of the Sanhedrin of Tiberias, and his secret Judaism, are grounded on this tale of Caracalla. I take the opportunity of expressing my obligation to this work, which has been of the greatest use in the composition of this last volume of my History. I differ from Jost, who is a pupil of Eichhorn, on many points, particu-

larly on the composition of the older Scriptures, but I gladly bear testimony to the high value of his work, which, both in depth of research and arrangement, is far superior to the desultory, and by no means trustworthy, volumes of Basnage. (*Note in former editions.*) The later book of Jost (Geschichte des Judenthums) is the more mature work of an indefatigable and eminently fair writer. Of course, as a Jew, he presents the doctrines and usages of his race in a favourable light, but he always fully deserves a respectful and candid hearing.

[k] The Jews confounded the best and first with the last and worst of the Antonines. Lightfoot and Selden were misled by David Ganz. The chrono-

attached to his Jewish playmates, as to have shed tears when one of them was whipped by order of the Emperor. Indeed for several reigns Judaism might boast its influence on the Imperial throne. Among the strange medley of foreign superstitions with which the filthy Heliogabalus offended even the easy and tolerant religion of his Roman subjects, he adopted the Jewish usages of circumcision and abstinence from swine's flesh.[l] And, in the reign of the good Alexander Severus, that beautiful oasis in the desert of this period of the Imperial history, the Jews enjoyed the equal protection and the favour of the virtuous sovereign. Abraham, as well as Christ, had his place in the Emperor's gallery of divinities, or men worthy of divine honours. Alexander was even called the Father of the Synagogue.[m]

In the mean time, the Patriarchal throne had been ascended by the most celebrated of the Rabbinical sovereigns. Jehuda, sometimes called the Nasi or Patriarch, sometimes the Holy, sometimes emphatically the Rabbi, succeeded his father, Simon, son of Gamaliel. Jehuda is said to have been born on the day on which R. Akiba died; an event predicted, according to his admirers, in the verse of Solomon—"*One sun ariseth and one sun goeth down.*" Akiba was the setting— Jehuda the dawning sun. He was secretly circumcised, in defiance of the law of Hadrian. His whole life was of the most spotless purity; hence he was called the Holy, or the Holiest of the Holy. R. Jehuda was the

logy makes any intercourse between Antoninus Pius and Jehuda the Holy impossible. See also Basnage, who gives, as said above, all the stories about Antoninus Pius, viii. p. 3.

Dion Cassius, lxxix. 11.

"Dicebat præterea Judæorum et

Samaritanorum religiones, et Christianam devotionem illuc transferendam ut omnium culturarum secretum Heliogabali sacerdotium teneret." Lamprid. Heliogab., H. A. S., p. 462.

[m] Lamprid. Alexander Severus, H A. S., p. 540.

author of a new constitution to the Jewish people. He embodied in the celebrated Mischna, or Code of Traditional Law, all the authorized interpretations of the Mosaic Law, the traditions, the decisions of the learned, and the precedents of the Courts or Schools.[n] It is singular that this period is distinguished by the labours of the great Roman lawyers in the formation of a Code of Jurisprudence for the whole empire. It might seem as if the Jews, constituting thus, as it were, an *imperium in imperio*, a state within a state, were ambitious of providing themselves with their own Pandects, either in emulation of their masters, or lest their subjects might discover the superior advantage of a written code over the arbitrary decisions of the Rabbinical interpreters of their original polity.[o] The sources from which the Mischna was derived, may give a fair view of the nature of the Rabbinical authority, and the manner in which it had superseded the original Mosaic Constitution. The Mischna was grounded, 1. On the Written Law of Moses. 2. On the Oral Law, received

---

[n] "From Moses, our Teacher, to our Holy Rabbi, no one had united in a single body of doctrine what was publicly taught as the Oral Law; but in each generation the Prince of the Sanhedrin, or the Prophet of his day, notes down in writing for his own use, and as an aid to his memory, the traditions which he had heard from his teachers; but in public he taught them only orally. In the same manner each transcribed that which best pleased him in the Commentaries and Expositions of the Law. As for those points on which changes took place as regards the judicial forms, they were derived rather from reason than tradition, and depended on the authority of the great Consistory. Such was the form of proceeding until our Rabbi the Holy (Jehuda), who first collected all the traditions, the judgements, the sentences, the expositions of the Law, heard by Moses our Master, and taught in each generation." Moses Maimonides, Preface to Mischna. The Mischna is derived from the Hebrew שָׁנָה, the repetition; in Greek δευτέρωσις.

[o] The Mischna was accepted in Babylonia as of equal authority with that which it had acquired in Palestine. It is the foundation of the Babylonian as of the Jerusalem Talmud.

by Moses on Mount Sinai; and handed down, it was
said, by uninterrupted tradition. 3. The decisions or
maxims of the Wise Men.[p] 4. Opinions of particular
individuals, on which the schools were divided, and
which still remained open. 5. Ancient usages and
customs. The distribution of the Mischna affords a
curious exemplification of the intimate manner in which
the religious and civil duties of the Jews were inter-
woven, and of the authority assumed by the Law over
every transaction of life.[q] The Mischna commenced
with rules for prayer, thanksgiving, ablutions; it is
impossible to conceive the minuteness or subtlety of
these rules, and the fine distinctions drawn by the
Rabbins. It was a question whether a man who ate
figs, grapes, and pomegranates, was to say one or three
graces (p. 23). The schools of Shammai and Hillel
differed on the points, whether the believer having
washed his hands, he should put the napkin on the
table, or on a cushion; whether he should sweep the
house and then wash his hands, or wash his hands and
then sweep the house (29). But there are nobler words.
"These are the things of which man has the usufruct
in this life, the reward in the life to come: honour
rendered to father and mother; beneficence; the propagation of peace among men. But the doctrine of the
Law is like all these." Against the tithing of "mint,

---

[p] Jost acknowledges that, excepting a few sayings ascribed to the pre-
Asmonean times, there is nothing older
in the Mischna than the age of Herod:
"Die in diese Werk niedergelegten
Lehrsätze reichen nicht über das He-
rodaische Zeitalter heraus, einige wenige
Sätze ausgenommen, die den vor-He-
rodaischen Lehrern zugeschrieben werden." iv. 105.

[q] The Mischna was published by
Surenhusius (Amsterdam, 1698) in
excellent print and with acknowledged
accuracy. It contains the Mischna,
with the commentaries of Bartenora
and Moses Maimonides, and notes by
Guisius, Surenhusius himself, and
other modern Hebraists.

anise, and cummin," may be set the rigid and generous provisions by which the corner of the field is set apart for the poor (De Angulo). There is a whole book (De Heterogeneis) as to what things may be sown together, or mingled together, and what may not; the strictest rules about the divisions in fields and gardens; the most ordinary, and what might seem the most unimportant, questions of cultivation are subject to the severest regulations, and are controverted between the schools. There is one on the Sabbatarian year, as if still rigidly observed by the cultivators of the soil, which it presumes that the Jews will for ever continue to be. The second book, which treats on the Sabbath, the festivals, and fasts, displays the whole religious life of the Jew. On the Sabbath, of course, there are the most precise and rigorous definitions of the innocence and guilt of every act, almost of every thought. This is characteristic of the tenet and of the people. If on the Sabbath one extinguishes a light from fear of the Gentiles, or of robbers, or on account of an evil spirit, or on account of a sick man who is asleep, he is guiltless; if he does it to save his oil or his candle, he is guilty (i p. 13). Throughout, as in all priest-ridden races (for the Rabbins were essentially a priesthood), there was the same strange admixture of the loftiest piety with the lowest superstition; there are solemn and imposing rites preserving the sacred memory of the wonderful events in their history, hedged round with the most puerile and servile provisions. The history of the Mosaic Law, intricate enough, as perhaps was necessary to keep asunder a half-barbarous people, is woven into an inextricable network of decrees, which left nothing to the free and enlightened conscience, and therefore nothing ennobling or praiseworthy in man. God, from a

wise taskmaster, sank to a petty tyrant. In the third
book are the rules on marriage and divorce, on the
charge of idolatry, on vows and Nazaritism. The
Levirate law is treated as of perpetual obligation; the
learned, however, seem to have been disposed to mitigate
its force, and to multiply the causes which justified
either party in eluding it. The Mischna fully admits
polygamy. If a man leaves many wives, the Law
determines that one only can claim the Levirate
right.[r] The first of two wives takes precedence, and
her children inherit. Yet these are rare instances,
and the impression of the whole book is that the
usage of the Jews was monogamy. The fourth book
treats, I. of Injuries. It is remarkable that the injuries
or damages are almost exclusively those of an agricultural people; their chief causes are—*a*, wells, as, if left
open, dangerous to life or limb; *b*, the ox, as goring or
hurting man or beast; *c*, trespass of men or cattle
(De Pascuis); *d*, fire, as consuming standing crops.
II. The Treatise Sanhedrin is full of historical matter on
the origin and power of those courts. Smaller crimes
were adjudged by three, the greater by twenty-three, the
greatest by the whole seventy-one. Every Israelite has a
portion in the world to come, except those who deny the
resurrection of the dead, and the Epicureans. Three
kings and four private men have no share in eternal
life: Jeroboam, Ahab, Manasseh; Balaam, Ahitophel,
Doeg, Gehasi. This tract assumes the power of capital
punishment. This is of four kinds, stoning, burning,
slaying by the sword, strangling. There are rules for
each. The other punishments in this, and in the smaller

---

[r] "Si multas reliquerit mulieres
uni ex illis tantum imponetur extrac-
tio calcei aut leviratio." This is the
comment of Maimonides, fol. i. In the
law of marriage—"si quis duas duxerit
uxores, et mortuus est." **91-95.**

tract (De Pœnis), are exile, fine, flagellation. Two trea-
tises follow, on Oaths and on Witnesses. The fifth book
is on sacrifices, offerings, vows, and the measurements
of the Temple. It is remarkable only for the elaborate
minuteness of its provisions. Finally, the sixth is on the
somewhat difficult subject of uncleanness and ablution;
it is rigid and particular to the utmost repulsiveness.

As the object of this great work was to fix, once for
all, on undoubted authority, the whole Unwritten Law,
some of the more zealous Rabbins reprobated this
measure of Jehuda the Holy, as tending to supersede
or invalidate their own personal power. But the
multiplication of written statutes enlarges rather than
contracts the province of the lawyer; a new field was
opened for ingenuity, and comment was speedily heaped
upon the Mischna, till it was buried under the weight,
as the Mosaic Law had been before by the Mischna.
The interpreters of the Mischna assumed a particular
name, the Tanaim. In fact, the acknowledgment of
the Mischna as a sort of new constitution, powerfully
contributed to the maintenance of the Rabbinical authority after the fall of the Patriarchate and the extinction of the Schools. It threw back the Written Law
into a sort of reverential and mysterious obscurity.
Never was such honour paid to the Books of Moses as
by the Rabbins of Tiberias, or such labour employed in
their preservation: every letter was counted, every dot,
every iota sanctified, as perhaps of the deepest import.
But they were dark oracles, whose profound meaning
could not be caught by the vulgar ear; while from
the formal, and as it were constitutional, recognition of
the Unwritten Law, as embodied in the Mischna, it
became the popular and practical code, until the more
voluminous Talmud superseded, in its turn, the Mischna.

Those ponderous tomes were at once the religious and civil institutes of the Jewish people, and swayed the Jews with an uncontested authority, in like manner as the Acts of the Saints and the Canon-law the nations of Christian Europe.

In the mean time the rival throne in Babylonia, that of the Prince of the Captivity, was rapidly rising to the state and dignity which perhaps did not attain its perfect height till under the Persian monarchs. There seems to have been some acknowledged hereditary claim in R. Hona, who now appears as the Prince of the Captivity, as if his descent from the house of David had been recognised by the willing credulity of his brethren: at least, if any reliance is to be placed in a speech attributed to R. Jehuda, that if R. Hona were to make his appearance, he should do homage to him.[a] Such submission would not, it may be thought, have been extorted from the Patriarch of Tiberias, even from the modest and humble R. Jehuda, unless general opinion had invested the rival chieftain with some peculiar sanctity. The Prince of the Captivity might recall in his splendour, particularly during his inauguration, some lofty reminiscences of the great Jewish monarchy under the ancestors from whom he claimed his descent, the holy David and the magnificent Solomon, though affectingly mingled with allusions to the present state of degradation. The ceremonial of his installation is thus described. The spiritual Heads of the people, the Masters of the learned schools, the Elders, and the

---

[a] Another version of this story shows the Rabbi in not so humble a light. To the wish of R. Jehuda, the learned Haja replied, " He is here."—R. Jehuda turned pale.—" His corpse is here." It might seem that the feeling that all true Jews ought to be buried in the Holy Land extended to the chiefs of Babylonia. Jost, Judenthum, ii. 116.

people, assembled in great multitudes within a stately chamber, adorned with rich curtains, in Babylon, where, during his days of splendour, the Resch-Glutha fixed his residence. The Prince was seated on a lofty throne. The heads of the schools of Sura and Pumbeditha were on his right hand and his left. These chiefs of the learned men, having laid their hands upon the Prince, with the sound of trumpets and other music, then delivered an address, exhorting the new monarch not to abuse his power; he was called to slavery rather than to sovereignty, for he was prince of a captive people. On the next Thursday he was inaugurated by the laying-on of hands, and the sound of trumpets, and acclamations. He was escorted to his palace with great pomp, and received magnificent presents from all his subjects. On the Sabbath all the principal people assembled before his house, he placed himself at their head, and, his face covered with a silken veil, proceeded to the synagogue.[t] Benedictions and hymns of thanksgiving announced his entrance. They then brought him the Book of the Law, out of which he read the first line; afterwards he addressed the assembly, with his eyes closed out of respect. He exhorted them to charity, and he set the example by offering liberal alms to the poor. The ceremony closed with new acclamations and prayers to God that, under the new Prince, He would be pleased to put an end to their calamities. The Prince gave his blessing to the people, and prayed for each province

---

[t] There is a description of the installation of the Resch-Glutha in the Schevet Judah: "Die Jovis in sacram ædem frequenter conveniebant, ubi dum Academiæ rectores Principi manus suas imponerent, alii interea tubis, alii vero cornibus accinebant, cuncti autem bene ominantes festâ voce acclamabant, ‘Noster vivat Princeps vigeatque æternùm! Ille Princeps noster, ille exulum caput est, exulum caput est Israelitarum,’ &c., &c." p. 302.

that it might be preserved from war and famine. He
concluded his orisons in a low voice, lest his prayer
should be repeated to the jealous ears of the native
monarchs, for he prayed for the restoration of the
kingdom of Israel, which could not rise but on the
ruins of their empire. The Prince returned to his
palace, where he gave a splendid banquet to the chief
persons of the community. After that day he lived in
a sort of stately Oriental seclusion, never quitting his
palace except to go to the schools of the learned, where,
as he entered, the whole assembly rose, and continued
standing till he took his seat. He sometimes paid a
visit to the native Sovereign in Babylon (Bagdad).
This probably refers to a somewhat later period. On
these great occasions his imperial host sent his own
chariot for his guest; but the Prince of the Captivity
dared not accept the invidious distinction; he walked in
humble and submissive modesty behind the chariot.
Yet his own state was by no means wanting in splendour: he was arrayed in cloth of gold; fifty guards
marched before him ; all the Jews, who met him on the
way, paid their homage, and fell behind into his train.
He was received by the eunuchs, who conducted him to
the throne, while one of his officers, as he marched slowly
along, distributed gold and silver on all sides. As the
Prince approached the imperial throne, he prostrated himself on the ground, in token of vassalage. The eunuchs
raised him and placed him on the left hand of the Sovereign. After the first salutation, the Prince represented
the grievances or discussed the affairs of his people.

   The Court of the Resch-Glutha is described as equally
splendid ; in imitation of his Persian master, he had
his officers, counsellors, and cupbearers. Rabbins were
appointed as satraps over the different communities.

This state, it is probable, was maintained by a tribute raised from the body of the people, and substituted for that which, in ancient times, was paid for the Temple in Jerusalem.[u] His subjects in Babylonia were many of them wealthy. They were husbandmen, shepherds, and artizans. The Babylonian garments were still famous in the West, and probably great part of that lucrative manufacture was carried on by the Jews. Asinai and Asilai, it will be recollected, were weavers. It is said, indeed, in the usual figurative style, of a Jew merchant of Babylon, that he had 1000 vessels on the sea, and 1000 cities on land. They prided themselves on their learning as well as on their wealth. Though the Palestinian Jews affected to speak with contempt of Babylonian wisdom, yet in general estimation the schools of Nahardea, Sura, and Pumbeditha, might compete with Sepphoris and Tiberias.[x]

Whether the authority of the Prince of the Captivity extended beyond Babylonia and the adjacent districts is uncertain. The limits of Persia form an insuperable barrier to our knowledge, and almost all the rest of Asia, during this period, is covered, as it were, with impenetrable darkness. Many Jews were no doubt settled in Arabia. Mohammed found them both numerous and powerful, and a Jewish dynasty had long sat on one of the native thrones; but this subject will come

---

[u] Jost supposes that when the Jewish settlements passed under the Parthian and Persian dominion, the Jews continued to pay to their own Prince the Temple tribute, exacted from them by the Romans. iv. 267.

[x] Jost, both in his Israeliter and Judenthum, enlarges on the succession of famous Doctors who maintained the renown of the Babylonian Schools, their ambition to surpass the Resch-Glutha in power and influence, their internal jealousies and rivalries, and their rivalries with the Palestinean teachers. The Mischna was received and acknowledged as of equal authority in Nahardea and Pumbeditha as in Tiberias.

under our notice when we consider the influence of the
progress of Mohammedanism as connected with the
History of the Jews. All other accounts of Oriental Jews,
at this early period, are so obscure,[7] so entirely or so
nearly fabulous, that they may wisely be dismissed; but
there is one curious point, which, as it seems to rest on
better evidence, demands more particular notice, the
establishment of a Jewish colony in China, if not an-
terior, certainly immediately subsequent, to the time of
our Lord. This singular discovery was made known to
Europe by the Jesuit missionaries, but unfortunately
the Father Gozani, who had the best opportunity of obtaining accurate information both as to their history
and the manuscripts of the Law which they possessed,
was ignorant of the Hebrew language. It was inferred
from their tradition, in my opinion, somewhat hastily,
that Jews had been settled in the country 249 years
before the Christian Era. More authentic statements
fixed their introduction into the empire towards
the close of the reign of Mingti, of the dynasty of
Han, who reigned from 58 to 75 A.C. They were
originally 70 *sings*, or families, and settled in the cities
of Nimpo, Ninghin, Hamtcheu, Peking, and Caifong-
fou. Only seven remained in the middle of the seventeenth century, all in the latter city, the capital of
Honan. They came from Si-yu, the west country, and
their Hebrew language betrayed evident signs of corruption from the introduction of Persian words. They
could not have been of the earlier dispersion, for they

---

[7] That there were Parthian as well
as Elamite (Persian) and Mesopotamian Jews, is clear from the Acts of
the Apostles; the traditions of Christianity assert the early propagation of
the faith in those regions, which intimates, I am inclined to think, that
the Jews were numerous; but little
is known which is either distinct or
certain.

had the Book of Ezra, and highly reverenced his name.
They knew nothing, or at least had preserved no knowledge of Christ or his religion. They were employed in
agriculture and traffic. They had cultivated learning
with success, and some of them, as was attested by
extant inscriptions, had been highly honoured with the
imperial favour, and had attained the rank of Manda-
rins. One of these inscriptions, bearing date in 1515,
praises the Jews for their integrity and fidelity, in
agricultural pursuits, in traffic, in the magistracy, and
in the army, and their punctual observance of their
own religious ceremonies: it assures them of the Emperor's high esteem. They paid great respect to the
name of Confucius, and after the Chinese customs
preserved the memory of their fathers with religious
reverence, on tablets inscribed with their names. In
other respects they were strict Jews: they observed the
Sabbath, lighting no fire, and preparing their food on
the preceding day: they practised circumcision on the
eighth day: they intermarried only among themselves.
They believe (so writes the Jesuit) in Purgatory,
Hell, Paradise, the Resurrection, and the Last Judgement; in Angels, Cherubim and Seraphin. They neither make, nor attempt to make, proselytes. Their
sacred edifice (a remarkable fact) resembles much more
the Temple than the modern synagogue. It is situated
in an open space, among pavilions or avenues of trees.
It consists of a nave and two aisles; the centre is divided
into a Holy Place, and a Holy of Holies, which is square
without and circular within; here are deposited the
Books of the Law,[z] and the sacred chamber is entered

---

z Notice d'un Manuscrit du Penta-
teuque conservé dans la Synagogue des
Juifs de Cai-fong Fou. Notices et

Extraits des MS. de la Bibl. du Roi,
vol. iv

The learned Baron de Sacy has

only by the Chief Priest.   The Chief Priest is not distinguished by any splendour of apparel, only by a red belt of silk, which passes over his right and under his left shoulder.   They chant the sacred Scripture and

---

clearly shown that the existing copies of the sacred writings among the Chinese Jews, imperfect as they are, are not older than the year 1620 A.C. Their former sacred books had been destroyed, first by an inundation of the great Yellow River in 1446, afterwards by a fire about 1600, and lastly, those they possess were greatly damaged by a second inundation in 1642.

Compare J. de Guignes, Mémoires de l'Académie, t. xlviii. See also, in Trigaultii de Christianâ Expeditione apud Sinas, a curious account of an interview between a Chinese Jew and Father Ricci the Jesuit, p. 118. The Jew recognised the Hebrew characters in a printed Bible, but could not read them. The Jews, it was said, had ten or twelve families in Pekin, with a synagogue, which they had just repaired at the cost of 10,000 pieces of gold. They had the Pentateuch wrapt up and kept with great care; they had possessed it, they said, five or six hundred years. In Hamcheu, they said, they had many more Jews, with their synagogues. In other places in China they were dying out from want of synagogues.

In a memoir of Ignatius Kugler, reprinted by De Murr (Halæ ad Salam), it appears that the Chinese Jews called the Pentateuch the Canonical Book: but they had Esther, as well as Ezra, and the Book of the Maccabees. They had not Job, Proverbs, Canticles, or Ecclesiastes. They were said to

date from the Seleucidæ! (?)

See also an excellent memoir in Brotier's Notes on Tacitus.

Barrow conceived it possible that the Jews may have introduced silk into China. "Many of them, indeed, forsake the religion of their forefathers, and arrive at high employments in the State. Few among them, I understand, except the Rabbis, have any knowledge of the Hebrew language; and they have been so long intermingled with the Chinese, that the priests at the present day are said to find some difficulty in keeping up their congregations. So different are the effects produced by suffering instead of persecuting religious opinions." p. 438. Barrow concludes, from their knowing no Jesus but the son of Sirach, that they were the followers of Alexander's army !—a curious illustration of the common fault of intelligent travellers writing about that of which they know nothing. Those Jews of whom Barrow wrote may be, for all which appears, very modern immigrants.

The best recent summary of this question with which I am acquainted is in Delitzsch (Zur Geschichte der Judischen Poesie, von Franz Delitzsch, Leipsic, 1836), especially a note (p. 59) describing the Synagogue, and a passage about their Book of Prayer. Their language is a jargon of mingled Hebrew and Chinese. See on their present low state the concluding chapter of this work.

their prayers, as Father Gozani had heard the Jews in Italy. They entertain distinct though remote hopes of the coming of the Messiah.

Such, in a brief outline, is the history of one branch of this extraordinary people, thus, in the eastern as well as the western extremity of the Old World, resisting the common laws by which nations seem to be absorbed into each other. However opposite the institutions, the usages, the manners of the people among whom they dwell; whether the government be mild or intolerant, the Jews, equally inflexible and unsocial, maintain their seclusion from the rest of mankind. The same principles operate on the banks of the Yellow River, and on those of the Tiber or the Seine. The Jew, severed for ages from all intercourse with his brethren, amid the inaccessible regions of the Celestial Empire, in most respects, remains as he would have remained, if he had continued to inhabit the valleys of Palestine, under the constant and immediate superintendence of the national chief of his religion, the Patriarch of Tiberias.

END OF VOL. II.

LONDON: PRINTED BY WILLIAM CLOWES AND SONS, LIMITED,
STAMFORD STREET AND CHARING CROSS.

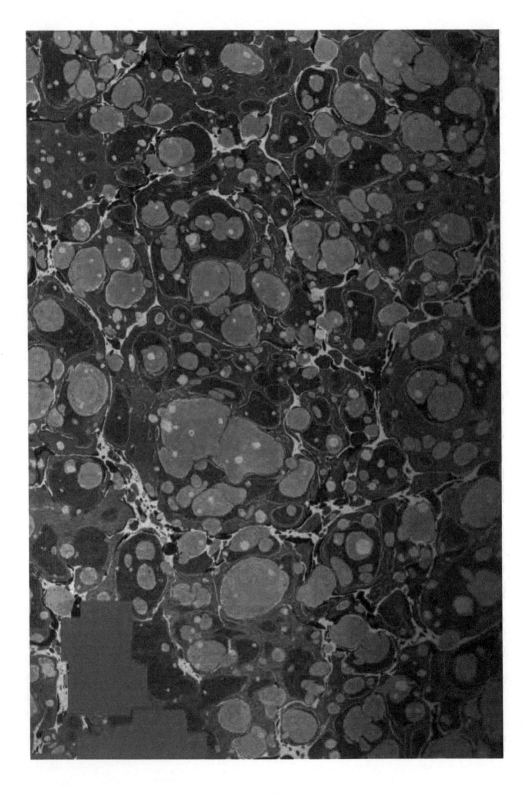

Lightning Source UK Ltd.
Milton Keynes UK
UKHW020630200721
387437UK00002B/107